Contents:

READINESS / KINDERGARTEN

MULTIYEAR EDUCATION

EXTRA LEARNING TIME

TEACHING ACROSS THE CURRICULUM

LEARNING & UNDERSTANDING

BEHAVIOR & DISCIPLINE

SPECIAL NEEDS

ASSESSMENT

RESOURCES / BIBLIOGRAPHY

Teachers Make the Difference.
SDE Sourcebook. © Copyright 1997 by The Society For Developmental Education.
All rights reserved. Printed in the United States of America.
Published by The Society For Developmental Education, Ten Sharon Road, PO Box 577, Peterborough, New Hampshire 03458.
Phone 1-800-924-9621
FAX 1-800-337-9929
e-mail: sde.csb@worldnet.att.net
website: www.socdeved.com

TENTH EDITION

President: Jay LaRoche
Executive Director: Jim Grant
Program Director: Irv Richardson
Publishing Manager: Lorraine Walker
Editor: Aldene Fredenburg
Cover and Book Design: Susan Dunholter
Cover Illustrations: Nathan Bundy
Production Coordinator: Christine Landry
Type Compositor: Laura Taylor

ISBN 1-884548-15-6

ERIC Clearinghouse on Elementary and
Early Childhood Education

Readiness /
Kindergarten

University of Illinois • 805 W. Pennsylvania Ave. • Urbana, IL 61801-4897
(217) 333-1386 • (800) 583-4135 • ericeece@uiuc.edu

ERIC DIGEST
December 1995 • EDO-PS-95-15

School Readiness and Children's Developmental Status

Nicholas Zill, Mary Collins, Jerry West, and Elvie Germino Hausken

Kindergarten is now a nearly universal experience for children in the United States, with 98% of all children attending kindergarten prior to entering first grade. However, the population of children that comes to kindergarten is increasingly diverse. Growing numbers of children in the United States come from different racial, ethnic, and cultural backgrounds; family types; parent education levels; income strata; and language backgrounds. The majority of children come to kindergarten with some experience in center-based programs (such as child care centers or preschools), but the percentage of children with such experience and the quality of these experiences vary across the backgrounds and other characteristics listed above.

Schools in the United States are expected to respond to this diversity in children's backgrounds and educational needs by providing all children with appropriate activities and instruction to ensure that each child begins his or her schooling with a good start. Knowing the range of developmental accomplishments and difficulties that children bring with them when they arrive at kindergarten can help us understand the demands being placed on schools to meet the needs of the entering children. Indeed, some of the difficulties discussed here are not experienced as difficulties until children enter school.

Parents of a national sample of 4,423 children from 3 to 5 years of age who had not yet started kindergarten were asked about specific accomplishments and difficulties of their children. Parents, usually the mother, were asked to rate how well their child demonstrated behaviors indicating emerging literacy and numeracy skills, such as pretending to read stories or counting to 20, and small-motor skills, such as buttoning clothes and holding a pencil properly. Parents were also asked to rate the extent to which their child showed signs of difficulties in physical activity or attention, such as restlessness and inattention, speech difficulties, and less than optimal health. These data were collected in early 1993 as part of a U.S. Department of Education study (Zill et al., 1995).

Accomplishments and Difficulties

Three- to five-year-olds. The percentage of children displaying signs of emerging literacy and small-motor skills increased with age within the 3- to 5-year-old population and within months of age among 4-year-olds. For example, the percentage of preschoolers reported as able to write their own name more than tripled between ages 3 and 4, while the percentage recognizing most letters of the alphabet more than doubled. Other accomplishments showed more moderate age differences. Developmental difficulties showed much smaller changes across ages, and difficulties in some developmental areas showed no change.

More girls than boys demonstrated each of the literacy and small-motor skills covered in the survey, and more boys than girls exhibited signs of difficulties with physical activity, attention, or speech. Though differences between boys and girls were widespread, they were not large.

Hispanic preschoolers were reported to show fewer signs of emerging literacy and more indication of difficulties with physical activity or attention, and to be in less good general health than White or Black children. Controlling for related risk factors, such as a mother with limited education and minority language status, reduced these ethnic differences but did not eliminate them. Black preschoolers showed fewer signs of emerging literacy and were more likely to be reported as in less than good health than White preschoolers. Differences between races were wholly accounted for by related risk factors, such as low maternal education, poverty, and single parenthood.

Four-year-olds. A majority of the 4-year-olds in the study displayed each of the small-motor skills and signs of emerging literacy asked about in the survey. The proportion of children displaying each of these behaviors varied greatly across specific accomplishments, however. More than 9 out of 10 were able to button their own clothes and hold a pencil properly, and more than 8 out of 10 were able to identify the primary colors by name. Fewer, about 6 in 10, could count to 20 or recognize most letters of the alphabet.

Much smaller proportions of preschoolers exhibited any developmental difficulties, although a substantial minority displayed signs of difficulties with physical activity or attention. At age 4, nearly 3 in 10 were reported to be very restless and fidgety and nearly 1 in 4 to have short attention spans. Nearly 1 in 8 was reported by their parents to be in less than very good health. About 1 in 13 were reported to stutter, stammer, or speak in a way that is not understandable to a stranger.

Family Risk Factors and 4-Year-Olds

Sociodemographic risk factors that have been found to be associated with problems in learning after children start school are also correlated with the accomplishments and difficulties children bring with them when they arrive at kindergarten. Five family risk factors were examined:

- mother has less than a high school education;
- family is below the official poverty line;
- mother speaks a language other than English as her primary language;
- mother was unmarried at the time of the child's birth; and
- only one parent is present in the home.

Half of today's preschoolers are affected by at least one of these risk factors, and 15% are affected by three or more of them.

The risk factors are found to be associated with fewer accomplishments and more difficulties in children, even after other child and family characteristics are taken into account. The relative importance of individual risk factors varies across developmental domains. Nevertheless, low maternal education and minority language status are most consistently associated with fewer signs of emerging literacy and a greater number of difficulties in preschoolers.

Attending Head Start, prekindergarten, or other center-based preschool programs was linked to higher emerging literacy scores in 4-year-olds. This correlation remained statistically significant when other child and family characteristics were taken into account. This benefit of preschool attendance accrued to children from both high-risk and low-risk family backgrounds. On the other hand, preschool attendance was found not to be associated with fewer behavioral or speech difficulties or with better health status in preschoolers.

Conclusion

The results of the study point to a need for innovative approaches in providing early education services for children from low-socioeconomic circumstances. As previous studies have shown, existing preschool programs have beneficial effects in the area of emerging literacy and numeracy. But they do not appear to be ameliorating the behavioral, speech, and health difficulties of preschoolers.

The survey results also emphasize the value of a multifaceted concept of educational risk. Five different risk factors were employed in the present study. All were found to have some relationship to preschoolers' accomplishments and difficulties, although the pattern of relationships varied across developmental domains. Many observers believe that low family income is the key factor behind educational failure, but the results of this research do not support this view. When compared to low family income, the risk factors of low maternal education, minority language status, and family structure were often as good

or better predictors of the child's developmental accomplishments and difficulties.

By showing the considerable variation that exists in the accomplishments and difficulties of children about to start school, the study highlights the challenges that kindergarten teachers face in meeting the needs of children who are not only demographically but also developmentally diverse. Teachers must maintain the interest and promote the growth of children who have already demonstrated signs of early literacy and numeracy while simultaneously encouraging the development of these behaviors in children who have not yet acquired them. Similarly, they must meet the needs of children with difficulties while reserving sufficient attention and effort for those with few or no difficulties. Although there has always been variation in the characteristics of children entering kindergarten, the commitment to meeting the educational and developmental needs of all children in an increasingly diverse society presents great challenges to teachers, schools, and communities.

Adapted from: Zill, Nicholas, Mary Collins, Jerry West, and Elvie Germino Hausken. (1995). Approaching Kindergarten: A Look at Preschoolers in the United States. *Young Children* 51(1, Nov): 35-38. PS 524 215. Adapted with permission of *Young Children* and the authors.

For More Information

Hofferth, Sandra L, Jerry West, Robin Henke, and Phillip Kaufman. (1994). *Access to Early Childhood Programs for Children at Risk*. Washington, DC: National Center for Education Statistics. ED 370 715.

West, Jerry, Elvie Germino Hauskin, and Mary Collins. (1993). *Profile of Preschool Children's Child Care and Early Program Participation*. Washington, DC: National Center for Education Statistics. ED 355 046.

West, Jerry, Elvie Germino Hauskin, and Mary Collins. (1993). *Readiness for Kindergarten: Parent and Teacher Beliefs*. Washington, DC: National Center for Education Statistics. ED 363 249.

Zill, Nicholas, Mary Collins, Jerry West, and Elvie Germino Hausken. (1995). *Approaching Kindergarten: A Look at Preschoolers in the United States. National Household Education Survey*. Washington, DC: National Center for Education Statistics. PS 023 767.

This publication was funded by the Office of Educational Research and Improvement, U.S. Department of Education, under contract no. DERR93002007. The opinions expressed in this report do not necessarily reflect the positions or policies of OERI. ERIC Digests are in the public domain and may be freely reproduced.

Factors That Influence Developmental Diversity

College of Education and Human Services Wright State University
Dayton, OH 45435 • (513) 873-3231

The school bells ring in late summer and thousands of children march through the school house doors without anyone having given any thought as to whether or not these children are ready — physically, socially, emotionally, academically — for the curriculum awaiting them. This document aims to provide you, the parent, with a number of major elements which should be considered as you make this vital decision. These same considerations are also relevant when parents are thinking about giving their child the *gift of time,* another year in the current grade in order to grow and mature, or a year in a readiness, K or a transition K-1 program. Too often parents and school officials alike confuse verbal brightness with readiness for school. *Being bright and being ready for school are not the same thing!* An inappropriate start in school too often "tarnishes" that brightness.

Today's K-3 curriculum has been pushed down by our American "faster is better" culture to the point that what is often found in today's kindergarten was found in late first or early second grade just three decades ago! Many schools are trying to change from the "sit-still, paper-pencil" approach of the present to a more active, involved, manipulative curriculum which enables young children to learn best. However, until this latter learning environment is available for your child, you must consider whether or not the child is ready. The material which follows is presented to help you make this very tough decision!

Each of the following factors indicates a potential for problems. The more of these factors which apply to an individual child, the more likely he/she is to encounter difficulty — academically, socially, emotionally, and/or physically — and each of these areas is crucial to a well-rounded human being. No one factor should be the only basis for making a decision. Look at all of the factors, then decide.

Readiness Factors

Chronological Age at School Entrance: My own research and that of many others indicates that children who are less than five and one-half years of age at the time of school entrance into kindergarten are much more likely to encounter problems. This would put the date at about March 25th for many schools. The younger the child is, the more likely the current academic paper/pencil kindergarten curriculum is inappropriate.

Problems at Birth: When labor lasts a long time or is less than four hours; or when labor is unusually difficult, the child is more likely to experience problems. Long labor too often results in reduced oxygen and/or nourishment for the child just before birth. Some studies have found birth trauma to be associated with later emotional problems including, in the extreme, suicidal tendencies.

Early General Health & Nutrition: Poor nutrition in the pre-school years puts the child at greater risk in terms of school success. The child who experiences many serious ear infections during these years has been found to have more difficulty in learning to read. Allergies, asthma, and other similar problems can also inhibit such learning. Any type of illness or problem which results in a passive child — in bed or just "being very quiet" day after day — is more likely to result in a physically delayed development. Lack of body and muscle control can be a major problem for learners.

Family Status: Any act which lessens the stability of the child's family security is a problem and the closer such acts/events occur to the start of school, the more likely that start is to be a negative one. Such destabilizers as the following should be considered.

1. **Death** of anyone close to the child. This includes family, friends, neighbors, pets, etc.
2. **Moves** from one house/apartment to another even though the adults may see it as a positive relocation—more space, own bedroom for child, etc. The child may miss friends, neighbors, the dog next door, etc.
3. **Separation** from parents or close family members whether by jobs, military duty, divorce, prison, remarriage, moves, etc., can create problems for child in early school experiences.
4. **Birth of a Sibling** or the addition of new step-family members can be very upsetting.

Birth Order: If the gap between child #1 and #2 is less than three years, then #2 is more likely to have problems in school. When there are more than 3 children in a family, the baby of the family (last born) often experiences less independence and initiative. There are exceptions to these factors as with the others, but they remain as predictors, never-the-less.

Low Birth Weight: A premature child with low weight often experi-

5

ences significant delays in many aspects of his/her development.

Sex: Boys are about one month behind girls in physiological development at birth; about 6 months behind at age 5; and about 24 months behind girls at age 11-12. (Some contend that we males never catch up!) Boys need extra time more than girls, but research shows that girls actually benefit from it more. Their eyes, motor skills, etc., etc., are ahead by nature, and when given time become even "aheader"! Boys fail far more often than do girls and have many more school problems than do girls.

Vision: Being able to see clearly does *not* mean that a child's vision is ready for school work. It is not until age 8 that 90% of children have sufficient eye-muscle development to do *with ease* what reading demands of the eyes. The younger the child is, the more likely he/she does *not* have all of the vision development required. For example, many children have problems with focusing. Their eyes work like a zoom lens on a projector zooming in and out until a sharp focus is obtained. Much time can be spent in this process and much is missed while focusing is taking place. Other eye problems include the muscle ability to maintain focus and smooth movement from left to right, lazy eye, and midline problems.

Memory Level: If a child has difficulty remembering such common items as prayers, commercials, home address/telephone number, etc., then the child may well experience problems with the typical primary grade curriculum. Many times memory success is associated with one's ability to concentrate—attention span, thus this factor is related to the next one.

Attention Span: Research has clearly shown a strong connection between the amount of time a child spends working on skill content (three Rs) and the achievement level reached. The child who is easily distracted and finds it difficult to focus attention for 10-15 minutes at a time on a single activity is also a child who is probably

going to experience much frustration in school. Discipline problems are likely, as are academic ones. Sitting still is very difficult for the typical 5½- to 6½-year-old child and this normal physiological condition is at great odds with the typical sit still/paper-pencil curriculum imposed after Sputnik went up over 30 years ago!

Social Skills: The child with delayed social development is often reluctant to leave the security of a known situation (home/sitter/preschool/etc.). This child is very hesitant about mixing with other children, is passive, and slow to become involved. Noninvolvement is often associated with lower learning levels. Tears, urinary "accidents," morning tummy aches, a return to thumb sucking, etc., are all signals of such a delay. Some research has found correlations between short labor deliveries and problems such as these.

Speaking Skills: The ability of a child to communicate clearly is closely related to maturation. In order to pronounce sounds distinctly and correctly, muscle control is essential. Hearing must also be of good quality and this has often been reduced by early ear infections, allergies, etc. Inappropriate speech patterns (baby talk) and/or incorrect articulation (an "r" sounds like a "w") are major concern signals.

Reading Interest: If a child does not like to be read to, has little desire to watch a TV story all the way through, or rarely picks up a book to read to him/herself, then the odds are high that this child is not ready for the curriculum of the typical kindergarten. Few of us do well those things in which we are not yet interested and our children are no different!

Small Motor Skills: The ability to cut, draw, paste, and manipulate pencils, colors, etc., are very important in today's pushed-down kindergarten. The child who has some difficulty with these, uses an awkward grip on the pencil (ice-pick, one or no fingertips on the pencil, etc.), and/or has trouble holding small cards in the hand during a game is a candidate for frus-

trations. Eye/hand coordination is vital for a high degree of success.

Large Motor Skills: It is typical for a 5- to 6-year-old child to "trip over a piece of string," yet the typical curriculum assumes major control over one's body movements. Ability to skip, jump on one foot at a time, walk a balance beam, hop, jump from a standing position, etc., is an ability which research has found to be related to overall success with some particular skills tested just before starting school predicting reading success levels in 5th and 8th grades!

Summary

"Is my child ready for school?" is a major question for parents to answer. This small document merely highlights some of the key factors one should consider when making such a decision. I urge all schools to adopt a thorough assessment procedure which checks all of these factors so as to provide parents with more information upon which to base their decisions.

A child's self-concept needs to be positive. He/she should see school as a good place to be, a place where he/she finds success and support. Giving the child the best start in school demands that the parent and school work together to be sure that the curriculum available will enable this child to find success and positive experiences. Parents can also provide support for the school in its efforts to reduce the amount of paper work in the early grades. Working together, the home and the school can help each child establish a firm foundation for a lifetime of learning.

For more information on transition and readiness programs, see Dr. Uphoff's book Real Facts from Real Schools, *published by Programs for Education, 1994.*

The book provides a historical perspective on the development of readiness and transition programs, presents an in-depth look at the major issues raised by attacks on such programs, and summarizes more than three dozen research studies.

ERIC Clearinghouse on Elementary and
Early Childhood Education

University of Illinois at Urbana-Champaign
Children's Research Center, 51 Gerty Drive, Champaign, IL 61820-7469
(217) 333-1386; (800) 583-4135; fax (217) 333-3767
ericeece@uiuc.edu

ERIC Digest

Readiness: Children and Schools

Lilian G. Katz

EDO-PS-91-4

Concern for the readiness of America's children to profit from school experience was expressed by the President of the United States and the National Governors' Association at their summit meeting in February, 1990. The first of six educational goals outlined at the meeting was that "all children will start school ready to learn" by the year 2000. Three objectives emerged from discussion of ways to achieve this goal. Communities and schools must:

☐ provide disadvantaged and disabled children with access to high quality and developmentally appropriate preschool programs designed to help prepare them for school.

☐ recognize that parents are children's first teachers and encourage them to spend time daily to help their preschool children learn; provide parents with training and support.

☐ enhance prenatal health systems to reduce the number of low birthweight babies; ensure that children receive the nutrition and health care they need to arrive at school with healthy minds and bodies.

The Concept of Readiness

Consideration of the readiness goal and the more precise objectives raises questions about the concept of readiness and its meaning to policymakers and educators. This concept has been debated for more than a century (Kagan, 1990). The main issue debated is the extent to which development and learning are determined by the biological processes involved in growth versus the experiences children have with parents, peers, and their environments. Those who emphasize internal developmental processes believe that the passage of time during which growth occurs renders the child more or less able to benefit from formal instruction. Those who emphasize experience take the position that virtually all human beings are born with a powerful built-in disposition to learn and that inherent growth processes and experience both contribute to children's learning.

The quantity and rate of learning in the first few years of life are nothing short of spectacular. The fact that by three or four years of age, most children can understand and use the language of those around them is just one example of learning that takes place long before children begin school.

However, what children learn, how they learn, and how much they learn depend on many factors. Among the most important factors are the child's physical well-being, and his emotional and cognitive relationships with those who care for him. The school readiness goal reflects two concerns about the education of young children. The first is that increasing numbers of young children live in poverty, in single-parent households, have limited proficiency in English, are affected by the drug abuse of their parents, have poor nutrition, and receive inadequate health care.

The second area of concern involves such matters as the high rates of retention in kindergarten and the primary grades, delayed school entry in some districts, segregated transition classes in others, and the increasing use of standardized tests to determine children's readiness to enter school. Standardized tests used to deny children entrance to school or place them in special classes are inappropriate for children younger than six. These trends are due largely to the fact that an academic curriculum and direct instruction teaching practices that are appropriate for the upper grades have gradually been moved down into the kindergarten and first grade.

These two areas of concern suggest that reaching the school readiness goal will require a twofold strategy: one part focused on supporting families in their efforts to help their children get ready for school, and the second on helping the schools to be responsive to the wide range of developmental levels, backgrounds, experiences, and needs children bring to school with them.

Getting Children Ready for School

The term *readiness* is commonly used to mean *readiness to learn to read*. However, children's general social development and intellectual backgrounds should also be taken into account in any consideration of ways to help children prepare for school.

- ☐ *Social readiness.* Children are more likely to cope successfully with their first school experience if they have had positive experience in being in a group away from their home and familiar adults. Young children can approach new relationships with confidence if they have already had some positive experience in accepting authority from adults outside of their family. They are also more likely to adjust easily to school life if they have experienced satisfying interaction with a group of peers and have thereby acquired such social skills as taking turns, making compromises, and approaching unfamiliar children. Parents and preschool teachers can contribute to social readiness by offering children positive experiences in group settings outside of the home, and by helping children strengthen their social skills and understanding (Katz & McClellan).

- ☐ *Intellectual readiness.* Children are more likely to feel competent in school if they can understand and use the language of the peers and the adults they meet in school. They are also more likely to have confidence in their own ability to cope with school if they can relate to the ideas and topics introduced by the teacher and other children in class discussion and activities.

   Parents and preschool teachers can strengthen intellectual preparedness by providing children ample opportunity for conversation, discussion, and cooperative work and play with peers who are likely to start school with them. Parents of children not enrolled in a preschool program can help by talking to the staff at the child's future school about the kinds of stories, songs, and special activities and field trips usually offered at the school, and by introducing related topics to their children.

Getting the School Ready for the Children

The most important strategy for addressing the school readiness goal is to prepare the school to be responsive to the wide range of experiences, backgrounds and needs of the children who are starting school.

☐ *Appropriate curriculum.* A position statement on school readiness issued by the National Association for the Education of Young Children (1990) points out that, given the nature of children's development, "the curriculum in the early grades must provide meaningful contexts for children's learning rather than focusing primarily on isolated skill acquisitions" (p.22). The curriculum should emphasize informal work and play, a wide range of activities related to the children's direct, firsthand experience, ample opportunity to apply skills being learned in meaningful contexts, and a wide variety of teaching methods.

☐ *Appropriate staffing.* Teachers are more likely to be able to accommodate the diversity of experiences, backgrounds, languages, and interests of their pupils if their classes are small, or if they have the services of a qualified full-time aide. Having two adults in each class makes it easier to staff classes with speakers of more than one language. Small child/staff ratios provide teachers with the opportunity to spend unhurried time with every child, to address each child's unique needs, and to develop good relationships with parents.

☐ *Age considerations.* The National Association for the Education of Young Children's Position Statement on School Readiness points out that contrary to what is commonly assumed, there are no tests by which to determine reliably whether a child is "ready" to begin school. "Therefore, the only legally and ethically defensible criterion for determining school entry is whether the child has reached the legal chronological age of school entry" (p.22). Some schools and districts are experimenting with mixed-age grouping as a way of reducing grade retention rates, and encouraging children to help each other in all areas of learning (Katz, and others, 1990).

Realizing the goal of having all our children ready for school and all our schools ready for the children by the year 2000 will require the best efforts of all involved: parents, teachers, administrators and everyone in the community who has a stake in the welfare of its children. And that's just about everybody!

For More Information

Kagan, Sharon Lynn. Readiness 2000: Rethinking Rhetoric and Responsibility. *Phi delta kappan.* (December, 1990): 272-279.

Katz, Lilian G., and Diane McClellan. *The Teacher's Role in Children's Social Development.* Urbana, Illinois: ERIC Clearinghouse on Elementary and Early Childhood Education, 1991.

Katz, Lilian G., Demetra Evangelou, and Jeanette Allison Hartman. *The Case for Mixed-Age Grouping in Early Childhood.* Washington, D.C.: National Association for the Education of Young Children, 1990.

National Association for the Education of Young Children. NAEYC Position Statement on School Readiness. *Young Children.* (November, 1990): 21-23.

This publication was funded by the Office of Educational Research and Improvement, U.S. Department of Education, under contract no. OERI 88-0620-12. Opinions expressed in this report do not necessarily reflect the positions or policies of OERI. ERIC Digests are in the public domain and may be freely reproduced and disseminated.

About ERIC/EECE Digests....

ERIC/EECE Digests are short reports on topics of current interest in education. Digests are targeted to teachers, administrators, parents, policy makers, and other practitioners. They are designed to provide an overview of information on a given topic and references to items that provide more detailed information. Reviewed by subject experts who are content specialists in the field, the digests are funded by the Office of Educational Research and Improvement (OERI) of the U.S. Department of Education.

All ERIC/EECE Digests are available free in original printed form directly from the clearinghouse. For additional information on this topic, please contact ERIC/EECE directly at ericeece@uiuc.edu or 1-800-583-4135.

Return to the ReadyWeb home page.
Return to the Getting Schools Ready for Children introductory page

TRANSITIONAL
Classrooms

BY ANTHONY COLETTA

Transitional classrooms are designed for normal children who need more time to acquire the maturity, learning habits, motivation, and attention span needed to succeed in school. For such children, the extra year of time and stimulation promotes success and supports positive self-esteem. These children, according to language consultant Katrina deHirsch, develop slowly despite excellent intelligence, and fare better if their school entrance is deferred, "since one more year would make the difference between success and failure."

Participants are placed either in a readiness class prior to kindergarten, or a transitional first between kindergarten and first grade. After completing the readiness class, students enter kindergarten. The transitional first grade is for students who have finished kindergarten but who have been identified as needing extra time before entering first grade.

The additional year is provided within a child-centered environment. In many schools, transitional classrooms provide a model for primary-grade teachers interested in creating a "developmentally appropriate curriculum." Susan Sweitzer, Director of Education and Training for

Clearly, children do not languish or "mark time" in these programs.
A well-planned transition class is intellectually stimulating.
Moreover, the curriculum does not repeat what the students have experienced the year before.
Instead, the concepts are extended and elaborated upon.

the Gesell Institute in New Haven, Connecticut, recommends the use of traditional classrooms as a "transition" to developmentally appropriate practice. She states: "Until we get to the point where these practices are extended up to the early grades, there have to be some options."

Clearly, children do not languish or "mark time" in these programs. A well-planned transition class is intellectually stimulating. Moreover, the curriculum does not repeat what the students have experienced the year before. Instead, the concepts are extended and elaborated upon. The additional year allows the children to mature in all areas of development while they are exposed to stimulating learning experiences. As Harvard University Professor Jerome Bruner, author of ***Towards a Theory of Instruction***, says about readiness, the teacher "provides opportunities for its nurture."

As early as 1958, Gordon Liddle and Dale Long reported in the ***Elementary School Journal*** that transitional classrooms were valuable in improving academic performance. During the 1970s and 1980s, students in New Hampshire's public schools consistently achieved the highest scores on the Scholastic Aptitude Test (SAT), even though New

Hampshire ranks 50th in state aid to public schools. In **All Grown Up & No Place to Go**, David Elkind writes that "In New Hampshire children are not hurried. It is one of the few states in the nation that provides 'readiness' classes for children who have completed kindergarten but who are not yet ready for first grade."

Research on Transitional Classrooms

The extent to which extra-year programs yield academic gains is subject to controversy, but their beneficial effect on social growth and self-esteem seems clear. As Robert Lichtenstein states in a paper entitled, "Reanalysis of Research on Early Retention and Extra Year Programs," transitional classrooms "offer significant advantages in non-academic areas (e.g., self-concept, adjustment, attitude toward school)."

Jonathan Sandoval, Professor of Education at the University of California, published research in which he studied high school students who years ago had completed the transitional (junior) first grade. The results showed beneficial outcomes. The children placed in the transitional class were superior to the control group on three out of four indicators of academic progress. The students also had favorable attitudes about the transitional program, indicating that the experiences helped them do better socially and emotionally, as well as academically. Sandoval speculated that without the transitional program, they might not have done as well.

A much publicized 1985 study, conducted by Professors Lorrie Shepard and Mary Lee Smith, concluded that transitional classrooms, though not harmful, do not boost academic performance in schools as had been expected. They conducted a study of 80 children in Boulder, Colorado, which led them to state there were no clear advantages to having an extra year of school prior to first grade. However, even they found a slight difference in achievement test scores in favor of the extra-year students. And, Shepard and Smith's published conclusions omitted the positive social-emotional effects of giving children more time to grow. Their original study includes figures showing that in every area of "Teacher Ratings" (reading, math, social maturity, learner self-concept, and attention), the group receiving the extra year (the "retained" group) scored higher. Most important, the figures were especially higher in the areas of social maturity and learner self-concept. The Shepard and Smith study also does not separate those children who repeated kindergarten from those who were placed in transition programs. All were part of the "retained" group.

Shepard and Smith contend in their book, **Flunking Grades**, that the study of extra-year programs is "limited by the lack of systematic investigation of long-term effects." However, they do not mention Betty McCarty's eight-year study of the effect of kindergarten non-promotion on developmentally immature children. McCarty's results indicated that non-promotion of developmentally young kindergarten children had a positive effect on subsequent levels of peer acceptance, academic attitude, classroom adjustment, and academic achievement.

In general, studies which have reported negative effects of transitional classrooms, such as those described in Gilbert Gredler's article, "Transitional Classes," studied children who were academically at risk. It must, however, be remembered that a transitional program is not intended for remediation. It is developmental, and therefore is based on the premise that children have not yet acquired academic skills.

More than 25 studies of transitional classroom programs are summarized in Dr. James K. Uphoff's **School Readiness and Transition Programs: Real Facts From Real Schools.** According to Uphoff, these studies show that students in transitional classes have at least done as well as fellow students in regard to academic achievement in later years, and in many cases they have surpassed the national averages. The classes have also produced very positive benefits in regard to student self-concept, and emotional and social maturity. Further, there has been overwhelmingly strong satisfaction and support for transitional classes among parents whose children participated in such classes.

The Transitional Class Debate

Transitional classrooms have become a controversial issue. Supporters view them favorably because they help children who might do poorly in a rigid, academic curriculum, by providing instead the opportunity to be successful in a more relaxed, developmentally appropriate environment. Extra-year programs are therefore seen as a clear alternative to grade retention.

Critics, however, argue that such classrooms often become a "dumping ground" for children with low abilities and emotional problems. There may be merit to this argument if schools use transitional classrooms for children who have handicaps or learning problems, or if they inaccurately identify children using techniques and instruments which are insensitive to maturational factors.

Critics also argue that transitional classrooms are a form of retention in which children are stigmatized because they do not progress directly to the next grade. However, as Dr. James Uphoff writes in the article "Proving Your Program Works," "Clearly there is a tremendous difference between a child whose school experience has been one of failure, and a child in a success-oriented program providing time to grow.

The National Association for the Education of Young Children (NAEYC) opposes transitional classrooms because it believes lack of school readiness is most often due to rigid, inappropriate curriculums. NAEYC argues the schools should change so children do not need extra time in order to succeed. They have proposed a shift toward more developmentally appropriate practices in kindergarten and in the primary grades as a way of reducing the large number of children deemed to be unready for school. In an NAEYC publication titled, **Kindergarten Policies: What Is Best for Children,** co-author Johanne Peck states that instead of increasing the age of school entry, "resources and energy should instead be redirected to offering a good program." Many supporters of this position feel that transitional programs impede progress toward the goal of creating appropriate curriculums for all students.

There may be some truth to this, but I am not aware of any hard data which supports this position. And, eliminating readiness and transition classes does not mean that a school will quickly or even eventually implement a developmental curriculum. Many schools will have great difficulty changing to a system that requires additional teacher training and smaller class sizes.

Robert Wood, director of the Northeast Foundation for Children and co-author of **A Notebook for Teachers**, believes that kindergarten teachers are hard-pressed to create a curriculum that meets the individual needs of children, when the developmental age range in a typical class may vary as much as three years. In an average kindergarten, where some children behave like 4 year-olds and others like 5 or 6 year-olds, responding to individual student needs requires high levels of diagnostic teaching skills and more specialized preparation than teachers normally receive.

School personnel interested in providing a developmentally appropriate curriculum for all students realize it is a worthwhile goal that may take time to achieve. In the meantime, many of these schools have established, or are considering, transitional classrooms. To be effective, such programs must be carefully implemented. A series of guidelines that can help parents and educators prepare for success are included in my book, **What's Best for Kids.**

PROPER PLACEMENT
in the beginning
Assures Success
AT THE END

BY JIM GRANT

When I graduated from Keene State College in 1967, I found a job teaching 5th grade in a small, rural community in New Hampshire. My first year as a teacher was a tremendous experience, and I felt I had achieved a lot of success. When I went back for my second year, the Assistant Superintendent of Schools came to see me. He said, "Jim, we're pleased with you, and we want to give you a chance to experience upward mobility. We're going to make you Principal of the Temple Elementary School."

"Well," I said, "I may not look very bright, but I am gifted in math, and I know that would make me Temple's fifth principal in twenty-four months. I'm not sure I can stand that kind of upward mobility." In spite of my reservations, when I woke up the following Monday, I was the principal of an elementary school.

The teacher of the first/second multiage classroom presented me with my first challenge. "I don't know what I'm going to do with my twenty-five children," she said. "They're all over the place. I have trouble getting them to slow down long enough for me to teach them."

I went to her classroom, opened the door, and quickly

56

"A child who is eager and ready for kindergarten and first grade is likely to become a lifelong learner.
A child who is pushed to do too much too soon will never really like school and is likely to have problems all the way through.
These are your child's formative years, and starting school should be a positive, rewarding experience."

— Judy Keshner,
Starting School

closed it. Nothing in my teacher education classes or one year of actual teaching experience had prepared me to deal with what I saw.

It was then that I brought in my former teacher, Nancy Richard, as an early childhood consultant who could advise me on the children's development. She observed the class and said, "You have second graders doing third grade work, second graders doing second grade work, second graders doing first grade work, first graders doing second grade work, first graders doing first grade work, first graders doing no work at all, and then there are two boys in the corner who aren't toilet trained after lunch."

"Some of these children," she continued, "aren't yet ready to do first grade work. Chronologically, they are 6, but developmentally they are still too young to succeed in that class." She then suggested I take a course on "developmental readiness."

In that course, I was surprised to learn that up to twenty-five percent of the children in American schools repeat a grade, and as many as another twenty-five percent are often struggling and not succeeding in their current grade. I checked the registers covering a six-year period at my school and proved those statistics were flawed. In my school, thirty-three percent of the kids had repeated! This informal survey also showed that most of the children who repeated were boys, and the grade most children repeated was first grade.

Being a bright, young, "overplaced" principal, I immediately made two brilliant deductions: boys are stupid, and first grade teachers are incompetent. Further reflection, observation, and discussion led me to some different conclusions, however. I began to consider the possibility that girls tended to develop more rapidly in certain respects than boys, and that these differences reached the crisis point in first grade, when all the children were expected to learn how to read and write.

One September in the late 1960's, we began to screen children to help determine their developmental readiness for a first grade experience. We discovered that many of the children eligible for first grade on the basis of their age that year were at risk for a traditional first grade program. When I shared that news with their parents and recommended that the developmentally young children remain in kindergarten for another year, the parents were very unhappy. They decided to send all of those late-blooming children into first grade together, thinking that the children being together would somehow make a difference in their developmental readiness for the demands of first grade.

Of course, it did not. By the middle of October, several of the children had been withdrawn from first grade at their parents' request and moved back to kindergarten. The problems that were surfacing at home and at school made the parents realize that these children really did need more time to grow and prepare for first grade. The rest of the developmentally young children ended up taking two years to complete first grade.

The next year, when we assessed the entering children's developmental levels, we did more to inform the parents — at PTA meetings, in one-on-one meetings, through literature. That year, many children who were developmentally young stayed in kindergarten for an extra year, and then entered first grade when most were 7-years-old. That first group of children, who had the advantage of an extra year to grow, graduated from high school in 1982, and many went on to graduate from college in 1986. We've been using this developmental approach in schools across New Hampshire for well over two decades — with success.

Nationwide, thousands of schools also began providing developmentally young children with extra-time options during the 1960's, helping tens of thousands of students master the curriculum and achieve success in school. This concept, which was formulated in 1911 and formalized as a Title III government program in New Hampshire in 1966, spread rapidly as teachers and parents recognized firsthand how much some children benefited from having an extra year to develop, which then gave them a much greater chance to succeed in school.

Now, when many parents and politicians are demanding stricter standards and measurements of progress, at the same time that many young children are feeling the effects of the disintegration of families and communities, there is a greater need than ever to provide extra-time options for children who are developmentally too young to succeed in a particular grade or program.

Time-flexibility Options

Programs that provide children with an extra year of growing time have many different names, but they share a number of common features. A good time-flexibility program offers reasonable class sizes, an environment rich in materials, and a room with space for movement. Here children can develop their physical and motor capabilities, learn social skills, work with hands-on math and science materials, practice listening and speaking, gain experience with different types of literature, explore the creative arts, and develop problem-solving abilities. As a result, children in these programs can develop the habits of success and a positive attitude toward school.

These programs emphasize an interest-based approach to learning rather than a curriculum based on text books and "time-on-task," access to a wide variety of literature instead of just basal readers and workbooks, and the use of authentic assessments rather than standardized achievement tests. All of these characteristics should be found in any of the time-flexibility options described below:

Readiness Classes for "Young 5's"

Many schools continue to find that a large number of entering students are developmentally too young to learn and succeed in kindergarten. This may be due to a child's innate but still normal rate of development, or environmental factors which have left a child unprepared to work well in a kindergarten class. Readiness classes provide the time needed to grow and make the transition to the school environment in a supportive setting, which then makes kindergarten a much more positive and educational experience. This is particularly important because, as kindergarten teacher Judy Keshner explains in her booklet, *Starting School*, kindergarten "is not a preview of what is to come — it is the foundation on which the following years will grow. Each grade builds on the one that came before, and kindergarten sets the pattern and the tone."

Developmental "Two-tier" Kindergarten

In this type of program, all 5-year-olds enter kindergarten at the same time, based on the legal entrance age, but some stay for one year and some stay for two. After enrollment, each child is developmentally assessed and continues to be observed throughout the year, so that detailed information about children's rate and stage of development is available. At the end of the school year, those children who are developmentally ready move on to first grade. Children who need more time to develop in order to enhance their experience in first grade can remain in kindergarten for a second year, or move into the sort of pre-first or transition class described below.

Pre-first Grade, Transition Grade, Bridge Classes

Call it what you will, this sort of extra-year option has been adopted by concerned parents, teachers, and administrators across America. It provides developmentally young 6-year-olds with a continuous-progress, full-day program in which they have extra time to grow and learn. This helps them make the very difficult and important transition from the play-oriented learning of kindergarten to the more formal "academic tasks" which become increasingly important in first grade. Developmentally young children who have had this extra-year experience are then much better prepared to enter first grade with confidence and a reasonable expectation of success.

Readiness/First Grade (R/1) Configuration

This approach acknowledges the reality that continues to exist in most first grade classes: children who need extra time to grow are blended with those who are developmentally ready for first grade. What makes the R/1 configuration different is that the parents of children who need extra time know from the very beginning that their children can have two years to complete this blended first grade, if needed. This takes the pressure off everyone — students, teachers, and mom and dad. There are no high-stakes campaigns to pass "or else," and no end-of-the-year trauma for children who just need more time to grow and develop.

Some schools chose the R/1 configuration to save money — by not having a separate readiness class, they save on classroom space, staffing, and materials. Other schools choose this option because it is the one the educators prefer and the community accepts. It also provides many benefits of the multi-age classes described below, such as allowing developmentally young students to work closely with and learn from more experienced students during their first year, and then to become the models for new students during their second year.

Multi-age Primary Classes

An increasing number of schools now offer multi-age primary classrooms, in which children of different ages work and learn together, staying together with the teacher for a multi-year placement. These classrooms eliminate the artificial time constraints created by having separate grades from kindergarten through third grade.

One important result is that more time is available for teaching and learning, especially at the start of the year, as teachers and students don't have to spend time getting to know one another and learning to work well together. This approach also eliminates worries about "running out of time" to complete the curriculum by the end of each year, and it eliminates many high-stakes decisions which otherwise have to be made each year. In addition, if a child needs extra time to develop and complete the curriculum before moving on, a multi-age class works particularly well because it already contains a wide range of age levels and a flexible timetable, rather than a rigid, lock-step grade structure.

Multi-age classrooms decrease the risk of failure for all children, because these classes allow students to develop and learn at their own rate in a much less hurried environment. Staying in the same class with the same teacher and classmates for more than one year also provides a sense of consistency and belonging, which can be particularly helpful for the many children who now grow up in fast-changing families and communities. And, the developmental diversity that naturally occurs in a multi-age classroom makes it easier for transfer and special-needs students to be included in them.

An Extra Year of Preschool

Unfortunately, too many parents have to cope with schools which do not offer viable extra-time options for children who are developmentally too young to succeed in kindergarten. Under these circumstances, allowing developmentally young children to spend an extra year in preschool can be a very positive alternative to sending them off to kindergarten and waiting to find out if they "sink or swim." Having an extra year to grow and learn in a supportive preschool environment greatly decreases the odds that such children will flounder and need rescuing in the primary grades.

High-quality preschools provide children with a range of developmentally appropriate activities that foster continued growth and learning. And, the mixed age levels found in most preschools makes it easy for developmentally young children to fit in, just as in a multi-age class. This sort of environment also tends to make preschool teachers aware of the importance of readiness and adept at working with children who are at various developmental levels. Unfortunately, in most cases this option is only available to financially advantaged parents.

An Extra Year at Home

Some parents may prefer to provide their late bloomer with day care and learning experiences at home for an extra year. In situations where there is a parent at home every day who has the time, inclination, and understanding to work with a child in this way, it can be a viable alternative, especially now that more materials and support networks have been developed for the small but growing number of parents who opt to provide their children's entire education at home.

In many cases, parents can simply notify the local school of their intent and send children to kindergarten when they are 6-years-old. However, young children need opportunities to grow and learn with their peers, which contribute in many ways to a child's overall development. And, well-trained preschool and elementary school teachers can often provide a wider range of supportive and educational learning experiences for a developmentally young child than a parent.

Dropping Out and "Stopping Out"

When developmentally young children do not take extra time early in their educational career, they tend to take the time later on. They may repeat a grade in middle school or high school, or flunk out or drop out altogether. They may also obtain their high school diploma but feel the need to take time off before going to college. Some "stop out" — a phrase used to describe students who take a leave of absence while at college. Statistics show that a large number of students do take time off during college, and interestingly enough, the percentage is about the same as the percentage of children found to need extra time when they start school!

Some young people may be ready to put the extra time to better use when they are older, but too many end up with negative attitudes, low self-esteem, and poor skills that interfere with their ability to create productive and fulfilling lives. Early intervention in a positive and supportive way can be far more effective than a wait-and-see approach.

Readiness for Kindergarten
PARENT OBSERVATION FORM
General Knowledge

1. **Does your child know the names of four or more colors?**
   ☐ Yes   ☐ Not at this time

2. **Please check all colors your child knows:**
   ☐ Red   ☐ Green   ☐ White
   ☐ Brown   ☐ Orange   ☐ Blue
   ☐ Pink   ☐ Gold   ☐ Yellow
   ☐ Purple   ☐ Black   ☐ Tan

   Comments: _____

   _____

3. **Does your child show interest in numbers?**

   ☐ Yes   ☐ Sometimes   ☐ Not at this time

4. **Does your child recognize some numbers?**

   ☐ Yes   ☐ Not at this time

   Comments: _____

   _____

5. **How high can your child count?**

   ☐ Not at all   ☐ Up to twenty
   ☐ Up to five   ☐ Up to forty
   ☐ Up to ten   ☐ Up to sixty or more

6. **Can your child count four or more objects?**

   ☐ Yes   ☐ Not at this time

7. **My/our child is able to count _____ objects.**

   Comments: _____

   _____

8. **Can your child repeat a series of four numbers after hearing them once? (example: 3-5-4-7)**

   ☐ Yes   ☐ Not at this time

9. **Can your child draw or copy a square?**
   ☐ Yes   ☐ Not at this time   ☐

10. **Does your child know the names of the following shapes?**

    Circle ◯   ☐ Yes   ☐ Not at this time

    Triangle △   ☐ Yes   ☐ Not at this time

    Diamond ◇   ☐ Yes   ☐ Not at this time

    Cross ✛   ☐ Yes   ☐ Not at this time

    Comments: _____

    _____

11. **Does your child show interest in the letters of the alphabet?**
    ☐ Yes   ☐ Sometimes   ☐ Not at this time

    Comments: _____

    _____

12. **Can your child sing the alphabet song?**

    ☐ Yes   ☐ Not at this time

    Comments: _____

    _____

13. **Can your child recite the alphabet?**

    ☐ Yes   ☐ Not at this time

    Comments: _____

    _____

14. **Does your child recognize some letters of the alphabet?**

    ☐ Yes   ☐ Not at this time

    Comments: _____

    _____

We feel very strongly that children entering kindergarten should have some base of knowledge. This knowledge comes from the child's first teachers — the parents or guardians.

1. Does your child know the names of four or more colors?

2. Please check all colors your child knows.

It is reasonable to expect a parent to teach children about common colors.

3. Does your child show an interest in numbers?

By five years old the child should be showing an interest in numbers.

4. Does your child recognize some numbers?

A five-year-old should be able to recognize some numbers, both in and out of context.

5. How high can your child count?

Children entering kindergarten should be able to count to 20; many are able to count beyond that.

6. Can your child count four or more objects?

7. My child is able to count _____ objects.

A child entering kindergarten should be able to count four or more objects by touching or manipulating them. This counting skill is very different from the memorization of numbers shown in question 5, and exhibits the beginning of an understanding of math concepts.

8. Can your child repeat a series of four numbers after hearing them once? (example: 3-5-4-7)

This tests both memorization and sequencing skills.

9. Can your child copy or draw a square?

10. Does your child know the names of the following shapes? (circle, triangle, diamond, cross)

A five-year-old should be able to draw or copy a square and know that it's a square. A five-year-old child is not expected to be able to draw a circle, triangle, diamond or cross, but should be able to name some of these geometric shapes.

11. Does your child show interest in the letters of the alphabet?

12. Can your child sing the alphabet song?

13. Can your child recite the alphabet?

14. Does your child recognize some letters of the alphabet?

Five-year-old children are curious, and at this age should be showing an interest in letters, be able to sing the alphabet song, recite the alphabet, and recognize some letters of the alphabet out of context, particularly some letters in the child's own first name.

15. Does your child look at books with pictures and pretend to read?

16. When he or she pretends to read books: it sounds like a story/there isn't much connection between the story my child is telling and what's in each picture.

17. Can your child actually read the words written in the book?

18. Is your child able to retell a story in order of the way things happened?

At age five, the child should enjoy looking at books and pretending to read. He or she might talk or sing to the pictures while going through the book.

When the child pretends to read, the pictures the child is interpreting should actually make sense and sound like a story, and there should be a connection between each picture. (The story may be a different one than is actually written in the book; that's okay, as long as the story the child is telling makes sense according to the pictures.)

Some children who are gifted, precocious, or advantaged may be able to sit down at age five and read a simple book; however, it is important to stress that in no way is reading to be expected of a five-year-old entering kindergarten. At this point, children should know how a book works: how to pick a book up and hold it, how to go from front to back, and so on.

When a parent reads a book to a five-year old child, the child should be able to summarize the story's events in the order they happened.

19. Does your child recognize common sounds such as: church bells, birds singing, car horns, water running, train, sirens, airplane, vacuum cleaner?

A child should be able to identify common everyday sounds, interpret what the sounds mean, and make important connections. For instance: a church bell ringing means that a church service is about to begin; a siren means that a police car, fire truck, or ambulance is coming.

Factors and Circumstances That May Influence Developmental Readiness

1. Chronological age at entrance
2. Gender
3. Low birth weight
4. Prematurity
5. Mother's level of education *
6. Living below the poverty level *
7. Non-English speaking mother *
8. Mother unmarried at time of the child's birth *
9. Single parent family *
10. Homelessness
11. High mobility rate (excessive absences)
12. Difficult/traumatic birth/forcep birth
13. Lack of health care, i.e., untreated ear infections, lack of dental and vision care
14. Lack of prenatal care
15. Traumatized, i.e., divorce, violence, death of a family member, abuse/neglect
16. Smoking/alcohol/drugs prenatally
17. Lack of pre-school experience
18. Family in crisis
19. Malnutrition
20. Chemically injured, i.e., lead, pesticides, etc.

* Top Five Family Risk Factors (One half of today's preschoolers are affected by at least one of these risk factors and fifteen percent are affected by three or more of them. Children with one or more of these characteristics may be educationally disadvantaged or "at-risk" of school failure. — *National Center for Educational Statistics*)

Note: Some factors are not considered to be a root cause of unreadiness in children, however they may exacerbate the condition.

The chronologically younger children in any grade are far more likely than the older children in that grade to:

1. have failed a grade
2. become dropouts
3. be referred for testing for special services and special education
4. be diagnosed as Learning Disabled
5. be sent to the principal's office for discipline problems even when in high school
6. be receiving various types of counseling services
7. be receiving lower grades than their ability scores would indicate as reasonable
8. be behind their grade peers in athletic skill level
9. be chosen less frequently for leadership roles by peers or adults
10. be in special service programs such as Title I
11. be in speech therapy programs
12. be slower in social development
13. rank lower in their graduating class
14. be a suicide victim
15. be more of a follower than a leader
16. be less attentive in class
17. earn lower grades
18. score lower on achievement tests

School Readiness and Transition Programs: Real Facts From Real Schools
by James K. Uphoff, Ed.D

Jim Grant/Bob Johnson/Char Forsten

HOW DIVERSE IS YOUR CLASSROOM?
Factors and Circumstances That May Influence School Preparedness

Teacher: _____

# of Class Members: _____

Grade(s) or Program: _____

School Year: _____

Column headers (factors and circumstances):

- Boy/Girl (Chronologically young)
- Low birthweight (U.S. 5 lbs. or less)
- Premature birth
- Lives at or below the poverty level
- ESL student
- Family is/was in crisis *
- Transient family
- High absenteeism
- No preschool experience
- Mother has less than a high school education
- Abused/neglected/traumatized
- Single parent family
- Is/was homeless
- Lacks health care
- Seems depressed
- Difficult/traumatic birth
- Seems hyperactive
- May have attention deficit
- Identified learning disability/learning disabled
- Qualifies for Title I
- Takes medication (i.e. Ritalin, prozac, etc.)
- Parent(s) in jail
- Mother was unmarried at the time of baby's birth
- Seems to be a slower learner (70-89 IQ range)
- Has health related problems
- Child may have been damaged by drugs prenatally
- Child abuse alcohol/drugs
- Family member abuse alcohol/drugs
- Mother did not have adequate prenatal care
- Difficult child
- Behavior disorder
- Emotional disorder
- Total # of factors & circumstances
- Notes

Students

Student	Boy/Girl	Total # of factors & circumstances
Skippy Richardson	B (circled) G	17

(Rows marked B G for subsequent blank student entries)

Percent of students in each category

Please check all areas that apply. Leave blank any area you are unsure of. Circle B or G to indicate boy or girl.

* Family is going through a divorce for instance, parent(s) in jail, etc.

© Jim Grant and Bob Johnson.

Jim Grant/Bob Johnson

The Society For
Developmental Education
10 Sharon Road • Box 577 • Peterborough, NH 03458

How the Two-Year Looping Classroom Works: Promoting Teachers with Their Students

What Looping Is

Looping is sometimes called multiyear teaching or multiyear placement. It is a two or more year placement for the teacher as well as the students. The students have the same teacher for two or more successive years. Looping involves a partnership of at least two teachers, who teach two different grade levels, but in alternate years.

For example, in the initial year, Teacher A teaches first grade and Teacher B teaches second grade. At the end of the year both Teacher A and the first graders are "promoted" to second grade. Teacher A and her students are together for the second year, but this time as a second grade.

At the end of the second year, Teacher A's students move on to third grade, and the following fall, Teacher A will begin the cycle again with a new crop of first graders.

Meanwhile, at the end of the first year, Teacher B's second graders move on to third grade, and at the beginning of the second year she welcomes a new class of first graders. At the end of the second year Teacher B is "promoted" to second grade and continues with the same class the next year. (See Figure 1)

In schools where kindergarten is half-day, only half of the kindergartners will continue with the same teacher. The other half will have another first-grade teacher. The half that stay in the loop could be either from the morning group or the afternoon group. Or, they can be chosen by lot from among those whose parents indicated they would like them to stay with the same teacher.

Although our example is of first and second grade, looping will work with any two contiguous grades: second and third grade, third and fourth, fourth and fifth. It can be started with any two grades where two teachers are willing to get together and give it a try.

What Looping Is Not

Looping is not a multiage configuration. It does, however, open up an appealing window of opportunity for creating a continuous progress program. Over the two-year span, the teacher can see and take advantage of a child's development in a less fragmented, more natural way. In moving toward implementing multiage continuous progress practices, looping offers teachers, parents, and administrators the chance to see, experience and appreciate what can happen when a teacher and a student work together for more than one year.

What Looping Makes Possible

"My teacher" is an important person in a young child's life. For a lot of children today, their teacher is often the most stable, predictable adult in their lives. If "my teacher" waves goodbye at the end of 180 days, come September a whole new relationship with a brand new teacher has to be slowly established. Moving into a new grade can be a scary transition for children.

When "my teacher" is the same person for two years, there is stability that the child can build on. By the middle of the first year, the child knows what the teacher expects of him or her, knows what the rules are, knows what pleases *and* what annoys the teacher. Teacher and child have established a working relationship that the child can count on. As the child becomes comfortable in the relationship

Jim Grant/Bob Johnson/Char Forsten

and begins to count on its stability, s/he can release the tension and energy that have gone into trying to understand the teacher.

It is a jump start from the teacher's point of view as well. It takes time to find out the interests, abilities and learning styles of each student in the classroom. All aspects of classroom planning are affected by this knowledge. At the beginning of the second year, the teacher already has in-depth information and can build on it. S/he knows who is shy, who is aggressive, who is an emergent reader, and who finds reading easy. A few reminders, some review, and both teacher and children are ready to pick up where they left off at the end of the last grade and move ahead.

Looping is effective and efficient. Teachers like being able to spread certain themes over a longer period of time. They report that, in the second year, children frequently mention activities and experiences from the previous year that relate to present activities. Teachers can help children carry over information and build on these connections. The two-year curriculum becomes woven together.

Looping's Effect on High-Stake Decisions

In the spring every teacher has to make high-stake decisions based on evaluation of what each child has accomplished during the year. Some children in the class are clearly ready for the next grade. One or two may have learning disabilities and been referred for special evaluation. But what of the others? Are they "late bloomers"? Do they just need a little more time — "cheddar cheese kids" who simply need to age to be their best? What about borderline children? What should happen with a very verbal girl, for instance, who has mastered words but seems quite young developmentally in other ways? Looping reduces the stakes in decisions made at the end of the first year. A teacher can keep watching and evaluating these children.

At the end of the two-year loop, a child who is developmentally young and needs an extra year of time may be accommodated by moving laterally. S/he could remain in the same grade but with a different teacher in a different classroom.

Where there is the goal of including differently-abled children in the classroom, the stability and continuity of looping is very helpful. A two-year program can be somewhat more flexible than a time-bound single grade where the curriculum tends to be unforgiving to children who are differently-abled.

"Something Easy That Works Well"

Looping allows teachers and administrators to move into a change that produces a minimum of fear, anxiety, and frustration, not only for children, but for parents and themselves. It begins with the concept of the teacher simply moving with the children up one grade. It involves a philosophical change but not a major school restructuring. It requires no new building or alterations in physical space. Most teachers don't need a great deal of retraining to begin looping.

Many teachers find this a very manageable change. It is a challenge, but it can be done. We have had several teachers tell us that it was particularly satisfying. Typical of these comments are:

"It was refreshing, re-energizing to be able to do something innovative that works so well."

"It made me reflect on my teaching and move in a new direction."

"Did I want the same children for two years? Could I create a seamless curriculum? I found out I both liked it and did it well."

"I wasn't so sure when I agreed to do this, because I never thought of myself as a very versatile person. But to my surprise, this brought out a side of me I didn't think I had."

Jim Grant/Bob Johnson/Char Forsten

Making a change that works tends to boost teachers' confidence and open them up to the possibilities that a multiage continuous progress classroom has to offer. Having experience teaching a two-year looping cycle, they know they can bond with a family of children and enjoy having them over a longer period of time. They have had experience in creating a semiseamless, integrated curriculum over two or more grade levels. They have proven to themselves that they can comfortably handle a multiyear program.

What Is Required to Make Looping Work

The first requirement is two teachers who want to try looping. Our advice to principals is to start with good teachers and give them the support they need. In practical terms, this translates into enough materials and enough time to plan and organize a two-year curriculum cycle, time to share day-to-day planning and, later on, their experience and problems. The looping partnership is one opportunity for teachers to collaborate. Though each teacher is in his or her own room, looping encourages ongoing collaboration and mutual support between teachers.

Communicating with parents can be particularly rewarding in a multiyear program. It takes some parents most of the year to become comfortable with a teacher. Multiyear teachers often find that parents who may have been standoffish in the first year will begin to participate in events the second year, volunteer in the classroom, or help in other ways.

Some Hazards of Looping

Every teacher we have ever worked with recalls times when a whole class was in trouble. We remember one class that we called "the year of the summer-born boys." The class was top-heavy with males, almost every one of whom was chronologically young. It was an exceptionally difficult, disjointed year. The individual children would not have been problems in themselves but having so many in the same class threw it out of balance.

If, by October or November, there are clear signs that a class is out of balance and is a difficult, disjointed group of children, plan to divide up the class in the second year. It does not help any children in such a class to keep them together for two years.

When possible, teachers should not feel required to keep a difficult child more than one year. However, a difficult child is often one who is particularly in need of the stability and continuity that a two-year looping program offers. There is no one right answer to this dilemma. This is one of those tough decisions!

There is also the occasional problem of the difficult parent who may be endured for one year but should not have to be endured for two.

In looping, the teacher may spot some borderline children who might or might not need referral for special services. There is some advantage in having more time to make these decisions. The down side of that is the risk of delaying referral for special services. A two-year delay could be disastrous for a child who really needs special services.

Have you ever considered moving up a grade with your class?

"Kindergarten Teachers— Move Up to First Grade!"

Elise A. Harding

© Terri Gonzalez

My kindergarten class one year was an especially nice group. It wasn't that the children were overly bright or even unusually well behaved, but they had a certain chemistry. They all seemed to fit together as a team. I thought it would be an interesting experience to follow this group of children into the first grade.

I needed a special project for a course I was taking as part of my graduate degree work; being this group's teacher for *two* years seemed like a worthwhile project. "Would it be better," I contemplated, "for the children to have the same teacher for two years?"

My principal okayed the idea but would not give me permission to tell the students or parents of the plan. I conferenced especially carefully at the end of the school year and sent home summer packets of work. The packets included my home address so that the children could write to me over the summer. Colleagues warned me about getting "too involved," so giving my home address was certainly forward.

August came and the principal wisely moved my classroom next door to the other first-grade classes. The afternoon of the school preview open house arrived. I was nervous! Would the parents be happy, sad, or perhaps even angry? What if they didn't like me and thought this was a terrible idea? What if the children said, "Oh, no, not her again!"

As the first group of children arrived with hugs and smiles, I found my fears unjustified. Parents and children alike were delighted that we were together again.

A stress-free first day

Children often are nervous about beginning a new school year. I thought if a child had the same friends and teacher, there would be fewer first-day jitters and less stress upon coming to school each day, and this was true. The children settled down together, and we were off to a quicker, more efficient start because there was far less testing-type behavior than is typical for some children when getting to know a new teacher.

Another positive aspect of this plan was the continuity it provided for children in special education programs. Those whom I had referred in kindergarten went smoothly into their part-time SLD (specific learning disabilities) and speech classes. The SLD teacher remarked on the ease of transition for these children in contrast to the adjustment for those who had to get to know a new classroom teacher. Also, some children were borderline SLD referrals in kindergarten, and because I knew the problems they had had earlier, I was able to get help started quickly in the first grade.

One child in particular is a success story. The testing in kindergarten showed she had many needs and should be placed in a full-time SLD classroom. Because I knew the child well, I was able to successfully advocate for placing her in a part-time, less-

Elise A. Harding, E.D.S., is a kindergarten teacher at Poinciana Math/Science/Technology School in Palm Beach County, Florida. She also serves as a curriculum writer for the kindergarten program.

restrictive program. Her mother trusted me enough to back my recommendation. The child ended up making fantastic progress and exited SLD by the time she entered third grade.

Of course, some new students joined our class. Two new girls adjusted well and never seemed to notice that the other children already knew each other. One boy, however, complained about being "the new kid" even as the year went by and more children joined our class. That was the only negative problem at the beginning of the year.

Starting teaching that first week of school was very efficient. I had to spend far less time evaluating and reading cumulative records; academically, this was a positive aspect of the program.

Satisfactions and comforts

Probably, the most satisfying part of the experience for me was the deeper relationships I was able to build, not only with the children but with the parents as well. Conferences were much more comfortable and interesting. Parents shared things with me that helped me understand when their child was having trouble. In many ways I became part of the family. I knew all of the siblings who attended our school. The teachers of siblings sometimes would come to me for insight into the families that I knew so well.

Another positive part of this research project was knowing the names of many first graders who were not in my class. This was an unexpected but very satisfying aspect of the program. In a school of more than 1,000 students, it made me feel more competent to be familiar with so many of the children I saw each day.

I wanted to continue the moving-up program into the second grade. I had a great deal of parental support. Eighteen parents wrote letters requesting the program's continuance, but the principal declined to approve their requests. Unfortunately, her reasons were never explained.

Making the program better

Looking back and considering how the program could have been better, I strongly suggest giving parents a voice in whether or not they want the same teacher for their child. Most parents were very happy, but a couple of them told me that they would have liked being asked permission. I agreed because I think that, more than ever, parents need to be an integral part of their children's education.

Certainly this plan is not for all teachers. I would not want an administrator to keep students and teacher together without the teacher's support and knowledge: educational plans work best when you believe in them. I urge more principals and teachers to encourage this option for those who would like to try it.

* * *

As an epilogue to my two years together with my class, my husband planned for me a surprise birthday swim party in July. Imagine my delight when I opened my front door and saw the wonderful faces of my students and their brothers, sisters, moms, and dads. We all really were a family! It was an experience I will always treasure.

Editor's note: What age do *you* teach? "Moving up" can be done with a group of infants, threes, second graders— *many* young children benefit from being with the same teacher for two years. Would *you* like to try this? Will you propose the idea to your principal or director?

Voices

America cannot afford to waste resources by failing to prevent and curb the national human deficit, which cripples our children's welfare today and costs billions in later remedial and custodial dollars. Every dollar we invest in preventive health care for mothers and children saves more than $3 later. Every dollar put into quality preschool education like Head Start saves $4.75 later. It costs more than twice as much to place a child in foster care as to provide family preservation services. The question is not whether we can afford to invest in every child; it is whether we can afford not to.

Edelman, Marian Wright, from *The Measure of Our Success: A Letter to My Children and Yours.* New York: HarperPerennial, 1992.

Managing the Change to Multiage: "How Do I Get There From Here?"

Changing from a graded structure to a multiage structure involves shifting people's ideas about school. It also means implementing policies and procedures that do not rely on grade levels as a method of grouping students and as a way to organize curriculum.

Because the lock-step graded structure is such a part of how we view education, it is often difficult for people to consider "school" without specific grade levels. It is interesting to note how important grade level designation can be when describing children between the ages of five and eight. More often than not children are defined by their grade level attainment — "Jamie is a third grader," for example. The notion of grade levels becomes much less important after graduation from high school. None of us would consider asking another adult his current grade.

To begin the change to multiage, a first step is to research the topic of multiage by reading professional literature and by attending conferences and workshops. It can also be beneficial to visit schools which have successfully implemented multiage programs to discuss their change process and to examine the beliefs and structure of their multiage program.

After obtaining a solid foundation of multiage practices and philosophy, educators must work with community members to decide whether or not a multiage structure will benefit the students enrolled in that school system. If a school decides to implement a multiage program, then the members of the school community must begin to plan for the transition from a one-year, single-grade, timebound organization to a multiage continuous progress structure.

Our Best Advice ✔

Understanding and following the various elements of the change process is the beginning point for all reform efforts. The change process enables stakeholders to clearly focus on the shared vision to create multiage continuous progress programs.

I magine a farmer who wants to harvest his crops in a fraction of the usual time. To do this, he plants the seeds, waters them without stopping for two weeks, spends the next week weeding, fertilizes, and then harvests. It sounds silly, for we all know that it takes a certain period of time to harvest a crop — even with good agricultural practices.

Growing a good multiage program also takes time. The foundation for any good early childhood education program must be a staff that is knowledgeable about developmentally appropriate practices. With knowledge about child development, appropriate curricula and teaching strategies, and a love for children, educators have the requisite skills to implement a strong multiage program.

With a strong foundation in appropriate education and support from the school community and parents, some educators choose to implement multiage programs. The decision to implement is made by teachers, administrators, and community members. The decision is made after considerable research about multiage philosophy and multiage programs that function well. Most schools investigate the multiage philosophy for at least a year before implementing a multiage program.

Taking the time to investigate multiage, making the decision to start a multiage program, choosing the staff, making the necessary adjustments to curriculum and launching the program can take a year or more. It may take another four years to iron out wrinkles and get the program running smoothly.

Take Your Time When Implementing a Multiage Classroom

Steps to Success

1. Attend an awareness session on multiage practices.
2. Present your plans to create a multiage classroom to your parent group, and invite them to participate in the process.
3. Form a multiage study team to do the following:
   - Read and discuss articles, professional books, and journals, review videos and audiotapes on multiage practices.
   - Attend workshops, conferences and various staff development opportunities.

4. Secure administrative, fellow staff, school board, and broad community support.

5. Investigate and visit successful multiage models that would be appropriate for your community.

6. Assign willing teachers to staff the multiage classroom.

7. Budget appropriate financial resources for training, related costs, curriculum development, travel, professional books, furniture, classroom remodeling, etc.

8. Select a well-balanced, heterogeneous student population and secure permission from parents to include their children in the multiage classroom.

Our Best Advice ✔

The more time taken to carefully plan and implement multiage practices, the greater is the likelihood of your program having longevity. The faster you implement your program the more likely you will have overlooked very important elements necessary to the program's well-being. High-speed implementation usually results in high-speed unraveling, leading to the eventual dismantling of your program.

Plan Ahead — But Allow for Change

Peter Drucker, a prominent business management consultant, states that "planning is invaluable. Plans are useless." This quotation is a succinct way of explaining the importance of being organized and proactive when planning educational programs . . . and the difficulty of forecasting the future.

In a rapidly changing world, it's hard to predict what issues will be important in a year or two. We all have experienced the futility of trying to plan five years into the future while having to deal with one-year budgets and a rapid turnover rate among teaching staff. Although we can't plan the future, there is no substitute for developing the knowledge and process skills that will help you implement and improve a multiage program, should the opportunity arise. If you are aware of what it takes to be successful, and you have the skills to be successful, then you are much more likely to succeed.

Although no two schools go about implementing multiage programs in exactly the same manner, the following is a plan for implementation that many school districts have found successful.

A Suggested Implementation Plan

A. Create staff knowledge of developmentally appropriate practices
   1. Knowledge about children
   2. Knowledge of appropriate curricula and experience with appropriate pedagogy
   3. Knowledge and skill about appropriate assessment
   4. Knowledge about what constitutes a strong, resilient school culture

B. Create staff and community awareness of multiage structures
   1. Explore advantages and disadvantages for staff, parents, and students
   2. Provide staff development on multiage practices
      a. Attend conferences/seminars/forums/networking groups
      b. Visit different multiage configurations
      c. Read professional literature on multiage practices

C. Make a decision about whether or not to begin a multiage program
  1. Who is responsible for the decision?
  2. Who will implement the decision?
  3. Who has the expertise/knowledge to make a good decision?
  4. Who has an interest in the outcome of the decision?

D. Organize for the multiage program
  1. Consider the transition from a one-year single grade to a multiyear/multiage program
  2. Consider staffing of the program
  3. Consider how students will be selected for the program
  4. Work with specialists to define their role in the program
  5. Consider the logistics of space, scheduling, facilities, grades to be blended, class size, etc.

E. Collect the resources necessary to instruct students
  1. Appropriate curricula
  2. Appropriate materials
  3. Appropriate assessment procedures and assessment materials
  4. Appropriate instructional teaching techniques

F. Promote the school/home partnership and community partnership
  1. Parent awareness of multiage practices
  2. Parent involvement in program design and implementation
  3. Parent participation in public relations

G. Implement the program and prepare to monitor program for adjustments
  1. Provide strong administrative support
  2. Provide time for reflection/assessment/improvements
  3. Provide for ongoing staff development

— Irv Richardson, © 1995

Our Best Advice ✔

A well-articulated plan keeps your program together and assures that all stakeholders are moving in the same direction. Think of such a plan as a road map that leads us to a common destination.

Q.
What is looping?

A. Looping is a practice which allows single-grade teachers to remain with the same class for a period of two or more years. It generally requires a partnership of two teachers in contiguous grades; a first-grade teacher, for instance, decides to progress with her students to grade two, while the second-grade teacher moves to first grade and begins a new two-year cycle.

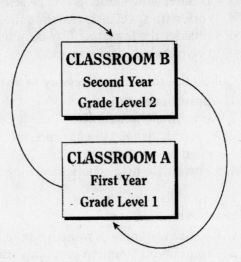

CLASSROOM B
Second Year
Grade Level 2

CLASSROOM A
First Year
Grade Level 1

The concept of looping is not new. In 1913, the Department of the Interior recommended this same practice, but referred to it as "teacher retention." Since then, other terms have been used to describe looping, including: teacher-student progression; two-cycle teaching; multiyear teaching; and the twenty-month classroom.

No matter what its name, the practice is the same. In a looping classroom, the teacher is the heart and the students are the focus.

A. Looping is a very simple concept, but with profound benefits. Dr. Joseph Rappa, Superintendent of the Attleboro School District in Massachusetts, reports that students who have the same teacher for two years tend to enjoy school more, have fewer discipline problems, fewer absences, are referred to special education placement less often, and are less apt to be retained in a grade for lack of academic achievement.*

At the heart of a successful looping classroom are the continuity of relationship and the learning environment. Many of today's children are on a fast track along with their families, moving from home to school, to after-school activities, to day care, adapting to parents' job schedules along the way. Additionally, many children come from single-parent homes. Many children today lack continuity in their lives. Often the five-and-a-half hour period that children spend in school is the most stable and predictable part of their day. Keeping children with the same caring, concerned teacher over a two-year period provides the stable foundation that many children need.

Looping allows a teacher and children to get to know one another. Children learn the expectations of their teacher, while the teacher gets to know the needs and the strengths of individual students over this two-year period. The extended relationship gives the teacher time to respond to problems, academic or otherwise, that a child may have. With the additional year, teachers can focus more on learning, rather than "covering" the curriculum.

The looping classroom is time-efficient. Built into the looping relationship is extra time; most teachers find that their students start the second year of class as if it were the 181st day of school, needing virtually no period of adjustment before getting into the swing of learning. Teachers estimate that they gain at least a solid month of instructional time at the beginning of the second year of a looping cycle.

Teachers also have a head start in the second year with their relationships with parents. Bonds formed in the first year are strengthened during the second year. Many teachers report strong,

Q.
What are the benefits of looping?

---

* Grant, Jim; Richardson, Irv; and Johnson, Bob. *The Looping Handbook: Teachers and Students Progressing Together*. Peterborough, NH: Crystal Springs Books, 1996, p. 15.

lasting friendships with the parents of children in a multiyear class.

Discipline is much better in a looping classroom. By the second year of a two-year classroom, children know what is expected of them. They know the classroom routines and trust that they're in a consistent, stable environment. They've developed strong ties with their classmates and respond to positive peer modeling and peer pressure. Many teachers report that discipline problems drop dramatically in the second year of a multiyear arrangement.

The strong parent-teacher relationship that tends to form in a looping situation lets the child know that the teacher and parents are working together for his or her best interests. Also, the strong parental involvement that often accompanies a looping arrangement gives the child a sense of well-being that makes "acting out" less of an emotional necessity.

Student attendance tends to improve in a looping classroom. By the second year, teacher and students know what to expect from each other, and many strong friendships have been forged. With this sense of relationship and belonging, children want to come to school. Parents and teachers report fewer tummyaches, fewer lost gloves and shoes, and generally more enthusiasm for school. In Attleboro, Massachusetts, student attendance in grades two through eight has increased from 92% ADA to 97.2% ADA.*

Many of the instructional strategies that multiyear teachers find successful — thematic teaching, cooperative learning, learning centers, among others — make the looping classroom a place where children want to be.

Looping tends to reduce special education referrals. The two-year classroom gives children a longer academic runway. In a single-grade, single-year classroom, the teacher keeps a worried eye on the child who is not up to par as he nears the end of the school year. The looping teacher knows she has more time to work with the child before making such a high-stakes decision as a special education referral. The extra instructional time provided by the looping structure may be just enough to put many children over the top academically.

The looping arrangement also provides greater opportunity to observe children and determine their needs, and to better match the curriculum to those needs. A looping teacher can often devise effec-

* *The Looping Handbook*, p. 15

tive strategies the second year which are based on numerous observations from the previous year.

A growing concern among educators is that too many children are being referred for special education for academic problems that may simply reflect a normal variance in the rate at which children learn. Looping takes much of the time pressure off the teacher and reduces the chance of unnecessary referrals.

That being said, we must remind people that looping is not a substitute for special education. While it will provide many children with the extra time and support they need, it will not in and of itself resolve learning disabilities, and it will not end the need for adaptations due to physical disabilities. There is a danger that, given the forgiving nature of the looping classroom, a child may miss being referred to special ed services that she may need.

One alarming development is that some states are considering capping the number of children allowed to receive special education services. This is a response to the extremely high cost of providing federally mandated special education services. If these caps are allowed to be created, school systems will find themselves doing triage on their students; looping may optimize the time spent in the regular classroom for those students who no longer qualify for special ed services.

Looping reduces (but does not eliminate) grade level retentions.
When teachers have children for two years, they don't have to make retention decisions at the end of the first year, because that barrier no longer exists. The teacher can use the two-year span to help bring children up to grade level academically.

Often children who are lagging behind don't need to repeat an entire grade; they just need a little more time to better understand concepts. With the extra learning time provided in the beginning of the second year, and with the teacher's increased understanding of the child's needs, strengths, and weaknesses, the trauma of grade-level retention often isn't necessary.

Sometimes, a child's lagging abilities may not be so much an academic problem as a problem of readiness. If a child, especially a kindergarten or first-grade child, is developmentally young, retention may be the appropriate solution.

Children Progress Through School on a Broken Front

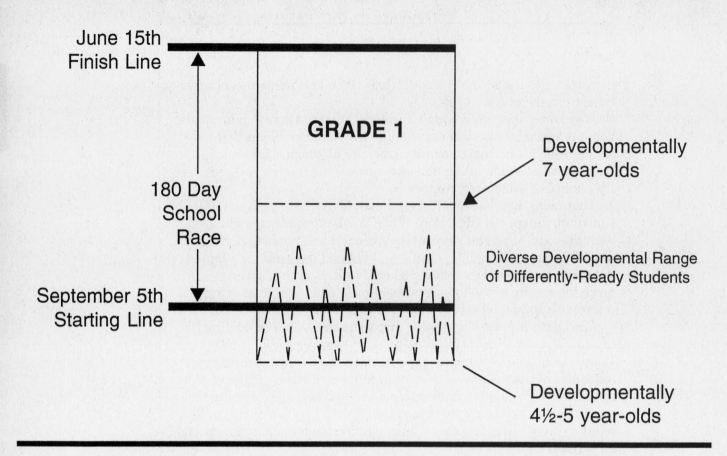

June 15th
Finish Line

180 Day
School
Race

September 5th
Starting Line

GRADE 1

Developmentally
7 year-olds

Diverse Developmental Range
of Differently-Ready Students

Developmentally
4½-5 year-olds

Children Enter School on a Broken Front

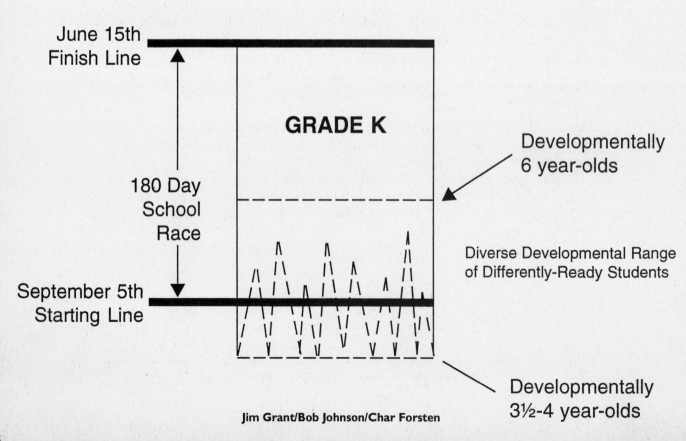

June 15th
Finish Line

180 Day
School
Race

September 5th
Starting Line

GRADE K

Developmentally
6 year-olds

Diverse Developmental Range
of Differently-Ready Students

Developmentally
3½-4 year-olds

Jim Grant/Bob Johnson/Char Forsten

Looping Requires a Two-Teacher Partnership

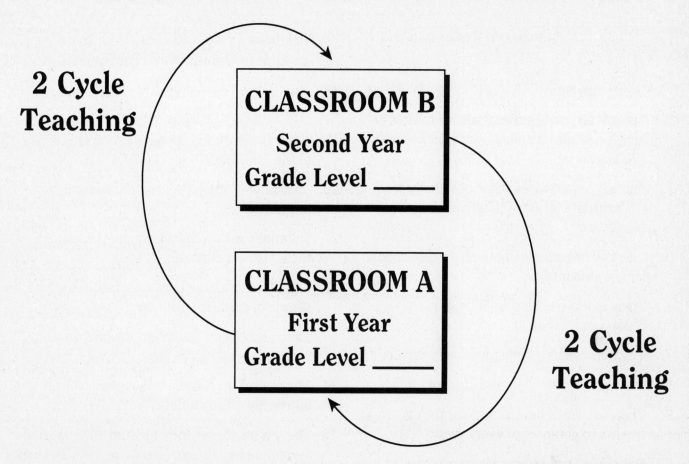

2 Cycle Teaching

CLASSROOM B
Second Year
Grade Level _____

CLASSROOM A
First Year
Grade Level _____

2 Cycle Teaching

The classroom A teacher is "promoted" to classroom B with the class and keeps students for a second year. The classroom B teacher returns to classroom A to pick up a new class and begins another two-year cycle. **Note:** This is a multiyear continuous progress configuration and is <u>not</u> a true multiage classroom.

Looping Facts

- Student attendance in grades 2 through 8 has increased from 92% average daily attendance (ADA) to 97.2% ADA.

- Retention rates have decreased by over 43% in those same grades.

- Discipline and suspensions, especially at the middle schools (grades 5 through 8), have declined significantly.

- Special education referrals have decreased by over 55%.

- Staff attendance has improved markedly from an average of seven days per staff member per year, to less than three.

Joseph B. Rappa, ED.D., Provided by the Attleboro, Massachusetts School System

Jim Grant/Bob Johnson/Char Forsten

Multiple Year Classroom Benefits

1. There are fewer student/teacher transitions

2. Multiyear relationships create a cohesive family atmosphere

3. There is an increased cooperative spirit between students and between students and teacher(s)

4. There is an increased sense of stability for students as a result of classroom routine and consistency

5. There is an increase in mental health benefits for the students

6. There is less pressure and stress on the classroom teacher

7. Teachers report a higher level of discipline

8. Principals report improved student attendance

9. There are fewer new parents for the classroom teacher to get to know every year

10. Principals and teachers report an increase in parent involvement

11. There are fewer new students for the teacher to get to know every other year

12. The teacher has increased student observation time

13. Teachers are not pressured to make high stakes decisions and may postpone these important decisions until they have more observation and instructional time with the students

14. There tends to be decrease in special needs referrals

15. Educators report fewer grade level retentions

16. A multiple year configuration allows for semi-seamless curriculum

17. Multiple year classrooms are more time efficient instructionally

Numbers 18-26 are classroom benefits unique to the multiage configuration

18. "Old-timers" eavesdrop and revisit concepts taught to newcomers

19. "First-timers" eavesdrop on concepts taught to the "old-timers"

20. "Old-timers" model appropriate behavior to newcomers

21. The more knowledgeable students assist the less knowledgeable

22. Extra learning time is provided without the stigma of grade level failure

23. There is a higher ceiling on the curriculum every other year

24. The classroom is more inclusionary for differently-abled students

25. There is an opportunity for students to reach "senior citizen" status every two or three years

26. There is a broader age-range of friends

Jim Grant/Bob Johnson/Char Forsten

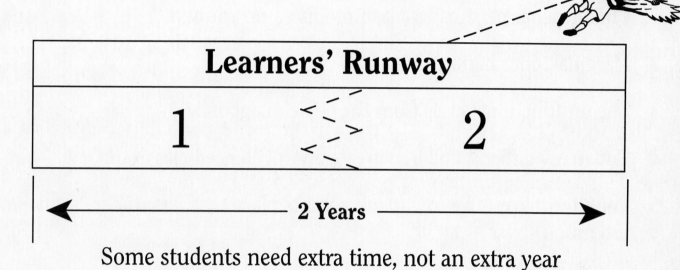

Learners' Runway

1   2

← —————— **2 Years** —————— →

Some students need extra time, not an extra year

Sources for Looping Information

Publications

1. Grant, Jim and Bob Johnson. ***A Common Sense Guide to Multiage Practices.*** Columbus, OH: Teachers' Publishing Group, 1995. 128 pp. *

2. Grant, Jim; Bob Johnson and Irv Richardson. ***The Looping Handbook: Teachers and Students Progressing Together.*** Peterborough, NH: Crystal Springs Books, 1996, 157 pp. *

3. Grant, Jim; Bob Johnson and Irv Richardson. ***The Multiage Handbook: A Comprehensive Guide to Multiage Practices.*** Peterborough, NH: Crystal Springs Books, 1996. 157 pp. *

4. Grant, Jim; Char Forsten, Bob Johnson and Irv Richardson. ***Looping Q&A: 75 Answers to Your Most Pressing Questions.*** Peterborough, NH: Crystal Springs Books, 1996. 128 pp. *

5. Jankowski, Elizabeth. ***Perceptions of the Effect of Looping on Classroom Relationships and Continuity in Learning.*** A Dissertation. Sarasota, FL: University of Sarasota, 1996. 97 pp. **

Video

1. **The Looping Classroom** *featuring Jim Grant.* Available in a Teacher/Administrator Edition (52 minutes) and Parent Edition (28 minutes). *

* Available from Crystal Springs Books, Ten Sharon Road, Box 500, Peterborough, NH 03458 • 1-800-321-0401.

** Available from Betty Jankowski, Ed.D, Hilton Head Elementary School, Hilton Head, SC 29926

Jim Grant/Bob Johnson/Char Forsten

Caution . . . the road to the multiyear classroom has some potholes

1. Child/teacher personality clash produces no winners

2. Marginal, poor performing teacher

3. The dysfunctional class from the "Black Lagoon"

4. Too many difficult children create an unbalanced classroom

5. Long term exposure to difficult parents place teachers under too much stress

6. The multiyear classroom may mask a learning disability

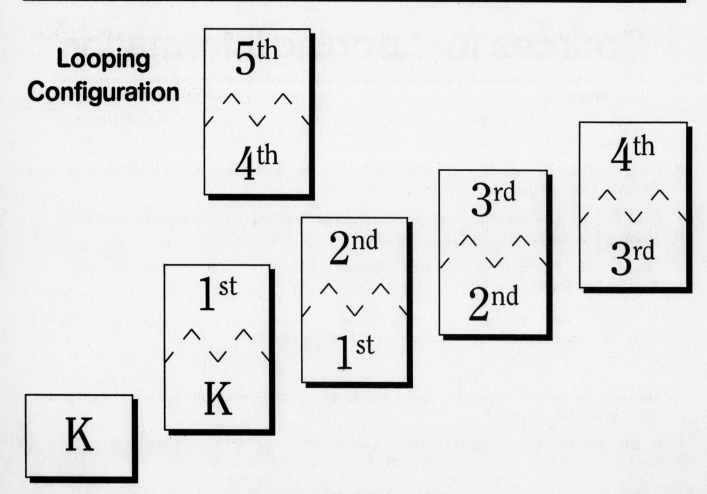

Looping Configuration

Looping with Kindergarten (½ day) and First Grade

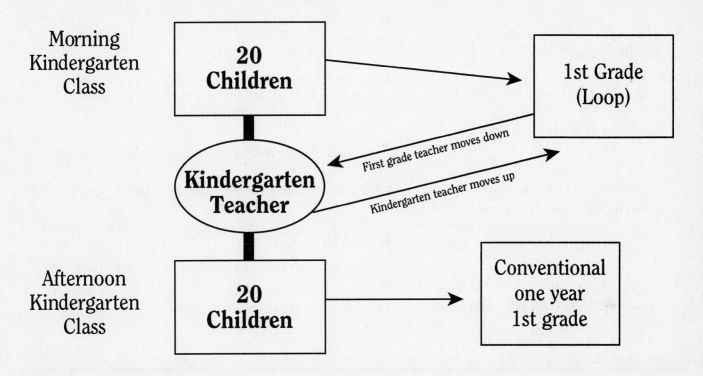

Morning Kindergarten Class — **20 Children** — **Kindergarten Teacher** — → **1st Grade (Loop)**

First grade teacher moves down

Kindergarten teacher moves up

Afternoon Kindergarten Class — **20 Children** — → Conventional one year 1st grade

Note: Looping with a two session ½ day kindergarten program requires two first grades.

Student Selection

- The AM class can loop

- The PM class can loop

- 10 students from the AM plus 10 students from the PM can loop

- Select 20 out of 40 AM/PM student to loop (random selection)

The Positive Aspects of Implementing Looping

1. Career(s) are not placed at risk

2. Short lead time is required for implementation

3. No extensive training is necessary

4. Builds a teacher's confidence

5. Low stress level for teachers

6. Curriculum changes are minimal

7. Additional physical space is not required

8. Midyear decision allows the teacher who moves up to "road test" the class

9. A 100% obstacle free reform

10. All down sides are totally correctable

11. Program termination is possible without being "noticed"

12. Prerequisite ground work for future multiage configuration

13. There are minimal things to go wrong

14. Looping with a partial class is permissible

15. Minimal financial resources are required

16. The only permission necessary to secure is from the parents of the future second year students

The Hidden Consequences of Looping

Teachers:

1. who change grade levels may lose their teaching assistant

2. must learn the curriculum of a new grade

3. may need special training for: Health, DARE, etc.

4. must learn the ages and stages of the students at the new grade level

5. may move to a grade with mandated:
   • Testing
   • Curriculum content
   • Promotional standards

6. may need to change pods (located in another wing), thus becoming separated from established teacher colleagues

7. may move up to "high pressure" grade level (i.e., 1st or 3rd grade)

8. may move to a grade level that is not child-centered philosophy (i.e. departmentalized situation)

9. may change to a grade level and be required to increase class size

10. may find a high number of pre-first graders identified as differently-abled when they move up to 1st grade

11. may find that their state requires 2 teacher certification

12. may find that some local teacher unions require posting positions before allowing a teacher to change grade levels.

Jim Grant/Bob Johnson/Char Forsten

The Role of Administrators in a Looping and/or Multiage Classroom

1. The administration should secure waiver(s):
   - To change the timeframe and sequence for teaching mandated grade specific curriculum content
   - To eliminate promotional gates
   - Requiring teachers to hold dual certifications (i.e., kindergarten and elementary certification)
   - To postpone group standardized testing

2. Principals must permit teachers to deemphasize the traditional grade barrier at the end of the first year.

3. The administration needs to work with the Teachers' Union to ease the union rule that a classroom position must be posted and open to all before automatically allowing a looping teacher to change grade levels.

4. The principal should actively participate in school board, staff and parental presentations.

5. The principal needs to be proactive and take measures to reduce/minimize/eliminate staff dissension.

6. The administration should secure adequate funding for supplemental materials, training, research, substitutes, etc.

7. The principal needs to create opportunities for teachers to:
   - Visit the next grade
   - Visit model programs
   - Attend seminars/conferences
   - Have collaborative planning time

8. The principal needs to assure that multiyear classrooms have balanced, teachable student populations.

9. The principal must provide options for giving some students an additional year of learning time.

10. The school administration should "guarantee" the rights of teachers to have a "voice" in creating his/her workplace.

Multiyear Teachers' Bill of Rights

— Teachers are not mandated to teach in a multiyear classroom against his/her will.

— Teachers have a right to take a hiatus from teaching in a multiyear classroom if his/her life's circumstances change.

— Teachers have the right to transfer a student to another class if a personality clash is unable to be resolved.

— Teachers are not required to keep an unreasonable or disgruntled parent for more than <u>one</u> year.

— Teachers are <u>not</u> required to keep a dysfunctional class for more than one year.

— Teachers have the right to create a classroom with a balanced student population.

— Teachers who agree to take a disproportionately higher number of high needs students will be provided additional classroom support as well as a reduced class size.

Jim Grant/Bob Johnson/Char Forsten

Multiage Configuration

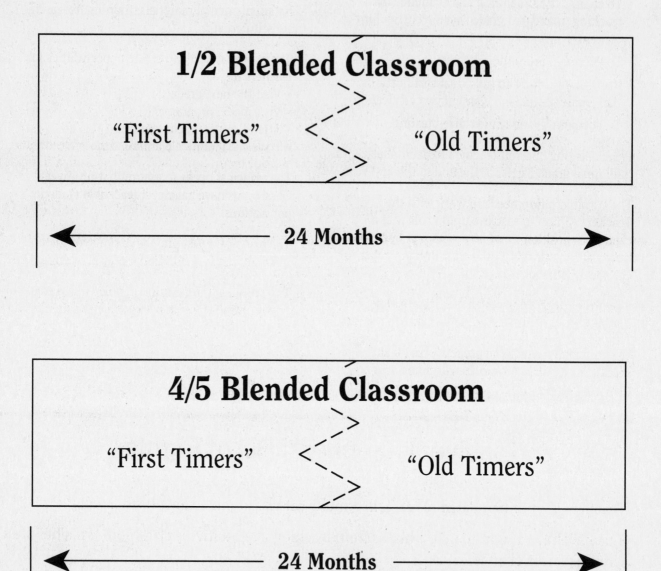

Note: Any required grade specific group standardized testing should be postponed until the end of the second year.

Comparisons of Graded and Nongraded Schools

Anderson and Pavan reviewed 64 research studies published between 1968-90 which compared nongraded and graded schools. The studies most frequently favored nongradedness on standardized measures of academic achievement, mental health and positive attitude toward school.

Specifically, regarding **academic achievement:**

58%   of the studies favored nongraded groups
33%   of the studies showed no difference
9%   of the studies showed nongraded groups performed not as well

Regarding, **mental health and positive school attitude:**

52%   of the studies favored nongraded groups
43%   of the studies showed the groups to be similar in performance
5%   of the studies showed nongraded groups performed not as well

The studies also showed that boys, African-Americans, underachievers, and students from lower socioeconomic status were more likely to perform better and feel more positive about themselves and their schools in a nongraded environment.

Sources: _Nongradedness: Helping It To Happen;_ Robert H. Anderson and Barbara Nelson Pavan, Technomic Pub. Co., 1992, Page 46.

Doable Format to Teach Grade Level
Mandated Content in a Dual Year Classroom

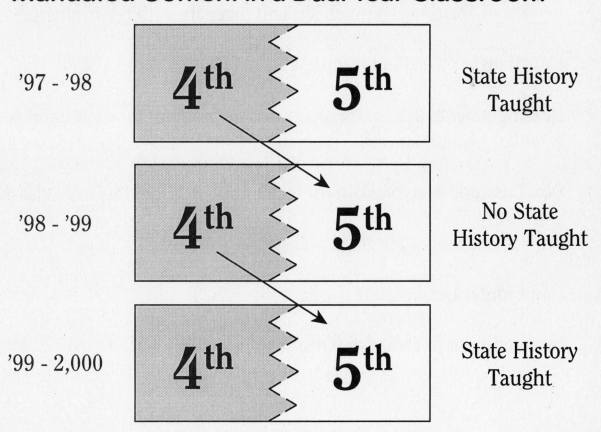

'97 - '98 — 4th / 5th — State History Taught

'98 - '99 — 4th / 5th — No State History Taught

'99 - 2,000 — 4th / 5th — State History Taught

Note: School officials should secure a test waiver to move testing to the end of Grade 5

Jim Grant/Bob Johnson/Char Forsten

How to Avoid Disaster in the Multiage Classroom

1. Change Process

    A. Create a shared vision with all stakeholders
    B. Provide adequate staff development
    C. Provide initiatives/incentives
    D. Be willing to pay for educational reforms
    E. Develop an action plan

2. Don't expect multiage practices to solve every problem in your class

3. Avoid using inaccurate or inflammatory terms when defining your program

4. Consider class size

5. Beware of creating too much student diversity within a multiage setting

6. Pay attention to school readiness issues when placing a child

7. Offering parents the choice of a multiage program for their child is essential — but can create problems

8. Don't assume everyone can (or wants to) teach in a multiage classroom

9. Provide challenges for gifted students

10. Don't forget the research

11. Be careful not to create staff dissension

Jim Grant/Bob Johnson/Char Forsten

The Graded Classroom
("Parts List")

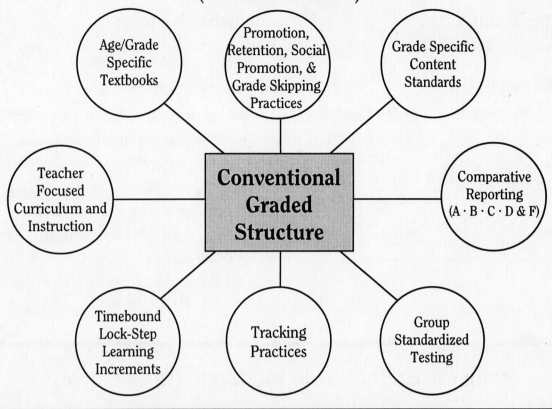

Age/Grade Specific Textbooks

Promotion, Retention, Social Promotion, & Grade Skipping Practices

Grade Specific Content Standards

Teacher Focused Curriculum and Instruction

Conventional Graded Structure

Comparative Reporting (A · B · C · D & F)

Timebound Lock-Step Learning Increments

Tracking Practices

Group Standardized Testing

The Multiage Classroom
("Parts List")

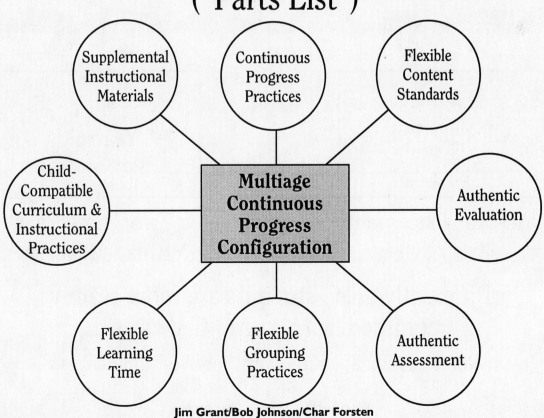

Supplemental Instructional Materials

Continuous Progress Practices

Flexible Content Standards

Child-Compatible Curriculum & Instructional Practices

Multiage Continuous Progress Configuration

Authentic Evaluation

Flexible Learning Time

Flexible Grouping Practices

Authentic Assessment

Jim Grant/Bob Johnson/Char Forsten

Gifted and Talented Students

Conventional One Year/Single Grade Classroom

- Extended learning program
- Tutoring opportunities offer a "teaching role"

That's all, folks!

Multiage Classroom

- Extended learning program
- Tutoring opportunities offer a "teaching role" **and**
- There are younger students to socialize with
- Student can gain "senior citizen" status
- The older more knowledgeable students have the chance to practice being in a leadership role
- Multiage classrooms have a higher ceiling on the curriculum
- First-timers can be more readily accelerated into the next years' curriculum

Inclusion Education in the Multiage Classroom

GRADE ONE

One-Year Placement

5 · 6 · 7 · 8 Year-olds
One/Two Blend

Two/Three Year-Multiage Placement

Differently-abled students are more readily accommodated in a multiage setting

Notes: A multiage classroom "forgives" differences

Jim Grant/Bob Johnson/Char Forsten

Class Size

Compared to large classes:

- small classes ameliorate the effects of large schools
- fewer students are held back a grade
- while small classes benefit all students, minority students benefit the most
- students receive more individual attention
- smaller classes are friendlier and more intimate
- there are fewer discipline problems in smaller classes
- students are more likely to participate in activities

Consider some potential cost savings from using small classes in grades K-2 or K-3

- There are fewer retentions
- Less need for remediation and /or special education
- Improved behavior
- Increased achievement

Center of Excellence for Research in Basic Skills · Tennessee State University
330 Tenth Avenue North, Suite J · Nashville, TN 37203 · 615-963-7238

Contact Jayne Zaharias for more information on the Student/Teacher Achievment Ratio Project (Project STAR). The project has studied the effect of class size on learning.

Guidelines to balancing the multiyear classroom

- Equal number of students from each grade level *
- Equal number of boys and girls
- Racially/culturally/linguistically balanced
- Socio-economically balanced
- Equal range of ability levels
- The percent of special needs students is the same as other conventional classrooms

Note: Remember, it is not always possible to achieve the above ideal guidelines.

* Does not pertain to single grade looping classrooms

Jim Grant/Bob Johnson/Char Forsten

Perceived Advantages of a Kindergarten/First Grade Blend

- Mixed-age eavesdropping opportunities
- There is a higher ceiling on the curriculum
- There are peer modeling opportunities
- There are over a dozen multiyear placement benefits
- There can be an additional year of learning time without the stigma of "staying back"
- Grade one is afforded more play opportunities
- There is additional time available for "kid watching"
- In some schools kindergartners go home at noon reducing the class size for first grade in the PM
- There are real benefits to proximal development
- There are tutoring opportunities for both groups
- There are 50% fewer new first graders to teach to read

Perceived Disadvantages of a Kindergarten/First Grade Blend

- Kindergartners may be denied play opportunities
- Many of today's kindergartners have very high needs
- Class is too diverse developmentally
- First graders may be shortchanged academically
- Some schools have four-year-olds in kindergarten due to a late entrance date
- The needs of five-year-olds are very different from six-year-olds
- Kindergartners may be overwhelmed by more experienced first graders
- There may not be enough quality kid watching time
- Kindergarten is time intensive to teach
- Some entire kindergarten classes are to disjointed to keep together as a group for multiple years
- Kindergartners who are learning handicapped, yet unidentified, may not qualify for special needs intervention
- If there is an AM and PM kindergarten (2 groups) there may be too much lost time transitioning

Various Factors to Consider Before Blending Kindergarten and First Grade

- Class size
- Entrance date
- Program support: Parents, teachers, administrators, school board
- Condition of the student population
- Number of non-English speaking children
- Conflicting mandates from the state, country, and local education officials
- Grade specific curriculum requirements
- Number of identified special needs children
- Number of children with "invisible" disabilities

Kindergarten/First Grade Configuration Options

Caution: The special needs population tends to be overrepresented in transition classes.

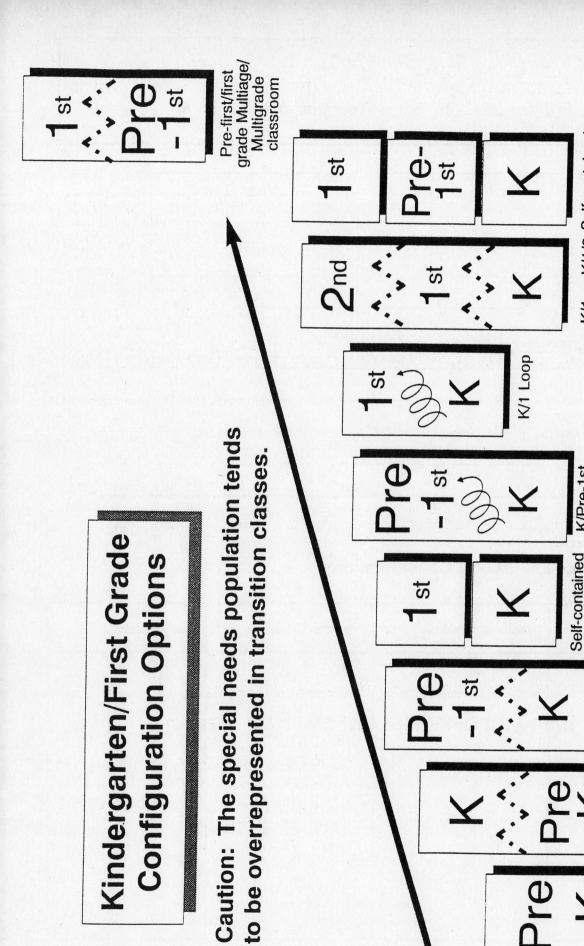

Pre-K for "Young Fives"

Pre-K/K Multiage/Multigrade classroom

K/Pre-1st Multiage/Multigrade classroom

Self-contained classroom for Kindergarten and first grade

K/Pre-1st Loop

K/1 Loop

K/1 or K/1/2 Multiage/Multigrade classroom (one teacher or team teachers)

Self-contained Kindergarten, Pre-1st and first grade

Pre-first/first grade Multiage/Multigrade classroom

Jim Grant / Bob Johnson / Char Forsten

51

LOOPING

Single Grade Progresses With Same Teacher(s) for 2 or More Years

Year One		Year Two
Grade _____	→	Grade _____

Compelling Reasons to Loop:

_____

_____

_____

_____

_____

_____

Cautions & Decision-Making Considerations:

	Previous Grade: _____	Present Grade: _____	Next Grade: _____
Curriculum:			
Learners:			
Staff:			
Expectations:			
Other:			

Society for Developmental Education   1-800-924-9621

Looping Continuum

Single-Grade
Single-Year

School-Wide Looping

Factors That Influence Looping Structure:

- school culture
- space & resource constraints
- teacher style & input
- parental involvement & input
- student population
- school officials & policy
- other...

Change Is Not Always a Forward Motion

1. ⟶

2. ⟵

3. ⟶

Any Kind of Change is Stressful!

Char Forsten   Society for Developmental Education   1-800-924-9621

Look Before You Loop

READY???

- Read about the topic.

- Explore and visit successful models of looping configurations.

- Assess your parent, administrative, & staff support.

- Determine if you or your school should proceed.

- Yield to a plan of action that focuses on your situation.

SET???

- Start drafting a plan and creating a realistic time line.

- Educate staff, students, & parents.

- Take-charge & determine staff development needs.

GO!!!

- Get your room(s) and materials ready.

- Oversee and assess your progress.

Char Forsten   Society for Developmental Education   1-800-924-9621

ACTION PLAN: READY? SET? IMPLEMENT...

1. READY?

Gather Information:
- Read books & articles;
- Attend conferences;
- Make school visits where multiyear practices are used;
- Network on the *Internet* & with other multiyear educators .
- Other...

Testing the Waters:
- Discuss with principal & colleagues;
- Implement some multiyear techniques - cross-age groups, cooperative groups, mentoring, center work, etc.;
- Switch places with colleagues at other grade levels.
- Other...

2. SET? Decision-Making:

- Develop Flexible 2-year Plan (proposal) Who will be affected? How will It work? How will you assess?:

    Staff:

    Students:

    Curriculum:

    Parents -

        Information Letter/Night:

        On-going Involvement:

- Complete a Needs Assessment:

    Training:

    Materials:

    Physical Space:

    Planning Time:

Char Forsten

3. GO!   Implementation:

Building Level:

- ☐ **Present plan & needs assessment to administration, colleagues, & school board;**
- ☐ **Secure administrative & peer support & establish:**

  On-going Discussion Forum:

  Staff Roles/Involvement:

  Student Placement Guidelines:

  Other:

- ☐ **Prepare a tentative calendar.**

- ☐ **Other...**

Personal Level (Needs/Support Assessment)

- ☐ **Physical Space:**

- ☐ **Organization of Materials:**

- ☐ **Organizing Students:**

- ☐ **Planning**

- ☐ **Assessment:**

- ☐ **Other:**

SAMPLE: PREPLANNING CALENDAR (Fill in Tentative Dates)

	Jan.	Feb.	Mar.	Apr.	May	June	July	Aug.	Sept.	Oct.	Nov.	Dec.
1. Gather Information- Test the Waters-												
2. Draft: 2-Year Plan: Staff: Students: Curriculum: Parents: Needs Assessment-												
3. Building Level: Presentation(s)- Staff Meetings: Roles- Student Placement- Other-												
Personal: Classroom Space- Materials- Student Concerns- Curriculum Help- Assessment-												

©Char Forsten   Society for Developmental Education   1-800-924-9621

57

Looping Benefits

Based on positive, long-term student/teacher/parent relationships & more effective & efficient use of instructional time:

BENEFITS	STRATEGIES TO HELP ACHIEVE BENEFITS
Fewer & smoother transitions produce less student/teacher/ parent stress.	
Two-year classrooms increase instructional time & decrease "down" or repetitive time.	
Consistency of rules, routines, & traditions has positive effect on discipline, attendance, & academic performance.	
Two-year classrooms allow for in-depth understanding of child's strengths & weaknesses.	
Increased time allows for better-informed decisions concerning students. Fewer special ed. referrals & retentions reported.	
Two-year classrooms can lead to improved parent involvement.	
Family atmosphere builds interdependence & cooperation.	
Time allows for more meaningful *semi-seamless* curriculum.	

Looping Obstacles

POTENTIAL OBSTACLES	SPECIFIC STRATEGIES TO HELP AVOID OBSTACLES:
Lack of understanding the change process	
Lack of adequate planning and ongoing assessment	
Lack of Support	
Child/teacher or parent/teacher personality conflict that is unresolvable Dysfunctional class	
Class imbalance: too many difficult and/or special needs children	
Staff Dissension	
Ineffective Teacher	
Multiyear classroom might mask learning disability.	

Char Forsten   Society for Developmental Education   1-800-924-9621

A STUDENT PLACEMENT PROCESS

Decision-Making Considerations for Staff & Administrators:

- Classroom Configurations - Does your school have choices in classroom configurations? (multiage, looping, teams, conventional, etc.) What criteria will you use to place students in different configurations?

- Parent Roles - Will parents have a role in the placement process? Will you survey parents for information about their children or for placement in particular configurations?

- Classroom Balance (Equity) -- How will you place students so that a balance is achieved according to gender, ability, class size, grades (if multiage), special needs, learning disabilities, & diversity, etc.

- Changes in Classroom Assignments - How will requests for change be handled after the placement process is completed? To ensure balance, a guideline could be: Any requests for changes in assignments receive final approval from administrator & staff members affected by change. (This point needs to be addressed in your placement guidelines. Two messages are sent to staff members involved in the process if class lists are randomly changed: their time & recommendations are not respected.

- Opt Out Clause - Will "opting out" at the end of the first year be an option in your plan? How will this be handled? What circumstances will warrant a decision to not continue with a particular classroom or configuration?

- Incoming/New Students - How will new students be placed in classrooms? You might establish a "Getting to Know You" time period for the first two weeks of the school year, or a set time period for incoming students once the school year has started. This will allow observation & decision-making time to make alternative recommendations.

    Note: Some teachers might opt to begin the year with a greater number of students, with the condition that new students will be placed in other classrooms. This reduces chances for disruption of instruction and classroom dynamics, especially when teachers are teaching in a multiage or other modified setting.

Char Forsten   Society for Developmental Education   1-800-924-9621

Teacher:_____   School Year: _____

	A.D.D.	Emotional Difficulties	Independent Learner	Motivated
Gifted	■ (girl)		□ (boy)	■ (girl)
Above Level		□ (boy)	□ (boy) / ■ (girl)	
At Level	□ (boy)	■ (girl)	□ (boy)	□ (boy) ■ (girl) / □ (boy)
Below Level	□ (boy) ■ (girl)		■ (girl) □ (boy)	
Title I		■ (girl)	□ (boy) ■ (girl)	
L.D.	■ (girl) □ (boy)			□ (boy) ■ (girl)

■ = girls   □ = boys

Char Forsten

61

REFLECTING...

a)	1	2	3	4	5	6	7	8	9	10
b)	1	2	3	4	5	6	7	8	9	10
c)	1	2	3	4	5	6	7	8	9	10
d)	1	2	3	4	5	6	7	8	9	10
e)	1	2	3	4	5	6	7	8	9	10

CLARIFYING...

1. Describe Change:_____

_____

2. Why?_____

_____

3. Strengths? _____

_____

4. Obstacles? _____

_____

HOW AM I DOING?

	GREAT!	PROGRESSING	WELL?...	WHAT PLAN?
Change Area:				

Char Forsten   Society for Developmental Education   1-800-924-9621

PLANNING AND ASSESSING YOUR LOOPING PROGRESS

Change Area:	1. WHERE AM I NOW?	3. WHAT IS MY PLAN?	4. WHAT RESOURCES DO I NEED?	2. WHERE DO I WANT TO BE?	5. HOW AM I DOING? ...HOW DID I DO?
Explore Looping					
Develop Proposal					
Parent Education					
Staff Involvement					
Placement Guidelines					
Assessment					
Thematic Instruction					
Learning Centers					
Grouping					
Management					
Multiple Intelligences					

REFLECT: WHAT   RESPOND: ACTION   REACH OUT   REFLECT: WHY   ASSESS & REVISE

This is a *sample* planner. It can be enlarged and customized to fit individual school and classroom needs.

©Char Forsten   Society for Developmental Education   1-800-924-9621

64

ASSESSING YOUR LOOPING PROGRAM

Directions: Why are you implementing looping? The compelling reasons that influenced your decision to explore looping should serve as the basis for your assessment and evaluation. Use the chart below to create an assessment tool for your unique Program:

Looping Goals	How Will I Know There Is Progress?	Assessment Tool
1. Example: More effective use of instructional time	The first day of the second year will seem like the 181st day of the school year. I will not need to re-teach rules & routines. Time will not be spent on unnecessary review.	Personal Journal/ Questionnaire
2.		
3.		
4.		
5.		

©Char Forsten, 1997

65

Z. Best Elementary School
Education Place
Universal Studies, USA

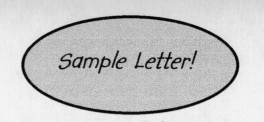
Sample Letter!

May 22, 1994

Dear Parents,

I couldn't let the school year draw to a close without commenting on what I believe is a very unique class. We have had an exciting and productive year!

I am also writing to let you know that your child will progress to second grade with me in a *"looping configuration."* "A WHAT?" you might ask. *Looping* or *student/teacher progression* is a concept that allows me to teach students over a two-year time period.

The benefits of having the same teacher for two years are quite extraordinary. Your child and I have developed a relationship that can only continue to grow. We have begun to establish trust and understanding that is the foundation to a powerful learning atmosphere. Also, consider the academic growth that can take place immediately upon arrival in the Fall, because students are already familiar with everyday classroom procedures. These benefits are just to name a few! It is and can be a very exciting option.

There are pros and cons to every issue, though. One con could be that you/your child is not comfortable with me or my teaching style. If that is the case, I am asking that you let D. Principal, know as soon as possible so she can place your child appropriately next year.

If you have questions/concerns, please feel free to call me or D. Principal.

Thank you! I look forward to seeing you in the Fall!

Love,
Ms. M.A. Teacher

*Note: Parent letters adapted from a number of educators' correspondence

Char Forsten   Society for Developmental Education

September 25, 1997

Dear Parents,

How often have you wished your children could remain with their teacher for more than one year? During the past year, we have been investigating an educational concept called "looping." This means that the same class of students are taught by the same teacher for two consecutive years.

There are compelling reasons to consider looping. We would like to share these with you on October 1st, (Wednesday evening) at 7:00 p.m. in the school library. We also want to listen to any questions and concerns you might have about looping.

At Z Best Elementary School, we are pleased that we have a number of teachers presently studying this concept, who are interested in implementing this 2-year cycle of teaching, beginning next school year.

We look forward to meeting with you and discussing this student-centered concept of spending two years with the same teacher. If you cannot attend, please fill in the agreement below and return it with your child.

Sincerely,

D. Principal

My child's name: _____

My child's grade next fall: _____

_____ I would like my child to be considered for placement in a looping classroom, beginning the 1998-99 school year.

(I understand that if my child is selected to be in a looping classroom, he/she will have the same teacher for 2 consecutive school years. I also understand that at the end of the first school year, either the school or I can choose to remove my child from the looping class without consequence.

_____ I would not like my child placed in a looping classroom.

_____
Parent Signature   Date

Char Forsten

LOOPING SURVEY*

Please circle A for Agree, D for Disagree, or U for Unsure in response to these questions about your child being with the same teacher for two years:

My child enjoyed being with the same teacher for two years.	A D U
My child enjoyed being with the same classmates for two years.	A D U
Starting the second year was less stressful for my child.	A D U
The second year was less stressful for me as a parent.	A D U
I had a better understanding of my child's education after two years with the same teacher.	A D U
At the beginning of the second year, my child understood what was expected of him/her.	A D U
The teacher better understood my child's strengths and needs the second year.	A D U
The summer between the two years was less stressful for my child.	A D U
I felt more comfortable communicating with my child's teacher the second year.	A D U
If I had it to do over, I would choose looping for my child.	A D U
I would recommend looping to other parents.	A D U

Comments: _____

_____

_____

*Adapted from surveys from a collection of sources

Char Forsten

Three Grouping Strategies

Whole Class

Group conferences
Appropriate group lessons
Introductions
Reading to class
Instructional games
Etc.

Small Group Instruction

Group

Skills development
Interest
Work habits
Social
Random
Task/Activity

Other students

Contracts
Centers
Stations
Peer tutoring
Parent volunteers
Choices

Individual Instruction

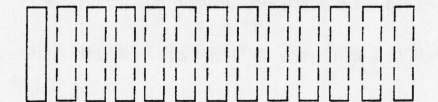

Contracts, centers, stations, peer tutoring, choices, volunteers, projects

U.S.A. TODAY

Date: 3/14/97   Special: *Art, 10:30*
Day of School Year: *144*   Fraction: *144/180*
News: *Class: Sally's dog had a litter of 9 puppies.*
         World: President Clinton injured his knee.

Class Math: *Multiplication - Rename the Date*
- Math Whiz Kids: *p. 234 (prime # examples), Krypto*
- Marvelous Multipliers: *Meet with Ms. F*
  Math Maniacs: *Activity "Multiplying Mysteries." Center 1*

Class Reading: *Ms. F. - Read Aloud: Stuart Little*
- *Fantastic Mr. Fox: Literature Circle: chapters 8 & 9.*
- *Charlotte's Web: Activity: Point of View, Ind. Project*
- *Cricket in Times Square: Meet with Ms. F.*

Spelling:
- Mighty Spellers: *Pretest - plan*
- Spelling Bees: *Newspaper Scavenger Hunt*
- Spellbound: *Syllable Game*

Writing: *Diary Entries "Pioneers," Research Reports*

Social Studies: *"Pioneers" - cooperative groups pack*
                begin to pack wagon trains.
Science: *Mammals - mid-1800s*

Challenge: *How did Portland, Oregon get its name?*

Other: *Mr. Clark will present "Artist of the Month" today.*

Reminders: *Book money due Friday*

Char Forsten   Society for Developmental Education   1-800-924-9621

Example: PRE-PLANNING WORKSHEET FOR THEME OR UNIT OF STUDY

THEME: The Community

DISCIPLINES:	READING	WRITING	SPELLING	SOCIAL STUDIES	MATH	SCIENCE	MUSIC	ART	PE
Concepts/Content:	(The Little House) -non-fiction -biographies -poetry	-reports -journals -editorials	-community words -science words -reg. spell. program	(Hands-On Geography) -maps -community roles -current events	-scale of miles -measurement -money (economics)	-animal community -food chain/food web	-original songs - local musicians	-mural & model of community	-food web game
Skills:	-fact & opinion -similes & metaphors -main idea & supporting facts -character traits	-research skills -business letter -syllables (haiku & limericks) -rhyme & free verse	-endings "er," "or," & "ar" (roles) -ongoing spell. rules	-map symbols, key, & scale -cardinal directions -local laws	-linear measure -add/sub money -nonstandard measure	-scientific method -food chain roles	-beats, measure -rhythm	-perspective -proportion	
Multiple Intelligences:	-oral history skits -visit library	-biographical sketch -"Poet Tea" -class newsletter	-word searches -riddles	-make relief maps -dioramas -role playing	-keep checkbook -visit bank -board games	-act out food web -essay on pollution	-write lyrics -compose music	-dioramas -make models	-movement -games
Real World Connections:	-surveys -debates	-interview local writers & journalists	-find words in newspapers	-community guest speakers	-field trip to bank	-report to local conservation com.	-visit radio station	-contact local artists	-community sports

Roles In Daily Lives →

© Char Forsten   Society for Developmental Education   1-800-924-9621

PRE-PLANNING WORKSHEET FOR THEME OR UNIT OF STUDY*

THEME:

DISCIPLINES:	READING	WRITING	MECHANICS SPELLING	SOCIAL STUDIES	MATH	SCIENCE	MUSIC	ART	PE
Concepts/ Content:									
Skills:									
Multiple Intelligences:									
Real World Connections:									

*Recommendation: For better results, enlarge chart on photocopier before using.

© Char Forsten

Society for Developmental Education

1-800-924-9621

"PERMANENT" SUBJECT & REFERENCE CENTERS

SUBJECT: | **SUGGESTED MATERIALS:**

Reading
Classroom library, reading logs & reviews, magazines, newspapers;

Writing/Spelling
Assorted paper, writing process chart, writing folders, publication sheets, thesauruses, rhyming, spelling, & standard dictionaries, pre-writing materials;

Listening/Music
Cassette player with set of headphones, recorded book & music cassettes, blank tapes, biographies of composers;

Social Studies
Maps, atlas, almanacs, travel brochures, geography/history magazines;

Math/Science
Problem solving charts, games, puzzles, dice, calculators, manipulatives for geometry, measurement, probability & statistics, number sense, etc. Also, weather station hand lenses, science manipulatives, observation ...es, math & science magazines, blocks;

Art
Assorted paper, crayons, markers, pencils, scissors, glue, paste, paints, recyclables, art prints, artist biographies.

Char Forsten

Society for Developmental Education

1-800-924-9621

"PERMANENT" SUBJECT & REFERENCE CENTERS

Sample Room Plan

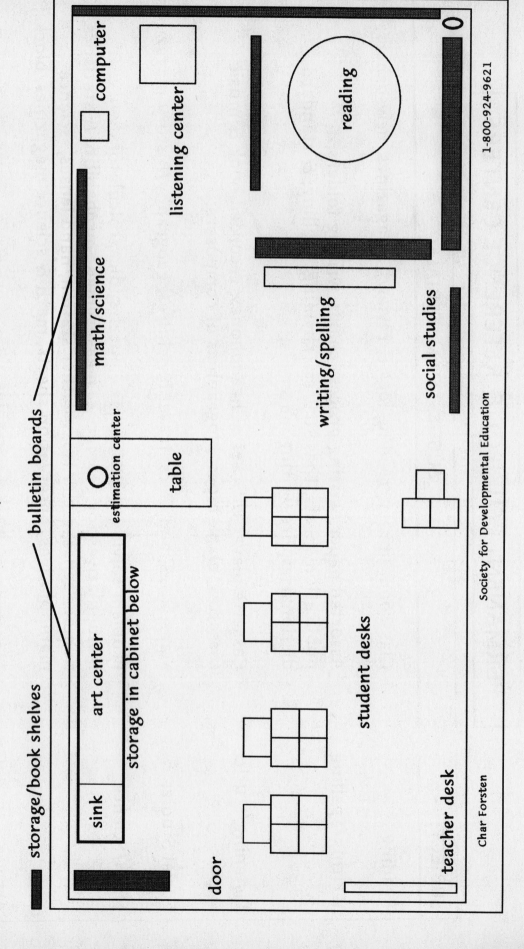

storage/book shelves

bulletin boards

computer

math/science

listening center

reading

estimation center

table

art center

storage in cabinet below

sink

door

student desks

writing/spelling

social studies

teacher desk

Char Forsten   Society for Developmental Education   1-800-924-9621

Teaching Full Circle:

Organizing Your Instruction & Incorporating Multiple Intelligences

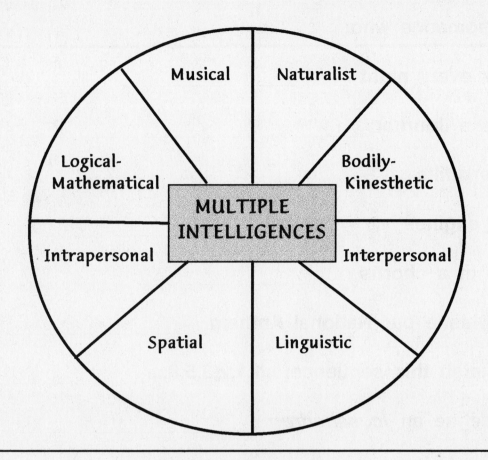

Multiple Intelligences*

As you plan your instruction, incorporate activities that teach to the strengths of a wide range of intelligences among your students. Use this chart to help in your planning:

Logical Mathematical - Numbers, Logic, Puzzles, Scientific Method
Linguistic - Reading, Writing, Speaking, Storytelling, Poetry
Musical - Singing, Music Appreciation, Imagery, Composing, Music Software
Spatial - Charts, Graphs, & Diagrams, Painting & Drawing, Photography, Geometry
Bodily-Kinesthetic - Movement, Skits & Plays, Hands-On Activities, Manipulatives
Interpersonal - Cooperative Groups, Simulations, Conflict Resolution, Clubs
Intrapersonal - Private Space, Journals, Independent Study, Self-Awareness
                      Activities
Naturalist Ecology, Nature, & Outdoor Activities, Global Themes, Real World
                      Connections

*Gardner, Howard. *Frames of Mind: The Theory of Multiple Intelligences,* 1983.
_____*Multiple Intelligences: The Theory in Practice.* Basic Books, 1993.

MULTIPLE INTELLIGENCE SCAVENGER HUNT

Find someone who:

Reads every night _____

Keeps a Journal _____

Makes quilts _____

Fixes engines _____

Sings in a chorus _____

Can whistle our National Anthem_____

Can finish this sequence: 1,1,2,3,5,8,..._____

Can define an *icosahedron*_____

Will recite a short poem_____

Plays a sport _____

Takes dance lessons _____

Plays an instrument_____

Loves to entertain_____

Can juggle_____

Makes Art: _____

Enjoys Hiking or Camping_____

Char Forsten   Society for Developmental Education   1-800-924-9621

WINDOWS OF LEARNING

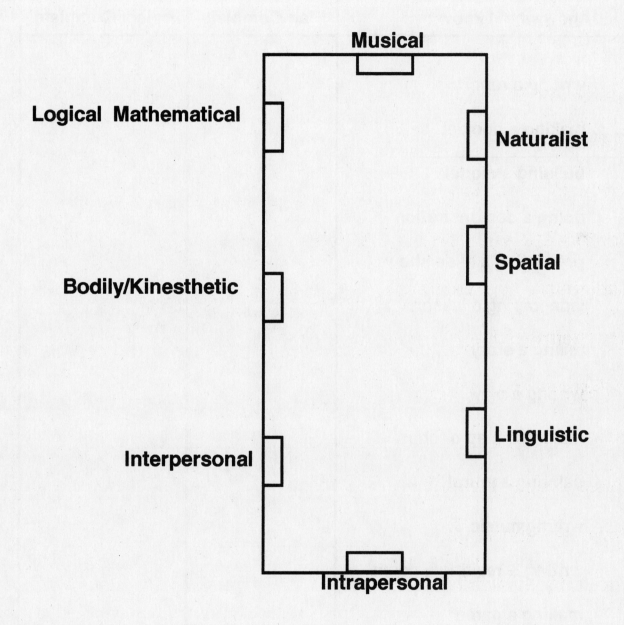

Char Forsten   Society for Developmental Education   1-800-924-9621

LEARNING CONTRACT

Name: _____   Date:_____

I will show what I know by:	Plan Complete	Project Complete
writing a report		
making a booklet		
building a model		
doing a demonstration		
presenting a slide show		
videotaping a lesson		
telling a story		
writing a play		
making a map or chart		
painting a mural		
writing music		
writing & reciting a poem		
making a game		
teaching a younger student		
Other: _____		

Char Forsten   Society for Developmental Education   1-800-924-9621

FOCUS FRAME

DIRECTIONS: Use the "Focus Frame" pattern below to cut out pieces of posterboard or another type of heavy weight paper. Cut along the dotted line of frame section "A." Insert "B" into section "A" to form a movable box. Slide the "Focus Frame" to adjust for amount of space needed.

Student slides focus frame to fit the present problem,

eliminating unnecessary information or distractions →

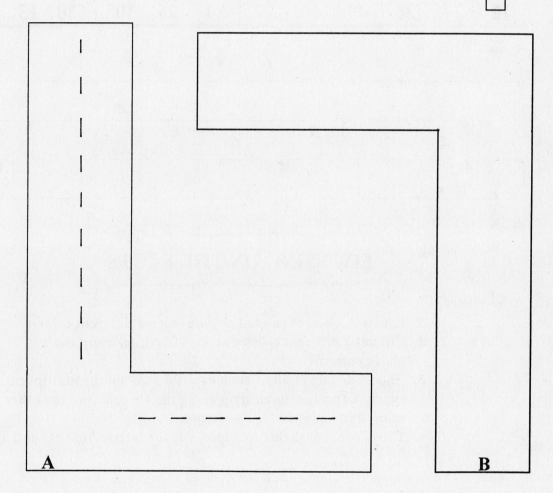

Society for Developmental Education   1-800-924-9621

1	2	3	4	5	6	7	8	9	10	11	12
2	4	6	8	10	12	14	16	18	20	22	24
3	6	9	12	15	18	21	24	27	30	33	36
4	8	12	16	20	24	28	32	36	40	44	48
5	10	15	20	25	30	35	40	45	50	55	60
6	12	18	24	30	36	42	48	54	60	66	72
7	14	21	28	35	42	49	56	63	70	77	84
8	16	24	32	40	48	56	64	72	80	88	96
9	18	27	36	45	54	63	72	81	90	99	108
10	20	30	40	50	60	70	80	90	100	110	120
11	22	33	44	55	66	77	88	99	110	121	132
12	24	36	48	60	72	84	96	108	120	132	144

FOCUSING ON THE FACTS

Directions:

1. Locate 2 sheets of colored acetate (each a different color);
2. Cut out 2 different colored strips of acetate, using the above patterns;
3. Choose a "fact family," such as *4 X 7 = 28* on the multiplication chart. Lay one colored strip along the 4's row, and the other colored strip down the 7's column.
4. The product or dividend appears at the intersection of the 2 strips.

| Student Name: _____ |
| Teacher: _____ |
| Grade: _____ |
| Report Period: _____ |

Spelling Level: _____

    Program: _____

    Progress: C P N /

    Effort: C P N /

Comments: _____

_____

Listening:

  Follows Directions: C P N /

  Shows Understanding: C P N /

  Enjoys stories   C P N /

Comments: _____

_____

Speaking:

  Expresses Self Clearly: C P N /

  Uses Good Diction: C P N /

  Joins Discussions: C P N /

Comments: _____

_____

Writing:

  Writes interesting leads: C P N /

  Sequences ideas: C P N /

  Develops Theme: C P N /

  Uses "voice" in Stories: C P N /

  Uses grammatical rules: C P N /

  Uses legible penmanship: C P N /

  Writes strong endings: C P N /

Comments: _____

_____

Social/Emotional Growth:

  Is Cooperative: C P N /

  Accepts Responsibility: C P N /

  Accepts Rules & Limits   C P N /

  Uses Self-Control: C P N /

Comments: _____

_____

Reading Level: _____

Reading Program: _____

  Selects Books at Level: C P N /

  Reads Independently: C P N /

  Reads for Meaning: C P N /

  Self-Corrects: C P N /

  Shows Understanding: C P N /

  Sustains Silent Reading: C P N /

  Enjoys Reading: C P N /

  Reads Different Genre: C P N /

Comments: _____

_____

Math Concept(s): _____

Approximate Level: _____

  Number Facts: C P N /

  Number Sense: C P N /

  Addition: C P N /

  Subtraction: C P N /

  Multiplication: C P N /

  Division: C P N /

  Geometry: C P N /

  Measurement: C P N /

  Problem Solving: C P N /

Comments: _____

_____

Social Studies/Science Theme(s): _____

  Participates: C P N /

  Understands Concepts: C P N /

  Effort: C P N /

Comments: _____

_____

Study & Work Habits:

  Stays on Task: C P N /

  Completes Assignments: C P N /

  Works Neatly   C P N /

  Works Independently: C P N /

  Stays Organized   C P N /

Comments: _____

_____

COMPONENTS OF A QUALITY MATH PROGRAM

(Based on the National Council of Teachers of Mathematics *Standards*)

Goals

Students should learn to:
- Value mathematics;
- Communicate mathematically;
- Reason mathematically.

Students should become:
- Confident about their ability to do mathematics;
- Mathematical problem solvers.

STRANDS

1. Problem Solving
2. Using Mathematics to Communicate Information
3. Using Mathematics to Reason
4. Making Connections with Mathematics
5. Estimation
6. Number Sense and Numeration
7. Concepts of Whole Number Operations
8. Whole Number Computation
9. Geometry and Spatial Sense
10. Measurement
11. Statistics and Probability
12. Fractions and Decimals
13. Patterns and Relationships

Irv Richardson/Char Forsten   Society for Developmental Education   1-800-924-9621

PROBLEM SOLVING CHART

Name:	Group:	Date:

PROBLEM:

RELEVANT FACTS:

CONDITIONS:

STRATEGY:

SOLUTION:

REASONABLE ANSWER?

SOCIAL SKILLS ASSESSMENT

CONTRIBUTIONS TO GROUP:

ENCOURAGING WORDS:

WAYS WE COOPERATED:

Char Forsten   Society for Developmental Education   1-800-924-9621

SKILL BUILDER CHART

NAME:_____

DATE	SHEET	SCORE	DATE	SHEET	SCORE

Society for Developmental Education   1-800-924-9621

100					
98					
96					
94					
92					
90					
88					
86					
84					
82					
80					
78					
76					
74					
72					
70					
68					
66					
64					
62					
60					
58					
56					
54					
52					
50					
48					
46					
44					
42					
40					
38					
36					
34					
32					
30					
28					
26					
24					
22					
20					
18					
16					
14					
12					
10					
8					
6					
4					
2	Monday	Tuesday	Wednesday	Thursday	Friday

Name:_____   **Week of** _____

Skill Builder Bar Graph

Recommended Math Materials

compiled by Char Forsten

> **Key**
> P = Primary
> M = Middle

Children's Books

Anno, Masaichiro and Mitsumasa. *Anno's Math Games I, II, & III, Anno's Counting House, Anno's Mysterious Multiplying Jar.* Philomel Books. (Delightful series in which age range varies, P - M)

Allen, Pamela. *Mr. Archimedes' Bath.* Angus & Robertson, 1980. (P)

Base, Graeme. *The Eleventh Hour.* Harry N. Abrams, Inc., 1989. (M+)

Baum, Arline & Joseph. *Opt, An Illusionary Tale.* Puffin, 1987. (M)

Briggs, Raymond. *Jim and the Beanstalk.* Sandcastle Books, 1970. (P, P+)

Burns, Marilyn. *The Greedy Triangle.* Scholastic, 1994. (P - M)

Connell, David D. & Jim Thurman. *Mathnet: The Map with a Gap.* W.H. Freeman; Children's Television Workshop, 1994. (Entire series available) (P+, M)

Dyches, Richerd W. & Jean M. Shaw. *First Math Dictionary.* Franklin Watts, 1991. (P, M)

Ehlert, Lois. *Fish Eyes, A Book You Can Count On.* Harcourt, Brace & Co., 1990. (P)

Facklam, Margery & Margaret Thomas. *The Kid's World Almanac of Amazing Facts About Numbers, Math and Money.* World Almanac, 1992. (M)

Friedman, Aileen. *A Cloak for the Dreamer.* Scholastic, 1994. (P, M)

_____. *The King's Commissioners.* Scholastic, 1994. (P, P+)

Godfrey, Neale S. *The Kids' Money Book.* Scholastic, 1991.

Marzollo, Jean and Walter Wick. *I Spy Fantasy — A Book of Picture Riddles.* Scholastic, 1994. (Wonderful series!! P - M)

Myller, Rolf. *How Big is a Foot?* Young Yearling — Dell, 1990. (P, P+)

Pappas, Theoni. *Math Talk: Mathematical Ideas in Poems for Two Voices.* World Wide Publishing, 1991. (M)

Pittman, Helena Clare. *A Grain of Rice.* Bantam Skylark, 1986. (P+,M)

Schwartz, David M. *How Much Is a Million?* Lothrop, Lee & Shepard, 1985. (P, M)

_____. *If You Made a Million.* Lothrop, Lee & Shepard, 1989. (M)

Scieszka, Jon and Lane Smith. *Math Curse.* Viking, 1995. (P+, M)

Simon, Seymour. *The Optical Illusion Book.* Beech Tree Books, 1976. (M)

Tahan, Malba. *The Man Who Counted.* W.W. Norton, 1993. (M)

Viorst, Judith. *Alexander, Who Used to Be Rich Last Sunday.* Alladin, 1978. (P, P+)

Professional and Activity Books That Develop Thinking and Problem Solving Skills

Allen, Roger E. & Stephen D. Allen. *Winnie-the-Pooh on Problem Solving.* Dutton, 1995. (P+, M)

Ary, Daniel W. *Middle School Math Challenge.* Learning Works, 1995. (M)

Brumbaugh, Allyne. *Do-It-Yourself Math Stories.* Scholastic, 1991. (M)

Burns, Marilyn. *The Book of Think.* Little, Brown & Co., 1976. (M)

Burns, Marilyn & Bonnie Tank. *A Collection of Math Lessons from Grades 1 Through 3.* Math Solutions Publications, 1988. (P)

Burns, Marilyn. *A Collection of Math Lessons from Grades 3 Through 6.* Math Solutions Publications, 1987. (M)

_____. *The I Hate Mathematics Book.* Scholastic, 1994. (M)

_____. *Math for Smarty Pants.* Scholastic, 1995. (M)

Cheney, Martha & Diane Bockwoldt. *Puzzles and Games for Critical and Creative Thinking.* The Lowell House (Juvenile), 1994. (P+)

Cook, Marcy. *Mathematics Problems of the Day.* Creative Publications, 1982. (M)

Forsten, Char. *Teaching Thinking and Problem Solving in Math.* Scholastic, 1992. (P+, M)

Greenberg, Dan. *30 Wild and Wonderful Math Stories.* Scholastic, 1992. (M)

Problem Solver, The. Creative Publications. (Series available for grades one through eight)

Risby, Bonnie. *Logic Liftoff.* Dandy Lion, 1987. (M)

Schoenfield, Mark & Jeanette Rosenblatt. *Adventures with Logic.* David S. Lake Publishers, 1985. (Grades 5-7)

_____. *Discovering Logic.* David S. Lake Publishers, 1985. (Grades 4-6)

_____. *Playing with Logic.* David S. Lake Publishers, 1985. (Grades 3-5)

Seymour, Dale & Ed Beardslee. *Critical Thinking Activities.* Dale Seymour Publications, 1988. (M)

Silbert, Jack. *Math Mysteries.* Scholastic, 1995. (P - M)

Vydra, Joan & Jean McCall. *No Problem!* Dandy Lion, 1989. (M)

Books that enhance arithmetic, number sense, geometry, probability, measurement & calculators, etc.

Abrohms, Alison. *Literature-Based Math Activities.* Scholastic. 1992. (K-3)

_____. *1001 Instant Manipulatives for Math.* Scholastic. 1993. (P)

Bacarella, Dawn Hickman. *1-100 Activity Book.* Learning Resources, 1990. (P)

Brumbaugh, Allyne. *Big Magic Number Puzzles.* Scholastic, 1992. (M)

Burns, Marilyn. *The Good Time Math Event Book.* Creative Publications. 1977. (M)

_____. *This Book Is About Time.* Little, Brown & Co., 1978. (M)

Donald in Mathmagic Land. Walt Disney Mini Classic Video, Color - 27 min., (P - M)

Forsten, Char. *Using Calculators Is Easy!* Scholastic, 1992. (P, M)

Garland, Trudi Hammel. *Fascinating Fibonaccis — Mystery and Magic in Numbers.* Dale Seymour Publications, 1987. (M)

Goldish, Meish. *Making Multiplication Easy.* Scholastic. 1991. (P+, M)

Hope, Jack A. et al. *Mental Math in the Middle Grades.* Dale Seymour Publications, 1987. (M)

Jones, Graham A. and Carol A. Thornton. *Data, Chance & Probability.* Learning Resources, 1993. (M)

Kenda, Margaret and Phyllis S. Williams. *Math Wizardry for Kids.* Barron's 1995. (P - M)

Lee, Martin and Marcia Miller. *Great Graphing.* Scholastic, 1993. (P+, M)

Miller, Marcia and Martin Lee. *Estimation Investigations.* Scholastic, 1994. (M)

Morton, Lone. *My First Design Book.* Barron's, 1993. (P)

Piccirilli, Richard S. *Mental Math.* Scholastic, 1994. (M)

Ranucci, E.R. and J.L. Teeters. *Creating Escher-Type Drawings.* Creative Publications, 1977. (M)

Spann, Mary Beth. *Exploring the Numbers 1-100.* Scholastic, 1993. (P)

VanCleave, Janice. *Janice VanCleave's Geometry for Every Kid.* John Wiley & Sons, 1994. (M) (Janice VanCleave writes wonderful science & math books)

Whitin, David J. and Sandra Wilde. *Read Any Good Math Lately?* Heinemann, 1992. (P - M)

Zaslavsky, Claudia. *Multicultural Math.* Scholastic, 1994. (P+ - M)

Reference, resource and background books for teachers

Blum, Raymond. *Mathemagic.* Sterling Publication, 1991. (M)

Burns, Marilyn. *About Teaching Mathematics — A K-8 Resource.* Math Solutions, 1992. (P - M)

Curriculum and Evaluation: Standards for School Mathematics. National Council of Teachers of Mathematics, 1989. (P - H)

Dictionary of Mathematics. London: Penguin Books, 1989.

Ferrell, Edmund. *Math-O-pedia.* OMNI Books, 1994.

Pappas, Theoni. *More Joy of Mathematics.* Wide World Publishing, 1991.

_____. *Fractals, Googols, and Other Mathematical Tales.* Wide World Publishing. 1993. (M)

_____. *The Magic of Mathematics.* Wide World Publishing, 1994. (M)

Paulos, John Allen. *Innumeracy, Mathematical Illiteracy and Its Consequences.* Vintage Books. 1988.

Silver Burdett Mathematical Dictionary. Silver Burdett., 1979.

Stenmark, Jean Kerr et al. *Family Math.* Lawrence Hall of Science, University of CA, 1986. (P - M)

Char Forsten

Time on Their Side

If social promotion doesn't work, is retention the answer? Well, sometimes

BY JIM GRANT

Did you consider keeping your young son or daughter home an extra year before starting school? Did you or someone in your family take more than four years to complete a college degree? Do you know someone who took a year off between high school and college? If you answer Yes to any of these questions, you know that time can indeed work in favor of some students.

Anyone who has spent time in a classroom knows that sometimes it makes sense for a child to spend an extra year in the same grade and sometimes it doesn't. Anyone who has spent time in a classroom knows, too, that not all the children coming to school today are ready to learn: They're coming with a host of physical, social, and psychological problems the likes of which we haven't seen before.

In the face of such complexity, many school systems have jumped on board the social promotion bandwagon, where they simply have to eyeball the date on a child's birth certificate before moving the child along to the next grade. And in doing so, they've put some of our most vulnerable children at risk.

In over their heads

If you need a sign that social promotion isn't working, just ask your fourth, fifth, and sixth-grade teachers. The students coming into their classes today don't know their times tables, haven't mastered cursive writing, and wouldn't know how to sound a word out if they tripped over it. That's the result of social promotion. That's what happens when we insist that every child has precisely 36 weeks to master all the material in first, second, or whatever grade.

It's also the result of placing children in the wrong grade to begin with. With two genders, 365 different birth dates, and a single cutoff date in September, school districts can't

Jim Grant is the founder and executive director of the Society for Developmental Education, Peterborough, N.H.

help but put some children in the wrong grade level. In fact, most research estimates that about 20 percent of school children are in the wrong grade, an estimate I think is quite low. In fact, large numbers of the children diagnosed with attention deficit disorder or learning disabilities are younger than their grade-level peers. For many of them, the only real problem is that some adult—a teacher, a principal, or a parent—put them in the wrong grade to begin with.

How could that happen? Schools are set up in 13 grades, school years last 180 days, and school days run for five and a quarter hours. That's the system we cling to, even though most of us don't know where it came from. In truth, the system is based on a Prussian military-industrial model that Horace Mann happened upon in 1843. Mann imported the idea to the United States, put the model into place in Quincy, Mass., and the modern school was born. Today, then, we perpetuate a 154-year-old system that was devised before the age of steam and electricity, a system that says, "Sure, let's collect children by age, segregate them by grade, and move them along in 36-week increments."

But common sense tells us that uniform grades and a uniform curriculum require uniform students, and we know that what we have today are nonstandardized children—children of poverty, children who don't speak English as their native language, children with severe physical and mental disabilities, children who were born with low birth weights, children whose parents have split up, if they were ever together at all.

Faced with this kind of diversity, what do we do? In effect, we resort to astrology: We decide when a child will start school on the basis on how many moons have passed since the child was born. We have an age and grade-specific curriculum in our schools today, and we bring kids in regardless of their level of readiness.

The following scenario is all too familiar: It's September, the start of the new school year in Any District, U.S.A., where the cutoff date for enrollment is a birthday before Sept. 1. In comes Jenny a 7-year-old first-grader born Sept.

2. Jenny is right-handed, well-behaved, and the apple of her middle-class parents' eyes. Her hobby is counting by threes, and she writes with an unbitten pencil. All in all, Jennie will be easy to teach.

Then there's Skippy, born Aug. 31 at 11:59 p.m. Skippy, who goes to school a full year early, is left-handed, was born premature, and lives in poverty. His parents are divorced.

How far apart are these two children? So far apart that even if you massage the curriculum and teach developmentally, the two of them will look at each other across the same divide in June, ready to be sentenced to Grade 2.

Any teacher or principal could tell you: The youngest children in the classroom are generally those who end up being retained in grade, dropping out, or being referred to special education. They are the children who are diagnosed as learning disabled and sent to the principal's office for discipline. They receive a variety of counseling services, earn lower grades than their abilities would suggest, pay less attention than other students in class, fall behind their peers in athletic skills, and rank lower in their graduating class. And we've made them that way.

The youngest children in the classroom are generally those who end up being retained in grade

Developmentally appropriate?

Some school systems, of course, say the answer is developmentally appropriate practice. If teachers would simply teach in a more developmentally appropriate fashion, these school systems say, all children would catch up by third grade.

I haven't visited a single school system in the United States that's been successful with this approach. And though I've been a street fighter for developmentally appropriate practice for years, I've become convinced that substituting developmentally appropriate practice for more time in grade is really just a way to save the district money. Developmentally appropriate practice doesn't eliminate a child's need for additional learning time.

Too often, in fact, school systems that adopt developmentally appropriate practices simply water down their curricula. In these districts it's understood that for a number of students, the first-grade curriculum will be more like kindergarten and the second grade will be something like first grade. But a developmentally appropriate curriculum is not the great equalizer. Rather, it is only one piece of a much larger puzzle. Such curricula meet the needs of children from the neck up, but they don't address the social, physical, and emotional baggage so many of our students carry with them.

A better solution is to offer our youngest children a variety of ways to spend an extra year—just one extra year—in grade. Take the practice of looping, for example, which a number of school systems are beginning to adopt. In looping, a first-grade teacher gets promoted with her students and becomes their second-grade teacher. In the traditional system, children might have been held back if they weren't reading fluently. With looping, the teacher has two full years to work with these children; she doesn't have to make a decision at the end of Grade 1. And kids generally benefit from having the same routine and consistency from one grade to the next. (Loops between kindergarten and Grade 1 are useful, too.) Or schools might consider having a sequence that includes pre-kindergarten, kindergarten, and pre-first grade classes.

Schools should also give parents choices. Some parents beg to have their child with the same teacher two years in a row. Others say one year is plenty. Still others don't want their children in school at all. We ought to have arrangements for as many different parents as we can.

The option of last resort

So where does retention fit? It fits in as one of a number of options schools need to consider. But it's never the only option, and often it's not the best option.

Retention doesn't work, for example, as an IQ booster—it never has and never will. So if you're thinking of retaining a child simply because of the child's low ability level, think again. The child might be more comfortable having the same teacher next year, but that comfort isn't going to make a difference in the child's achievement. If you retain this child, chances are that next year you will simply have a larger child with a low IQ in the same grade.

Retention isn't a good way to motivate children either. I've run into only two truly lazy kids in my life; the rest were shut down because of circumstances at home. More important, I've never seen a case where retention motivated the child to be a good student. If children are not motivated, retention will probably finish them off.

I also believe you gain nothing by retaining a child who's

simply a slow learner or a child who is emotionally disturbed. And there's no use thinking that retention will correct a child's behavioral disorder either, unless you have proof that the behavior is tied to being placed in the wrong grade.

Is retention a solution for high absenteesim? Again, don't count on it. If you retain a child because of attendance problems, I guarantee you'll have a dropout on your hands. Missing school isn't the child's fault, it's the parents' fault, and retention does nothing to correct parental behavior. Two final injunctions are worth remembering as well: Retention isn't the solution for the child with a multiple number of complex problems, and it's not a cure-all for the child with low self-esteem.

The children who flourish

Retention works best for children who are average to above average in ability but who are among the youngest of their classmates. It also can work for children who started school biologically, socially, emotionally, and physically behind, and for children whose only problem is that some adult put them in the wrong grade. But before I gave any child an extra year of instruction, I'd want to make certain that I had the parents' support, and I'd also want to be sure the child hadn't already been given another year before.

If your schools are rethinking the policy and practice of retention, I'd offer the following advice as well:

• No one person should decide whether to retain a child. Instead, the decision should be up to an ad hoc study team that includes the child's parents, the teacher, the school principal, and a counselor.

• Never retain a child instead of providing special education services. Retention and special education are two separate interventions.

• If you're going to retain a child, do it early. In fact, I'm most comfortable retaining children in kindergarten, first, second, and third grade. In fact, the handful of studies that support retention agree: Early is better. Never retain a child in an upper grade unless you have the youngster's unconditional support.

• Let parents cast the deciding vote on retention. Superintendents, of course, have the legal right to place a child, and they delegate that right to the building principal. But it's a wise principal who doesn't exercise that right over a parent's objection. In my experience, retention will never work if the parents don't buy into the concept.

• Never retain a child for more than one year. Ever. If you're looking at more than one year, you're looking at a child with a variety of complex problems, none of which will be solved by retention.

Retention won't change the color of a child's skin, and it won't change family circumstances. It won't change a kid's language to English, it won't improve attendance, and it won't make a poor child affluent. It's dramatic, it's traumatic, and it's an intervention of last resort.

But for the right child, in the right circumstances, it works, and it's up to us adults to have the courage to use it wisely. ⬛

Voices

*We must use time creatively . . .
and forever realize that the
time is ripe to do great things.*

— *Martin Luther King, Jr.*

When Compared to Boys . . .

<u>Girls entering kindergarten are more likely to:</u>

- Hold a pencil correctly
- Button their clothes
- Write or draw rather than scribble
- Be able to identify more colors
- Count to 20 or beyond
- Write their own name
- Recognize more letters of the alphabet
- Have a longer attention span
- Fidget less
- Show an interest in reading
- Have speech understandable to a stranger
- Not stutter or stammer

On-Time Bloomers Have More Assets

<u>They:</u>

- Seem to cope better emotionally
- Often are older and more mature
- Seem better able to focus and attend
- Seem to have the physical stamina to sustain a demanding school experience
- Often have a greater general knowledge base
- Seem better able to complete tasks
- Seem to have higher social abilities
- Have more school related accomplishments
- Tend to have fewer school related difficulties

Jim Grant/Bob Johnson

Additional Learning Time Options

Transition Kindergarten

1st Grade

Kindergarten

Pre-Kindergarten

Transition First Grade

1st Grade

Pre-1st Grade

Kindergarten

Transition Second Grade

2nd Grade

Pre-2nd Grade

1st Grade

Transition Third Grade

3rd Grade

Pre-3rd Grade

2nd Grade

Note: Children should only take one additional year of learning time. These configurations allow a child to take an extra year of learning time without the stigma of school failure.

Jim Grant/Bob Johnson

94

Factors and Circumstances that Place a Student at Serious Risk of School Failure

1. Highly transient

2. Low academic achievement (Reading one or more years below grade level)*

3. Low socio-economic status

4. Poor school attendance*

5. Behavioral problems*

6. Live in a single-parent family

7. Attends school with many other poor children

8. May be a member of a minority, racial or ethnic group

9. Been retained in grade*

* These circumstances often result from being placed in the wrong grade

Additional Learning Time Option for "Young Sixes"

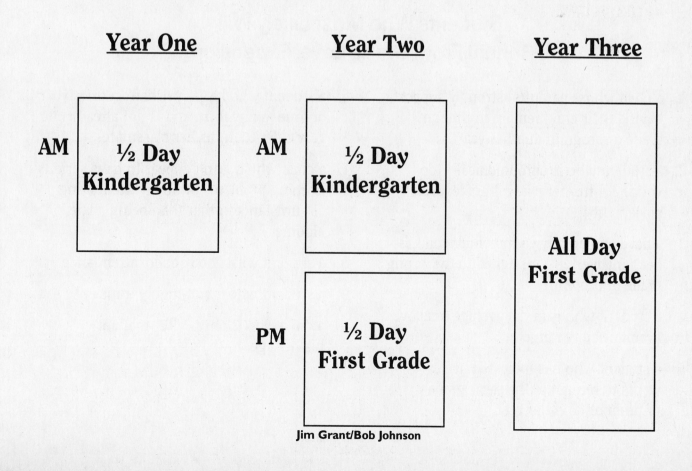

Year One	Year Two	Year Three
AM ½ Day Kindergarten	AM ½ Day Kindergarten	All Day First Grade
	PM ½ Day First Grade	

Jim Grant/Bob Johnson

LOOK BEFORE YOU LEAP!
Some students may be placed at-risk when remaining in the same grade for a second year

1. A student whose parent(s) are opposed to an additional year of learning time through grade level retention

2. An unmotivated student

3. An emotionally disturbed student (Note: Some students exhibit emotional problems from being in over their heads.)

4. A student with a behavior disorder (Note: Some students exhibit behavior problems as a result of being in over their heads.)

5. Some children who are raised in poverty

6. A student who has a history of excessive absenteeism

7. A student who is below average in ability (slower learners)

8. A student who is already one year older than his/her peers

9. A student who is considered too "street wise" for his/her age

10. A student who has a multitude of complex problems

11. A child with very low self-esteem (Note: In many, if not most, cases students in the wrong grade exhibit signs of low self-esteem.)

12. A child from a highly transient family

13. Some linguistically different students

Note: Some of these students may show some level of improvement when retained as a result of the stress of being in the wrong grade being removed. These are cautions and not a rigid list of students to eliminate from consideration for an extra year of learning time

---

Students Who Most Likely Will Benefit From Grade Level Expansion:

1. a child whose parent(s) strongly support having their child remain in the same grade or program another year

2. a student who is chronologically too young for his/her present grade level placement

3. a developmentally young child who has been inadvertently assigned to the wrong grade or program

4. a student who is in the average or above average ability range

5. a student who has indicated he/she wants to remain in the same grade or program another year.

6. a student who has never had an extra year of time in any form and is not already one year older than his/her classmates

7. a child who doesn't appear to have serious learning problems or other extenuating circumstances other than being a late bloomer

8. a student with good school attendance

9. a student who is not highly transient

10. a child who is physically small for his/her age

Jim Grant/Bob Johnson

Common Sense Tips to Make an Informed Grade Level Retention Decision for Individual Students

1. Always present parents with multiple placement options from which to choose. Children with very different beginnings need very different beginnings!

2. Always explore alternatives to grade level retention first. Think of grade level retention as the intervention strategy of last resort.

3. Parent(s) should never be pressured to retain a child against their wishes. Forced retentions simply do not work.

4. Don't cause students to be two years older than their classmates. Students two or more years over-age are most likely to drop out of school.

5. Always make high stakes decisions with an ad hoc child study team, i.e., parents, teacher, principal, counselor, etc.

6. Don't substitute grade level retention in place of special education intervention. They are two very different interventions.

7. Do not make a grade level retention decision based on a single factor, i.e., standardized tests, chronological age, reading level, etc.

8. If a student needs more time in grade, do it during the early childhood years.

9. Don't hesitate to change a child's placement mid-year (grade re-placement).

10. Only retain an upper grade student if you have his/her unconditional support.

11. Provide retained students remedial support services when needed. Many developmentally young students also have learning problems.

12. When possible, allow the child to stay with the same teacher a second year. Take the child's feelings into account when making this decision.

13. Parents must be allowed the right to cast the deciding vote to retain or not to retain their child.

14. Create and adopt flexible grade level retention guidelines versus a rigid grade level retention policy. A no retention policy is an extremist position leaving no room to make case by case individual decisions. Such an absolute position denies the existence of students placed in the wrong grade.

15. Remember, grade level retention research is reported as an average of a group. An individual retention is a very personal one child, one family at a time decision, and is NOT a group activity.

16. Bear in mind that keeping students in a grade or program another year without changing the curriculum and instruction will most likely produce dismal results.

17. Don't overstate the benefits of retention. Be modest in your claims.

18. Remember, people stigmatize people. (A stigma is an adult "gift" to children!)

19. The social promotion fad of recent years is not without consequences and generally created a host of other problems.

20. Taking an extra year of learning time in a transition class is not the same experience as grade level retention. This is not "another form of retention!"

21. Remaining an extra year in a multiage continuous progress classroom is not considered grade level retention. This also is not "another form of retention!"

22. All students will come to school ready to learn by the year 2000. A noble goal that is very unlikely to happen. Until this goal is met it is likely that different students will need different amounts of learning time to participate success-fully in school.

Jim Grant/Bob Johnson

4-Year-Olds

Signs and Signals of Preschool Stress

Child's Name _____ Birthdate _____

At Home – A 4-year-old suffering from preschool-related stress may:

		Often	Never	Rarely
1.	not want to leave Mom/Dad			
2.	hide shoes so as not to have to go to preschool			
3.	complain about stomachaches or headaches			
4.	have bathroom "accidents"			
5.	come home exhausted			
6.	have nightmares			

At Preschool – A 4-year-old experiencing the stress of being in the wrong group or program may:

1.	have difficulty separating from Mom/Dad			
2.	cling to the teacher, showing a high degree of dependency			
3.	not participate in "cooperative" play — instead, his or her play is "isolated" (child plays alone) or "parallel" (playing next to other children but not with them)			
4.	not like the other children			
5.	show "young" fine-motor coordination while cutting, gluing, drawing, etc.			
6.	demonstrate a lack of awareness of appropriate behavior in the "classroom"			
7.	not catch on to "classroom" routines, which more mature classmates adapt to easily			
8.	find it difficult to select activities and stick with them			
9.	become "outspoken" and/or want to leave when asked to perform a task that is too difficult			

In General – A 4-year-old who is under excessive amount of stress at preschool may:

1.	cry easily			
2.	lack self-control or self-discipline (biting, hitting and kicking)			
3.	appear to be "shy"			
4.	revert to thumbsucking, nail biting or "baby talk"			
5.	become aggressive during games and other activities involving the taking of turns or sharing			

Note: All children display some stress signs at times. Severe stress is indicated when a child consistently displays several stress signs over an extended period of time.

Excerpted from "I Hate School! Revised and Updated for the 1990's Some Common Sense Answers for Educators & Parents Who Want To Know Why & What To Do About It" by Jim Grant. © 1994 Modern Learning Press, Rosemont, NJ 08556

5-Year-Olds
Signs and Signals of School Stress

Child's Name _____ Birthdate _____

At Home – How often does this 5-year-old child:

		Often	Never	Rarely
1.	not want to leave Mom/Dad			
2.	not want to go to school			
3.	suffer from stomach aches or headaches, particularly in the morning before school			
4.	dislike school or complain that school is "dumb"			
5.	complain that the teacher does not allow enough time to finish his or her school work			
6.	need to rest, but resist taking a nap			
7.	revert to bedwetting			

At School – How often does this 5-year-old child:

1.	show little interest in kindergarten "academics"			
2.	ask if it's time to go home			
3.	seem unable to hold scissors as directed by the teacher			
4.	worry that Mom/Dad will forget to pick him or her up after school			
5.	have a difficult time following the daily routine			
6.	talk incessantly			
7.	complain that school work is "too hard" ("I can't do it,") or "too easy" ("It's so easy I'm not going to do it," or "too boring")			
8.	interrupt the teacher constantly			
9.	seem unable to shift easily from one task to the next			
10.	seem overly restless during class and frequently in motion when supposed to be working at a task			

In General – How often does this 5-year-old child:

1.	become withdrawn			
2.	revert to thumbsucking or infantile speech			
3.	compare herself negatively to other children ("They can do it, but I can't")			
4.	complain that she has no friends			
5.	cry easily and frequently			
6.	make up stories			
7.	bite his or her nails			
8.	seem depressed			

Note: All children display some stress signs at times. Severe stress is indicated when a child consistently displays several stress signs over an extended period of time.

Excerpted from "I Hate School! Revised and Updated for the 1990's Some Common Sense Answers for Educators & Parents Who Want To Know Why & What To Do About It" by Jim Grant. © 1994 Modern Learning Press, Rosemont, NJ 08556

6-Year-Olds
Signs and Signals of School Stress

Child's Name_____ Birthdate_____

At Home – **How often does this 6-year-old child:**

		Never	Rarely	Often
1.	complain of before-school stomach aches			
2.	revert to bed-wetting			
3.	behave in a manner that seems out of character to the parent			
4.	ask to stay at home			

At School – **How often does this 6-year-old child:**

		Never	Rarely	Often
1.	want to play with 5-year-olds			
2.	want to play with toys during class time			
3.	choose recess, gym and music as favorite subjects			
4.	feel overwhelmed by the size and activity level in the lunchroom			
5.	have a high rate of absenteeism			
6.	try to take frequent "in-house field trips" to the pencil sharpener, bathroom, school nurse, custodian, etc.			
7.	mark papers randomly			
8.	"act out" on the playground			
9.	reverse, invert, substitute, or omit letters and numbers when reading and/or writing (this is also not unusual for properly placed students either			
10.	complain about being bored with school work, when in reality he or she cannot do the work			
11.	have a short attention span — unable to stay focused on a twenty minute reading lesson			
12.	have difficulty understanding the teacher's instructions			

In General – **How often does this 6-year-old child:**

		Never	Rarely	Often
1.	cry easily or frequently			
2.	tire quickly			
3.	need constant reassurance and praise			
4.	become withdrawn and shy			
5.	develop a nervous tic — a twitching eye, a nervous cough, frequent clearing of the throat or twirling of hair			
6.	return to thumbsucking			
7.	lie or "adjust the truth" about school			
8.	revert to soiling his or her pants			
9.	make restless body movements, such as rocking in a chair, jiggling legs, etc.			
10.	dawdle			
11.	seem depressed			
12.	feel harried / hurried			

Excerpted from "I Hate School! Revised and Updated for the 1990's Some Common Sense Answers for Educators & Parents Who Want To Know Why & What To Do About It" by Jim Grant. © 1994 Modern Learning Press, Rosemont, NJ 08556

Signs and Signals of Depression

Please check all signs and signals that apply to: _____

How often does this student:

	Often	Rarely	Never
Appear not to have fun or enjoy school			
Cry easily or frequently			
Appear to be sad			
Tend to be a loner with few friends			
Tend to be non-participatory in school activities			
Seem disengaged			
Seem to not care about his/her personal hygiene			
Have trouble sleeping			
Appear irritable and/or angry			
Tend to mope about			
Lack enthusiasm about things in general			
Seem overly pessimistic about life			
Have excessive absenteeism			
Complain about being tired, all the time			

In extreme cases of depression, a child may exhibit self-destructive behaviors such as:

Bulimia/Anorexia	☐ Yes ☐ No	Talk of suicide	☐ Yes ☐ No
Pulling out hair	☐ Yes ☐ No	Alcohol/drug abuse	☐ Yes ☐ No
Digging/scratching/cutting of skin	☐ Yes ☐ No	Other _____

A yes on any of the above areas indicates a top priority referral for this student.

Note: Many students display a few signs and signals of depression at times. Serious concern is warranted when a student displays multiple signs of depression over an extended period of time. Certain signs and signals of depression may also be indicative of other problems or conditions such as social difficulty, low self-concept, slower learner, school-related stress, emotional difficulty, behavior problems, ADD, as well as learning disabilities. None of these signs and signals of depression are absolute.

Caution: Do not use this information to identify, diagnose or label any student as being depressed. The use of this information should be strictly for discussion purposes only. Diagnosis and subsequent treatment for depression should only be provided by a medical doctor.

Name of the person(s) who provided this information:

_____ Date _____

_____ Date _____

Excerpted from *The Before Retention Checklist* by Jim Grant

Jim Grant/Bob Johnson

Spotting a Possible Learning Disability

Please check all traits that apply to: _____

Student's name

How often does this student:	Often	Rarely	Never
Experience difficulty retaining knowledge taught			
Require a number of repetitions of taught materials (rate of acquisition and knowledge retention are lower than those of age-appropriate peers)			
Lack organizational strategies to work independently			
Seem unable to discriminate between important facts and details and unnecessary facts			
Seem unable to remain attentive and focused on learning			
Experience difficulties with expressive and receptive language			
Lack motivation			
Exhibit inappropriate social skills			
Experience difficulty memorizing and applying new information			
Require work load and time allowances to be adapted to specific need			
Display poor judgment calls			
Seem unable to transition from one activity to another			

The above excerpt was contributed by Gretchen Goodman and adapted from the book, *Our Best Advice: The Multiage Problem Solving Handbook,* by Jim Grant, Bob Johnson, and Irv Richardson. Peterborough, NH: Crystal Springs Books, 1996.

Caution: Do not use this information to identify, diagnose or label any student learning disabled. The use of this information should be strictly for discussion purposes. A diagnosis of learning disabilities should only be made by a psychologist in conjunction with a pediatrician or family doctor.

Excerpted from *The Before Retention Checklist* by Jim Grant

Signs of Attention Deficit Disorder

Please check all signs that apply to: _____
Student's name

How often does this student:	Often	Rarely	Never
Blurt things out in class			
Tend to be forgetful			
Daydream or "space out"			
Have difficulty focusing on a single task			
Become impatient			
Have difficulty delaying gratification			
Tend to forget things			
Produce messy school work			
Exhibit poor fine motor control			
Lose things (i.e., toys, clothes, books, etc.)			
Tend to be in constant motion			
Become easily discouraged			
Lack self-control			
Appear disorganized			

Note: Many students may display some signs of ADD at times. Serious concern is warranted when a student exhibits multiple signs of ADD over an extended period of time. Some of these signs of ADD may also be indicative of other problems or conditions such as: depression, emotional difficulty, developmental immaturity, as well as being a slower learner. None of these signs of ADD are absolute.

Caution: Do not use this information to identify, diagnose or label any student as having ADD. A diagnosis of ADD should only be made by a psychologist in conjunction with a pediatrician or family doctor.

Name of the person(s) who provided this information:

_____ Date _____

_____ Date _____

Excerpted from *The Before Retention Checklist* by Jim Grant

Attributes of a Slower Learner*

Please check all attributes that apply to: _____

Student's name

How often does this student:	Often	Rarely	Never
Seem to have a poor memory for details			
Tend not to catch on to new concepts easily			
Have difficulty following instruction			
Become easily frustrated and upset when he/she seems unable to do his/her homework			
Take an inordinate amount of time to do his/her work			
Become confused with changes in routine or plans			
Have difficulty concentrating on most school work			
Have difficulty focusing on a task			
Have difficulty paying attention			
Seem "lost in space" during group instruction			
Complain about too much school work			
Complain about not having enough time to do his/her school work			
Have trouble remembering the rules to games			
Tend to be a spectator rather than a participant in activities			
Approach each day as if it were the first day of school			

Note: Some students may display a few attributes of a slower learner at times. Serious concern is warranted when a student has multiple attributes of a slower learner. Certain attributes of a slower learner may also be indicative of other problems or conditions such as: ADD, depression, school-related stress, learning disabilities, as well as developmental immaturity. Referral for a comprehensive evaluation by a child psychologist should be conducted immediately to determine the nature of this child's problem or condition.

Caution: Do not use this information to identify, diagnose or label any student a slow learner. The purpose of this information should be strictly for discussion purposes only. The determination of a child's index of intelligence should only be conducted by a trained psychologist.

Name of the person(s) who provided this information:

_____ Date _____

_____ Date _____

* 70-89 IQ Range

Excerpted from *The Before Retention Checklist* by Jim Grant

Jim Grant/Bob Johnson

Some Schools Enforce Some or All of the Following Rules:

- All potential retentions must be reported to the principal's office by March 15

- Former Reading Recovery students are not allowed to be retained in grade

- Retained students are automatically excluded from the Reading Recovery program

- Students identified as learning disabled are not allowed to be retained (No Double Dipping)

- Retained students are not allowed any form of special eduction services (No Double Dipping)

- No grade level retentions permitted at the kindergarten and first grade levels

- Students who take on an additional year of learning time in a transition program or remain an extra year in a multiage program are officially noted as retentions in the school register and are reported to the state as a grade level retention

- All students shall be socially promoted. There will be no additional learning time available in the form of an extra year for any student for any reason

- Teachers are not allowed to acknowledge the concept of "wrong grade placement" with parents and are asked not to suggest retention

- Once class rosters are set, no student can have their placement changed

---

Negative Impact on Children Who Are in Over Their Heads in the Wrong Grade

They may:

- exhibit behavior problems

- have difficulty paying attention

- have difficulty learning routine tasks

- have high absenteeism

- have low academic performance

- feel hurried/harried/stressed

- be depressed

- have a poor self-concept

- be easily discouraged

- have low stamina both physically and emotionally

- display emotional problems

- have difficulty socially

- in extreme cases have self-destructive behaviors

Many of these children require remedial and counseling services as a direct result of being in the wrong grade.

Jim Grant/Bob Johnson

The State of the Children in YOUR Classroom	Number of Children	Percent of Children	Percent of children automatically socially promoted	Number expected to pass grade level standards
Chronologically Young Children (late birthdate)			100%	100%
Developmentally Young Children			100%	100%
Slower Learners			100%	100%
Poor Children			100%	100%
Children with Learning Problems			100%	100%
Lacking Predictable Parental Support			100%	100%

Jim Grant/Bob Johnson

Best Practices to Reduce Special Education Referrals

- Provide early intervention programs

- Small class size (18-20 students)

- Implement multiage grouping

- Implement looping configurations

- Implement transition grades (i.e., pre-K, pre-1st, pre-2nd, pre-3rd, pre-4th)

- Change to child compatible curriculum and instructional strategies

- Provide health care services for all

- Provide adaptations through modification and accommodation of the curriculum and instruction

- Change the school entrance date back to September 1st

- Provide remedial and support services for unidentified "gray-area" students

---

How to Make a Child "Learning Disabled"

1. Escalated curriculum

2. Fixed point curriculum . . . in a fixed time frame

3. Irrelevant curriculum

4. Too much curriculum

5. Textbook-bound instruction

6. "Ditto" based instruction

7. Time on task practices

8. Too much board copying

9. Departmentalization of elementary schools

10. No recess policy

11. Lock-step, time-bound graded structure

12. Tracking practices

13. Unfair competition

14. Group standardized testing

15. Large class size

16. Narrow instructional approach

17. Narrow critical period to learn certain basic skills

18. Placement of students in the wrong grade

19. Change to a new education fad every week

20. Adoption of conflicting mandates

Jim Grant/Bob Johnson

Departmentalization:

1. Defeats the benefits gained by being placed with a significant adult in a consistent setting over time

2. Defeats the benefits of students being together in a school family over time

3. Is an inefficient use of instructional time

4. Creates "stop and go" teaching blocks

5. Sends the wrong message! All things in life are somehow unrelated and unconnected

6. Distorts curriculum planning

7. Creates too many transitions

8. Contributes to the harried/hurried child syndrome

9. Allows no one person to be accountable

10. Doesn't allow teachers to know children deeply

11. Is a major obstacle to integrating the curriculums

Books That Give Insight into Departmentalization at the Elementary Level

The Hurried Child by David Elkind

Yardsticks by Chip Wood

ITI: The Model by Susan Kovalik

A Place Called School by John Goodlad

Accommodations and Modification Ideas That Work

1. Seat the student near the front

2. Use high interest reading material

3. Seat the student in close proximity to the teacher

4. Utilize color overlays over printed materials

5. Require shortened/adjusted assignments

6. Provide a desk carrel

7. Utilize noise suppressing headsets

8. Seat the student away from the door or windows

9. Utilize talking books

10. Use 3-sided rubber pencil grips

11. Use student contracts

12. Minimize board copying

13. Provide cooperative learning opportunities

14. Have reports dictated on cassettes vs. writing

15. Provide erasable ink pens

16. Use high quality white bonded paper that allows for easy erasing

17. Utilize highlighting tape and markers

18. Provide two sets of textbooks, one for school, one for home

19. Reduce auditory and visual distractions

20. Provide and maintain a quiet work space

21. Provide direct instruction when appropriate

22. Use a variety of alternative assessments to evaluate student work

23. Accept oral recordings as an alternative to writing assignments

24. Provide a multiplication/division table chart

25. Provide a desktop cursive writing line

Jim Grant/Bob Johnson/Char Forsten

Various Ways to Reduce Grade Level Retentions

- Provide pre-school programs
- Adapt Reading Recovery type strategies
- Expand head-start enrollments
- Provide a full-day kindergarten program
- Provide summer school (for at-risk children)
- Expand Title I support services
- Create looping classrooms
- Create multiage classrooms
- Provide accelerated learning opportunities
- Adopt the Success for All reading program

- Provide remedial math and literacy services
- Private tutoring (outside of school)
- Change the school entrance date (move it back)
- Modify the school calendar, i.e.,
  - Extend the school year
  - Lengthen the school day
  - Space school vacation out over the school year
- Change to a child-centered curriculum
- Eliminate grade-level promotional gates
- Eliminate all-group standardized testing before grade four

Options to Eliminate Grade Level Retentions

- Stay at home (one year) *
- Extra year of pre-school *
- Expand head-start enrollments
- Home schooling *
- Pre-kindergarten program (for young fives)

- Pre-first grade (young sixes)
- Pre-second grade (young sevens)
- Remain 3 years in a two year multiage continuous progress classroom

* These options are usually available only to financially advantaged parents

Integrating the Curriculum with Parallel Block Scheduling

Innovations like whole language and interdisciplinary instruction demand scheduling flexibility.

HARRIET J. HOPKINS AND ROBERT LYNN CANADY

The principles of parallel block scheduling (PBS), employed by many elementary schools during the past 25 years, have produced the following results:

- Smaller class size during critical instructional periods in reading and mathematics;
- Less reliance on strict ability grouping;
- Less fragmentation of the school day due to better integration of support programs such as special education, gifted education, and Title I;
- More efficient and effective use of instructional staff;
- Significantly higher student engagement rates in learning activities; and
- Increased test scores.

While parallel block scheduling continues to produce these improvements, it faces a challenge in adapting to meet the needs of new educational programs, notably whole language and interdisciplinary instruction.

The Basic PBS Model

Parallel block scheduling is a way of structuring how time is used within a school day to facilitate instruction and reduce the pupil-teacher ratio during designated time periods. It also gives classroom teachers blocks of uninterrupted time to provide critical instruction.

In the model illustrated in *Figure 1*, large blocks of time are reserved for various grade levels of language arts/social studies and science/math throughout the day. During most of that time, teachers have their entire class present for direct instruction.

In addition to these whole-class periods, teachers can divide their classes to provide smaller groups of students with enrichment and remediation opportunities. While one group moves from the classroom to the extension center, the other group remains behind for individ-

Harriet J. Hopkins is coordinator of elementary programs for Area III of the Fairfax County Public Schools in Dunn Loring, Virginia.

Robert Lynn Canady is a professor at the University of Virginia's Curry School of Education in Charlottesville.

ualized remediation instruction or to work on applications of concepts previously taught. At the end of this period, the first group returns to the classroom, and the second group moves to the extension center.

The extension center teacher, in collaboration with the various classroom teachers, provides activities designed to apply, extend, or reinforce what is currently being taught. Students who need to be pulled out for special education, gifted and talented instruction, band, chorus, or remedial help in speech, language, or reading are taken only from the extension center. In many schools using full inclusion, students with disabilities also are serviced in the extension center.

Meeting Curriculum Challenges

As the elementary curriculum continues to change, it seems that more is always being added while little, if anything, is taken away. Teachers are asked to teach more content in the same amount of time, and this is particularly true of whole language and interdisciplinary instruction. But parallel block scheduling can easily be adapted to include both. *Figure 2* shows how blocks of time could be distributed among four teachers in Grade 4 to give each teacher 100 minutes a day for whole-group instruction in language arts and social studies, in addition to 50 minutes each with smaller groups for reading and writing.

During the whole-group time, the classroom teacher might use social studies content to teach a whole language unit on research skills. The students could then practice those skills in small groups during reading/writing time and in the extension center. Or they might be assigned to go to the library, where the media specialist could show them how to use the card catalog or conduct an online computer search. Another option could involve students using computers to write and edit.

Other whole language activities that could be performed in these time blocks include teaching reading skills through the use of novels and trade books related to social studies content. These might in-

"INTEGRATING SCIENCE AND MATH INSTRUCTION DURING A LARGE BLOCK OF TIME ALLOWS FOR ENRICHED CONTENT. . ."

clude the sequencing of ideas and events, classifying information, and identifying characters and their relationships. In much the same way, parallel block scheduling can expedite the teaching of writing skills, such as planning, drafting, revising, and editing.

There may be days, however, when the teacher wants to devote the entire 100-minute block of time to social studies or language arts—or to cooperative learning, a large-group project, or a play in which students practice oral language skills. The entire period may be used with confidence that all students will be there and that there will be no interruptions. If a larger block of time is necessary, the teacher may choose not to send students to the extension center that day, combining both small-group peri-

Robert Finken

Robert Finken

ods for an extra 100 minutes with the entire class.

These are only a few of the options available with the flexibility of parallel block scheduling. It also creates greater opportunities for teachers to collaborate in planning and exchanging ideas to provide stronger and more focused instructional programs.

PBS for Science and Math

Integrating science and math instruction during a large block of time allows for enriched content and provides opportunities for the skills and content taught in one subject to be applied and reinforced in another. For example, a teacher may plan a graphing unit in math while teaching a unit on pendulums in science. By having students

---

FIGURE 1

An Elementary School Model

Grade	8:15 – 9:50	9:50 – 10:50	10:50 – 11:40	11:40 – 12:40	12:40 – 1:50	1:50 – 2:50
K	Plan		Lunch and Recess			
1	Language/Social Studies	RWG	Recess and Lunch	RWG	Math/Science	Plan
2	RWG	RWG	Language/Social Studies	Recess and Lunch	Plan	Science/Math
3	Math/Science	Language/Social Studies		Plan	Recess and Lunch	RWG / RWG
4	Science/Math	Plan	Language/Social Studies	Lunch and Recess	RWG	RWG
5	Plan	Science/Math	RWG	Lunch and Recess	RWG	Language/Social Studies
Math Access to Computer Lab	Grade 3	Grade 4	Grade 5	Computer Lab time available on special needs basis (100 minutes)	Grade 1	Kinder-garten / Grade 2

RWG = Reduced reading/writing group
Plan = Planning time for classroom teachers while students are scheduled for physical education, art, or music.
Math Access to Computer Lab = During these periods, teachers may send approximately half their students to the computer lab for math assistance.

FIGURE 2

Integrating Language Arts and Social Studies

Teachers	50 minutes	50 minutes	50 minutes	50 minutes
Teacher A	Language Arts & Social Studies (Reading-Writing Groups 1 & 2)		Reading-Writing Group 1	Reading-Writing Group 2
Teacher B	Language Arts & Social Studies (Reading-Writing Groups 3 & 4)		Reading-Writing Group 3	Reading-Writing Group 4
Teacher C	Reading-Writing Group 5	Reading-Writing Group 6	Language Arts & Social Studies (Reading-Writing Groups 5 & 6)	
Teacher D	Reading-Writing Group 7	Reading-Writing Group 8	Language Arts & Social Studies (Reading-Writing Groups 7 & 8)	
Extension Center	Reading-Writing Groups 6 & 8	Reading-Writing Groups 5 & 7	Reading-Writing Groups 2 & 4	Reading-Writing Groups 1 & 3

graph the number of times a pendulum with a long string swings in a given amount of time, and comparing it to the number of times a pendulum with a shorter string swings in the same amount of time, the science concept is communicated graphically and the math concept becomes more meaningful. Other examples of combining science and math concepts might include the averaging of observed natural phenomena, and integrating the use of angles and circles with mapping skills.

The parallel block scheduling model also can be used to integrate math and science in several other ways. For example, the 100-minute math/science block shown in *Figure 1* could be divided into three 30-minute blocks, with five minutes between blocks for students to move from one room to another. With this schedule, a classroom teacher could use the first 30 minutes to teach a concept (*e.g.*, double-digit division) to all students. At the end of 30 minutes, the class moves to the computer lab or extension center where they reinforce what they have learned while the classroom teacher works with a smaller group. At the end of the second 30-minute period, the two groups change places.

Another way to use the math/science block is to divide the 100 minutes into two 50-minute periods. In each period, the classroom teacher teaches half the class while the other half goes to the extension center. This model offers the continuity of teaching a math or science unit every day to completion before moving to another unit.

Some schools use the split math/science block to have classroom teachers teach math while the extension teacher teaches science. Other options are to alternate whole- and reduced-group instruction on alternate days or weeks, or to rotate the teaching of science and math units.

These are but a few of the ways in which schools can use parallel block scheduling to enhance and improve instruction. PBS has proven that it can be adapted to the innovations and changes in instruction currently taking place in elementary schools, particularly the introduction of whole language and interdisciplinary instruction. Parallel block scheduling makes it possible to provide, enhance, and improve efficient instruction for *all* students in large and small groups throughout the school year. ☐

REFERENCES

Butler, A.; and Turbill, J. *Towards a Reading-Writing Classroom*. Portsmouth, N.H.: Heinemann Educational Books, 1985.

Calkins, L. M.; and Harwayne, S. *Living Between the Lines*. Portsmouth, N.H.: Heinemann Educational Books, 1991.

Canady, R. L. "A Cure for Fragmented School Schedules in Elementary Schools." *Educational Leadership* 46 (October 1988): 65–67.

Canady, R. L. "Designing Scheduling Structures to Increase Student Learning." *Focus in Change* 1, 2 (March 1989): 1–2, 7–8.

Canady, R. L. "Parallel Block Scheduling: A Better Way to Organize a School." *Principal* 69:3 (January 1990): 34-36.

Canady, R. L.; and Reina, J. M. "Parallel Bock Scheduling: An Alternative Structure." *Principal* 72:3 (January 1993): 26–29.

Jacobs, H. H. "Planning for Curriculum Integration." *Educational Leadership* 49:2 (October 1991): 27–28.

National Education Commission on Time and Learning. *Prisoners of Time: Commission on Time and Learning*. Washington, D.C.: U.S. Government Printing Office, 1994.

Rettig, M. D.; and Canady, R. L. "When Can I Have Your Kids? Scheduling Specialist Teachers." *Here's How* 14:2, National Association of Elementary School Principals, December 1995.

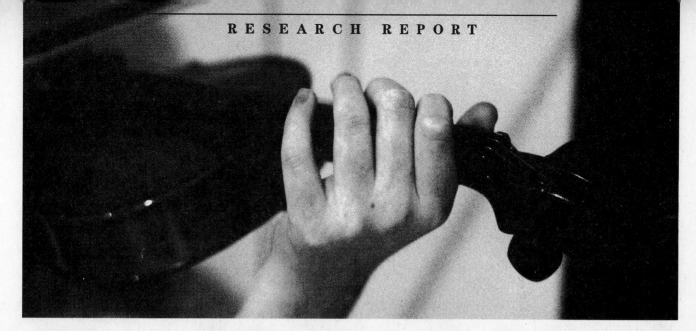

The Musical Mind

Training in music, researchers find,
has a positive effect on cognitive development

BY SUSAN BLACK

Music helps kids' brains grow. Carole Walker, an elementary school music teacher in Auburn, Maine, knows that, and to spread the word, she's likely to show up for a presentation wearing a hard hat and carrying signs that say "Slow Down—Work in Progress" or "Caution—Dendrites Growing Here."

Similarly, Lucille Croscup, an elementary music teacher in Bennington, Vt., and Janet Hanratty, a junior high school music teacher in Elmira, N.Y., can't help talking about neurons and synapses when they talk about their teaching. "I think of the seventh and eighth-graders in my instrumental music class and chorus as being part of my big brain bash," says Hanratty, whose graduate thesis explores the latest neurological research on brain development and its relationship to music education. "When I'm conducting, I can almost see the kids' brains glowing inside their heads as the music excites firing patterns in the cortex."

And in fact, showing brains in living color is exactly how Donald Hodges, professor of music at the University of Texas at San Antonio, presents the latest discoveries on neuromusical research. Hodges demonstrates what he calls the "musical brain" with slides of what goes on inside people's brains as they listen to music. The pictures are taken

Susan Black is an education research consultant in Hammondsport, N.Y.

using such techniques as magnetic resonance imaging (MRI) and positron emission tomography (PET). "Music actually changes the organization of the brain," says Hodges. "Now we can see what happens when a person listens to Bach," he says, pointing to vivid hues that show the research subject's active motor cortex.

Along with studies being done by other neuroscientists, Hodges' research dismantles some misconceptions while building new theories about music. One widespread misconception is that musicians are exclusively "right-brained"—that is, that they draw primarily on the right hemisphere of the brain, which dominates functions such as imagination, creativity, and artistic endeavors. But, as Hodges' compelling images show, music is distributed across locally specialized regions on both sides of the brain. Just how much musical ability is lateralized throughout the whole brain is subject to more study, Hodges says. But he says it shouldn't be surprising to learn that both brain hemispheres are involved in musical processing. Musical experiences are, to use Hodges' term, "multimodal"—that is, they involve auditory, visual, cognitive, affective, and motor systems.

"Think of what it takes to be a violinist," says Hodges, "and you'll realize that a musician relies on different brain systems to read symbols on a page, tune the instrument to the correct pitch, and coordinate finger and arm movements."

Neuromusical investigations also are yielding new findings that, in turn, are creating new theories. For example, on the basis of observations and experiments with newborns, neuroscientists now know that infants are born with neural mechanisms devoted exclusively to music. And, perhaps most important for music teachers, studies show that early and ongoing musical training helps organize and develop children's brains.

A 'learning window'

"Music," says Harvard University's Howard Gardner, "might be a special intelligence which should be viewed differently from other intelligences." Gardner, renowned for his theory of multiple intelligences first described in *Frames of Mind*, says musical intelligence probably carries more emotional, spiritual, and cultural weight than the other intelligences he has described (verbal/linguistic, mathematical/logical, spatial, bodily/kinesthetic, interpersonal, and intrapersonal).

But perhaps most important, Gardner says, is that music helps some people organize the way they think and work by helping them develop in other areas, such as math, language, and spatial reasoning.

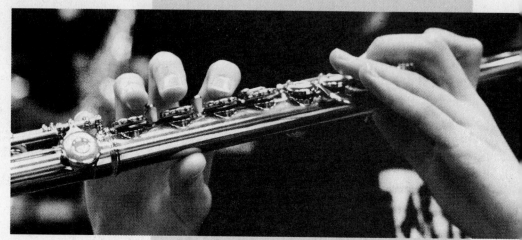

The work of Frances Rauscher of the University of Wisconsin at Oshkosh (formerly at the Center for Neurobiology and Memory at the University of California at Irvine) bears that claim out. The 100 billion neurons in a baby's brain are eager and willing to learn and grow, Rauscher's studies show, but to do so they need stimulation and enrichment to form connections (synapses) and to grow branching extensions (dendrites). And when their little brains are nourished with music, Rauscher and other researchers say, young children grow more connections and extensions. In effect, they get smarter.

In a study involving 3-year-olds, Rauscher and her colleague at Irvine Gordon Shaw demonstrate how musical training helps develop preschoolers' spatial reasoning skills. The children, some from an inner-city day-care center and some from a school for the arts, were given music training involving group singing classes or keyboard lessons. After the music lessons, the spatial reasoning scores of both groups of children nearly doubled. The value of such studies, which Rauscher is continuing on more extensive populations of children, lies in understanding higher brain functions (the firing patterns by groups of neurons over large regions of cortex, for instance) and understanding how to help children develop such functions.

"Through our studies, we're opening windows and looking in on children's learning," says Rauscher. "Music might be considered a pre-language which, while children are very young, excites inherent brain patterns and promotes their use in complex reasoning tasks. Based on our findings, we predict that music training at an early age—when the connections in the brain are most plastic—provides exercise for higher brain functions. Perhaps, when all our work is completed, we will be able to say that music should

be introduced in preschools and should continue as an integral part of a school's curriculum."

The Mozart effect

Music not only exercises the brain, it also is capable of arousing strong emotion. Donald Hodges' slides of brain activity show distinct responses in the limbic system, the area of the brain that responds with feeling, when people listen to a soaring Bach crescendo or a moody passage in a minor key. Some people claim they're almost "addicted to music" and must have their favorite radio station or CDs playing in the background while they work. "I need music to think," says a cardiovascular surgeon who spends hours each day mapping out surgical procedures for his patients. "Music seems to fill up a space inside my head, but at the same

Music's pathway

Neuroscientists may someday be able to describe precisely how our brains take in and respond to music, but for now the pathways music travels are part speculation and part science. Science writer Sandra Blakeslee describes that path this way: As sounds reach the cochlea (a part of the inner ear), they're converted into nerve impulses that flow to the auditory cortex on the right side of the brain, where they're analyzed for features such as pitch and timbre before they're transmitted to other brain areas which, in a complex interactive network, control such features as memory and emotion.

During this intake procedure, sounds are being mapped onto tissue in the brain. Jamshed Bharucha, a psychologist at Dartmouth College in New Hampshire, believes that in the future we will know more about how the sounds of music and language—which share pathways into the brain—eventually diverge and are understood as separate and distinct sounds and patterns. At this point, according to Harvard neurobiologist Mark Tramo, we can say that music is an "inborn human trait" and that brains have specialized circuits to encode speech and music. But exactly how, when, and where sounds associated with music and language separate and follow their own pathways is not yet known.—*S.B.*

time it clears out the cobwebs and lets me think clearly—and with complete concentration."

And research supports such statements. In a now-famous study that produced the so-called Mozart effect, Frances Rauscher and Gordon Shaw found that college students' spatial IQ scores rose significantly after listening to *Mozart's Piano Sonata K448*. Doubtful at first, two teachers familiar with the study agreed to play classical music in their classrooms to "see what might happen." Erika Bourget, who teaches teen mothers in an alternative school in Augusta, Maine, reports that her students liked the idea of playing music in the background but complained about classical music. Relenting, Bourget allowed her students to bring in their own choice of music—including rock, heavy metal, and country. "I couldn't believe it!," Bourget says. "After just 10 minutes of listening to hard-driving rock, one of the teens quietly got up, ejected the tape, and inserted a tape with segments from works by Vivaldi, Haydn, Chopin, and Liszt. There was a collective sigh (of relief, I would say), and everyone settled down and went right back to work."

In a similar experiment with fifth-graders in a small, rural school, Kim Gardner began playing classical music during students' lessons. "The kids just mellowed out," Gardner says. Two weeks later, kids began bringing in classical music, and some students have asked their teacher to make copies of the music so they can listen to it while doing their schoolwork at home. "I'm thrilled—and a bit overwhelmed," says Gardner. "For one thing, I had assumed that my students wouldn't like classical music and that they would rebel. I was so wrong!"

For more information

Blakeslee, Sandra. "The Mystery of Music: How it Works in the Brain." *The New York Times: Science Times*, May 16, 1995, pp. 1, 209, 225.

Bower, Bruce. "Brain Images Reveal Cerebral Side of Music." *Science News*, April 23, 1994, pp. 145, 260.

Gardner, Howard. Keynote Address. *Ithaca Conference 96: Music as Intelligence*, Ithaca College School of Music, Ithaca, N.Y., Sept. 20-21, 1996.

Hodges, Donald A. "Neuromusical Research: A Review of the Literature." *Handbook of Music Psychology*, 2nd edition. University of Texas at San Antonio: IMR Press, 1996, pp. 197-284.

Jennings-Welch, Patricia, et al. *The Richest Cousin: Integrating Music Education Across an Interdisciplinary Curriculum.* Salem, Mass: Greenhouse School, 1996, pp. 1-21.

Leng, Xiaodan, and Shaw, Gordon L. "Toward a Neural Theory of Higher Brain Function Using Music as a Window." *Concepts in Neuroscience*, 2, 1991, pp. 229-58.

Mazourek, Katherine M. "The Relationship between Musical Intelligence and Academic Achievement in High School Students in Newfield Central School, New York." Unpublished Research Study, Elmira College, Elmira, N.Y., December 1995.

Rauscher, Frances H., et al. "Pilot Study Indicates Music Training of Three-Year-Olds Enhances Specific Spatial Reasoning Skills." Center for the Neurobiology of Learning and Memory, University of California-Irvine, August 1993, pp. 1-12.

Rauscher, Frances H., et al. "Listening to Mozart Enhances Spatial-Temporal Reasoning: Towards a Neurophysiological Basis." *Neuroscience Letters*, 1995, 185, pp. 44-47.

Weinberger, Norman M., ed. "Music and Cognitive Achievement in Children." *Musical Research Notes*, 1, Fall 1994, pp. 1-7.

These teachers describe the effects of background music on their students primarily in terms of behavior rather than achievement. "I can't really say that my students are doing a whole lot better in their studies," says Gardner. "But I can say, with confidence, that with the music on in our classroom, my students settle down quickly, stay on task, and go about their schoolwork in a calm and relaxed manner."

But music does seem to be linked to academic performance as well. Kathy Mazourek, a music teacher in Newfield, N.Y., analyzed the academic performance of 27 students enrolled in her high school band and chorus. "The patterns I saw when I looked at my students' grades in subjects such as English, math, science, physical education, and foreign language jumped right off the page," Mazourek says. "Almost every student my co-music teacher and I rated high in musicality was on the high honor roll. In math, my band kids almost go off the chart."

To many researchers, the best vantage point for studying the effects of musical training on children and young adults is within schools and classrooms. One such school is the Greenhouse School in Salem, Mass., a year-round primary school that serves mainly children from low-income families. There, with the help of principal Daniel Patrick Welch and researcher Patricia Jennings-Welch, teachers are trying to integrate music education throughout an interdisciplinary curriculum.

Some 60 students who would be assigned to grades kindergarten through six in other schools mingle and learn together in an open, ungraded classroom where music is woven into learning activities. Infants and toddlers from a nearby child-care center join the Greenhouse School kids for weekly group singing—an event where, teachers say, their integrated curriculum program begins. And while teachers are quick to acknowledge that they pay attention to multiple intelligences, they agree they think of music as special. Music provides the structure that, as Jennings-Welch puts it, makes the school "more organic, complex, lifelike—*human*."

Music also helps expand students' math and language learning, Greenhouse teachers say. Referring to a music matrix used to plan and assess curriculum, one teacher comments, "It might look jumbled up to a visitor, but kids are learning such things as patterns and symbols—the undergirding concepts that make math and reading possible."

So is music a necessary part of the school curriculum? Increasingly, educators agree that it is. "At Greenhouse School, we think of all the riches music can bring to our lives," the teachers there say, explaining why they called their booklet on music at Greenhouse *The Richest Cousin*. "At our school, music is definitely not thought of as a 'poor stepchild.'"

School districts that "lop off" music in a child's education are simply "arrogant" and unmindful of how humans have evolved with musical brains and intelligences, charges Howard Gardner. Students are entitled to all the artistic and cultural riches the human species has created, and schools should help kids understand these valuable gifts. Think of the highest aspirations possible for students, he says. Then think of those aspirations without music and art.

What's more, Gardner concludes, music can help students learn one of the most valuable lessons of all: that hard work and perseverance have their own rewards—and, in the case of music, at least—can even be fun. ∎

Teaching to Students' Needs

Our students are at different stages of development as readers and writers. Knowing where they have been and where they are going will help us create appropriate goals for them.

Characteristics of Emergent Readers and Writers

- understand the basic grammatical structure of the English language
- know the difference between print and pictures
- know that print carries the story
- use memory and pictures to "read" a story
- can imitate the reading and writing processes
- understand the nature and purpose of print
    - know that print carries a message
    - know that print represents meaning
- show an interest in print
- begin to understand print concepts
    - beginning and ending of a book
    - directionality: left to right, top to bottom, return sweep
    - one printed word represents one spoken word
    - differences among letters, words, and sentences
    - word segmentation
- understand some letter/sound correspondence
- recognize some environmental print
- recognize some names

Characteristics of Developing Readers and Writers

- give text more importance than picture cues
- have mastered print concepts
- have mastered letter/sound correspondence (consonants)
- begin to recognize vowel patterns and combinations
- are developing a sight vocabulary
- begin to utilize the three cueing systems
    - can use syntax and meaning to predict
    - can use initial letter/sound correspondence to predict and confirm
- have knowledge of simple structural analysis
    - can recognize most commonly used affixes (ing, ed, s)
    - can recognize compound words

Excerpted from *Making the Connection: Learning Skills Through Literature (K-2)*, by Patricia Pavelka. Peterborough, NH: Crystal Springs Books, 1996. Reprinted with permission; all rights reserved.

- understand conventions such as punctuation and capital letters at beginning of sentences
- know that reading always makes sense
    read for meaning
- begin to read silently
- use inventive spelling
    audience can read what has been written

Characteristics of Independent Readers and Writers

- recognize the majority of words at sight
- read with fluency
- use the three cueing systems simultaneously
- self-correct to gain meaning
- adjust meaning of words according to the context in which they are used
- read silently
- make inferences independently
- draw conclusions independently
- read to learn (informational books)
- fully understand story elements
- begin to rely on visual cues for spelling rather than auditory cues
- can write using a variety of different forms
- read a wide range of different genres

Characteristics of Reading Materials

Emergent

- short and predictable
- repetitive
- use natural language
- use rhyme and rhythm
- simple texts, easy to memorize
- pictures and text closely matched
- illustrations play a major role on each page

Developing

- longer
- more complex
- wide range of vocabulary
- text rather than illustrations play a more important role on each page

Independent

- illustrations are at a minimum
- vocabulary becomes increasingly challenging
- children need to infer meaning from the story
- more characters are introduced and developed
- story elements are more fully developed
- language challenges are introduced (metaphors, similes)
- chapters appear

Use Quality Children's Literature as the Heart of Your Skills Instruction.

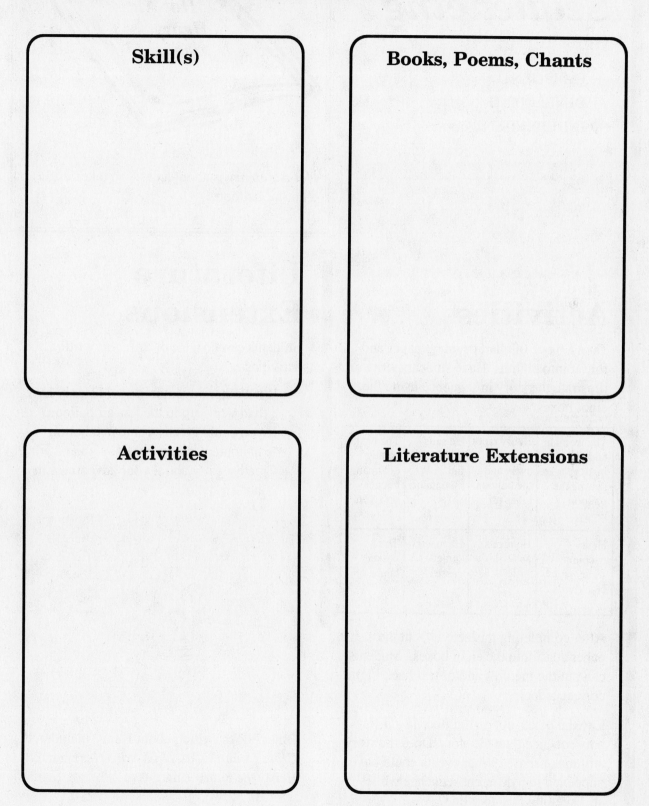

Skill(s)	Books, Poems, Chants

Activities	Literature Extensions

Sequencing

EMERGENT

DEVELOPING

→ **INDEPENDENT**

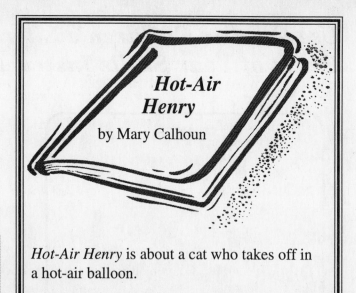

Hot-Air Henry by Mary Calhoun

Hot-Air Henry is about a cat who takes off in a hot-air balloon.

Activities

Take a piece of chart or mural paper and fold it into eighths. Have students write or illustrate the story in sequence using the eight boxes.

The woman and instructor are getting the balloon ready.	Henry races to stow away and the balloon takes off.	He sails toward the mountains.	The basket comes down and bounces up again.
Henry encounters some blackbirds.	He meets an eagle.	He meets some geese.	The basket lands.

After completing this activity, cut the paper apart into the eight boxes. Students can put the pictures and/or text back in the correct order.

Lay the boxes out on the floor in a different sequence than the story. Does the story still make sense? What events could have happened in a different sequence while still keeping the story line?

Add some boxes with new adventures for Henry.

Literature Extensions

Students can do a lot of different writing activities:

What other adventures could Henry have had while up in the hot-air balloon?

If you could go anywhere in a hot-air balloon, where would you go and why?

Create a story about your adventures in a hot-air balloon.

Other books written about Henry include: *Cross Country Cat, High-Wire Henry,* and *Henry the Sailor Cat.*

What other adventures besides ballooning, sailing, and skiing could Henry have? Write about one.

Strategies to Reinforce Skills and Accommodate for Different Abilities

In Part III of this book you will find a section that goes along with each skill and piece of literature called *Using Any Book*. These suggestions and activities deal with two issues:

1. varying levels of readers within our classrooms; and

2. reinforcement of skills throughout the year.

More specific information on dealing with struggling readers is included in Part IV.

Varying Levels of Readers

Within our classrooms there are students at varying levels of ability. Some can be reading significantly above grade level, and some at grade level; some may be nonreaders. Trying to accommodate each ability does seem overwhelming at times. Often at the upper primary level, students understand concepts that are introduced and taught at grade level, but then need to apply those concepts at their own reading level.

For example, when I was teaching at the fourth grade level, there was one child in the classroom reading at the primer level, some reading at a second-grade level, and some at grade level. Three were reading significantly above grade level. When we studied the skill *verbs,* most students could understand the concept of a verb, but needed to apply that concept at their independent level when working. So when an assignment was given to the class to look in the books they were reading and find examples of verbs, John was doing the activity using the book *Mr. Mitchell Brings the Mail,* an emergent-level book; Dale was using a Cam Jansen book; Caitlyn used *James and the Giant Peach*; and Jen used *Call it Courage.* When we met as a class, each child brought many samples of verbs that were found in their pieces of literature. All children could be a part of the activity, regardless of reading ability.

Reinforcement of Skills

I found myself very frustrated throughout the school year because my students were not remembering skills we had just worked on the week before, never mind something we had learned about months ago! I saw very little carryover of skills beyond the days or week we were concentrating on them.

For example: in October, when we were working on the skill of making words plurals, my students did a fantastic job on isolated skill sheets. Most achieved mastery of the skill by the end of the week it was taught. Some even applied it to their writing *that week*. But two months later, I could count on my right hand the number of students who were correctly using and spelling plurals. Most had forgotten how to apply the rules and skill. It was as if they had never been exposed to it.

In the section, *Using Any Book*, you will find ways to apply and reinforce concepts throughout the whole school year. For example, one year we had learned about adjectives and nouns in November. Every month after that, students were responsible for using the

Excerpted from *Making the Connection: Learning Skills Through Literature (3-6)*, by Patricia Pavelka. Peterborough, NH: Crystal Springs Books, 1997. Reprinted with permission; all rights reserved.

reproducibles found on pages 71, 72, and 77 to review and reinforce the concepts of adjectives and nouns; so in June, my students were still applying those concepts and skills that we had learned in September and October. They were also applying them in the context of the books they were reading, rather than on isolated skill sheets and workbook pages.

Skill Charts

Think of the number of skills your students are required to learn throughout the school year. It's no wonder that they forget to apply them weeks and/or months later. Even the students who have no difficulties learning and reading will often forget to use these skills and concepts. Some students need constant support in order to remember and apply these skills.

Using skill charts is a way of having skills and concepts available *all year* for students. Make a skill chart with your students for every skill learned throughout the whole year. Here are some charts that we made when learning about subjects and predicates, and about plurals.

It is imperative to give students an active role in making the charts. After we complete a unit on a skill, we make a chart. First, we brainstorm on the board all of the components of that skill. Next, we look at all of the information and decide how to condense, revise and organize it so that it makes sense and is usable. I do the final writing on the

chart, so that it is big and readable, but all of the information comes directly from the students.

You can keep three to four charts up at a time, depending on your wall space. When a new skill needs to go up, the oldest one comes down. It gets put onto a chart stand with rings. The information is still available for students to refer to *all year!*

Plurals

1. Add (s) to most nouns
   apple - apples   book - books

2. Add (es) to nouns ending in
   ch, sh, x, s
   gas - gases   patch - patches

3. When noun ends consonant y,
   change the y to (i) and add (es)
   party - parties   penny - pennies

4. When a noun ends in f or fe
   change the f, fe to (v) and add (es)

5. Some nouns completely change
   mouse - mice   child - children
   foot - feet   man - men

A sentence has 2 parts

Subject - who or what sentence is about

Predicate - what the subject is or does

The jazz (band) (played) its
favorite song.

A sea (gull) (is) about the
size of a pigeon.

Simple subject -   most important word
                   in subject

Simple predicate - verb

When I think about the line of students at my desk, many times their questions are about skills that we have already studied that the child forgot, or didn't apply properly. In the past, I would usually get a scrap of paper and say, "Remember when we did this . . . ?" Now when those questions come up, I can say to students, "Get the chart on [verbs] and review the information. If you still don't understand it, then come up to me with the chart."

The line at my desk has decreased dramatically. I can also hear my students say to each other, "Did you look at the chart? You know she's going to tell you to look at it or bring it up to her." Now when students come up to me, their questions are usually specific. Instead of that familiar saying, "I don't get it," they have a chart in hand and can pinpoint where the confusion is.

The first year we used skill charts I thought, "Great, now I won't have to ever make them again" . . . *wrong!* In order for students to really feel empowered and to take ownership of their own learning, they need to have an active role in making the charts. At the end of each year, I send the charts home with students and we begin again with the new class.

I also had some beautiful store-bought charts, but my students rarely used them because they didn't have any ownership in them.

Two excellent resources for students and teachers to help with skills are the books, *Write Source 2000* and *Writers INC*. Both are available through:

> Write Source
> Box 460
> Burlington, Wisconsin 53105
> 1-800-445-8613

If you use these books as resources in your classroom, add masking tape tabs to help students find information they need at their fingertips. Also, Crystal Springs Books has tabs that can be used instead of the masking tape. To order them, call 1-800-321-0401.

Modeling

As you use the ideas presented in this book, especially the reproducibles and open-ended activities, keep this in mind:

> Before asking students to do any activity independently, model it three times.

When thinking back to that constant line at my desk with students saying "I don't get it," I remember my feelings of frustration, and of never having enough time to get everything done. When I gave students their assignments or independent work to do, most of the time I just told them what to do. Yes, there were times that I did model something, but only once, and then I expected them to be able to do it on their own. And do it *well!*

Then I received a new pen and pencil set as a gift. When my pencil ran out of lead, I went to my brother Rich and asked him how to refill it. He took the pencil from me and demonstrated how to do it. I watched him and thought, I can do that. The next thing he did was to take the lead out and give me back the pencil and say, "Now you do it." Easy, I thought. I took it in my hands, looked at it and then said those four dreaded words my students always said:

"I don't get it!"

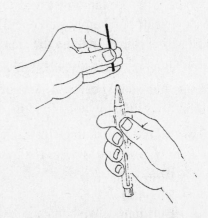

I then asked Rich to do it again so that I could watch him. After he modeled the procedure a number of times, I successfully completed the task. I immediately thought of my students and our usual scenario:

1. I would explain and/or model something once.
2. I would ask the students if everyone understood the task.
3. They would all shake their heads and say, "Uh, huh," with smiles on their faces.
4. I would give the assignment.
5. Without fail, the line began to form at my desk with students who didn't understand the assignment.

Now, when there are assignments that students will be doing throughout the whole year, such as the reproducibles and open-ended activities found in this book, I follow a format for modeling that consists of three basic steps:

First —

I put the assignment on an overhead projector and complete it as my students watch me. There is little or no student input at this time. Students watch me. As I complete the assignment I think aloud. I want students to get into my mind to see what I do to organize this specific task, and how I follow through.

Some of my students are very "task-oriented." They *go!* They do not take a moment to think about the task or to organize themselves for success. My own thinking aloud helps model that thought process to students.

Second —

I model the same assignment or task using different materials or pieces of literature. Now students begin to give me some input. We do the assignment together. I ask students to think aloud. As they give me suggestions and ideas, I want them to explain how and why they came up with them.

Third —

This time when I model the assignment I am basically my students' hands. They come up with all of the ideas and suggestions, and I write them down.

I do it.

We do it.

You do it.

Parts of Speech/ Adjectives

Activities

I find it easier for students to understand adjectives when I teach adjectives in conjunction with nouns. We talk about adjectives being the words that make nouns "come alive." They give us a clearer, more detailed picture of a person, place or thing.

Give students a piece of paper. Have them fold it in half. Write a noun on the board, and ask students to draw a picture of it on the left side of their paper. For example, write the word "apple" on the board. Students' pictures of the apple are all different: different colors, shapes, sizes, textures, etc. Then write the following on the board: "the small, green, rotten apple". Now have students draw a picture of this apple on the right side of their paper. The pictures are now more alike because of the adjectives.

After reading the story, have students work together or in groups to find pairs or groups of adjectives and nouns. For example:

> slow-flying geese
> small, white farmhouse
> old broom
> cold, autumn night
> moonlit sky
> tired broom
> lonely widow

The Widow's Broom
by Chris Van Allsburg

Minna, a lonely widow, finds a witch's broom and takes it home. The broom comes to life and begins helping Minna around the house. However, the neighbors aren't as happy about the broom as Minna.

Literature Extensions

Students can fill in the diamond on the following page using the directions on page 132. For example:

> Mystery
> third   person
> house   road   woods
> dark   eerie   moonlit   desolate
> Minna   Mr. Spivey   broom   witch   boys
> tired   old   harmless   helpful
> lonely   kind   brave
> shocked   confused
> surprised

Using Any Book

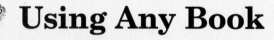

Usually two or three times a month, I ask students to fill in the noun and adjective reproducible (explained above), using the book they are reading. See the two examples on page 133.

Name: _____

Diamond: _____

Title: _____

Author: _____

_____

_____   _____

_____   _____   _____

_____   _____   _____   _____

_____   _____   _____   _____   _____

_____   _____   _____   _____

_____   _____   _____

_____   _____

_____

Story Diamond
Nouns and Adjectives

Line 1   Identify the genre

Line 2   Point of view

Line 3   Three nouns explaining the setting
          (Circle one of the nouns)

Line 4   Four adjectives describing the noun you circled

Line 5   Five important nouns in the story
                (2 proper, 3 common)
                Circle a common noun
                Circle a proper noun

Line 6   Four adjectives describing the common noun you circled

Line 7   Three adjectives describing the proper noun you circled

Line 8   Two words describing how you feel about the book

Line 9   One-word summary

This student used the book
Island of the Blue Dolphins
by Scott O'Dell

non-fiction

1st person

ocean   hut

iland   sandy   big   rocky   uninhabited   otter   dolphins
                                                        c   c

Karond   Ramo   wild dogs   fearce
            p   c

mean   big   hungry   sad

girl   alone   sad   realistic

lonly

This Student used the book
James and the Giant Peach
by Roald Dahl

fantasy

3rd person

air   hill   water   wet   deep

blue   little   enormous   Atlantic Ocean   Seagulls   air   lady bug
                                  p   c   c

Aunt Sponge   deep   black   red   friendly
p

good   blue   rocky

happy

funny

133

One of the foundations we need to establish in our classrooms is to help students become a community of learners, who work together as collaborators, not competitors. The following books all deal with issues that have an effect on learning. They help students build self-image, create acceptance, and respect individual differences.

Aekyung's Dream
by Min Paek

Arthur's Eyes
by Marc Brown

Be Good to Eddie Lee
by Virginia Fleming

Big Al
by Andrew Clements Yoshi

Boastful Bullfrog
by Keith Faulkner

Charlie the Caterpillar
by Dom DeLuise

Chrysanthemum
by Kevin Henkes

Crowboy
by Taro Yashima

Do I Have To Go To School Today?
by Larry Shles

Elephant and the Rainbow
by Keith Faulkner

Hallo-Wiener
by Dav Pilkey

I Like Me
by Nancy Carlson

I Wish I Were a Butterfly
by James Howe

Josh A Boy With Dyslexia
by Caroline Janover

Kids Explore the Gifts of Children with Special Needs
by Westridge Young Writers Workshop

Kittens Who Didn't Share
by Keith Faulkner

Leo the Late Bloomer
by Robert Kraus

Little Rabbit Who Wanted Red Wings
by Carolyn Sherwin Bailey

Mama Zooms
by Jane Cowen-Fletcher

Me First and the Gimme Gimmes
by Gerald G. Jampolsky & Diane V. Cirincione

My Buddy
by Audrey Osofsky

My Sister Is Different
by Betty Ren Wright

Old Henry
by Joan W. Blos

Original Warm Fuzzy Tale
by Claude Steiner

Our Brother Has Down's Syndrome
by Shelley Cairo

Owl and the Woodpecker
by Brian Wildsmith

Painting the Fire
by Liz Farrington & Jonathan Sherwood

People
by Peter Spier

Rainbow Fish and *Rainbow Fish to the Rescue*
by Marcus Pfister

Reach for the Moon
by Samantha Abeel

Royal Raven
by Hans Wilhelm

Santa's Book of Names
by David McPhail

Stellaluna
by Janell Cannon

Summer Tunes: A Martha's Vineyard Vacation
by Patricia McMahon

Table Where Rich People Sit
by Byrd Baylor

Tacky the Penguin and *Three Cheers for Tacky*
by Helen Lester

That's What a Friend Is
by P.K. Hallinan

What Do You Mean I Have a Learning Disability?
by Kathleen M. Dwyer

When Learning is Tough
by Cynthia Roby

We Can Do It
by Laura Dwight

Patricia Pavelka, M.Ed.

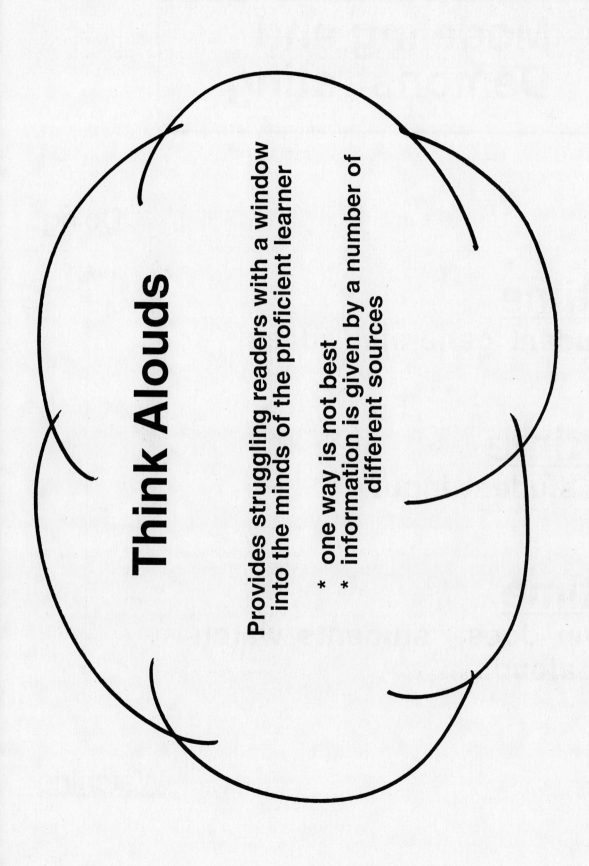

Think Alouds

Provides struggling readers with a window into the minds of the proficient learner

* one way is not best
* information is given by a number of different sources

paper cloud with headband to wear   cloud on overhead   ball to throw

Patricia Pavelka, M. Ed.

135

Modeling and Demonstrating

Doing

↑

3rd time
All student generated ideas

2nd time
Some student input

1st time
**Teacher does, students watch
Think alouds**

Watching

Patricia Pavelka, M. Ed.

Sight Vocabulary
Multiple Exposures

Books/Stories and Highlighting Tape
"I found <u>the,</u> <u>10</u> times."
Flip Books

Baggies

Glue Words

Clay/Playdough Words

Screenboards

Patricia Pavelka, M. Ed.

Flip Books

Take a piece of paper.

Fold it in half lengthwise.

Make 2-4 cuts on top side only.

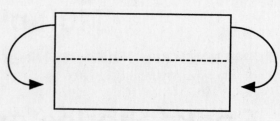

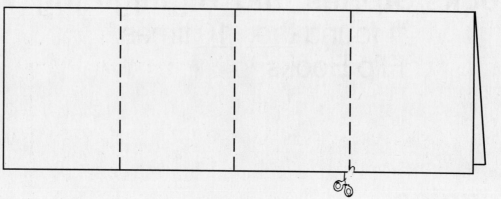

Descriptive Question

outside
words to describe

inside
prove it!
page #
sentences/phrases

Vocabulary

outside
words

inside
picture,
definition,antonyms,
synonyms, use it

Predictions

inside
make a prediction:
science experiment
events in a story

outside
Why?
What was prediction
based on?

Patricia Pavelka, M. Ed

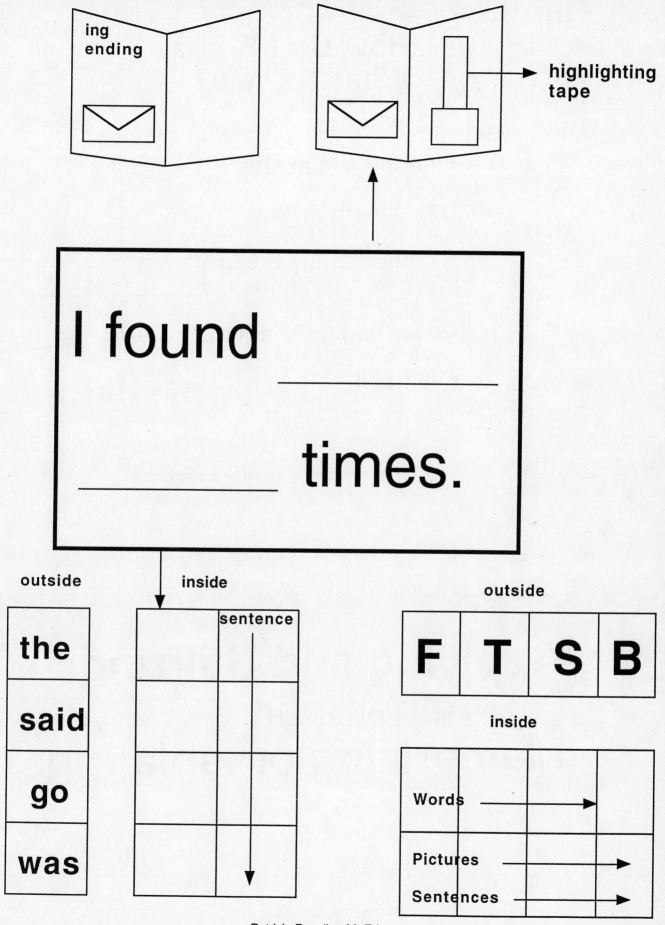

ing
ending

highlighting
tape

I found _____

_____ times.

outside

the

said

go

was

inside

sentence

outside

F T S B

inside

Words ⟶
Pictures ⟶
Sentences ⟶

Patricia Pavelka, M. Ed.

139

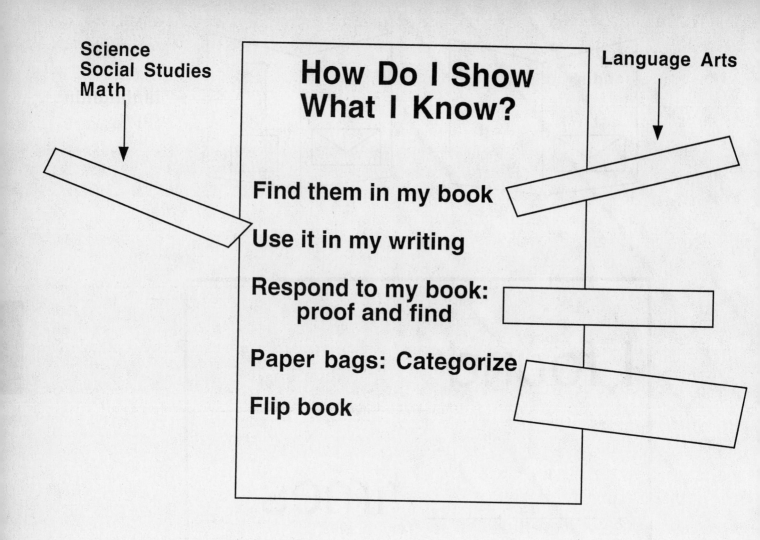

Science
Social Studies
Math

Language Arts

How Do I Show What I Know?

Find them in my book

Use it in my writing

Respond to my book:
   proof and find

Paper bags: Categorize

Flip book

Applying and Utilizing
rather than
Memorizing or Isolating

Patricia Pavelka, M. Ed.

First

1st

_____

_____

_____

Second

2nd

_____

_____

_____

_____

_____

_____

_____

_____

_____

Patricia Pavelka, M. Ed.

141

TEAM TEACHING
Beginnings

BY THE NORTHERN NEVADA WRITING PROJECT TEACHER- RESEARCHER GROUP

When the Nevada state legislature mandated a ratio of fifteen students to one teacher, it quickly became apparent that some major changes would have to take place, that classes and teachers would have to double up to comply with the law. Individual schools were allowed to determine who would team teach and where their classrooms would be located given the existing facilities.

The most visionary principals helped teachers form teams and subsequently responded to team needs. Professional teacher-training coordinators also scrambled to provide assistance. However, for the most part, teachers were expected to take on the responsibility of collaborating and becoming self-managed, successful teams. They were expected to develop the mutual respect and trust it takes to work together.

First-grade teachers were the first to deal with the challenge. Sherry recalled:

Partners were told on Thursday they were to combine students on the following Monday. I refused. "Give us at least one week." We were together a week

> We decided we would make this work. You can fight something and be miserable, or you can accept it and find the good. We will find the good. We have different styles of teaching, but I feel we will mesh very well. Also, we said we will not break up our friendship over this. We will communicate with each other.

from that Monday. There was no time before school, and [the change] was not funded in any way. We met for two hours while others took our classes.

Cami displayed some positive energy toward the prospect of team teaching.

We decided we would make this work. You can fight something and be miserable, or you can accept it and find the good. We will find the good. We have different styles of teaching, but I feel we will mesh very well. Also, we said we will not break up our friendship over this. We will communicate with each other.

Forming Teams

During those frantic, frenzied first days of team formation and initial team collaboration, and with the combination of time pressure and outside influences, it was difficult for those involved to make rational, focused decisions. As team teachers reflected on that time with us, most concurred that logical planning and careful choices were often tripped up by politics and fate.

Teachers within their own schools, particularly those who lacked job seniority, began looking for partners with compatible personalities and/or teaching styles. They talked openly with potential partners, with other staff members, with principals, and with significant others. Sara said,

> My partner and I started out last year thinking we would be teaching together, and we did a lot of discussing. Then when we took a trip together to San Francisco, we talked the whole way down and back, and it seemed like we were on the same wavelength in a lot of areas.

A few teachers began looking outside their own schools for partners. They hoped to obtain administrative approval once a possible arrangement had been secured.

Some considered asking friends to become their partners, since they already knew their friends' philosophies and styles of teaching. Margaret said, "I would want to pick someone who was a friend already instead of going in cold turkey with someone I didn't know at all." According to Virginia, "Dealing with a stranger might be easier, but working with a friend, you know what to expect, even if you don't like it." Other teachers decided against teaming with close friends, reasoning that the strain of being partners for at least seven hours a day could jeopardize their friendship. What if they discovered things about each other they couldn't respect?

Sometimes parents suggested possible teaching partners, sometimes counselors or other teachers did. Everyone became a potential matchmaker, knowing "just the right person for you."

In some cases, principals needed to hire team partners. Some did so unilaterally; others invited current staff members to be present during the interviews, either as silent observers or as participants. As several of our interviewees reflected on the selection process, they felt the partner-to-be of the new hire should insist on being present at the interview. Faye said, "I'd want to be in on the interview, especially if I was there first and they were bringing someone in to me. I'd want to be in on the interview and hear their answers."

Shannon extended that thought. "I'd like to interview them two or three times, not just a first time, because that first time they're always trying to be good. The second time you might really see what they're like." She said she would ask, "If you have report cards due to the principal on Wednesday morning and it's Friday afternoon and you and I are both going to be busy all weekend, would you be willing to stay Monday and Tuesday to get those report cards done?"

Dale warned about posing leading questions during an interview. "People are just as glib as they have always been. Some people give you the answers you want to hear."

Even though Angela had interviewed her current partner, it didn't work out. The next time in an interview, she plans to ask questions about classroom management, use of space, and planning strategies. "I would also like to know if they are flexible or structured. I feel that they should ask questions about me, too."

Teachers were also teamed up by chance: straws were drawn, names were put into a hat, and winners or losers, depending on your point of view, became a team.

Finding the Ideal Partner

If you accept the fact that no one is perfect, then the perfect teammate is not only elusive but nonexistent. Nevertheless, team teachers in our study had some definite ideas about who their ideal partner might be. Philosophies, classroom environments, methods of discipline, and personality types were their main concerns.

> "How would I choose a new partner?" Shannon reiterated the question.
> I'd have to sit down and really think about what I'd want to ask them. I'd like to interview them, go to lunch with them, then probably go to dinner with them, and then probably have breakfast with them, and probably never choose them because I honestly can't think of replacing my partner now. If she died tomorrow, I'd be in trouble. I'd probably try to get a single room. Even though my principal matched me with my partner, I don't trust that he could do that again. He just got lucky.

Phyllis said she would easily recognize her ideal partner.

> You know right off the bat. You could go into a school and sit with people and just listen and hear how they talk, see if they're tired and sick of their job and don't like children.

Virginia was concerned with less threatening issues, such as classroom arrangement. She would ask, "Does she use centers?

Does she like to have easels in her room? Does she like hands-on math?" Along similar lines, Pearl wanted to know whether the prospective partner prefers desks to tables.

Educational Philosophy

Sally felt that thinking about and articulating one's educational philosophy was especially important when the person was part of a team. Several respondents mentioned the need to have compatible philosophies, and some teachers specifically felt they needed to know whether a potential partner's teaching would be predominantly child-centered or curriculum-centered.

"I would look for a philosophy similar to mine," Eileen stated. "The way they teach isn't exactly it. Somebody who sees kids the way I do is closer. I would want their expectation level of kids to be similar to mine." Shannon said, "We should try to have a common goal: probably, it's teach the children as best we can, in the time that we're allowed, and have a good time."

Sonia said that partners would need to see eye to eye on their teaching methods and philosophies: how they group their students in reading or how they integrate a new child into the classroom. Gayle focused on methods of teaching reading and math; to her, these areas were the most important in first grade. Sara liked having a lot of books in the room and would like a partner who shared this desire. She felt there should be all sorts of books available and the students should have an opportunity to choose their own books. She would also look for a person who felt that

writing is an integral part of learning. Jill said that three concepts would be important to her in assessing a potential partner: educational philosophy of whole language versus phonics strategies; expectations of students; and teaching styles.

Renée mentioned these same three ideas more specifically: "I would hope that she was whole language [oriented] and that she had a developmental view of children as opposed to a skills-oriented view."

Twyla was concerned not only with a partner's educational philosophy, but also with personal beliefs:

> I've seen personal beliefs come into play this year, not just professional beliefs, but personal ones. If you don't agree with them, they can get in the way. If I don't like the way this person thinks, her prejudices can get in the way. Those beliefs will creep into your teaching in what you say or don't say. It will come out.

Others mentioned that they would look for partners who complemented them. When we interviewed Pearl, her partner was in the room, preparing for the next day. When Pearl stated, "Each of us has separate strengths," her partner chimed in, "I see that as a challenge. Pearl is good with crafts, and I like to think of projects. A lot of times, she'll know how to make it work. She's taken art classes, and that helps with the expertise. And Pearl helps me

spell." After a few giggles, Pearl continued, "My partner is good about positioning things. I'm [leading the class and] talking about things, and I may have visuals turned sideways so they aren't seen properly." Her partner concluded, "So we help each other."

Hillary wrote in her journal about days when fresh ideas eluded both partners. "To be completely honest, each of us has 'one of those days' about once a week." Helping each other was critical under these circumstances.

An ideal partner is versatile enough to cope with the unexpected situations that continually plague teachers. Hillary gave this example:

> On various occasions, one of us will get wrapped up in conversation with a parent, another teacher, the principal, the nurse, or the counselor. It seems as if we're always trying to contact or locate somebody for one reason or another. When you get them, you'd better communicate then, or it just gets put off. The other teacher will begin the lesson or activity until the partner returns. At an appropriate time, we will relay the information and clue each other in.

To uncover a prospective team partner's philosophy, Lynne would do several things:

> First, I would think about people I know: who they are, how they teach, and what they're like, probably someone who came out of

the University of Nevada about the same time I did and who would be on a similar wavelength. Next, I'd participate in the interview process by using the Professional Development Center's inventory that deals with rank-ordered issues. Then, I'd observe them in their classrooms and ask them whether they used or were familiar with particular programs like *Math Their Way* and *Come With Me Science*.

While there is no one common philosophical similarity identifiable to successful teams, the pervading notion of a "common view of the child" in a classroom dominated the teachers' ideas on how to find a compatible partner.

Classroom Climate

A second major area, classroom environment, also dominated responses on finding ideal partners. Some teachers focused on the importance of creating a positive, productive atmosphere; others were concerned with noise levels, neatness, and discipline.

Jill and her partner aspired to create a classroom where students, teachers, and others would want to spend time, a place where kids would feel safe and inspired, as evidenced by a great deal of student writing. Jill would look at a prospective partner's room to see if she felt happy and comfortable in it and if their standards of cleanliness were similar. Beth put it more directly. "I could not stand a total slob."

Summer echoed some of these ideas. She, too, would like to visit the prospective partner's classroom in order to observe the teacher-student interaction, listen to how the teacher talked to and with children, evaluate the teacher's expectations of the children, and determine whether the classroom seemed too structured or too lax. She would try to decide whether the purpose of the classroom decorations were adult-centered or were used to stimulate student thinking. As Lee Anne put it, "You can pick up a lot of things by seeing teachers with their kids — not just in the classroom, but other times, like computer time, music time, or just walking them down the hall."

Denise wanted to give prospective partners the same opportunity. "I'd want to see them in action, and I'd want them to see me in action, too."

While most partners did not make a value judgment on correct classroom climate, they emphasized that different climates needed to be able to coexist.

Discipline

A third key issue in selecting a teammate was classroom discipline. Phyllis said, "I'd look to a commitment — for manners and discipline in the classroom and high values." If she was given the opportunity to question a prospective partner, she would ask, "How do you want your children to behave in the classroom?" and "What would you do to achieve that?"

Showing her concern for children, Helen would wonder of her prospective partner, "Is screaming at students OK in the classroom?" Pearl added the following wish list:

I'd want a person who isn't afraid to discipline. I'm not a person who likes chaotic behavior. If a person was too lenient, that would bother me. You don't have to be exactly the same, but I think you have to see discipline in somewhat the same way. Be consistent and follow up on rules.

Although flexible about curriculum issues, Claire was not as willing to compromise her discipline strategies. For example, too much noise — even constructive noise — drives her to distraction. This year her partner, Gayle, who was more tolerant of student noise, accepted her partner's need for a quieter classroom.

Another team member, Clara, revealed, "I want someone who sees children as children and not as little robots who will sit [at] their desks all day long. Students need to get up and have some freedom, have some choices in what happens in the classroom." Bea said she wanted the teacher to have empathy for students, but at the same time help them to grow and change — "a steel rod in a velvet glove."

Personality Traits

There seemed to be a common set of personality attributes that the teachers in our study looked for when selecting a teammate.

Flexibility was a major concern. Pearl said, "I'd want a fairly flexible person, a person who is not afraid to try new things." Clara responded, "My partner should be somebody who will be somewhat spontaneous and doesn't get upset if we don't follow exactly what's in the lesson plan." Sharon summed up flexibility this way:

> Flexibility is a whole range of stuff. If we start something and it's just going dead, we look at each other and say, "It's not working." Then we go on to something else. When some people have changes in their schedules, they freak out. My partner and I just go with the flow.

A positive attitude was another necessary trait for many of the respondents. Claire wanted someone who was upbeat and animated. She definitely would not want a "deadpan" who would make her feel like a "goof." Pearl spoke for her partner and herself when she said, "Neither of us can stand negativity. I think when you're working with children, it's devastating if you're negative."

"There is something you sense when you walk into a classroom," Summer added. "You can feel if there is a positiveness about the class; you can sense that children and teachers want to be there learning." Sonia added, "Without positive self-esteem, communication will break down." Dale offered an example:

> Last week my partner and I were feeling rushed, and we found that we were both feeding each other's negativity on kids, on life, on school, on where we were going, on "let's hurry up

and get this school year over with." That hadn't happened to us generally over the previous years. Each day I found myself being more negative, and she was, too. We were feeding each other and causing it to compound. We have to watch for that. We have to help each other.

She suggested a solution. "Say to your partner, I know you're having a bad time, but I'm sure feeling bad, too, and I think we're hurting the kids. Our attitude needs a little adjustment here."

A third attribute, a sense of humor, was mentioned several times as an important trait. Renée said, "I'd want someone who likes to play in the classroom. Learning has to be fun." Toni suggested laughing together, while Jody recommended asking a potential teammate, "Do you consider yourself a humorous person?"

The attribute of trust is not only the most difficult to find in a teammate, but also seems the most difficult to develop in a partnership. Helen was adamant about the importance of trust. "I would absolutely have to trust that person," she said. "I would switch grades before I would team with someone I didn't trust." Irene pointed out that trust developed from working daily with a partner and seeing what the other did. However, Margaret stressed, "We come to any relationship with our own baggage, and that affects our dialogue in the relationship."

Sonia believed that issues of control and trust were common with beginning teams, but said that in her team the problem

lasted only four months. "As soon as we both felt comfortable with the knowledge that each team member knew her stuff, we relinquished the control factor." She also thought that the second year to-gether was very different from the first year. "The partners don't have to work out issues of trust and communication, and they are free to be both humane and fair to one another without losing their sense of self." These teachers felt lucky that their principal made it very clear to them in the beginning that they should remember at all times that they were equals. Jody concluded that team teaching can make both participants feel secure in their teaching.

Another trait some teachers sought in a teammate was personal compatibility. Gayle, wanting to be friends with her partner, might ask, "What would you like to do on Friday afternoon when we're finished teaching?" Similarly, Gladys revealed that she and her partner had "supportive personalities." She explained, "We want everything to be OK and we take charge of that. We are both mothering, that kind of personality."

An additional component for a potential teammate is the willingness to grow. Phyllis noted, "I'd want someone who wanted to learn — learn from the children, learn new methods of teaching, and be willing to try new things." Barbara added, "True professionals are those who are willing to grow."

For Joan, a compassionate and nurturing manner is a necessary factor. She said that while "realizing that everyone has cross moments," she felt that "kindness must be exhibited at all times." Melanie said that if she is irritated by something that happens during the day but ignores it, in a few days the irritation disappears because it will have been replaced by something positive her teammate has said or done. But Sharon said, "We believe that we have to let the other person know how we are feeling and what we're thinking, what we like and don't like, and we're very respectful of our individual differences."

Several team teachers focused on the need for a sense of equality and sharing. Sally warned that no one can completely own anything in a team classroom. And Margaret emphasized:

> I wouldn't want somebody who had to be the chief. I'd want someone who would balance my strengths. I love teaching reading, but I wouldn't want to be someone who said, "I love reading; it's my strength, so I'm going to do it all."

Gayle maintained that teachers have to let go of their own egos to appreciate the strengths and positive aspects of their partners. Margaret shared the following:

> Since I was doing remedial group work with students in a sectioned-off portion of the room, I felt isolated and felt I wasn't bonding with the kids the way I wanted to. I said several times to my partner, "I don't want to be your aide." Finally, one night after work we went to [a restaurant], and I burst into tears. She said that she felt what I was doing was the most important because if those little ones can't learn to read, they're sunk. So we changed

some stuff around and took turns doing the opening things, and then I found myself feeling ridiculous. They cared as much about me as they did her, and I decided to just let it go because I was getting behind and not able to get that first reading group going fast enough. So I told her, "I've changed my mind. Let's go back and do it the other way again." We try hard when discussing problems to say "I feel" instead of "You're doing."

Commitment was also emphasized by teachers in the study. Kelsey wanted her partner to have the same dedication to the job as she had. She stressed, "It can't be someone who comes at nine and leaves at three and is down in the lounge every recess." Two other teachers had similar views on this issue. Sharon reported, "My partner and I come out on weekends. On three-day weekends, we usually spend one of the three days either at her house or at school." Adele felt that a partner needs to be willing to spend time outside school getting the program set up. Mavis worried that if the team members were not balanced in their time commitment, the students would recognize it and perceive it as a weakness.

Another important consideration was a potential teammate's interaction with students. One teacher suggested observing the partner from a student's point of view. Sara proposed putting herself in a student's place, asking, "Would I like this person to be my teacher?" Joan thought that the rapport between student

and teacher was paramount. She would ask, "Do children seem to trust the person and go to [him or her] freely?" Phyllis would just listen to the language that teachers used while talking about children, asking herself such questions as "Did they seem tired of the job? Did they seem to like children?"

The ability to tolerate differences also seemed critical to successful teaming. Dale shared details about a team at her school:

> We never expected them to be successful because they were very, very different from each other. One is very religious; the other is a smoker, likes to go out and dance, is athletic, and pats you on the back. It's amazing how well they have done. I think the bottom line is that they respect each other. Each could say, "I would never have done that, but it sure did work!" Teammates must respect one another — which I think has to do with the way that they think about a child and the way that they approach their job.

Althier M. Lazar
Renee Weisberg

Inviting parents' perspectives: Building home-school partnerships to support children who struggle with literacy

What happens when parents are invited and encouraged to share their own knowledge and insight of their children's literacy development with teachers? This study suggests that such sharing can help teachers design instruction to better meet the needs of their students.

We were driving home one day last week. Normally Rachel sleeps, listens to music, or bugs her sister. This time she started reading the signs as we passed them, whether it was street signs, for sale signs, traffic signs, or store signs. The next time we used that same route, she knew where we were going.

Mrs. Jackson

This journal entry was written by Rachel's mother. It is a snapshot of Rachel as a reader, a sister, and a daughter. Descriptions like this reveal Rachel's purposeful use of print within the context of family life. Pieced together over time, they describe a youngster who is far more complex than her below-average grades indicate. By reading these journal entries, Rachel's teacher, Elaine, learned a great deal about this student and her ways of reading and writing at home. Elaine used the information to support Rachel's literacy development in and out of school.

When parents are invited to bring information about their child's involvement with print to the classroom, teachers can use it to understand their students as people and as literacy learners. This is especially important for teachers who want to help the children who concern them most. By inviting parent-teacher

Lazar, Althier M., & Weisberg, Renee K. (1996, November). Inviting parents' perspectives: Building home-school partnerships to support children who struggle with literacy. *The Reading Teacher,* 50(3), 228-237.

Parents can help teachers understand how their children relate to print outside the classroom.
Photo by Cleo Freelance Photo

communication within a college-based reading program for school-age children, we explored how parental input helped teachers support youngsters who struggle with reading.

Parent as outsider, parent as collaborator

News about a child's literacy behavior generally travels one way—from school to home, often through written reports and teacher conferences. Parents or other primary caregivers can respond to notes sent home or share insights about youngsters during school conferences, but most traditional school communication does not encourage this kind of input. Parents usually *receive* information about their child *from* teachers, rather than actively *contributing* to an emerging portrait of their child as a learner at home and at school. The prevailing model of parent-teacher communication does not take into account the value of parent input, even though information about children's everyday lives outside of school is important for understanding and supporting youngsters in school. Nevertheless, home

caregivers are uniquely situated as observers of children's out-of-school literacy activity:

> After all, parents see children reading and writing in many literacy contexts in the world outside of school. Because parents usually know their children better than anyone else, they can also supply important clues to help teachers adjust the literacy environment and instruction so their children can better succeed in school (Rhodes & Shanklin, 1993, p. 23).

Because parents connect with their children in personal ways across time, they can play a special role in helping teachers understand how their children relate to print outside of the classroom. The parent is able to achieve what Erickson and Mohatt (1982) describe as an "overall contextual perspective" that can "only come through intimate and continuous acquaintance" (Taylor, 1993, p. 15). Parents observe their children using language and print for a variety of purposes and can offer commentary on their children's range of experiences with the world outside of school.

Parents can also reveal how the family members function together in their transactions with print, offering a "between-heads" (Taylor,

1993) view of learning. In communicating about their children as literacy learners, parents can convey an image of themselves as observers of and participants in home literacy events. How parents structure, observe, and record family reading events tells much about their philosophies of learning, teaching, and literacy (Hedman, 1993).

Many of today's parents attended primary school 20 to 30 years ago, when subskill approaches to literacy teaching prevailed. Given the gradual shift from skill to holistic teaching over the last several years, one would expect to find growing differences in the ways parents and teachers view literacy teaching. Indeed, many parents view reading as a process of decoding and tend to focus on "sounding out" strategies as a primary means of identifying unknown words (Routman, 1991).

Some home-school programs focus on helping parents learn new trends in reading education, including providing lists of teaching ideas parents can try at home (McMackin, 1993; Vopat, 1994), in order to structure enjoyable and productive literacy experiences for their children. The information conveyed to parents may be useful, although it is not necessarily tailored to individual children and their particular family structures and circumstances.

Programs that encourage parents to *share* information with teachers about their children's literacy experiences outside of school (Burke, 1985; Cairney & Munsie, 1995; McGilp & Michael, 1994; Shockley, 1994) are based on the belief that parents have valuable information that might help teachers become better informed about their students. Rather than convincing parents to adopt teacher-generated literacy lessons, these programs provide a kind of cultural exchange between home and school environments aimed at supporting students' growth:

> The purpose in breaking down the barriers between home and school is not to coerce, or even persuade, parents to take on the literacy definitions held by teachers. Rather, it is to enable both teachers and parents to understand the way each defines, values, and uses literacy as part of cultural practices. In this way schooling can be adjusted to meet the needs of families. Parents, in turn, can observe and understand the definitions of literacy that schools support, which ultimately empower individuals to take their place in society. (Cairney & Munsie, 1995, p. 393)

Two-way communication between teachers and parents is one way of achieving mutual understanding of the cultural practices of home and school. This practice is a natural extension of ethnographic studies that have looked at the ways schools and communities differ culturally and the way these differences influence academic learning for school children (Erickson & Mohatt, 1982; Heath, 1983; Philips, 1972). These studies suggest that understanding cultural differences between schools and communities is critical to improving learning and teaching. Inviting parents to share what they know about their children provides an essential window into the home community.

Shockley (1994) initiated communication with the families of her first-grade classroom via home response journals. She began her school year inviting the parents to "tell about their children." This sparked ongoing correspondence as parents wrote about the books they read together and the stories they told to one another and also how their children responded to print at home. Through reading these entries and responding to parents' observations and insights, Shockley discovered how parent-teacher partnering maximized instructional support for each of her students.

> I was able to respond individually to issues regarding reading and writing development, sharing with parents my beliefs about literacy learning and ways to support that learning. Likewise, parents often informed me of their own strategies, beliefs, and insights. I learned to count on parents as co-teachers; there was now shared accountability and security in knowing each child had a one-to-one time with "a more capable peer".... (Shockley, 1994, p. 501)

By inviting parents to share their insights, Shockley extended her program of support into the home. Parent-teacher communication also influenced literacy learning in school as family-generated texts became the focus of many class discussions and projects. This experience points to the power of parent-teacher sharing, and it prompts the question of how parent-teacher communication can help children who have difficulty achieving success in school.

We explored this question by inviting the parents of children enrolled in a college-based reading program to write about their child's literacy activity in journals and to share these written entries with teachers. We asked how parent-teacher sharing would influence teachers' ways of supporting students at home and in the classroom.

The Reading-Language Arts Center

Each semester the Beaver College Reading-Language Arts Center (Glenside, Pennsylvania, USA) offers a program of literacy instruction for area school children in Grades 1 through 6 who live in the communities surrounding the college. The children are taught by graduate students who seek reading specialist certification through Beaver's Education Department. The children who attend classes at the Reading-Language Arts Center are a diverse group of African American, Asian American, and Caucasian youngsters of varying economic backgrounds. Teachers in surrounding school districts refer these children to the Center on the basis of a range of assessments: classroom observations, informal reading assessments, and standardized tests. These records show that most incoming students have difficulty meeting the expectations of the reading requirements in their regular schools.

The findings of this study were based on data gathered during the summer semester of 1994, when the Reading-Language Arts Center held classes Monday through Thursday mornings in July. Students were placed in groups of four according to age and grade and were assigned to one of eight teachers. Teachers collected initial information about their students' reading and writing behaviors through miscue analysis, retellings, response discussions, and writing samples. In addition, they collected information about students' attitudes toward literacy learning by interviewing children and having them respond to written questionnaires. When classes began, teachers took anecdotal notes of their students' classroom activity, and this information was placed in an assessment notebook. These data helped teachers plan instruction for their students.

Inviting parent-teacher correspondence

All of the teachers in the program had experiences communicating with parents through their work in public or private schools. When asked to describe these experiences, most recalled *sending* information to parents, in the form of newsletters, report cards, narrative progress reports, weekly work folders, letters, notices, conferences, back-to-school presentations, meetings, and telephone conversations. Teachers did not write about *receiving* parent

input. Even though they had not experienced reciprocal communication with parents, they were excited about doing so during the summer session.

We initiated a relationship with parents at the start of the semester. Teachers held individual interviews with parents, asking about each child's experiences, beliefs, practices, and goals around literacy. We also asked parents to attend an orientation meeting and invited them to share observations of their child's reading and writing outside of school.

During the meeting, parents provided examples of their children's literacy activity. These included reading license plates during long car trips, preparing grocery lists before shopping, and reading menus in restaurants. We explained that information like this might help teachers understand and plan for the children at the Center. We asked parents to record observations like these in a journal at least three times each week during the summer session. Parents were asked to bring the journals to their child's teacher at the Center so that the teacher could read the entries and write responses to parents the same day.

When asked to describe these experiences communicating with parents, most teachers recalled sending information to parents.

Approximately 60% of the parents participated in the journal writing project (17 of 28). After teachers read and responded to the parent journals each Thursday morning, they made notations in their assessment notebooks about the different issues raised by parents. Each Thursday afternoon, teachers shared with one another their thoughts about the journal writing project and what they might do with the information provided by parents.

"She's not reading the words!"

By reading and interpreting parent journal entries, assessment notebooks, transcripts of parent meetings and teacher seminars, and end-of-semester parent questionnaires, we generated some findings about the nature and significance of parent input. We found that parents expressed many concerns about their child's at-home reading behaviors. Many wrote detailed comments about their child's reluctance to read, their selection of "too easy" reading material, or their frequent hesitations and mistakes while reading. The following descriptions were excerpted from a few of the parent journals:

> Isn't sounding words out.
> Making up story and not reading the words.
> Not reading straight through.
> Depends on memory when reading.
> Skips words often.
> Is losing his sight words from last year.

Entries like these provided clues as to children's at-home reading as well as parents' interpretation of their children's reading. Note, for instance, how parents' comments reflected concern about getting the words "right" the first time, indicating their belief that skipping or memorizing words were ineffective strategies. These first impressions drawn from parent journal entries confirm Routman's (1991) assertion that many parents are concerned with word, sound, and letter identification.

We wanted to move beyond these observations and look at the contexts that prompted parental concern. It appeared that some events were more supportive of children's risk taking and enjoyment than others. Specifically, the ways in which parents responded to their child's fluency influenced the supportive nature of the reading event.

One of the teachers, Elaine, reflected on Rachel's home literacy activity by reading the journal entries written by Rachel's mother. Mrs. Jackson wrote about Rachel's reading experiences with different family members during the course of one week. Rachel's reactions to these reading events varied, depending on how different family members responded to her reading.

> When I pick Rachel up from class, she is always happy. Rachel tells me what she did in class. Sometimes Rachel will come home and read. Rachel and her younger sister read to each other before they go to sleep at night. Today, Rachel read some of her Samantha book. (7/11/94)

> Rachel was very excited about being able to bring home books. She read a very funny story to her father. They both had fun reading together. He said that Rachel had a few problems with some words but overall she did well. (7/12/94)

> Rachel had some problems reading tonight. She was making up her own story and not reading the words. Her father became impatient so she read with her sister. Over the weekend I may just have Rachel read to herself and have her tell me about what she just read. After that we will take turns reading the same story together. What are your views? (7/13/94)

Notice how Mrs. Jackson began the week's journal writing with entries that showed Rachel's success and enthusiasm for reading, especially while reading with her younger sister. She also noticed that when reading with her father, Rachel's "made-up story" and inability to "read the words" frustrated him. Mrs. Jackson seemed to recognize the tension surrounding this father-daughter reading event and altered plans for Rachel's reading at home. By reading alone first, the child could work through some of the difficult parts of the text prior to sharing the reading with an adult. Here, Mrs. Jackson planned changes aimed at helping her daughter read with greater confidence and enjoyment.

After reading about these events, Rachel's teacher, Elaine, was alerted to ways in which she might support Rachel's reading development both at home and at school. Elaine responded to Mrs. Jackson with the following note:

> Thank you for your notes! Very helpful! Rachel is a delightful girl! She has good answers in class when we discuss books! She is doing *very well*! We worked a little bit on the vowel sounds of *a* this week— still a little difficult to hear the difference— *cat, rain, star*. We're working on it!

> When Rachel has difficulty with a word, have her read the rest of the sentence. Ask her what would make sense. Then ask her if the sounds match the letters she sees. If the book is too hard, read it to her, then let her try to read some or all of it to you. Or you can let her read with you— kind of like partners—filling in where she can. If you read it to her, talk about the story, then let her try. Easy books will build up her confidence. (7/13/94)

Notice how Elaine's note included positive and reassuring comments about Rachel: "delightful," "good answers," "doing very well." Being familiar with Rachel's school record, Elaine knew that the Jacksons received many negative reports about Rachel's reading progress over the last few years. By noting Rachel's "good" participation during story discussions, Elaine presented a picture of how this youngster read meaningfully in class. During the first afternoon meeting, Elaine discussed the importance of parents' knowing about their child's achievements and successes in school. She felt her comments would help the Jacksons see their daughter's strengths in reading and that this would ultimately help Rachel see herself as a reader.

In the remaining paragraphs to Mrs. Jackson, Elaine offered suggestions for staging reading events at home. Elaine recommended that Rachel skip an unknown word and read the rest of the sentence to gather contextual information that might help her identify the word. She then suggested that Rachel use letter cues to make even more informed guesses to identify difficult words. Elaine's suggestion of having Rachel "fill in where she can" was aimed at helping Rachel make meaningful guesses while reading. Elaine also supported Rachel's reading of "easy" books to help build her confidence. These suggestions were tailored to Rachel's particular needs, based on the information acquired through the parent-teacher dialogue journal.

During the first seminar discussion, Elaine discussed her ideas for using Mrs. Jackson's commentary to help Rachel. Elaine felt it was important to tell Mrs. Jackson about some of the ways she might work with Rachel in class, especially since Mrs. Jackson was interested in receiving such support. At the end of the summer session, Rachel's mother commented that the journal writing experience helped her understand Rachel as a reader at school and at home:

> It (the journal project) helped us to share Rachel's experiences with her teacher, as well as how Rachel worked at home. I was able to know just what my daughter was reading daily. It gave me a chance to hear her read to her sister and to my husband. (8/4/94)

"No reading, no pool!"

Mrs. Fuller was another parent who shared detailed entries about her son, Ted, with a teacher named Sue. Like Mrs. Jackson, Mrs. Fuller wrote about the tension surrounding some of the reading events at home. Many of her entries described her own frustrations with her son's reading and the particular situations that prompted these negative feelings.

Mrs. Fuller's first three journal entries included statements about Ted's transactions with others around reading. The first describes Ted's reluctance to read with an older cousin, Aaron. The last two entries describe Ted's difficulty responding to his mother's requests to read:

> Ted is taking delight in his 10-year-old cousin's reading to him. When it's Ted's turn to read, he became self-conscious and embarrassed. Though Aaron was patient, positive, and reassuring, Ted quickly insisted that Aaron read instead. (7/9/94)

> While reading aloud to mother, appears *tense*, fidgety, and nervous. Positive reassurance and encouragement helping *somewhat*. Has lost some of the progress made this past spring, even sight word recognition. (7/11/94)

> Maybe he's tired, I don't know how to stimulate his interest today. He's very resistant to reading and is not doing well at all. What is coming out is with an attitude. I told him that he was *not* allowed to read for now (reverse psychology?), that reading could and should be enjoyed and that he may read later if he got some rest; he would be allowed the privilege of reading if his attitude changed. I'll let you know if it works. Forgive the tactics, but "no reading, no pool" worked. He read silently. (7/13/94)

After reading these journal entries, Sue was most struck by Mrs. Fuller's "no reading, no pool" rule and wondered why Mrs. Fuller used an ultimatum to get Ted to read. Sue also noted Mrs. Fuller's description of Ted being "tense, fidgety, and nervous" when he read aloud at home. Mrs. Fuller described Ted's lack of confidence and interest in reading and his difficulty with sight words. These impressions of Ted outside of class were quite different from Sue's impressions of Ted in class, as seen in her response to Mrs. Fuller:

> Thank you for your detailed comments on Ted. I am seeing a confident Ted in class, who on some occasions has been hesitant. His abilities have him in a "leader" role in the classroom, which I hope will help with his self-confidence. He participates often in class discussions. Keep me posted. Thanks again for the notes. Sue (7/14/94)

Sue emphasized Ted's positive qualities in her first note to Mrs. Fuller. She provided Mrs. Fuller with a picture of Ted as a confident, active student who, while occasionally hesitant, often played the role of leader in class. A complex and contradictory image of Ted emerged from this dialogue: Ted as a confident, skilled student in school and a hesitant, tense reader at home. Sue struggled with these contrasting images of Ted in her assessment notebook:

> Reading with his cousin seemed to be an activity he enjoyed; however, Mrs. Fuller alluded to a self-concept problem. I don't see this with Ted in the Center. He has the broadest range of skills of the students in his group, and this gives him confidence during classroom activities. Surprise.... Mrs. Fuller is concerned Ted is "losing" basic sight words. This may be causing Ted undue stress. I think my teaching environment should be nonthreatening/low stress. Sue (7/14/94)

As Sue tried to make sense of these conflicting views, she provided a possible reason why Mrs. Fuller's perception was different from her own. Sue wondered if Mrs. Fuller's emphasis on sight word mastery hindered Ted's enthusiasm for reading. His reluctance to read might have appeared as a "self-concept" problem. Mrs. Fuller's comments prompted Sue to look closely at Ted's responses to reading and consider some changes in the way she structured lessons.

In response to what seemed to be a "pressured" home environment, Sue planned a "nonthreatening/low stress" environment for Ted in the classroom. She also used Mrs. Fuller's comments about Ted reading with his cousin to consider changes in the way her students read in class. Sue thought she could help Ted become a more confident reader among his peers by organizing more partner reading experiences in the classroom. On the final questionnaire, Sue noted how Mrs. Fuller's input helped her understand and plan for Ted:

> Input on "hesitant while reading with cousin" helped me incorporate more partner reading to help overcome these insecurities. (8/1/94)

When Sue received information about Ted as a reader among family members (mother, cousin), she was able to make instructional decisions based on the particular nature of these relationships. A few weeks later, Sue wrote in her assessment notebook that Ted "worked well with his partner while reading" and "read with increased volume and confidence."

At home Mrs. Fuller continued to see Ted as a resistant reader and was concerned about his confidence. She did, however, write one journal entry that revealed Ted's confidence and enjoyment with reading to a younger neighbor:

> Two-and-a-half-year-old Emily (who adores "A-DORS" Ted) brought her bag of books and camped smack next to her Ted with admiring eyes until he could not refuse her. He read her Little Golden books hesitantly, but with expression and enjoyed her enthusiasm. (7/15/94)

> Read with some resistance. Still hesitates while reading, seems to lack confidence. Uncertain about content when encouraged to talk about story. (7/17/94)

> While reading, Ted skips words (even phrases) that he does not know. Chooses to read very elementary first grade readers. I don't refuse because I know he needs confidence and success. I want him to enjoy reading and not always feel like he has to labor,

but he must begin to move on. Any suggestions? (7/18/94)

In the entry dated July 15, Mrs. Fuller described Ted's reaction to his neighbor, Emily. His ability to read with expression and to appear happy about the experience provides some evidence that Ted responded well to certain kinds of reading contexts. Ted's willingness to read to this young, admiring toddler suggested that this event was less threatening, and perhaps more enjoyable, than the other reading situations described by Mrs. Fuller.

While Mrs. Fuller observed that her son responded positively to easy reading material, she was concerned that these kinds of texts would inhibit his progress in reading (entry 7/18/94). Mrs. Fuller struggled with Ted's need to build his confidence with "easy" reading material and her desire to see him read more demanding texts to help her son improve his reading ability.

Sue responded to Mrs. Fuller's call by reassuring her that easier books helped to inspire children to read and that Ted would indeed progress in his reading if he felt comfortable to do so. This message was intended to help Mrs. Fuller feel more at ease about Ted's choice of texts. Sue hoped that this would translate into less "pressured" home literacy events, which would help Ted take the risks he needed to grow as a reader.

At the end of the semester, Mrs. Fuller explained that having a system of communication to vent her concerns was extremely important to her. In the final questionnaire, Mrs. Fuller wrote:

> I appreciated the open communication with Susan. It was reassuring to know she understood and shared some of my concerns. Her suggestions were helpful. Home management is a constant, so any input is appreciated! (8/4/94)

Note how Mrs. Fuller appreciated the two-way exchange with Sue. This comment suggests that Mrs. Fuller viewed Sue as trusted professional with whom she could share concerns about her son. Even though their different frames of reference and ways of structuring learning gave rise to contradictory images of Ted, the project helped both adults consider specific ways to support this youngster's literacy growth.

Significance of the project

As a way of assessing the parent journal project, we asked parents to respond in writing to the following question: *What did it mean to you to keep a journal of your child's literacy experiences at home?* A sampling of their responses shows how the project helped them understand their children as readers at home and as students in the classroom:

> I had a better understanding of his specific achievements and problem areas. It helps me to give support where needed. R.

> The journal made me stop and really look at the progress Michele was making with her reading. The journal is also helpful as a tool for me to use later on as a reference to see how far she has come. C.

> I felt the journal gave me a feeling of knowing what was going on in the classroom, also to see their growing experiences and development. S.

> It provided the teacher with a knowledge of what Hope was doing at home and I taught the teacher a little about each child. M.

> I thought it was great, I was able to express some of my thoughts as they were happening. Because with my schedule, things can be easily forgotten. L.

> Keeping a journal of shared reading made me more aware of all the daily reading Matthew is involved with. E.

These descriptions show that the journal writing experience gave parents opportunities to think about their children as readers. Many parents made new, often positive, discoveries about their child's reading. Likewise, teachers used the journals in very much the same way—as tools for reflection. Teachers broadened their views of children and, in doing so, recognized the value of parent input:

> It's essential; parents have a unique view of their child that a classroom teacher may never see. B.

> They (parents) provide valuable information about their children's behaviors at home and share their own philosophies of literacy—anxieties, beliefs, experiences. I learn from the parents and they learn strategies from me. L.

> It gives the teacher insights into what the parent sees as important, and that may help explain some patterns you are seeing in the classroom. E.

> It was very useful and very relevant for setting up instructional lessons/material topics that would interest the student; I was keyed into weaknesses, past experiences, and strengths prior to our first meeting. S.

The comments reflect teachers' appreciation for just how much parents know about their children as literacy learners. Not only did teachers recognize the importance of parent input, they also welcomed it as a way to enhance their teaching. Recall how Mrs. Jackson helped Elaine understand Rachel's tendency to avoid words she didn't know. This prompted Elaine to expose Rachel to a broader repertoire of reading strategies for identifying unknown words. By reading Mrs. Fuller's journal entries, Sue found that Ted needed opportunities to enhance his self-confidence through partner reading, and she provided these opportunities in class.

We also felt parent input helped teachers think of ways to support students' reading outside of class. Elaine offered the Jacksons a few teaching strategies so they could help Rachel identify unknown words. Susan provided Mrs. Fuller with a rationale for allowing Ted to read easier, less demanding books. Both teachers presented positive images of what these students could do in class, helping parents to see their child's strengths in reading.

Teachers broadened their views of children and, in doing so, recognized the value of parent input.

The vignettes of family literacy activity allowed teachers to better understand family literacy events and their influence on students' reading. Mr. Jackson and Mrs. Fuller viewed fluent reading as a primary goal. When Rachel "made up her own words" while reading to her father, he became impatient. Likewise, Ted's mother was frustrated when Ted "skipped words" or "read hesitantly." The youngsters reacted by avoiding reading with these family members. However, both children enjoyed reading with younger, less skilled readers. Through the journal entries, teachers could view home literacy activity through a social-situational lens, capturing how children transacted with print in the company of significant others.

Classroom applications

While these findings point to the value of parent communication, teachers need to address some potential problems as they plan similar projects. First, the study raises important questions about the roles of parents as they observe or participate in literacy activity with their children and then share these observations with teachers. It's possible that parents' increased surveillance and reporting could embarrass or annoy youngsters and discourage them from engaging in home literacy activity. Teachers should caution against framing this as a project for parents to report on their children. One way would be to invite students to read and contribute to the parent-teacher exchange, providing their own perspectives about themselves as readers at home and at school. This would give students more ownership in the project, helping them think about their own literacy processes and practices.

In addition, teachers need to think about how the project is perceived by parents. In our study, almost one third of the parents did not participate in the journal writing project. In a final questionnaire to parents, a few reported that they expected journal writing would take up too much of their time.

We also considered the possibility that some parents might have been uncomfortable with writing. Even though we invited parents to write informally (lists, words, phrases), a project like this still assumes some proficiency with written language. Inviting parents to write to teachers takes for granted certain family literacy competencies. Before initiating a project like this, teachers need to be aware of the communities they serve and how parents feel about writing as a medium for communicating with teachers. This is especially critical for teachers in linguistically diverse school communities. When starting such a project, teachers and parents could explore a variety of means for exchanging information and select methods of communication that work best. Setting up telephone conversations with parents or inviting parents to bring in audio recordings of family reading events could substitute for written communication.

We recognize that keeping up a dialogue, whether oral or written, with the parents of 30 children each week might be unrealistic for some classroom teachers. To make the project more manageable, teachers could write to different families each week on a rotating basis. We caution against writing only to those parents whose children have difficulty with litera-

cy since this might stigmatize certain students and their families. Teachers could initiate face-to-face dialogues by inviting parents to informal get-togethers. In such a setting, parents can share their observations of home literacy activity with each other and with the teacher, as we did during our orientation meeting.

If journals are used, teachers can start by writing a letter to parents describing the uses of the journal they will receive. For example, one teacher in the Reading-Language Arts Center initiated a dialogue with parents by writing the following letter:

> Dear Parents,
> Each week your child will come home with this journal. This is a place where you and I may correspond with one another. You can use the journal to tell me about your child's reading at home or to ask me a question. Perhaps your child has had an interesting conversation with you or you see a change in attitude toward his or her reading or writing. Your thoughts and input will be very helpful to me. I will respond to your writing each week.

The teacher then wrote something positive about the child's reading at school that week and asked each parent what the child liked to read about at home. Notice that the teacher did not tell the parent what book to read at home or how much time to spend reading. Asking what the child liked to read at home was a low-risk question that served as a hook to encourage the parent to respond.

In addition to these practical issues, teachers also need to consider how parent dialogue journals fit within the wider literacy curriculum of schools. Parent journal projects are consistent with holistic, constructivist teaching since teachers can use parent input as the basis for selecting texts, materials, and methods that are relevant to children's ways of learning and life experiences. Donald Graves (1994) discusses the importance of "reading the world" as an inspiration for writing: "the writer's first act is to listen and observe the details of living" (p. 36).

For example, one parent wrote about a family wedding over the weekend to explain why she did not have time to read with her child. In class, the teacher asked the child to share her experiences about the wedding and then to write about the event. It was the first time the teacher observed this child writing more than just a few sentences! News about the wedding gave the teacher a place to begin a dialogue with this young writer, and this served as a rehearsal for her story writing.

Another consideration is the influence of adult modeling on literacy learning and teaching. Parent dialogue journals provide opportunities for adults to demonstrate the uses and functions of literacy. When parents and teachers communicate about real issues, they are reading and writing for authentic purposes. Demonstrations like these help students see how they can use dialogue journals to exchange stories, solve problems, or clarify issues with significant others.

This study illustrates how reciprocal communication between teachers and parents can advance a kind of cultural exchange between home and school. The use of parent communication projects is based on the idea that all families structure reading events differently, depending on the abilities, interests, and needs of children as well as the beliefs, practices, and plans of parents/guardians. Since this kind of program allows teachers to tailor classroom and home support to the specific needs of children and their families, it contrasts with programs that dispense generic information about how parents can assist their child's literacy development at home. Programs that encourage parents to use nonspecific instruction ignore the social-situational conditions that can influence how a child reads at home. By knowing the kinds of situations that can constrain or enhance reading at home, teachers are better positioned to support students, and consequently, parents may be more responsive to such support.

Teaching from the child's point of view (Taylor, 1993) depends on understanding the ways in which children relate to texts at home, among the people who matter most in their lives. Parents can provide these precious vignettes of home literacy activity. We can begin by moving beyond the traditional divide that positions parents and teachers in adversarial roles and begin to realize the tremendous potential of parent-teacher partnering.

Author note

This research was partially supported by a grant from the Pennsylvania Compact of the Pennsylvania Association of Colleges and Universities.

Lazar teaches courses in literacy education at West Chester University and facilitates contact between preservice teachers and parents in some Philadelphia school sites. She can be contacted at the Department of Childhood Studies and Reading, West Chester University, West Chester, PA 19383, USA. Weisberg coordinates the graduate reading program and directs the Reading-Language Arts Center at Beaver College in Glenside, Pennsylvania, USA.

References

Burke, C. (1985). Parenting, teaching, and learning as a collaborative venture. *Language Arts, 62,* 836 – 843.

Cairney, T.H., & Munsie, L. (1995). Parent participation in literacy learning. *The Reading Teacher, 48,* 392 – 403.

Erickson, F., & Mohatt, G. (1982). Cultural organization of participation structures in two classrooms of Indian students. In G. Spindler (Ed.), *Doing the ethnography of schooling* (pp. 132 – 174). New York: Holt.

Graves, D. (1994). *A fresh look at writing.* Portsmouth, NH: Heinemann.

Heath, S.B. (1983). *Ways with words: Language, life and work in communities and classrooms.* New York: Cambridge University Press.

Hedman, R. (1993). Parents and teachers as co-investigators. In S. Lytle & M. Cochran-Smith (Eds.), *Inside outside: Teacher research and knowledge* (pp. 220 – 230). New York: Teachers College Press.

McGilp, J., & Michael, M. (1994). *The home-school connection: Guidelines for working with parents.* Portsmouth, NH: Heinemann.

McMackin, M. (1993). The parent's role in literacy development. *Childhood Education, 69,* 142 – 145.

Philips, S.U. (1972). Participant structures and communicative competence: Warm Springs children in community and classroom. In C. Cazden, V.P. John, & D. Hymes (Eds.), *Functions of language in the classroom* (pp. 370 – 394). New York: Teachers College Press.

Rhodes, L., & Shanklin, N. (1993). *Windows into literacy: Assessing learners K–12.* Portsmouth, NH: Heinemann.

Routman, R. (1991). *Invitations: Changing as teachers and learners K–12.* Portsmouth, NH: Heinemann.

Shockley, B. (1994). Extending the literate community: Home-to-school and school-to-home. *The Reading Teacher, 47,* 500 – 502.

Taylor, D. (1993). *From the child's point of view.* Portsmouth, NH: Heinemann.

Vopat, J. (1994). *The parent project: A workshop approach to parent involvement.* York, ME: Stenhouse.

When Parents Serve as Writing Critics

Introducing the "Parent Writing Folder Review" – a strategy that increases the power of students' writing

BY KATHRYN HOWARD

Today's performance assessments require wider audiences. Beyond self-assessment and peer assessment, such things as student projects, presentations and portfolios make it highly desirable for us to have other audiences who can identify standards and criteria of accomplishment and process within the domain being assessed.

It was with this in mind that I began to search for a wider audience for my students' writing. I suspected that parents would be easily accessible and the most interested resource available. The next step was to ask my students' parents to assess the writing their children had produced in my class during the first seven months of the school year.

Portfolio culture. I felt comfortable with my decision because the atmosphere in which I worked encouraged teachers to try innovative ideas that would enhance students' thinking and talking about writing. This environment, which we call "portfolio culture," is a project of the Collaboratives for Humanities and Arts Teaching (CHART), which is funded by the Rockefeller Foundation with support from the Pittsburgh Foundation. (For more about CHART, see opposite page.)

In "portfolio culture," the learning and

H. ROBERT LOOMIS

Kathryn Howard teaches eighth grade language arts at Reizenstein Middle School in Pittsburgh, PA.

teaching of writing is merged with the assessment of writing. Students engage in conversations about writing standards, revisions and strategies; they share their writing with the classroom audience; and they develop a body of work that symbolizes to them membership in the community of writers.

As students become more comfortable with the community of writers idea, they begin to seek out a wider audience that will provide them with helpful feedback. In this context, students can make real meaning from what their parents have to say about their writing.

Keeping it simple. I did not do anything special to prepare the parents for their participation in the project, other than to let them know what the writing process is all about. I suppose I could have invited them to a coffee hour or a special presentation of some kind, but I preferred to keep it simple. After all, one of the objectives of the project was to find out what parents would do of their own volition, without any prior guidance from me.

I chose to pilot the Parent Writing Folder Review with my largest class of 33 students. I asked the students to take their writing folders home and have their parents read what they had written, discuss it with the children and respond in writing to the following questions:

• Which piece of writing in the folder tells you the most about your child's writing?

- What does it tell you?
- What do you see as the strengths in your child's writing?
- What do you see that needs to be addressed in your child's development as a writer?
- What suggestions do you have that might aid the class's growth as writers?
- Other comments or suggestions?

The quality of the parents' responses quickly and convincingly assured me that this activity had great power to enrich the conversation about my students' writing.

Obviously, I wanted to know if the parents would take the time required (one to two hours) to complete their task. Almost all of the parents did. I also wanted to know if the parents would find this a worthwhile experience. Again, most of them did. In fact, two parents volunteered to have family members who were published authors speak to the class, while a third parent sent in a reading list.

Folder and portfolio. One fundamental belief of portfolio culture is that encouraging students to interact with their writing allows them to develop ownership of that work. This is true whether we're considering the writing folder, which is the compilation of the student's writing for an academic year, or the self-reflective portfolio, which is used for presentations and assessments.

Students are accountable for both folder and portfolio. This accountability, among other factors, motivates most students to take greater responsibility for their writing and to work to improve it.

Because the parents, through the Folder Review, placed so much value on their children's writing, and because they were grateful for the opportunity to do it, the students seemed to accept the parents into the community of writers.

The critical issue in this activity is, of course, directly related to the validity of the parents' reflections about their children's writing. Four questions need to be asked:
- Will parents evaluate the writing in vocabulary that is the "shoptalk" of writing

A few words about CHART

In 11 large urban school systems and dozens of rural districts throughout the nation, teachers, artists, business and community leaders are working together to change teaching and learning about the arts and humanities. By reading, writing and experiencing their own and other cultures, students in CHART programs learn to communicate, think critically and meet personal, work and civic responsibilities throughout their lives. Each CHART project is locally designed to address major local needs. For example:

- A thematic course of study developed by teams of teachers in Los Angeles that crosses subject areas and encompasses the cultural and ethnic diversity of the student population.
- An interdisciplinary curriculum that focuses on local history, literature and culture, and links teachers in 28 South Carolina rural school districts with scholars at universities, museums and historical societies.
- An arts education program in Pittsburgh that features student exploration of the arts through perception, reflection and production, as well as documentation of student progress through portfolio development.

These and other CHART projects share a dedication to:

- providing stimulating arts and humanities learning opportunities to average students in impoverished urban and rural school districts
- developing teachers as the central agents of change
- creating models of substantive international and multicultural learning in the arts and humanities
- bringing together expertise and support from many sectors of the community in a collaborative approach
- implementing systemic changes in schools to accommodate the new content, methods and structures of successful arts and humanities teaching and learning.

CHART projects are funded in part by the Rockefeller Foundation and are supported locally by grants from many private and public foundations. For more information, contact CHART, 15 Tunnell Road, Somerset, NJ 08873; 908-249-7491; fax: 908-214-0110.

and conforms to the criteria the students are using when they talk and think about writing?
- Will they assess the content or concentrate on spelling and grammar?
- Can they critique the writing without criticizing the writers?
- And, finally, will they value such notions as growth over time, which were not specifically asked for in the activity but are essential to the idea of equitable assessment?

A content analysis of the parents' responses indicated that the answers to all questions were indeed positive. For example, the four most popular responses to the "strengths in writing" question were "expresses feelings, openness," "vocabulary," "creativity" and "ideas."

Continued on page 62

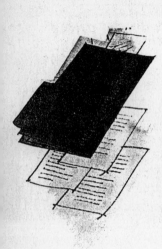

Additional responses included such descriptors as "use of detail," "ability to analyze," "use of evidence," "description" and "ability to write conclusions." This was the exact vocabulary we had used in both direct instruction and class discussions.

It works on one level when I model this vocabulary; it works on a deeper level when students begin to incorporate this language into their own conversations about writing; and it works on a still deeper level when students see this "shoptalk" modeled by an audience which in their eyes is far removed from the classroom setting. It's proof that they have discovered the language which all writers use to communicate. It's also proof that when we engage parents in meaningful, rich tasks, we get rich results.

Growth over time. Of particular interest was the fact that 14 parents noted "growth over time." This is significant not only because of its importance to assessments, but also because it was not specifically brought to the parents' attention.

The four most common responses to the "needs to be addressed" question were "vocabulary," "sentence structure," "organization of ideas" and "the reading/writing connection." It was satisfying to note that grammar and spelling issues did not appear at the top of the "needs" list, although they were mentioned by 11 parents.

Another essential factor in this activity is its humaneness. It was necessary for parents to assess their children's work in ways that were not harmful to the children's identities, either as writers or as young adults. Thus, as part of the content analysis, I evaluated the responses for a "feeling tone" of positive, neutral or negative.

The question which received the most negative responses was the "needs" question; even so, out of a total of 78 comments, only six were negative. No other question received more than three negative responses. The students indicated that none of them felt that their parents had treated them unfairly or in mean-spirited ways.

> "The quality of the parents' responses quickly and convincingly assured me that this activity had great power to enrich the conversation about my students' writing."

Even though the parents in this class performed admirably, this was not always the case. With other classes, I've had to guard against making this activity a cruel or punitive experience for some children.

Surrogate readers. To that end, I've assembled a group of "surrogate readers" – mostly school support personnel or teachers in other subject areas who are always ready to read a student's folder if he or she has real concerns about taking the folder home.

Most surrogate readers have been impressed with both the quality and quantity of the work in their student's folder and have not been hesitant to say so. This enhances the child's status both personally and in the school community.

After all of the students in the pilot class had completed the Writing Folder Review, I asked them to answer these four questions:
- What do you think your parents learned about you as a result of their reading your folders and discussing them with you?
- What did you learn about yourself as a writer as a result of your discussion?
- What surprised you most about the discussion?
- What suggestion do you have that might improve the discussion with your parents about your writing?

The responses told the real story of the negotiating process between reader and writer. Most students were amazed that their parents would celebrate their writing in such a sustained and formal way. Many – too many perhaps – had never shared their writing with their parents before and were awed by the positive feedback.

As we look toward assessment reform, here's a way we can involve parents early and constructively. The Writing Folder Review allows parents to learn about and trust authentic performance-based assessments. They come to appreciate what they learn about writing instruction. In essence, parents are welcomed into the educational process, making allies of those who have the greatest stake in the education of children. ↓

Art in Your Curriculum

Parents in the Workshop

Parents become advocates for change in your class-room when they experience learning for themselves.

Jason's mom had been coming to the Artist's Workshop to volunteer for several weeks when the children finally convinced her to make a picture with them. "I don't really have any ideas and I don't know what to use," Jason's mom told the third graders sitting at her table.

Samantha came to her rescue and walked her to the bookshelves. "You could copy a picture," she said as she flipped through a book. "This lion is everyone's favorite."

Samantha continued with her tour of the room, showing Jason's mom where to get paper, pencils and other supplies.

From Samantha and the other students, she learned how art could express meaning and expand her literacy. Through experience, she was learning about the importance of art in learning and life.

A page from Karen's sketch journal depicts parent-student interaction in the Workshop.

Why do they attend?
Here, parents can continue their education, learn about the changes we're making in education, and become our advocates for that change.

Parents learn about the Artist's Workshop in weekly PTA newsletter articles in which we explain

Karen Ernst teaches art at Kings Highway School, Westport, CT, and she is a Teaching Editor of *Teaching K-8.*

choice, uses of literature and art, the use of portfolios and why writing is an integral part of the process. We announce portfolio reviews and all-school exhibitions so parents begin to learn what's going on instead of being left to question what they don't understand.

Portfolios. When I tell parents artwork won't come home each week, but will instead remain in a portfolio at school, and if I explain why that's essential to a better assessment of their child's development, they begin to accept change. (Of course, if they wish, parents may come to the Workshop any time to see portfolios.)

When portfolios do go home, I include a letter that explains again about the Workshop process. In reviewing portfolios, parents hear the stories of pictures made by their child; they see their child develop confidence in self-expression and get ideas from artists and authors.

Exhibitions. I also educate others at all-school exhibitions. I include many signs on which I write explanations of the Workshop process – how we used sketch journals to observe in nature and then move from sketch to work of art, or how a

student repeats a picture, similar to professional artists.

When an exhibition goes up in the hallway, I'm conscious that we're going public with our product and process. I indicate that pages from artist notebooks and sketch journals are unedited drafts of thinking. This helps parents focus on ideas and not question the lack of focus on finished product.

Parent workshops. In the fall, I conduct workshops in which I invite parents to:

1 Look at children's work and listen to my description of how the arts are part of literacy, how students make decisions in the Artist's Workshop and how they think critically, read stories, paint poems and write pictures by using language.

2 Make pictures of their own and then write.

3 Volunteer in the Workshop, not during their child's art time necessarily, but early in the morning to help set up, or in the last hour to help clean up.

In the art room. Every week, more than 10 parents come in at an assigned time to do specific jobs such as bring out portfolios or unload the paint drying rack.

Parents are encouraged to listen as we meet on the rug and listen to a story or hear an artist share. They see for themselves the focus and independence of the children as they work; they hear the sound of sharing ideas and the chatter of a busy classroom.

That is how Jason's mom finally got the nerve to try her own picture, to ask Samantha for help, to keep her own portfolio, to write her own story, and to share it with the class.

This was not Jason's class – he's in fourth grade – this was his mom's third grade class. She was a member of their learning community. We needed her there. ↓

Reprinted with permission of the publisher, Teaching K-8, Norwalk, CT 06854, from the November/December 1996 issue of *Teaching K-8.*

THE SCIENCE CENTER

Mixing Primary Colors

Give opportunities for mixing primary colors by providing these materials in the center:

Colored icing on graham crackers:

- Mix vanilla icing with food coloring to provide the three primary colors.
- Place icing, graham crackers, tongue depressors for spreading, and directions in the center.
- Each child may mix and spread icing to get a variety of colors.

Jello or finger paint in plastic bags:

- Place two primary colors in each bag.
- Secure opening of bags with masking tape.
- Each bag may be squished and mushed to see the mixing of the colors.

Eyedroppers and colored water:

- Place three jars of colored water (food coloring and water). Use primary colors (red, blue, and yellow).
- Provide an eyedropper for each jar.
- Allow the children to drip colored water onto soft paper towels or coffee filters, seeing how the colors mix.

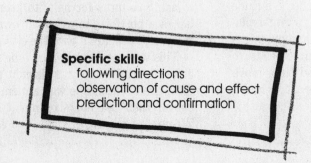

Specific skills
following directions
observation of cause and effect
prediction and confirmation

Create a Color Wheel

Teacher Preparation:

1. Mix primary colors (red, yellow, and blue) in three separate baby food jars by combining food coloring and water.

2. Create a color wheel on tagboard identical to the one in the diagram below.

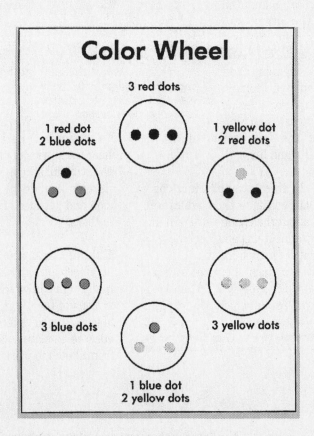

Color Wheel

3 red dots

1 red dot
2 blue dots

1 yellow dot
2 red dots

3 blue dots

1 blue dot
2 yellow dots

3 yellow dots

Excerpted from *Creating and Managing Learning Centers: A Thematic Approach,* by Phoebe Bell Ingraham. Peterborough, NH: Crystal Springs Books, 1996. Reprinted with permission; all rights reserved.

3. Laminate or cover with clear plastic contact paper.

4. Place the three baby food jars with the colored water on a tray in the learning center along with three eye-droppers, absorbent white paper towels, a toothpick, a pencil, and the laminated color wheel.

The Activity:

1. Demonstrate to the child how to drop colored water onto the colors of the laminated color wheel. Mix each puddle of colored water with the toothpick.

2. Write the child's name on a paper towel. Lay the towel over the laminated color wheel which contains the dots of colored water. Watch as the towel soaks up the water. The color wheel will appear on the towel.

3. Back the resulting color wheels with construction paper once they dry, if desired. The children can then write "color wheel" on the top of the paper.

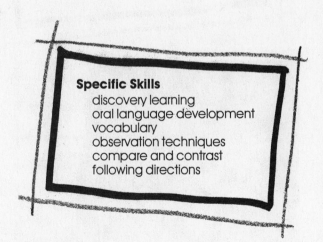

Specific Skills
discovery learning
oral language development
vocabulary
observation techniques
compare and contrast
following directions

- ▣ shelf with a large surface for displaying activities
- ▣ large table for extended work space
- ▣ small tables or desks to allow quiet space for individual investigations
- ▣ bookshelf for holding nonfiction books about specific topics
- ▣ windows, to tie science in with actual events just outside their window
- ▣ binoculars and clipboards hanging by the window to record sightings of birds, squirrels, changes in trees, etc.
- ▣ chart stands and board space for charts, posters, graphs, and pictures
- ▣ poetry charts, interactive charts, graphs, and posters for thematic units
- ▣ kitty litter box or sensory (water/sand) tables
- ▣ a computer with a CD-ROM encyclopedia for further study and independent investigations
- ▣ pets; books, charts, and graphs about the growth and care of these animals
- ▣ balance scales
- ▣ magnifying glasses
- ▣ stop watch or small clock with sweep second hand for timing experiments
- ▣ sand timers and kitchen timers
- ▣ trays for holding tasks carried from the shelf to the work tables
- ▣ a selection of science textbooks at various reading levels
- ▣ a selection of scoops, measuring spoons and cups, pitchers, funnels of different sizes, sifters, water pumps, magnets, manipulatives for self-discovery
- ▣ indoor/outdoor thermometer; weather graph
- ▣ tasks and materials specific to each unit
- ▣ plants: seeds (avocado), roots and tubers (sweet potato), and bulbs
- ▣ planters with glass or clear plastic sides for observing root development
- ▣ hand towels for cleaning up spills (sink and float, water table)

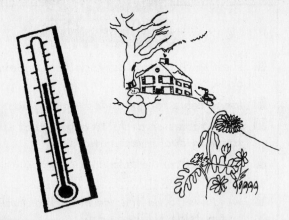

Recording the Temperature

Place an indoor/outdoor thermometer in a window near the science center. Keep a class graph of the temperature, with columns for recording both indoor and outdoor readings. When students work in the science center, it is their responsibility to check and record the temperatures onto the graph.

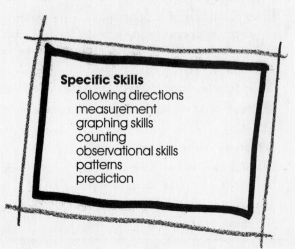

Modify this task for different levels by asking additional activities, such as:

- having the students make individual bar graphs at the end of each month, answering questions by interpreting the graph
- predicting what the average temperature will be next month
- figuring the average difference between the indoor and outdoor temperature

Specific Skills
  following directions
  measurement
  graphing skills
  counting
  observational skills
  patterns
  prediction

Measurement and Conservation

Place a measuring cup and clear plastic containers of different widths in the sand table along with dried beans, corn, or peas. Put rubber bands around the containers.

On sentence strips or a poster, print the following directions for the students to follow:

1. Measure 2 cups of beans.
2. Predict how high the beans will fill one container. Move the rubber band to that spot around the container.
3. Pour the beans into the container. Was your prediction close?
4. Try again with a new container.

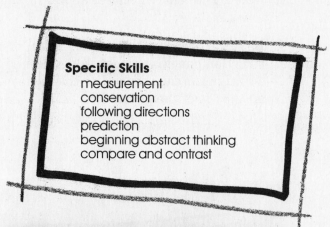

Specific Skills
  measurement
  conservation
  following directions
  prediction
  beginning abstract thinking
  compare and contrast

Science Observation

Place an item in your science center that is tied in some way to your thematic unit. For example, you might use:

- a fossil during a unit on earth science or dinosaurs
- a natural sponge during an ocean unit
- a seed pod during a unit on living things or plants
- a tadpole or caterpillar during a unit on changes

Model how to examine something as a scientist would, noticing every detail, taking notes and drawings, finding precise words to describe it. Introduce the microscope and the hand lens as tools that enable the scientist to observe details. List new vocabulary words the children give orally on a chart to place in the center. Ask a student to draw a picture of the object as the class notices details that should be included. Write a paragraph describing the item on a chart or board, using words generated from the list created by the children.

Show the children the observation form and explain that you would like them to be the scientist, using drawings and words to describe the object you have placed in the center. Provide drawing pencils, colored pencils, fine colored markers, large erasers, and whatever other tools the students suggest they might need.

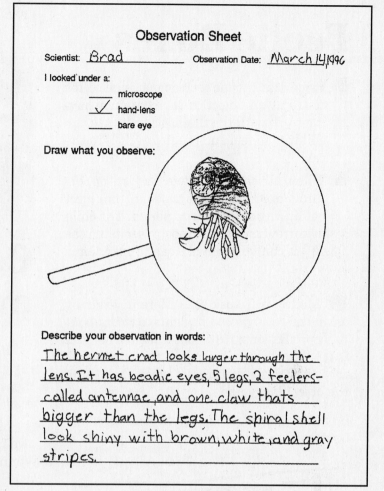

Observation Sheet

Scientist: _Brad_   Observation Date: _March 14, 1996_

I looked under a:

- ___ microscope
- _✓_ hand-lens
- ___ bare eye

Draw what you observe:

Describe your observation in words:

The hermit crab looks larger through the lens. It has beadie eyes, 5 legs, 2 feelers-called antennae, and one claw thats bigger than the legs. The spiral shell look shiny with brown, white, and gray stripes.

(Reproducible on page 186)

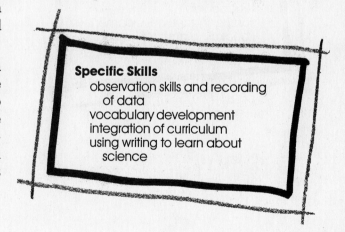

Specific Skills

observation skills and recording of data
vocabulary development
integration of curriculum
using writing to learn about science

Feelie Boxes

◎ Place a large tube sock over a small coffee can. Put an object in the container having to do with the thematic unit. Ask the children to feel and predict what is in the can.

◎ When all children have had an opportunity to complete this task, pull the object out during a total group period. The child who drew the picture most resembling the object can be given the can to take home to refill.

Ⓜ Modify this task for different levels by asking more advanced students to write about their predictions: How does it feel? What size is it? What shape is it? You might also ask that they draw pictures of what they think the object looks like.

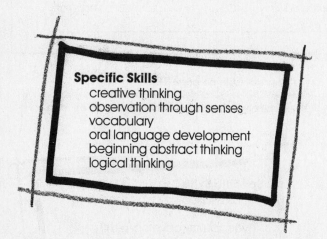

Specific Skills
creative thinking
observation through senses
vocabulary
oral language development
beginning abstract thinking
logical thinking

Compare and Contrast

Place two items on a tray with a magnifying glass, pencils, colored pencils or markers, measuring tape and ruler, scale, and Venn diagram sheets.

Model how to compare and contrast the two items, recording the comparisons on the Venn diagram. Demonstrate how to examine each item in a variety of ways, using the senses, the magnifying glass, a measuring tape or ruler, scale, etc.

Ⓜ Modify this task for different levels by requiring more writing, describing each item in detail. Some suggested items might include:

a hermit crab and a gerbil
a fossil and a stone
an acorn and a pine cone
a ramp and a pulley

Specific Skills
observational techniques and skills
recording data
following directions
compare and contrast
creative thinking strategies

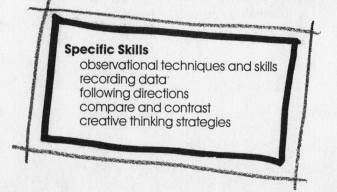

Examining Bones

◙ Collect old bones from your ham, turkey, and chicken dinners. Boil them and lay them out to dry for several days. When a good collection has been assembled, take them to school for your natural history unit. Place them in a tub, kitty litter box, or sand table. Let the students investigate them, predicting what animal they are from.

◙ Read books about dinosaur fossils and bones, such as *Bones, Bones, Dinosaur Bones,* by Byron Barton, or *My Visit to the Dinosaurs,* by Aliki. Model how to investigate the bones, showing how to:

- dig up bones placed in dirt or sand in the sand table (provide paintbrushes to uncover the bones, just as archaeologists do)

- weigh the bones

- classify the bones by what animal they came from or by similar shape

- draw and write about the bones found

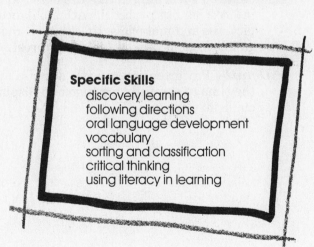

Specific Skills
discovery learning
following directions
oral language development
vocabulary
sorting and classification
critical thinking
using literacy in learning

Writing in Science

◙ List science-related vocabulary used in thematic units, or in science generally (such as *hypothesis, predict,* etc.), on a chart in the center. Ask students to choose from these words when writing in their thematic journals.

◙ Have students use these words in their writing activities within the science center, or in cooperative projects. Students can add new words to the list as they investigate a topic or as the class begins new units.

Ⓜ Modify this task for different levels by creating a class science dictionary, having each student choose a new word to add during each thematic unit.

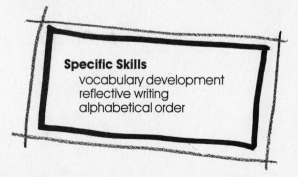

Specific Skills
vocabulary development
reflective writing
alphabetical order

Consider these three A's in designing environments for children:

Aesthetics is the love of beautiful things. Clearly, for children to learn to appreciate beautiful things, they must be surrounded by the best we can give them. According to research studies, children are happier, get along better, concentrate better, and have a more positive attitude about themselves and school when they are in a beautiful environment. The aesthetics in your school can be enhanced by following these guidelines:

Focus—Children, their activities, and their art should be the focus of the room. They should provide the color.

Light—Make the classroom as light as possible, with large, open windows. Pull up blinds and shades to capitalize on natural lighting.

Neutrals—Keep the walls light and use neutral colors. Use wooden furniture, shelves and equipment when possible.

Softness—Add pillows, soft sculpture, rugs, and window treatments to make the room look like home rather than an institution.

Nature—Bring the outside in with plants, pets, flowers, rocks, shells, and other natural objects.

Senses—A variety of textures, sounds, sights, and smells should surround children. Fresh air, flowers, evergreens, shaving cream for fingerpainting, and the aroma of food cooking will add a pleasant odor.

Order—Provide children with a sense of order and avoid clutter. Group like objects together and organize the classroom so children can take out materials and put them away independently.

Balance and Harmony—Too many toys, posters, and objects in the room create visual overload and interfere with children's learning. Make the classroom interesting but peaceful, with a balance of pictures and materials. Rotate toys and games to maintain children's interest.

Detail—Pay attention to little details. Take the time to carefully arrange and display children's art.

Ambiance refers to the mood, character, and atmosphere in the school. Children should be immersed in harmony, warmth, and acceptance when they walk through the door. Everything about the school, from the furniture to the artwork, should say, "This is a place for children. This is a place where children come first." These principles can have a positive effect on creating the ambiance you desire in your school:

Ownership—Create a truly child-centered classroom by including children in decisions about how to set up the classroom and decorate areas. Ask them which areas they like or dislike and why. How would they make the classroom better? What would they do if they were the teacher?

Size—Furniture, sinks, door handles, and other fixtures should fit the size of the children. Adapt equipment and spaces for children with special needs.

Eye Level—Display the children's art and materials at their eye level—not at the adult level.

Privacy—Create cozy spaces and distinct areas where children can play in small groups. (Children are more likely to run around with large, open areas.)

Sound—Don't overwhelm children with noise. Keep your voice down and the children will model you. Use classical music or other peaceful music to quiet children.

Safety and Security—Clean, safe environments will help keep children healthy and will make them feel secure.

Attitude suggests respect for individual children and their families. Children should be encouraged to make choices, laugh, play, and learn in their own unique ways. The classroom should be set up like a children's discovery museum with many open-ended activities. Attitude about children and how they learn is reflected in the following:

DAP—Use developmentally appropriate practices and materials to enable children to be independent, explore, and feel successful.

Play—Play is what children do best and enjoy most. It is their work, and should be integrated into all areas of the curriculum.

Friends—Encourage children to interact with their friends by talking, questioning, and helping each other. Use cooperative groups to work on projects.

Meaning—Provide children with authentic learning experiences that grow out of their interests and issues important to them.

Activity—Children learn by *doing!* They need to move, use their senses, talk, and interact with concrete materials.

Modeling—Modeling is one of the most powerful ways children learn. Demonstrate what you want children to do, and they will imitate you.

Repetition—Allow children to repeat activities and experience a wide variety of materials so skills are reinforced.

Success—It's true: nothing succeeds like success! Create an environment that is risk-free where all children can feel worthy and competent.

Diversity—reflect the diversity of all the people in our society with bias-free pictures, toys, books, and materials that represent different sexes, ages, abilities, and cultures. Celebrate how people are alike and how they are different!

Wholeness—Learning should be connected and integrated into all areas of the curriculum. Education should also be focused on the *whole* child by meeting his or her physical, social, emotional, and intellectual needs.

Invisible Walls and Wall Hangings

Here are some unique ideas to break down large areas and create cozy spaces. These hangings can also be used on walls to add softness and texture.

Handprint Sheets *

Materials:

⚘ old sheets (white works best)

⚘ paint

⚘ pie pans

Directions:

Pour the paint into the pie pans. Let the children dip their hands in the paint, then apply them on the sheet. Hang from the ceiling as a divider.

Variations:

Children can also decorate sheets with fabric crayons or markers. Older children could sew buttons, ribbons, lace, or felt shapes on old sheets to make wall hangings.

Fabric and Scarves *

Materials:

⚘ strips of bright-colored fabric or scarves

Directions:

Hang fabric or scarves from the ceiling to add softness and to separate areas.

To hang, insert jumbo paper clips in the top of the hanging, then tuck ends of paper clips under ceiling tile beams.

Window Treatments

Curtains, shades, and valances all soften a room and give it a home-like atmosphere.

Roman Shades

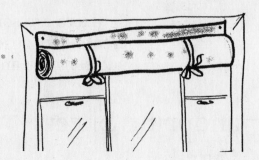

Materials:
- ❀ butcher paper
- ❀ paint and paintbrushes
- ❀ tacks, tape or stapler
- ❀ ribbon

Directions:

Cut the butcher paper as wide as the windows and three feet long. (If windows are wider than the butcher paper, then make several smaller sections and put them together.) Let the children spatter paint by throwing it on the paper. Tape or tack one end of the paper to the top of the window frame. Roll the bottom end and loosely tie it with two ribbons.

Variations:

You can make similar curtains by stapling fabric to the top of the window. Tie up with ribbons.

Cardboard Cornices

Materials:
- ❀ solid or juvenile print fabric
- ❀ cotton batting
- ❀ glue gun
- ❀ heavy cardboard or foam board
- ❀ scissors, hammer, nails

Directions:

Cut pieces of cardboard 8" wide and the length of the windows plus 4". Glue cotton batting to the front of the cardboard. Cut the fabric 14" wide and the length of the window plus 8". Cover the cardboard and padding with the fabric, then glue in place in the back. Nail panels to the tops of windows.

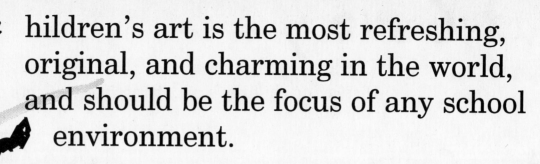

Children's art is the most refreshing, original, and charming in the world, and should be the focus of any school environment.

Rather than patterned projects and dittoes where everyone's looks the same, children need open-ended activities that allow them to think, experiment, problem-solve, and express themselves in unique ways. Art should be process-oriented, for children enjoy the moment and are not concerned with the final product. Since art is the child's outward expression of their inner world, it can also be an emotional release and can provide a vehicle for the development of thinking processes.

❋ **With art, there is no failure, but simply the joy of the experience.**

❋ **With art, there should be no comparison, for whatever the child creates is his or hers and should be cherished.**

❋ **With art, all children can experience success and grow!**

Why would you hang a commercial poster, cartoon character, or plastic cardboard animal drawn by an adult when you can hang an *original*—a one-of-a-kind by a very special child in your school! You'll find you will enjoy looking at the children's art much more than art by an anonymous adult, and the children will, too!

Art Gallery

Displaying children's art attractively reflects the importance of their work.

Artist Canvas

Materials:

❋ artist canvas
(available at craft and art shops)

❋ paints, brushes

❋ collage materials

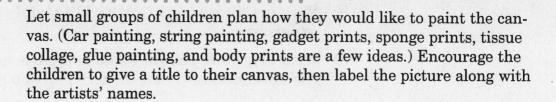

Directions:

Let small groups of children plan how they would like to paint the canvas. (Car painting, string painting, gadget prints, sponge prints, tissue collage, glue painting, and body prints are a few ideas.) Encourage the children to give a title to their canvas, then label the picture along with the artists' names.

Variations:

Photograph the children in the process of creating their canvas and display the photo beside the finished product.

Purchase large picture frames and rotate children's paintings in them.

Arrange several plastic box frames on a wall. Rotate children's stories and drawings in the frames.

Pedestals

Materials:

❋ plastic crate, stool, or cardboard box

❋ 1-2 yards of velvet, satin, taffeta, or other fabric

Directions:

Drape the fabric over the crate, stool or box in loose folds. Display sculptures or 3-dimensional projects on the pedestal.

Variations:

Stand up puppets made by children on a detergent bottle to display them.

Use an artist's easel to display different projects and paintings.

Sparkle and Shine

Children are attracted by things that glitter and shine, so this project is right up their alley.

Materials:

- ❀ clear contact paper
- ❀ tinsel
- ❀ foil paper
- ❀ sequins
- ❀ glitter
- ❀ ribbon scraps
- ❀ old Mylar balloons
- ❀ scissors

Directions:

Roll out a long sheet of contact paper (3'-5'). Let the children work together arranging shiny objects, such as tinsel, sequins, and glitter, on the contact paper. Give them scissors to cut objects from the foil paper and Mylar balloons. Place another sheet of clear contact paper on top to secure the objects. Hang from the ceiling, a window, or a wall.

Variations:

Let children make sticky collages by attaching tissue paper, leaves, flowers, and other small objects to contact paper.

Tape a large sheet of contact paper (sticky side out) on a wall and let children attach pieces of yarn, small pictures, paper scraps, etc., to it.

Dynamic Dioramas

Dioramas are a unique way for individuals or cooperative learning groups to display their creativity.

Materials:

- ❀ cardboard boxes (shoe boxes for individuals; corrugated cardboard boxes for group projects)
- ❀ paper scraps
- ❀ paint, paintbrushes
- ❀ glue, scissors, tape, string
- ❀ pipe cleaners, clay, foil, popsicle sticks, etc.
- ❀ collage materials, junk

Directions:

Ask the children to think of a favorite scene. It could be from a book, a place in their community, a period in history, a celebration, a habitat, etc. Let them paint the inside of the box, then create a three-dimensional scene using various art media. Objects can be suspended from the top of the box with string. Stand up characters and props with clay or glue. Characters and animals can be made from paper, clay or papier mache. Natural objects (rocks, sticks, nuts), small boxes, toys, and junk can also be used to build a diorama.

Variations:

Stack several dioramas on top of each other to create a fascinating display.

HINT!

This project can take several days or even weeks to create, so provide children with a place to work and store their dioramas.

The Napping House

Marvelous Murals

A mural is a wonderful project that encourages children to work together. Murals can be created with a wide variety of materials, and they provide an interesting focus on classroom walls and hallways.

Relate murals to a unit of study, season, or special interest of the children. Vary paint colors, and experiment with different types of paper and fabric.

When working on murals, hang the paper on the wall, put it on the floor, place it on a large table, or hang it from the playground fence.

Attach labels to murals that tell how children made them, or let the children dictate a story about the process. It's also interesting to take a photograph of the children working on the project to hang by the finished product.

Add borders to murals to create frames, then hang the murals at the children's eye level.

Feather Duster Mural

Materials:

❋ feather duster

❋ pie pans

❋ paint

❋ butcher paper

Directions:

Pour the paint into the pie pans, then let the children dip the feather duster in the paint and apply it to the paper.

Variation:

Give children individual feathers to paint a mural.

Bubble Painting

Materials:

❋ bottle of bubbles

❋ food coloring

❋ butcher paper

Directions:

Tape the paper to a playground fence. Add several big squirts of food coloring to the bubbles, then blow bubbles on the paper and watch them pop and make designs.

NEWS FLASH:
The Internet Has Arrived at Your School . . . or Will Be Arriving Shortly!

by Jim Moulton

This fact elicits one of two distinct reactions from America's teachers. Computer literate proponents of the Internet say, "Hooray! Just imagine what I can do with all these resources! We can get all the latest information!" There are also many less than enthusiastic educators who say, "Oh, no! Now I need to teach the Internet??!! What about my rain forest and community history units? I won't have time! And I'm not a high-tech computer nerd anyhow." Far more teachers have the latter reaction than the former.

These very valid feelings make it clear that before we put kids directly online, we need to make the teachers comfortable with working in this new environment. Only after teachers understand what information the Internet offers, and how to get to it, will we be able to make the Internet directly benefit our students. Fortunately, most teachers want to learn; learning is their business.

To get past the possible divisiveness involved in these diverse reactions to the Internet, it is helpful for teachers comfortable with the Internet to offer their assistance to those uncomfortable with the new technology. And those who are uncomfortable should not be afraid to ask the "techies" for help. It should work something like this:

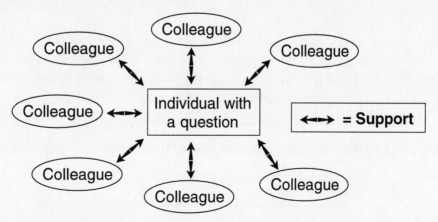

Ultimately, this reliance on the Internet is going to become part of the way schools do business. The genie cannot be put back into the bottle. At this point, the model of collaboration will need be slightly modified. Replacing the two camps, the techies and the intimidated, will be a community of educators with varying degrees of knowledge about specific resources on the Internet. Everyone will have the basic skills to use the Internet, but some teachers will know more about certain pieces, causing the model to evolve to look like this:

Now everyone from the the techno-savvy to the most novice will take his or her turn in the 'middle', as the question asker. We all will have questions, ranging from technical to curricular to methods, and like any other school-based effort, we will go to the people with the expertise to help us with our questions.

Resources on the Internet

Here is a sampling of online resources available to us over the Internet. Please use them and share them. And most of all . . . offer or ask for help!

There are several sites on the World Wide Web, the graphical portion of the Internet, which are designed specifically for teachers. At these sites you will find resources, often arranges by curriculum area and grade level, in ways that make immediate sense to teachers. They are a wonderful starting point for educators who are novices on the Internet, because these sites use the familiar language of teaching.

Here are the Uniform Resource Locators(URL) and site names, along with brief descriptions of a few of the many sites that cater specifically to the needs of teachers:

http://www.capecod.net/schrockguide/
Kathy Schrock's Guide for Educators

This site, as the audio introduction says, is a great place to locate resources and to grow professionally. It is updated regularly, and has curriculum and professional links.

http://www.classroom.net/
Classroom Connect

Another collection of materials of use to all teachers. Lesson plans and connections to other teachers are a few of the things offered.

http://www.ceismc.gatech.edu/BusyT/
The Busy Teacher

This site is designed for the person it is named for: you! Take a look here for things you can use right away.

http://www.pacificnet.net/mandel/index.html
Teachers Helping Teachers

This site is a place for teachers to share ideas and material. It is a great place to head if you have some ideas to share, or if you are looking for a new approach to teaching a concept or unit.

http://www.edbriefs.com/resource
Education Sites and Resources

This is a great collection of teacher stuff, all the way from curriculum to journals to professional growth. With a start here, you will be on your way!

The States Online

Studying Texas? Illinois? South Dakota? Every State is Online! Standards are part of every discussion in education these days and, luckily for educators and students, the states have adopted a standard for putting their state government online. To head for the state of Maine home page, go to this URL:

Go To: http://www.state.me.us

To visit the New Hampshire state government's web site, simply replace the 'me' with 'nh', and head for:

Go To: http://www.state.nh.us

As you can see, the URL for any state is: **http://www.state.xx.us**
with the 'xx' being replaced by the appropriate two-letter letter abbreviation, in lower case letters. Information available at these sites will vary from state to state, as does the way it is presented and organized. Just like license plates, each site is an attempt by the state to put its best foot forward, in

this case electronically, for the whole world to see. More and more of the states, realizing that these sites are used extensively by students doing research, are adding a 'Kids' Reference Section', where much of the information needed as a foundation for a state report can be found. Washington state is a good example of this, and undoubtedly as word spreads of this resource, other states will follow.

So . . . the next time you are studying a specific state or a region of the United States with your class, (or maybe planning a summer trip for yourself and your family), go online and collect some of your information here. (Please don't imagine that the site you visit can or should replace letters to the states' Departments of Tourism, interviews with people who have lived there, or the use of atlases and other library resources such as video or magazines. It cannot and should not. But do consider it one place no current research is complete without visiting!)

NASA Resources:
The latest information from this world and beyond . . .

Getting ready to do a Space or Flight unit? Go to your library and check the copyright dates of the collection of space, flight and aerodynamics research materials available. 1970's? 1980's? Earlier?

No matter how hard you and your librarian have worked to keep your school library stocked with current books, or how much you spend in dollars or book order bonus points to maintain your class-room collection, the latest volumes will contain information at least one or two years old, partly because of the time required to take printed material from creation to delivery.

Now consider this: Every time the Space Shuttle flies, NASA puts up a web site around that mission, at which they post the most current information in the form of text, images, sounds and videos from the preflight, launch, inflight activities and landing phases of the mission. This information is made available to you and your students minutes after the fact, if not in real time. Now *that* is current information!

Here Comes the Sun

NASA also keeps the public informed about astronomical events. If you hear a radio report on the way to school about a solar flare or some other discovery in space, you can be sure NASA will be following up with information online.

To begin using the massive resources NASA makes available over the Internet, head to NASA's web site at:

> Go To: `http://www.nasa.gov`

You'll be met by this menu of resources at the NASA home page:

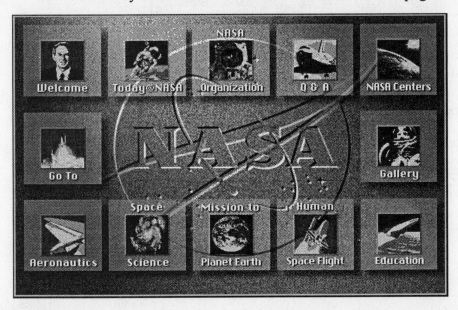

. . . with the education section described as follows way, further down the page:

> ● Education - If you're a student looking for information for a school paper or a teacher seeking material to add to your curriculum, this is the place to start.

NASA is a powerful model of the high-quality sites on the web today, full of images and data, projects and connections that can be used at any grade level. Do not expect to see the entire collection in one visit, but plan to wander through it several times, looking for resources that will fit with your classroom and your needs.

Studying the Rain Forest? — Searching the Internet

No matter what unit your students are studying, there are online resources to help, with more becoming available daily. To find resources for a specific unit, start with a visit to one of the many Search Engines available online. These sites maintain vast databases, composed of text and images, located on literally millions of WWW pages. By searching for a specific phrase you will be directed to a list of pages containing that phrase, and be confident that you will find within that list valuable resources.

Begin by heading for Digital's **AltaVista**, one of the most powerful search engines on the web by going to:

> Go To: http://www.altavista.digital.com/

When you reach the AltaVista home page, click in the search box, and type in something like this:

> "educational resources" +rainforest   Submit
>   Tip: Do not use AND or OR to combine words, simply type a few words or phrases.

By putting "educational resources" in quotes, you will force AltaVista to search for these two words as a phrase; by adding the '+rainforest' you are forcing it to find the word rainforest within 100 words of the original phrase. A quick tip is to do all of your Internet searching in lower case letters, as that tells the search engines not to be case sensitive.

Clicking on the "submit" button sends your request to the search engine's database, completes the search, and returns a linked list of resources. Here is a sample of what this AltaVista search returns:

> **The Rainforest Workshop**
>   Welcome To The Rainforest Workshop. This site uses HTML 3.0 tags. Visit the Temperate Rainforest. Visit the Tropical Rainforest. Visit our Educational...
>   http://kids.osd.wednet.edu/Marshall/rainforest_home_page.html - size 4K - 19 May 97

Note that by replacing the word "rainforest" with the unit you are searching for, be it 'flight' or 'france' (remember to use lower case!), you will find appropriate resources. When the list is returned, read the brief section of text that accompanies each link, and follow the ones that sound promising. Don't expect to find gold the first time, but keep at it, and refine the search if needed; with practice you will find incredible resources!

Another popular search engine is Yahoo, which can be found by heading for:

> Go To: http://www.yahoo.com/

Yahoo differs from AltaVista in that it allows you to work your way through a series of menus to approach your resources in a 'step by step' manner, closing in on them by saying, "Okay, I know that I want to start in the Science section, and from there I'll head into the Ecology section, and from there . . . ," as you approach the rainforest resources you are looking for. Here is the full trail:

> Top:Science:Ecology:Ecosystems:Forests:Rain Forests

Lo and behold, the list of resources includes many of the same resources found through AltaVista, the only difference being that we have approached them in a different way.

- Rain Forest Materials
- Rainforest Workshop - A student and teacher run link to rainforest information on the internet.
- Rainforests: Diversity and Destruction
- Skyrail Rainforest Cableway - Cairns, Australia

Two of the many other individual search engines available online can be found at:

Go To: http://www.webcrawler.com   Go To: http://www.infoseek.com

To search many search engines at the same time, head for:

Go To: http://www.dogpile.com/

or for even more options, try: Go To: http://www.regent.edu/~tedslat/tools.html

where you will be able to search more than twenty of the most powerful Internet search engines, all from a single site.

The Internet has fabulous resources to deliver to your school. Getting to them by using a browser like Netscape or Internet Explorer is the simplest piece and will in time become a natural part of the way you and your students access information.

But don't expect the Internet to change your classroom overnight. It is in how these resources are used to improve teaching and learning that the true challenge lies. This is where the collective imagination, experience, knowledge and enthusiasm of American teachers will have a tremendous impact.

So get involved, and take the time to see what this new tool has to offer you and your students. You'll learn that the Internet is not something you teach, but something that helps you teach. Ask for help if you need it, or offer help if you can. The Internet is coming to school, and it has some great resources for you!

Jim Moulton is currently the Staff Developer in the Community of Learners Network (http://www.col.k12.me.us), a Wide Area Network (WAN) connecting 21 schools across 3 districts and 6 communities in midcoast Maine. He is also active at the state level serving as Vice Chair of the Maine Internet Education Consortium (http://www.mstf.org/miec/). Jim's 8 years of classroom teaching experience in Grade 3 at Bowdoin Central School (http://www.col.k12.me.us/bcs/), which he blends with strong technical skills, is the greatest resource he brings to these positions as he helps real teachers find ways to make good use of the resources available online.

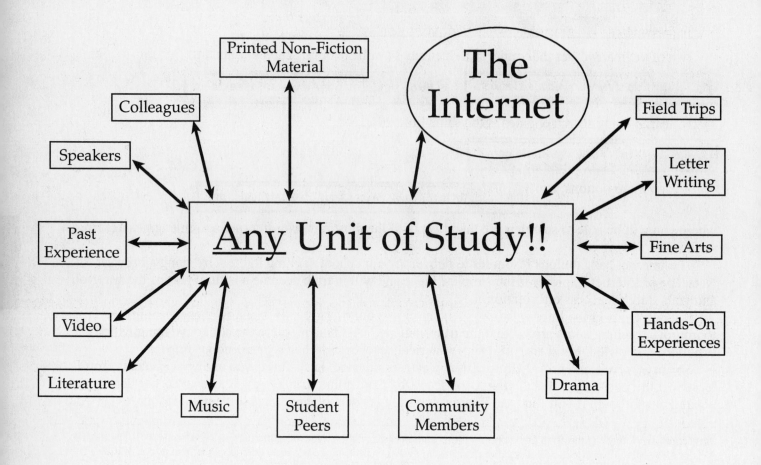

The Internet

Printed Non-Fiction Material

Colleagues

Speakers

Past Experience

Video

Literature

Music

Student Peers

Community Members

Drama

Hands-On Experiences

Fine Arts

Letter Writing

Field Trips

Any Unit of Study!!

The Internet - *One source to be used by **any** educator searching for resources to support **any** unit of study*

Some Internet *"Rules of Thumb"* for Teachers

What the Internet is

- Information — one important part of learning!
- A source for **current** information on virtually any topic
- A resource teachers can use for their students and for themselves
- Huge and confusing if taken in too large pieces!
- A topic **everyone** has opinions on

What the Internet isn't

- Education — you need **people** and **experiences** for that!
- A replacement for teachers
- An inherently good or bad place - it all depends on how it is used
- A place young children should spend time unsupervised

Beginning to learn about the Internet

- Find someone who is on-line, and ask to, "...see what it looks like"
- Learn about it with a friend to avoid the sense of going it alone
- Use it in your personal **and** professional life
- Take a course for re-certification
- Ask your students and their families
- Be curious!

Finding useful information on the Internet

- Look for Uniform Resource Locators (**URL**s), like **http://www.loc.gov** for the Library of Congress, in magazines, newspapers and professional journals as well as taking referrals from friends and colleagues
- Get a book, like the Internet Yellow Pages
- Take some time to explore!
- Make your own collection of useful URLs

Staying safe on the Internet

- Don't give out personal information on-line.... period!
- If a site doesn't feel right, leave it
- Consider screening software like SurfWatch, Cybersitter or NetNanny, but don't think it can replace direct adult involvement!
- Be honest with yourself, your family and your students about the good stuff **and** the bad stuff that is on-line. It is just like any major city, with lots of great reasons to go visit, but it also has places to stay away from!

Some Great Internet Web Sites for Teachers
Remember . . . this is just a start!

General Teacher Friendly Sites
- http://www.teachnet.com **Teachnet**
- http://www.ceismc.gatech.edu/BusyT/ **The Busy Teacher**
- http://tristate.pgh.net/~pinch13/ **The Homework Helper**
- http://www.capecod.net/schrockguide/ **Kathy Schrock's Guide**
- http://www.education-world.com/ **Education World**
- http://www.nea.org/ **National Education Association**
- http://www.aft.org//index.htm **American Federation of Teachers**

Great Current Events Sites
- http://www.nasa.gov **NASA**
- http://shuttle.nasa.gov **The Space Shuttle**
- http://www.cnn.com **CNN**
- http://www.usatoday.com **USA Today**

Classic Resource Sites
- http://www.si.edu **The Smithsonian Institution**
- http://shuttle.loc.gov **The Library of Congress**
- http://www.odci.gov/cia/ **The CIA Fact Book**

Search Engines
- http://www.dogpile.com **A Multi-Engine Search Utility**
- http://www.altavista.com **AltaVista**
- http://www.yahoo.com **Yahoo**

THE RESEARCH CENTER

Learning to research and report on information important to you uses a variety of domains. The type of research project I suggest is more than the typical effort of reading, writing about it, and handing it in.

My research center is designed around the *Self-Starter Kit for Independent Study*, by Edith Doherty and Louise Evans. In this program, each child designs his own specific project, investigating a very specific concept dealing with the thematic unit your class is currently studying. The kit explains the process in great detail, but I have adapted it for my own use.

You need to teach the process first, just as anything else. It might be wise to start with a class research project, to model the steps that individual children or small groups of children will complete as they design a project for their own use. The groups can work through individualized questions about one topic as you guide them through the first part of the process. The investigation can then be completed in cooperative groups, planning and completing a final, creative assignment to culminate the study.

1. First, a child chooses a topic to investigate in greater detail. For example, during a unit on tropical rain forests, a student wishes to learn more about three-toed sloths. Help him discover what he already knows about the animal: Why does he find it interesting enough to study in more detail? What kinds of things is he interested in learning about it? These will be his primary objectives.

2. When the child knows what he wishes to study, conference with him to make certain he has listed what he knows and

Name: Beth Ingraham   Date: Oct. 12

Fact Sheet for Independent Study: Bats

	Resource #1 Zipping, Zapping, Zooming Bats	Resource #2 C.D. Rom- Compton's Encycl.	Resource #3 Stellaluna
Question #1 What do bats eat?	mosquitoes gray bat - 3000 insects in 1 night moths, beetles, grasshoppers	brown bat- insects also fruit, flowers, sm. animals	fruit
Question #2 Are bats like birds?	long arm bones extra long finger bones like webbed hands "pups"- nurse (milk)	No - bats are mammals have hooks on wings	No! nocturnal don't land on feet hang upside down
Question #3 Are there really bats that suck blood?	Vampire Bats- only kind Usually from cows	Central & S. America Vampire Bats	___
Question #4 How do bats hang upside down?	by hooked claws on hands & toes	___	hooks catch on branches
Question #5 How do they fly safely in the dark?	"echolocation" bouncing sound waves	high-pitched cries send sound waves- reflected off obj. Ears are sensitive- react to waves	Use eyes to see - (?!) √ fact

© 1994 Phoebe B. Ingraham

Fig. 8-1

Excerpted from *Creating and Managing Learning Centers: A Thematic Approach*, by Phoebe Bell Ingraham. Peterborough, NH: Crystal Springs Books, 1996. Reprinted with permission; all rights reserved.

SUGGESTED MATERIALS

◻ a variety of papers

◻ writing tools

◻ a children's encyclopedia

◻ computer with a printer and CD-ROM (with encyclopedia)

◻ a variety of science textbooks

◻ nonfiction books dealing with concepts within the thematic unit

◻ trade books that teach information in the context of the story

◻ a selection of children's magazines such as *Ranger Rick, World,* and *Highlights for Children* that contain science articles related to your thematic unit

◻ models available that deal with the theme (such as earth-moon-sun or models of the human body

◻ charts and posters dealing with the theme

◻ library books, tapes, and recordings

◻ a variety of maps, atlases, and globes

◻ charts listing *Bloom's Taxonomy* verbs and steps in completing a research project, refined to meet the needs of your students (see page 147)

what he would like to learn. During the conference, help the student decide how much time he wishes to spend on this research project. The length of time the research will last will help determine how detailed the project can be. The student needs to plan how long he will spend investigating the material, then how much time will be spent creating a completed project.

3. Next, the student must find adequate resources for the investigation. Your school librarian can help, when she has available time, by assisting students in small groups. You can also supply your research center with many materials the students can use in the classroom.

4. Once the child has found ample resources, he may begin the research. I've given you a form (see Fig. 8-1; reproducible on page 192) that helps children learn how to take notes from multiple resources without simply copying sentences from each book. Because of the small space provided for each question, the child is limited to putting words and phrases in each box; he can then review his notes from all his resources together to answer each question.

As I said previously, independent research is probably best left for older children, but kindergartners and first graders can be guided through the research process and learn valuable skills while exploring topics of their own choosing.

5. Once all the research is completed, final objectives can be made for the project. First, the child chooses two to four objectives that require higher-level thinking strategies. He forms these by using a list of verbs that correspond to the levels of *Bloom's Taxonomy*. You can make a chart similar to the one on page 147 to assist the students in forming questions.

   For example, students may be required to write two objectives, one using a verb from the first three levels, and one using a verb from the second three. In this way, you are requiring each child to research the subject he chooses, write objectives that require higher-level thinking skills, and then plan a project that will address his objectives. This allows you to individualize instruction for each child in your class without designing a different curriculum for each child. The children are creating their own curriculum; you are providing the scaffolding they need in order to complete this task.

6. Once the child has written his objectives, he should schedule a conference with you to plan his culminating project. The objectives he has written will direct his reporting about the information he has learned, but the final project will enable him to share this information with the class. The child should plan to do or make something that will demonstrate what he has learned.

   It might be helpful in this stage to consider the seven intelligences.

   For example, consider the possible investigations chosen by different students during the unit on the rain forest:

   • A child who researches the three-toed sloth creates a diorama of a rain forest with a sloth in a tree. He places cards around the scene explaining the environment the sloth lives in. This child does not enjoy speaking in front of the class. He is free to choose a display with his written report.

   • A child who researches children's books written about the rain forest writes a book of her own, and records it on audiotape. Her book, along with a selection of books she found in her research, are displayed in the reading center for others to enjoy.

   • A child who researches endangered rain forest animals writes a song about them, and teaches it to the class. His report, along with the words and music to his song, is placed in the science center with a small electric keyboard so the students can learn to play the song.

   Remember that each child should be given an opportunity to share his/her knowledge in the most appropriate way for that child. After this is accomplished, it is important to schedule a short evaluation conference in order to encourage each child to reflect on her learning, and the process she went through in her research. She might set goals for improving the experience or modifying the culminating project for her next individual investigation.

   No activities need to be suggested, other than the description of the projects listed above, for each child designs his own research.

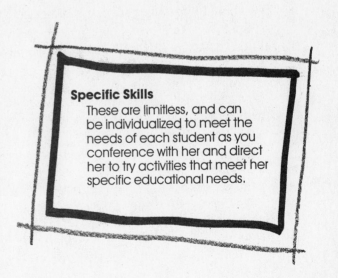

Specific Skills
These are limitless, and can be individualized to meet the needs of each student as you conference with her and direct her to try activities that meet her specific educational needs.

Words to Use to Plan Research Projects

Knowledge:	list	identify	define	match	state
Comprehension:	explain	locate	report	convert	paraphrase
Application:	predict	relate	change	graph	plan
Analysis:	web	infer	discover	analyze	distinguish
Synthesis:	create	rewrite	design	rearrange	compose
Evaluation:	select	criticize	judge	appraise	compare

CREATIVE DEVELOPMENT CENTERS

What Does It Mean to Be Smart?

by Robert J. Sternberg

A Yale study, based on the premise that intelligence has analytical, creative, and practical aspects, shows that if schools start valuing all three, they may find that thousands of kids are smarter than they think.

The most widely used circulated newspaper in Connecticut recently carried a story on the meteoric rise of the president of one of the major banks in the state. I might have passed over the story with a glance had the name of the bank president not caught my eye. He was someone with whom I had gone to school from 1st grade right up through high school. What especially caught my attention, though, was that he had been a *C* student — someone who didn't seem to have much to offer.

Were the bank president an isolated case it might not be cause for alarm. But one cannot help wondering how many such students conclude that they really do not have much to contribute — in school or in the world at large — and so never try.

The Cost of a Closed System

Our system of education is, to a large degree, a closed system. Students are tested and classified in terms of two kinds of abilities — their ability to memorize information and, to a lesser extent, their ability to analyze it. They are also taught and assessed in ways that emphasize memory and analysis. As a result, we label students who excel in these patterns of ability as smart or able. We may label students

who are weaker in these abilities as average or even slow or stupid.

Students may, however, excel in other abilities that are at least as important as those we now reward. Creativity and the practical application of information — ordinary common sense or "street smarts" — are two such abilities that go unappreciated and unrecognized. They are simply not considered relevant to conventional education.

The ability tests we currently use, whether to measure intelligence or achievement or to determine college admissions, also value memory and analytical abilities. These tests predict school performance reasonably well. They do so because they emphasize the same abilities that are emphasized in the classroom.

Thus, students who excel in memory and analytical abilities get good grades. Practically oriented learners, however, who are better able to learn a set of facts if they can see its relevance to their own lives, lose out. (Indeed, many teachers and administrators are themselves practical learners who simply tune out lectures or workshops they consider irrelevant to them.)

The consequences of this system are potentially devastating. Through grades and test scores, we may be rewarding only a fraction of the students who should be rewarded. Worse, we may be inadvertently

disenfranchising multitudes of students from learning. In fact, when researchers have examined the lives of enormously influential people, whether in creative domains (Gardner 1993), practical domains (Gardner 1995), or both, they have found that many of these people had been ordinary — or even mediocre — students.

Teaching in All Four Ways

At any grade level and in any subject, we can teach and assess in a way that enables students to use all four abilities (Sternberg 1994, Sternberg and Spear-Swerling 1996. See also Sternberg and Williams 1996, Williams et al. 1996). In other words, we can ask students to

■ Recall who did something, what was done, when it was done, where it was done, or how it was done;

■ Analyze, compare, evaluate, judge, or assess;

■ Create, invent, imagine, suppose, or design; and

■ Use, put into practice, implement, or show use.

In physical education, for example, competitors need to learn and remember various strategies for playing games, analyze their opponents' strategies, create their own strategies, and implement those strategies on the playing field. Figure 1 presents some examples of how teachers can do this in language arts, mathematics, social studies, and science.

When we use this framework, relatively few activities will end up requiring only one of these four abilities. On the contrary, most activities will be a mixture, as are the tasks we confront in everyday life. Notice that in this framework, instruction and assessment are closely related. Almost any activity that is used for the one can be used for the other.

In addition, no type of activity should be limited to students whose strength is in that area. On the contrary, we should teach all students in all four ways. In that way, each student will find at least some aspects of the instruction and assessment to be compatible with his or her preferred way of learning and other aspects to be challenging, if perhaps somewhat uncomfortable.

Teaching in all four ways also makes the teacher's job easier and more manageable. No teacher can

individualize instruction and assessment for each student in a large class, but any teacher can teach in a way that meets all students' needs.

Does This Work in Practice?

In the summer of 1993, we conducted a study of high school students to test our hypothesis that students learn and perform better when they are taught in a way that at least partially matches their own strengths (Sternberg 1996; Sternberg and Clinkenbeard 1995; Sternberg et al. 1996). Known as the Yale Summer Psychology Program, the study involved 199 students from high schools across the United States and some from abroad.

Each school had nominated students for the program. Interested nominees then took a test designed

to measure their analytical, creative, and practical abilities. The test included multiple-choice verbal, quantitative, and figural items, as well as analytical, creative, and practical essay items (Sternberg 1993). A sample of the items appears in Figure 2.

We then selected the students who fit into one of the five ability patterns: high analytical, high creative, high practical, high balanced (high in all three abilities), or low balanced (low in all three abilities). We based these judgments on both the individual student's patterns and the way these patterns compared to those of the other students.

We then placed each student into one of four differentiated instructional treatments. All included a

---

FIGURE 1

Teaching for Four Abilities

	Type of Skill		
Memory	**Analysis**	**Creativity**	**Practicality**
Language Arts Remember what a gerund is or what the name of Tom Sawyer's aunt was.	Compare the function of a gerund to that of a participle, or compare the personality of Tom Sawyer to that of Huckleberry Finn.	Invent a sentence that effectively uses a gerund, or write a very short story with Tom Sawyer as a character.	Find gerunds in a newspaper or magazine article and describe how they are used, or say what general lesson about persuasion can be learned from Tom Sawyer's way of persuading his friends to whitewash Aunt Polly's fence.
Mathematics Remember a mathematical formula (Distance = Rate x Time).	Solve a mathematical word problem (using the D=RT formula).	Create your own mathematical word problem using the D=RT formula.	Show how to use the D=RT formula to estimate driving time from one city to another near you.
Social Studies Remember a list of factors that led up to the U.S. Civil War.	Compare, contrast, and evaluate the arguments of those who supported slavery versus those who opposed it.	Write a page of a journal from the viewpoint of a soldier fighting for one or the other side during the Civil War.	Discuss the applicability of lessons of the Civil War for countries today that have strong internal divisions, such as the former Yugoslavia.
Science Name the main types of bacteria.	Analyze the means the immune system uses to fight bacterial infections.	Suggest ways to cope with the increasing immunity bacteria are showing to antibiotic drugs.	Suggest three steps that individuals might take to reduce the likelihood of bacterial infection.

---

morning lecture that balanced memory, analysis, creativity, and practical learning and thinking. All students used the same psychology text (Sternberg 1995), which was also balanced among the four types of learning and thinking. The treatments differed, however, in the afternoon discussion sections. There, we assigned students to a section that emphasized either memory, analysis, creativity, or practical learning and thinking.

The critical feature of this design was that, based on their ability patterns, some students were matched and others mismatched to the instructional emphasis of their section. Another important feature was that all students received at least some instruction emphasizing each type of ability.

We assessed student achievement through homework assignments, tests, and an independent project. We assessed memory specifically through multiple-choice tests, and we evaluated analytical, creative, and practical abilities through essays. For the essays we asked students questions such as "Discuss the advantages and disadvantages of having armed guards at school" (analysis); "Describe what your ideal school would be like" (creativity); and "Describe some problem you have been facing in your life and then give a practical solution" (practical use).

Because we assessed all students in exactly the same way, we could more easily compare the groups' performance. Had we used the more conventional forms of instruction and assessment, emphasizing memory and analysis, the creative and practical ability tests would probably not have told us much.

Some Surprises
The study yielded many findings, but four stand out:

1. Students whose instruction matched their pattern of abilities performed significantly better than the others. Even by partially matching instruction to abilities, we could improve student achievement.

FIGURE 2

Sample Multiple-Choice Questions from the Sternberg Triarchic Abilities Test

Analytical
Verbal

The vip was green, so I started to cross the street. Vip most likely means:
A. car
B. sign
C. light
D. tree

Creative
Quantitative

There is a new mathematical operation called graf. It is defined as follows:
x graf y = x + y, if x < y but
x graf y = x − y, if otherwise.
How much is 4 graf 7?
A. −3
B. 3
C. 11
D. −11

Practical
Figural
(Students are shown a map)

After attending a performance at the theater, you need to drive to House A. If you want to avoid the traffic jam at the intersection of Spruce Avenue and Willow Street and take the shortest alternative route, you will drive
A. west on Maple Avenue to Route 326.
B. west on Pine Street to Hickory Street.
C. east on Maple Avenue to Oak Street.
D. east on Pine Street to Oak Street.

---

2. By measuring creative and practical abilities, we significantly improved our ability to predict course performance.

3. To our surprise, our four high ability groups differed in their racial, ethnic, and socioeconomic composition. The high-analytic group was composed mostly of white, middle- to upper-middle-class students from well-known "good" schools. The high-creative and high-practical groups were much more diverse racially, ethnically, socioeconomically, and educationally. Our high-balanced group was in between. This pattern suggests that when we expand the range of abilities we test for, we also expand the range of students we identify as smart.

4. When we did a statistical analysis of the ability factors underlying performance on our ability test, we found no single general factor (sometimes called a *g* factor or an IQ). This suggests that the general ability factor that has been found to underlie many conventional ability tests may not be truly general, but general only in the narrow range of abilities that conventional tests assess.

A Clear-Eyed Sense of Accomplishment
By exposing students to instruction emphasizing each type of ability, we enable them to capitalize on their strengths while developing and improving new skills. This approach is also important because students need to learn that the world cannot always provide them with activities that suit their preferences. At the same time, if students are never presented with activities that suit them, they will never experience a sense of success and accomplishment. As a

result, they may tune out and never achieve their full potential.

On a personal note, I was primarily a creative learner in classes that were largely oriented toward memorizing information. When in college, I took an introductory psychology course that was so oriented; I got a *C*, leading my instructor to suggest that I might want to consider another career path. What's more, that instructor was a psychologist who specialized in learning and memory! I might add that never once in my career have I had to memorize a book or lecture. But I have continually needed to think analytically, creatively, and practically in my teaching, writing, and research.

Success in today's job market often requires creativity, flexibility, and a readiness to see things in new ways. Furthermore, students who graduate with *A*'s but who cannot apply what they have learned may find themselves failing on the job.

Creativity, in particular, has become even more important over time, just as other abilities have become less valuable. For example, with the advent of computers and calculators, both penmanship and arithmetic skills have been diminished in importance. Some standardized ability tests, such as the SAT, even allow students to use calculators. With the increasing availability of massive, rapid data-retrieval systems, the ability to memorize information will become even less important.

This is not to say that memory and analytical abilities are not important. Students need to learn and remember the core content of the curriculum, and they need to be able to analyze — to think critically about — the material. But the importance of these abilities should not be allowed to obfuscate what else is important.

In a pluralistic society, we cannot afford to have a monolithic conception of intelligence and schooling; it's simply a waste of talent. And, as I unexpectedly found in my study, it's no random waste. The more we teach and assess students based on a broader set of abilities, the more racially, ethnically, and socioeconomically diverse our achievers will be. We can easily change our closed system — and we should. We must take a more balanced approach to education to reach all of our students. ∎

Author's note: This research was supported under the Javits Act Program (Grant R206R50001), administered by the U.S. Department of Education's Office of Educational Research and Improvement. The findings and opinions expressed here do not reflect the Office's positions or policies.

References

Gardner, H. (1993) *Creating Minds*. New York: Basic Books.

Gardner, H. (1995) *Leading Minds*. New York: Basic Books.

Sternberg, R.J. (1993). "Sternberg Triarchic Abilities Test." Unpublished test.

Sternberg, R.J. (1994). "Diversifying Instruction and Assessment." *The Educational Forum* 59, 1: 47-53.

Sternberg, R.J. (1995). *In Search of the Human Mind*. Orlando, Fla.: Harcourt Brace College Publishers.

Sternberg, R.J. (1996). *Successful Intelligence*. New York: Simon & Schuster.

Sternberg, R.J. and P. Clinkenbeard. (May-June 1995). "A Triachic View of Identifying, Teaching, and Assessing Gifted Children." *Roeper Review* 17, 4: 255-260.

Sternberg, R.J., M. Ferran, P. Clinkenbeard, and E.L. Grigorenko. (1996). "Identification, Instruction, and Assessment of Gifted Children: A Construct Validation of a Triarchic Model." *Gifted Child Quarterly* 40: 129-137.

Sternberg, R.J. and L. Spear-Swerling. (1996). *Teaching for Thinking*. Washington, D.C.: American Psychological Association.

Sternberg, R.J., R.K. Wagner, W.M. Williams, and J.A. Hovarth (1995). "Testing Common Sense." *American Psychologist* 50, 11: 912-927.

Sternberg, R.J., and W.M. Williams. (1996). *How to Develop Student Creativity*. Alexandria, Va.: ASCD

Williams, W.M., T. Blyth, N. White, J. Li, R.J. Sternberg, and H.I. Gardner. (1996). *Practical Intelligence for School: A Handbook for Teachers of Grades 5-8*. New York: Harper Collins.

Robert J. Sternberg is a Professor in the Department of Psychology, Yale University, P.O. Box 20825, New Haven, CT 06520-8205 (e-mail: sterobj@yalevm.cis.yale.edu).

Voices

While most people possess the full spectrum of intelligence, each individual reveals distinctive cognitive features. We possess varying amounts of the seven intelligences and combine and use them in highly personal ways. Restricting educational programs to focusing on a preponderance of linguistic and mathematical intelligences minimizes the importance of other forms of knowing. Thus many students who fail to demonstrate the traditional academic intelligences are held in low esteem and their strengths may remain unrealized and lost to both the school and society at large.

From *Phonics That Work! New Strategies for the Reading/Writing Classroom* by Janet Wagstaff. NY: Scholastic.

Encouraging — and Challenging — Students' Understandings

by John A. Zahorik

In productive constructivism, the teacher's job is to fuse students' knowledge with what experts know, not to favor one over the other.

The notion that people don't simply discover knowledge but make or construct it has strong appeal. So, too, do the related ideas that knowledge results from disequilibrium, emerges from prior knowledge, and grows through exposure and feedback. For these reasons, constructivism is a growing trend; it is beginning to appear in the teaching of literacy, mathematics, science, and other areas. Yet because constructivism often clashes with more traditional practices, introducing it in a school is no easy matter.

Over the past several years, I have been working with teachers as they move toward constructivism. I have found that they encounter several problems. The most formidable is the tension between students' constructions — what students learn from group problem solving, laboratory experiments, and so forth — and the constructions of experts in that field.

Some teachers choose to emphasize students' understandings at the expense of experts' constructions,

while others do the opposite, minimizing the importance of what the students learn. Both groups are making a mistake; the teacher's job is to help the students integrate the two.

Experiencing and Revising

As constructivism posits, knowledge is not a static phenomenon; it changes as we engage in new experiences that test what we know. These new experiences may cause us to alter or add to our understanding, sometimes in subtle ways and sometimes dramatically. Or the experiences may affirm our understanding until another new experience again causes us to rethink our ideas.

All of us are constantly engaged in this process in our everyday lives, but this is also the process that scholars in every discipline follow. They seek new experiences to test, and they subsequently construct knowledge through inquiry and scholarly dialogue. The results are the revised understanding of the origin of stars, the cause of ulcers,

and the reason dinosaurs became extinct.

This is not to say that knowledge of nonexperts is unimportant. It is very important, because in disciplines ranging from history to science to math, the only thing we can know is our own understanding of the knowledge — our own construction of it. (In this sense, all of our constructions are, probably, misconceptions. If they appear to be true, it is only at a particular time and in a particular place.)

This brings us back to the problem teachers encounter. Here is a closer look at the two solutions some teachers adhere to, followed by other — more constructive — approaches to constructivism.

Erring on the Side of Students

Teachers who err on the side of students' constructions often engage students in group activities calling for problem solving, decision making, and invention. The students, either individually or in groups, develop their own understandings, which they then present to the class. The teacher considers these personal constructions as satisfying to the students and adequate for their purpose, knowing that as the students have new experiences, they will continue to develop these concepts.

An example of this type of constructivist teaching is the 4th grade teacher who taught a lesson on

A teacher does not promote understanding by permitting students' constructions to stand even though they clash with experts' constructions.

insects. She divided her class into groups of four or five and gave each group a box containing models of various insects. She announced that each group would do what scientists do: classify the bugs based on common characteristics — size, color, shape, type of wings and antennas. The groups then presented their schemes to the entire class. The teacher asked the students to discuss the various approaches and demonstrate the efficacy of their own categories. But the lesson ended there. The teacher did not introduce the scheme of distinguishing characteristics that scientists have agreed to use in classifying insects.

Erring on the Side of Scholars

Teachers who err on the side of constructions from the various disciplines also may begin the lesson with group activities calling for problem solving and related processes. These activities, however, function more as an introduction to and motivation for the major part of the lesson. The teacher gives the groups only a short time to investigate a problem or perform a task then report back to the class.

After listening to the reports — often with little discussion — the teacher presents knowledge from the disciplines, viewing it as constructed knowledge rather than as a discovered, stable reality. The message, however, is clear: Students' constructions are trivial and often wrong, and experts' constructions must be accepted. The teacher usually does not discuss the experts' constructions in depth, although he or she does provide examples and pose and respond to questions.

An economics lesson taught to another group of 4th graders exemplifies this approach. The teacher introduced the terms *goods, services, natural resources, labor* and *capital* by defining and providing examples of each. She then organized a scavenger hunt of sorts. Students were to look for examples of natural resources, labor and capital anywhere in the school, then

record their discoveries on a form the teacher provided. After a 20-minute hunt, the students returned and shared their results.

The teacher identified and corrected questionable examples. She then began a lecture on the economics principles underlying the relationship of natural resources, labor, and capital to goods and services. She noted, for example, that people's choices about what goods and services to buy and consume determine how resources will be used, and that people cannot have all the goods and services they want because productive resources are limited. She did not initiate a discussion of these principles, nor did she ask the students to draw conclusions about goods and services based on the examples they had found.

Integrating the Two

If the goal of teaching is to impart conceptual understanding, neither of these constructivist strategies is entirely productive. A teacher does not promote understanding by permitting students' constructions to stand even though they clash with experts' constructions. In fact, it is dangerous to ignore the concepts, conventions, and processes that are essential to the maintenance of our culture or to wait for them to emerge over time through random experiences. As Driver and colleagues (1994, p.6) point out, "Scientific entities and ideas, which are constructed, validated, and communicated through the cultural institutions of science, are unlikely to be discovered by individuals through their own empirical enquiry."

On the other hand, as Von Glaserfeld (1995, p. 5) reminds us, "Concepts cannot simply be transferred from teacher to students — they must be conceived." Students' experiences influence their perception and processing of new information.

Vygotsky (1986) stresses that both

Problem-solving tasks are critical to the growth of student constructions.

of these types of constructions are essential to understanding. He contends that students' constructions, or what he calls *spontaneous concepts*, and experts' constructions, or what he calls *scientific concepts*, develop in reverse directions. A spontaneous concept works its way up until it reaches a level that permits a person to absorb a scientific concept. Scientific concepts work their way down, supplying logic and structures to spontaneous concepts.

Activities in which students engage in problem-solving tasks — as individuals or in small groups — are critical to the growth of student constructions. These activities can also be useful as a way to present experts' knowledge in an indirect way.

What is essential for bringing the two types of constructions together, however, is teacher-student dialogue. As Leinhardt (1992, p. 24) says, when we use the classroom "as a social arena for the public examination of ideas . . . students naturally build on or refute old ideas as they are merged with new knowledge."

In Tobin and Tippens's (1993, p. 11) view, group interaction can "provide a milieu in which students can negotiate differences of opinion and seek consensus." Teachers must examine, discuss, critique, and challenge students' constructions in relation to those of both experts and other students. Conversely, teachers need to critique and discuss experts' constructions in relation to emerging student constructions.

Reconstructing the Lessons

Suppose we apply these recommendations to our two examples. In the lesson on insect characteristics, after the students share their classification schemes, the teacher introduces the experts' approaches to insect identification. She can do this directly or through a discovery activity.

The object is not to conclude the activity with the correct answer, but to extend the discussion. By comparing and contrasting their construction with the experts' construction, the students gain insights into both and begin to reconceptualize their constructions in the direction of those of the experts. If the students' original conceptions were viable but different from the expert opinions, they at least become aware that there is an agreed-upon classification scheme that scientists use as a standard convention in studying insects.

In the lesson on economics, the teacher asks her students to critique the economic principles that she has presented. She and other students may then critique the critiques (that is, the constructions), examining them for inadequacies and errors. This type of critical dialogue about knowledge in various disciplines is what Perkinson (1993) has labeled *critical teaching*.

Nurturing the Process

Some teachers may view the constructions of students and experts as irreconcilable. But, again, in a school setting, the teacher must fuse the two if conceptual understanding is to occur.

To some degree, students' and experts' constructions are already joined, no matter how the teacher organizes his or her lessons. Constructing knowledge is a constant, naturally occurring process as students view new information — such as experts' constructions — in terms of their prior knowledge. Teachers can nurture this process. They can help students negotiate meaning through discussions that bring the understandings of both of these groups together. ∎

References

Driver, R., H. Asoko, J. Leach, E. Mortimer, and P. Scott. (October 1994). "Constructing Scientific Knowledge in the Classroom." *Educational Researcher* 23: 5-12.

Leinhardt, G. (April 1992). "What Research on Learning Tells Us About Teaching." *Educational Leadership* 49, 7: 20-25.

Perkinson, H. (1993). *Teachers Without Goals, Students Without Purposes*. New York: McGraw-Hill.

Tobin, K., and D. Tippens (1993). "Constructivism as a Referent for Teaching and Learning." In *The Practice of Constructivism In Science Education*, edited by K. Tobin. Hillsdale, N.J.: Lawrence Erlbaum, pp. 3-21.

Von Glaserfeld, E. (1995). "A Constructivist Approach to Teaching." In *Constructivism in Education*, edited by L. Steffe and J. Gale. Hillsdale, N.J.: Lawrence Erlbaum, pp. 3-15.

Vygotsky, L. (1986). *Thought and Language*. Cambridge, Mass.: MIT Press.

John A. Zahorik is a Professor at the University of Wisconsin-Milwaukee, School of Education, Department of Curriculum and Instruction, Enderis Hall, P.O. Box 413, Milwaukee, WI 53201 (e-mail: jzahorik@soe.uwm.edu).

Voices

*P*aulo Trure (1985) argues that inquirers need to be problem-posers, not just problem-solvers. We saw that in our classrooms we were the problem-posers; our students were forced to become the problem-solvers, answering our questions. We realized that problem-solving and research are empty processes when the question is not one that really matters in the life of the inquirer. While there are many research strategies that support our lives as inquirers, focusing on learning those strategies is a waste of time if we don't first take time to find a significant question. Even then, we may not find a specific question, but an interest, an issue, or a general wondering that we want to pursue further. As we work through inquiry, we do not usually end with one answer or even a set of answers. Inquiry does not narrow our perspective; it gives us more understandings, questions, and possibilities than when we started. Inquiry isn't just asking and answering a question. It involves searching for significant questions and figuring out how to explore those questions from many perspectives.

From *Learning Together Through Inquiry: From Columbus to Integrated Curriculum*, by Kathy G. Short, Jean Schroeder, Julie Laird, Gloria Kauffman, Margaret J. Ferguson, and Kathleen Marie Crawford. York, ME: Stenhouse, 1996.

Reading Styles Times Twenty

by Marie Carbo

Research shows that reading styles instruction can help even the least academically talented youngsters become proficient readers.

Twenty years of experience with reading styles have taught us well. We now know the importance of teaching to the students' strengths and accommodating their interests. We know how to select, adapt, and manage the best reading methods for different learners. And we know beyond a doubt that there is no single best way to teach every youngster to read even though some state legislatures are headed toward the potentially disastrous decision to mandate phonics for all.

During the past 20 years, my colleagues and I have learned how to accelerate literacy levels so that students learn to love reading and become lifelong readers. We have seen districtwide reading gains of two stanines in rural Appalachia (Snyder 1994), a bilingual school that rose from 61st of 65 schools academically to 9th, and special education students who increased their reading comprehension from 2 to 20 times. We have seen student motivation increase dramatically, and we have seen teachers become more confident, competent, and effective (Barber, Carbo, and Thomasson 1994; Carbo 1997b; Skipper 1997; Snyder 1994).

Working across the United States with thousands of students K-12 — a great many of them in the bottom third academically — my colleagues and I see the "big picture" of reading styles teaching and offer some effective strategies for increasing literacy.

Guiding Principles and Recommendations

Reading styles programs send a strong message to students that we respect them as learners. The programs, which capitalize on their strengths and interests, incorporate the following 10 guiding principals.

1. It is natural for children to enjoy reading and to be motivated to read.

Highly motivated students become more responsible about reading and are more likely to read regularly. Because students' learning accelerates when they are relaxed, open, and receptive (Hart 1993), we must provide comfortable environments and flexible groups. Most students prefer and respond to a wide range of reading choices.

Recommendations:

■ Provide a relaxing, literature-rich reading environment. Design warm, inviting reading centers. Rotate groups of students so that each youngster has access to the center at least once a week. Stock classroom libraries with books, magazines, newspapers, TV and movie schedules, catalogs, menus, reference materials, and so on. If funds are short ask for donations, check garage sales and resale shops, or hold PTA-sponsored book drives or fundraisers.

■ Give students a wide range of reading choices. Ask students about their interests, and stock class libraries accordingly (Trelease 1989). Use short stories and books with unmotivated students to provide more choices. Hold book discussions and invite authors to visit to generate student interest in reading.

2. Students need to be challenged with high-level reading materials.

If we don't expose students to high-level materials, it is unlikely that they will ever be able to read or understand them.

Recommendations:

■ Provide sufficient modeling. Modeling calls for a competent reader to read aloud while less able readers listen and look at the words as they are read. Make certain that less able readers can see the words (use charts, chalkboards, or oversized books). Point to the words or phrases as they are being read; reread sections two or three times. After sufficient modeling, encourage students to read aloud in small groups before they advance to reading aloud individually (Carbo 1996).

■ Challenge students. The Carbo Recorded-Book Method (see box on next page) increases fluency, comprehension, and word recognition quickly; it challenges students with more difficult materials while providing a recording that they can review as many times as needed (Carbo 1989). This method has been particularly effective with youngsters who have difficulty learning with phonics, with older students and adults who have become "turned off" to reading, and with children who have poor language proficiency.

3. Every student has a special style for reading.

Students learn to read more easily and enjoy it more when instructional techniques match their styles. We use observation techniques and the Reading Style Inventory® (Carbo 1982, 1994) to identify students' learning styles during the act of reading. Then we create reading programs that accommodate their strengths while compensating for any weaknesses.

Reading styles helped prevent state intervention at Horace Mann Middle School in Amarillo, Texas. The students helped plan appropriate instruction and testing environments. They could take the untimed statewide achievement test in rooms with or without music, and were permitted snacks, pillows, colored overlays, and highlighters to break lengthy passages into smaller, workable chunks. Reading scores at Horace Mann climbed an average of 33 percentage points! Three years later, the scores remained high. Best of all, students repeatedly commented on how much more relaxed and better prepared they felt than in previous years.

Recommendations:

■ Observe your students carefully and use the Reading Style Inventory (RSI) to identify strengths and needs. (The RSI is a questionnaire that describes a learner's strengths and physical needs, and identifies the appropriate reading strategies.) Begin by accommodating students' reading styles with comfortable reading arenas, snacks, some reduced lighting, and choices of activities. Learn a variety of methods to teach reading and apply them flexibly. If a child cannot learn with one method, adapt it or use a

different method. Try multisensory teaching, and accommodate students' global and analytical needs.

■ Use colored overlays to minimize visual problems. For some youngsters, letters and words reverse, swirl, or slide off the page (Irlen 1991). Experiment by placing different overlays over the text. The right color for a youngster can dramatically improve reading by reducing letter movement. Also try using colored notebook paper, colored chalk, and colored transparencies.

4. Reading style strengths and preferences develop at different times and rates.

Some educators believe that a particular method such as phonics should be taught to all children as early as kindergarten. But "early" is not the ideal time for all children. We provide every youngster with

> **Students learn to read more easily and enjoy it more when instructional techniques match their styles.**

decoding skills (phonics, context clues, syllabication, prefixes, suffixes), but we don't assign children tasks they are neither ready for nor able to accomplish. A child who has great difficulty learning phonics in kindergarten might breeze through it in 2nd grade. Timing is vitally important.

Recommendations:

■ Select the right reading method at the right time. If a student does poorly on a phonics test, he or she might not be developmentally ready to learn phonics. Or the child might not have the necessary strengths to learn (can't hear phonics sounds, associate sounds with letters, or blend them). Each youngster has a different inner clock and a different reading style.

■ Don't label students as "slow" because they are primarily tactile and kinesthetic (T-K). While most young children appear to be tactile and kinesthetic, some students continue to prefer that style throughout their lives. These students often are placed in lower tracks simply because their learning needs have not been met. We strongly recommend that teachers create files of tactile and kinesthetic activities to use with these learners (Carbo 1996, Gilbert 1977, Martin 1996, Thomasson 1993).

5. Students who understand their own reading styles can learn to work through their strengths and develop respect for the styles of others.

We teach our students that their own reading styles must not infringe on the styles of others. For example, if some students learn through discussion, they cannot confer with one another near youngsters who require quiet. Students learn to accommodate one another's strengths and compensate for weaknesses.

In Chatham County, North Carolina, for example, AD/HD students (Attention Deficit/Hyperactivity Disorder) are provided the movement they need to remain alert. One AD/HD 2nd grader who fell asleep often during the day now sits on a therapy ball alongside his classmates. Bouncing gently on the big ball helps him stay focused. When he gets up, he simply pushes the ball under his desk.

Recommendations:

■ Teach the concept of reading styles to students. We recommend that teachers read their students books that accentuate differences in styles. Consider, for example, *Rose and Tulip* (Fels 1993) and *Gregory the Terrible Eater* (Sharmat 1980) for elementary students and *The Bedspread* for secondary students.

No one reading method or set of reading materials is ideal for all students.

■ Encourage students to plan strategies that capitalize on their reading styles. We use many techniques — including cooperative groups — that provide problem situations related to reading styles. Consider this example: Explain to your students that 17 of the 25 students in your classroom prefer quiet while reading and the remaining 8 prefer music. Have them think about how they would meet the needs of both groups. Do they foresee any problems? Such activities encourage students to become part of the decision-making process.

6. The predominant reading style of primary children and struggling readers is global, tactile and kinesthetic.

These hands-on learners need holistic methods, active learning, and emotional involvement. Generally, we have accelerated such students' reading with holistic programs that emphasize fun and movement. These include allowing them to select stories of their choice, providing role models, using sufficient modeling of stories, and emphasizing skills related to the stories and to students' needs. We tend to teach these skills in flexible groups with hands-on materials.

Recommendations:

■ Emphasize holistic, thematic teaching and modeling. Global learners relate to stories and situations that are exciting, fun, humorous, and personal. To do their best, they must be interested in what they read. We expose children to a wide variety of authors and books; we read short passages aloud, invite authors to visit, and use reading volunteers. Global students, in particular, often lose interest quickly when taught solely through such analytical approaches as phonics and linguistics.

■ Provide many different opportunities for movement. We think of active learning on four levels. Many classrooms operate at only the first level, but all four are necessary, especially for highly tactile and

kinesthetic learners. Level 1 provides a physical break separate from learning (move to get needed materials, sharpen pencils, get a drink, distribute papers). At Level 2, students may move while they work (play a tape recording, work an overhead projector, stand at a desk, or sit on a rug). At Level 3, students work with manipulatives and games to learn concepts and information. Finally, at Level 4, youngsters engage in real-life or simulated experiences (pantomime, puppets, role playing).

7. Every reading method, strategy, and set of materials is biased in favor of particular reading styles.

No one reading method or set of reading materials is ideal for all students. Some children have many strengths and can learn with practically any reading approach. Others have many weaknesses and need instruction that capitalizes on the strengths they do possess. We use the results of the Reading Style Inventory as a guide for combining and adapting a wide range of reading methods. Those that are inappropriate for a student are quickly replaced so little time is wasted.

Recommendations:

■ Use reading styles strategies with basal readers. Many teachers' manuals prescribe activities for auditory and analytic learners. To make adaptations for global, tactile, and kinesthetic learners, try the following: Provide a human interest story about the author or illustrator, have children pantomime or role-play the story, create vocabulary task cards, or tape record the story. Include humor in your presentation. Give students the choice of working alone, in pairs, or with small groups. Eliminate any stories or workbook pages that children dislike or find boring. When possible, allow students to choose the story they will read.

■ Adapt and combine reading methods when appropriate. Remember, the learner — not the method — is important. Ask very low-level readers to dictate stories of two or three sentences. These very short stories take only a few minutes to record, and they're easy for students to remember and build on. Each day, have students add another "page" to their book and listen several times to their new, expanded story. Include all the stories in the class library for students to share.

8. Successful reading styles programs are student-centered and stress active learning.

They require high levels of organization and management skills. We emphasize organization and management strategies so that children become increasingly independent and teachers become facilitators who provide many minilessons and some whole-class instruction. And, as students enjoy more choices and greater freedom, they learn self-discipline. If they abuse privileges, they lose them until they are able to handle them.

Recommendations:
■ Begin by providing activity-based, multisensory, whole-class lessons. Consider the following model lesson that improves spelling and vocabulary while demonstrating the high motivation levels and excitement produced by activity-based learning: Provide each student with a packet of blank laminated cards and a crayon. Have students write one spelling word on each card and spread the cards out on their desks. Ask them to find a particular word, or synonym or antonym. Students find the word, hold it up toward the teacher, and whisper the word. In a later activity, students might use the word in a sentence and spell it aloud.
■ Develop learning centers that contain clear directions and assessment devices. Learning centers allow controlled movement within a classroom. We develop reading centers that contain reading materials, recorded books, book games, card readers, tape players, and listening areas. Some reading styles schools have schoolwide reading centers. Assessments may take the form of games, writing, artwork, or

oral conferences. Teachers use checklists or charts to schedule students into the center and to manage materials. Student, parent, or grandparent volunteers can help develop materials for the learning centers.

9. Successful reading styles programs are content intensive and require extensive staff development efforts.

We have trained more than 110,000 educators in reading styles philosophy and strategies. Most require training in reading methodology, identifying and matching student strengths, redesigning the classroom environment, and applying and adapting effective reading strategies and management techniques. Reading styles instruction is more than merely adding a few pillows, games, recordings, and a center or two to the classroom. Students' strengths and interests must drive the program. Teachers must have many effective reading strategies at their fingertips, and they must be able to adapt these strategies to the strengths and interests of their students.

Recommendations:
■ Plan for in-depth staff training in reading styles.
■ Continue training and monitor staff progress for at least three years. Teachers and administrators need time to learn new strategies, share successes and failures, develop materials and management techniques, and work with parents. And they need mentors throughout the process. We have found that the change process accelerates considerably when teachers observe and analyze model lessons, develop buddy systems, are assisted by on-site facilitators, make interclass visits, and enjoy the support of administrators.

10. Parental and administrative support is essential for maximum student progress.

The greatest increases in literacy rates occur when the reading styles

approach guides all reading instruction. We provide administrators with the skills they need to organize and develop a successful reading styles program (Carbo 1997a). We also help teachers and administrators work with parents and encourage them to become facilitators and supporters of the reading styles program.

Recommendations:
■ Provide administrators with training in reading styles. The program benefits when administrators become active supporters and facilitators.
■ Help parents understand reading styles. Hold evening sessions for parents. Invite parents to workshops where they can create samples of hands-on materials. The staff at R.E. Baker Elementary (a reading styles model school in Bentonville, Arkansas) started an innovative Saturday Parent University. Topics covered grew out of a parent survey. Teachers provided child care, and parents could attend three of the five 35-minute sessions. Parents learned about their children's reading styles and saw the methods and materials being used to meet the needs of different learners.

We have learned a great deal in our 20 years with the reading styles program. We have learned that children written off as unteachable are capable of learning. When students learn through their strengths, when they gain self-confidence, when teachers believe they can learn and know how to teach them, they can make astonishing gains.

We can have literate citizenry. Reading is well within the power of every young person. And the key to literacy lies in reading styles. That key can unlock the strengths, interests, and abilities of each student. ■

References
Barber, L., M. Carbo, and R. Thomasson. (1994). *A Comparative Study of the Reading Styles Program to Extant Programs of Teaching Reading.* Syosset, N.Y.: National Reading Styles Institute.

Carbo, M. (1982, 1994). *Reading Styles Inventory.* Syosset, N.Y.: National Reading Styles Institute.

Carbo, M. (1989). *How to Record Books for Maximum Reading Gains.* Syosset, N.Y.: National Reading Styles Institute.

Carbo, M. (1996). "Selecting the Right Reading Method." *Teaching K-8* 27, 1: 84, 86-87.

Carbo, M. (1997a). *What Every Principal Should Know About Teaching Reading.* Syosset, N.Y.: National Reading Styles Institute.

Carbo, M. (1997b). "Every Child a Reader." *The American School Board Journal* 184: 33-35. National Reading Styles Institute.

Fair, S. (1982). *The Bedspread.* New York: William Morrow.

Fels, C. (1993). *Rose and Tulip.* Syosset, N.Y.: National Reading Styles Institute.

Gilbert, A. (1977). *Teaching in the Three R's Through Movement Experiences.* New York: Macmillan.

Hart, L. (1983). "Programs, Patterns, and Downshifting in Learning to Read." *The Reading Teacher* 37: 4-11.

Irlen, H. (1991). *Reading by the Colors: Overcoming Dyslexia and Other Reading Disabilities Through the Irlen Method.* Garden Park, N.Y.: Avery Publishing Group, Inc.

Martin, J. (1996). *Sight Words that Stick.* Syosset, N.Y.: National Reading Styles Institute.

Sharmat, M. (1980). *Gregory the Terrible Eater.* New York: Scholastic.

Skipper, B. (1997). "Reading with Style." *The American School Board Journal* 184: 36-37.

Snyder, A. (1994). "On the Road to Reading Recovery." *The School Administrator* 51, 1: 23-24.

Thomasson, R. (1993). *Patterns for Hands-on Learning.* Syosset, N.Y.: National Reading Styles Institute.

Trelease, J. (1989). *The New Read-Aloud Handbook.* New York: Penguin.

Copyright © 1997 by Marie Carbo.

Marie Carbo is Founder and Executive Director of the National Reading Styles Institute, P.O. Box 737, Syosset, NY 11791 (e-mail: nrsi@mindspring.com). Contributors to this article included Beverly Crotts, Karen Floro, Rita Foust, Jill Haney, Meridel Hedges, Cynthia Hernandez, Barbara Hinds, Stephanie Lane, Lois LaShell, Jenette Norton, Kay Pantier, Brenda Perkins, Linda Queiruga, and Rebecca Thomasson.

Voices

When students are able successfully to use all cues available to them as readers and writers, they make amazing gains; I've seen it in my own students' progress. The strategies have proven to be beneficial to all learners, even those who were really struggling. They have provided better access to reading and writing for my advanced students as well. Even I have benefited. As a poor speller, I have noticed how my understanding of the strategies has changed the way I tackle spelling problems.

From *Teaching and Learning Through Multiple Intelligences* by Linda Campbell, Bruce Campbell, and Dee Dickinson. Needham Heights, MA: Allyn & Bacon, 1996.

Dear Parent(s),

This is your child's I CAN READ poetry folder. It is a vital part of your child's reading program as it contains the familiar print from the poems, songs and rhymes we have been learning in our classroom.

Each poem, rhyme, or song is first learned orally. This gives the oral language to call upon when we later connect the poem, song or rhyme to enlarged print during our Shared Reading time. Once the children are familiar with the print, they receive their own individual copy of the passage so that it can be illustrated and added to their notebook. Each week children will add 2-3 new passages to their notebook. By the end of the year your child will successfully read this wonderful collection.

Your child takes home this notebook once a week for reading pleasure and practice. It is helpful if a family member reads the passage first, if needed. That way your child again <u>hears</u> the flow of language and is better able to predict unknown words. A natural part of your child's reading development is memorization. As children practice reading the passages, they continue to recognize more words in print and also gain fluency. It is helpful to guide your child's hand or finger along the print while reading, so the oral language continues to be connected to print.

Children need help with their reading when they are having difficulty. The type of help we give is important. We want to keep children thinking as they are reading and teach them problem-solving strategies when they encounter unknown words.

These reading and thinking strategies include:
- Giving children "think time" to see what they attempt to do themselves.
- Asking children what would make sense there.
- Using the picture to figure the word out.
- Skipping the word and coming back to it, using initial and or final sounds.
- Going back to the beginning of the sentence and trying again after completing the reading.
- Substituting another word that makes sense.
- Telling children the word.

We find the least useful strategy for children (especially beginning readers) is to "sound it out." This stops the flow of the reading process and no longer enables children to read for meaning.

Once you and your child have enjoyed the notebook at home, return it to school the next morning. Please remind your child to return the folder in good condition, and it always needs to be transported to and from school in a bookbag!

Your role as <u>Parents as Partners in Developing Literacy</u> is so appreciated. Due to our work together, your child will celebrate the <u>pleasure</u> and <u>joy</u> in becoming a <u>lifelong</u> reader.

Sincerely,

Kathy Skinner

WEEKLY POETRY ROUTINE

Day One: Introduce new poem. Pass out copies to students and read poem to class. Read chorally and practice using expression. Discuss particular skill using highlighter markers, highlighter tape or crayons and the poem on chart paper.

Day Two: Practice previously introduced poem. Have students read lines or verses individually or by category. ("Read the next verse if you are wearing tennis shoes today.")

Day Three: Introduce new poem following the same routine as day one. Discuss particular skill using overhead projector and "magic" paddle.

Day Four: Review and practice previously introduced poems. Discuss vocabulary and related skills. Have students illustrate both poems.

Day Five: Poetry Theatre. Allow student volunteers to read or recite poems of their choice in front of the class. Give volunteers positive feedback and suggestions for improvement.

Kathy Skinner

Reader's Choice Conference Sheet

NAME: _____

Date	Book Title	Comments

Writing

Step One — Getting Ready

1. Gather materials and references
2. Conference corners, centers, stations
3. Baskets/cart for editing and final copies
4. Permanent files
5. Working files
   - Titles and dates of finished pieces
   - "Things I can do . . ." sheet
   - Five-step editing sheet
6. Status of the class chart
7. Record keeping

Step Two — Getting Ready

1. **Time** — at least 3 hours per week
2. **Ownership**
   - Allow choices
   - Allow to abandon
   - Stay away from deadlines
3. **Response**
   - Listen first!
   - Be courteous and gentle

Writing Workshop

1. **Mini-lesson**
   - Procedures
   - Mechanics/Conventions
   - Craft/Style/Genre
2. **Workshop**
3. **Group Share**

Kathy Skinner

Five-step Editing

1. Did I put spaces between words?
2. Did I use one of these to end a sentence? (. ? !)
3. Did I begin sentences with capital letters?
4. Did I begin peoples', pets' and places' names with capital letters?
5. Did I check my spelling?

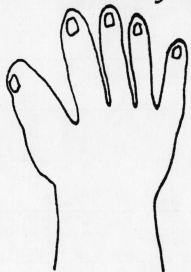

Revising and Editing Marks

_____ take away

∧ add something

≡ capitalize

Things I Can Do As A Writer . . .

- _____
- _____
- _____
- _____
- _____
- _____
- _____
- _____
- _____
- _____
- _____
- _____
- _____
- _____

Kathy Skinner

Finished Pieces/Date

- _____ _____

- _____ _____

- _____ _____

- _____ _____

- _____ _____

- _____ _____

- _____ _____

- _____ _____

- _____ _____

- _____ _____

- _____ _____

- _____ _____

- _____ _____

- _____ _____

Kathy Skinner

Writing Centers

- Dramatic play
- Play dough/clay
- Magnetic ABC letters
- Salt trays
- Shaving cream
- Sandpaper/yarn letters
- Hole punches
- "Sewing" cards
- Paint in baggies
- Paint brushes/H_2O
- Language master
- Chalkboard
- Typewriters

- Drymark board
- Letter/word stamps
- Stencils
- Computer
- Overhead
- Briefcases
- Stationery & postcards
- "Free stuff" books
- Message board
- "Magic" letter
- Triaramas
- Music/poetry

Kathy Skinner

HAVE-A-GO

1ST ATTEMPT	2ND ATTEMPT	STANDARD SPELLING

Self-Evaluation Sheet for Writing

Name: _____ Date: _____

What score do you give this piece of writing? (circle one)

1   2   3   4   5

Why did you give yourself this score?

_____

_____

_____

Would you do anything differently on your next piece of writing?

_____

_____

_____

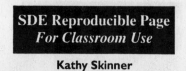

SDE Reproducible Page
For Classroom Use

Kathy Skinner

"The main source of good discipline is growing up in a loving family, being loved and learning to love in return."
_Benjamin Spock

Categories of Families

- Healthy

- Faltering

- Troubled

- Chaotic

Supporting Acceptance

Unique Student of the Week

- names in hat/jar
- poster for each child
- brainstorm as class
- share items for poster
- "unique" privileges
- "I Love Myself" song
  by Jack Hartmann

Feelings Formula

- make chart
- incorporate daily
- model
- encourage use throughout the school day

Feelings Corner

- pillows
- books
- dolls/stuffed animals
- music
- egg cartons
- mini-trampoline
- paper/pencils/crayons

FEELINGS FORMULA

I feel _____

when_____

because_____

and I wish _____

Establish Relationships

Two things these children need:

1. Structure

2. Nurture

Levels of Attachment

Securely attached

Insecurely attached

Poorly attached

Unattached

Recognizing Children
with Attachment Problems

Poor Eye Contact:

Over-Competency:

Withdrawal:

Lack of Self-Awareness:

Chronic Anxiety:

Control Battles:

Aggressive and/or Hyperactive:

Delayed Moral Development:

Indiscriminate Affection:

Cognitive Dysfunction:

Prerequisites to Creating a Safe Environment

Must have a <u>responsible adult</u>!

- Will deal with the moment given to them.

- Ability to respond to the current situation.

- Will see the moment as "an opportunity to teach!"

Must have a <u>loving adult</u>!

- Will focus energy on the positive.

- Will focus on what is wanted instead of what is not wanted.

- Will give to others what is desired within self.

Must have a <u>connected child</u>!

- Will have to establish a school family (community).

- Will have to meet the needs of the children with unmet needs!

Focus is on the Rules

"Fear"

Removal

Obedience

Rules

Consequences

Rejection

Focus is on Community

"Love"

Rules & Consequences

Problem Solvers

Community/Connected

Communication

Acceptance

I Love You Rituals

3 minutes a day/child
Has to be 1:1/building a bond

Time
Place
Name

* Rituals last 30 seconds to one minute

* Approximate bonding is 6-8 weeks

Stages of Bonding

Stage One:
The Ability to look, listen and stay calm
- Calm and relaxed
- Make eye contact
- Focus attention
- Enjoy touch

Stage Two:
Falling in love with you
- Cling on
- Reaches out emotionally
- Looks at face
- Increased interest

Stage Three:
Develops intentional communication
- Wide range of emotions
- More sad than angry
- Initiates fun
- Explores environment

Stage Four:
Emergence of self
- Uses words
- Accepts limits
- Communicates emotions in organized manners
- Recovers from anger quicker

NEEDS

EXTROVERTS

Time with others

Feedback

People to help them think

INTROVERTS

Time alone

Physical space

Time to reflect

Uninterrupted work time

EXTROVERTS

Draw their energy from others.

Talk, share ideas and experiences immediately

They have to tell you all that's happening and will follow you around and keep talking non-stop.

IDENTIFICATION

Gregarious and outgoing

Enjoys others and is energized by a group

Wants to share immediately

Thinks by talking

Talks a lot and easily initiates conversations

Hates being sent to room to be alone and comes to "cheer you up"

Lets you know what she's thinking and feeling

Needs lots of approval

Kathy Skinner

INTROVERTS

Get their energy by being alone or with one or two special people.

Prefer to interact with world on the inside by
reflecting on thoughts and feelings before sharing.

You have to ask questions because they don't readily share information.

IDENTIFICATION

Prefers to watch or listen before joining in

Prefers doing things by self or with best-friend

Becomes grouchy if around people too long

Being with strangers is draining

Doesn't like to discuss days' events until later

Strong sense of personal space

Doesn't mind going to room to sit alone

Difficult to share feelings

Guests or substitutes are "invasive"

May talk a lot with family members but is quieter among outsiders

TEMPERAMENT TRAITS

Intensity

Persistence

Sensitivity

Perceptiveness

Adaptability

Regularity

Energy

First Reaction

Mood

Kathy Skinner

Old Negative Labels | New Exciting Labels

Old Negative Labels	New Exciting Labels
Manipulative	Charismatic
Impatient	Compelling
Anxious	Cautious
Explosive	Dramatic
Picky	Selective
Whiny	Analytical
Distractible	Perceptive
Stubborn	Assertive, a willingness to persist in the face of difficulties
Nosy	Curious
Wild	Energetic
Extreme	Tenderhearted
Inflexible	Traditional
Demanding	Holds high standards
Unpredictable	Flexible, a creative problem solver
Loud	Enthusiastic and zestful
Argumentative	Opinionated, strongly committed to one's goals

Kathy Skinner

Teaching Tips:

EXTROVERTS:

Your extroverted child needs other people to help her recharge.

Provide her with lots of feedback.

Spend time talking with her to help her think through problems.

Understand that her need for people and feedback is not a reflection of low self-esteem.

INTROVERTS:

Make sure your introverted child has an opportunity to pull out of the action and refuel by being alone.

Help your child to understand that she needs space and can ask for it without pushing others away.

Allow your introverted child time to think before you expect a response.

Avoid interrupting her when she is working.

Kathy Skinner

Poetry Anthology

- *Once Upon Ice and Other Frozen Poems* selected by Jane Yolen

- *The Gooch Machine - Poems for Children to Perform* by Brod Bagert

- *Fathers, Mothers, Sisters, Brothers* by Mary Ann Hoberman

- *Flamingo Knees* by Carolyn Lesser

- *Good Books, Good Times!* selected by Lee Bennett Hopkins

- *Something Big Has Been Here* by Jack Prelutsky

- *Sweet Dreams of the Wild - Poems for Bedtime* by Rebecca Kai Dotlich

- *The Sun Is Up - A Child's Year of Poems* compiled by William Jay Smith and Carol Ra

- *The Sky Is Not So Far Away - Night Poems for Children* by Margaret Hillert

- *Sun Through the Window* by Marci Ridlon

- *Joyful Noise - Poems for Two Voices* by Paul Fleischman

- *A Small Treasury of Easter Poems and Prayers* illustrated by Susan Spellma

- *A Jar of Tiny Stars - Poems by NCTE Award-Winning Poets* selected by children

- *Mother Earth Father Sky - Poems of Our Planets* selected by Jane Yolen

- *Sky Scrape/City Scrape - Poems of City Life* selected by Jane Yolen

- *Come Play With Me* by Margaret Hillert

- *Don't Read This Book, Whatever You Do! - More Poems About School* by Kalli Dakos

- *If You're Not Here, Please Raise Your Hand - Poems About School* by Kalli Dakos

- *Yo!Yes?* by Chris Raschka

- *A Thousand Cousins - Poems of Family Life* by David L. Harrison

- *I Never Said I Wasn't Difficult* by Sara Holbrook

- *The Dog Ate My Homework* by Sara Holbrook

© Kathy Skinner, Educational Consultant

Recommended Reading

Professional and Personal Growth

- *There's Gotta Be A Better Way . . . Discipline That Works* by Dr. Becky Bailey
- *I Love You Rituals* by Dr. Becky Bailey
- *Punished by Rewards* by Alfie Kohn
- *Raising Your Spirited Child* by Mary Sheedy Kurcinka
- *Good Morning Class - I Love You!* by Esther Wright
- *Endangered Minds . . . Why Children Don't Think and What We Can Do About It* by Jane M. Healy, Ph.D.
- *A Celebration of Neurons . . . An Educator's Guide to the Human Brain* by Robert Sylwester
- *Please Understand Me . . . Character and Temperament Types* by David Keirsey and Marilyn Bates
- *Spel . . . Is A Four-Letter Word* by Richard Gentry
- *Hey! Listen To This . . .* by Jim Trelease
- *The Celestine Prophecy* by James Redfield
- *The Universal Schoolhouse* by James Moffett
- *A Return to Love* by Marianne Williamson
- *Real Magic* by Dr. Wayne W. Dyer
- *Conversations With God* by Neale Donald Walsch
- *Homecoming* by John Bradshaw
- *Creating Love* by John Bradshaw
- *The Seven Spiritual Laws of Success* by Deepak Chopra
- *Perfect Health* by Deepak Chopra

Educational Strategies and Techniques

- *Invitations* by Regie Routman
- *Write on Target* by Cindy Merrilees and Pam Haack
- *Spinning Inward . . . Using Guided Imagery with Children for Learning, Creativity and Relaxation* by Maureen Murdock
- *In the Middle . . . Writing, Reading, and Learning With Adolescents* by Nancie Atwell
- *The Foundations of Literacy* by Don Holdaway
- *The Whole Story* by Brian Cambourne

ADD and ADHD

- *ADD* by Glen Hunsucker
- *Driven to Distraction* by Edward M. Hallowell, MD and John J. Ratey, MD
- *Why Johnny Can't Concentrate* by Robert A. Moss, MD

Components of a Balanced Literacy Curriculum

Reading to Children

Language Experience

Shared Reading

Guided Reading

Independent Reading

Writing

Sharing Responses

Kathryn L. Cloonan

Daily Schedule

8:50 Welcome
"Base Groups" — Getting Organized
Teacher — attendance / lunch money, etc.
Managers — Book check, snack table
Independent Writing / Independent Study

9:20 Morning Meeting

9:35 Super Readers

9:45 Literature Block
Shared Reading

Writer's Workshop
mini-lesson
writers' write
teacher conferencing

10:15 Guided Writing

10:30 Recess

10:45 Language Arts Block
Small Group Instruction
Interest or needs or skills

| Morning Centers | Literature |
| Buddy Reading | Extension |

11:45 Story / Songs / Book Talk

12:00 Lunch / Recess

12:30 Read Aloud

12:45 Math

Math Centers
and small group instruction

1:15 Thematic Study   Science / Social Studies

2:00 Art / Music / P.E.

2:30 Open Centers

3:00 Clean Up / Songs / Story / Discuss the Day

3:20

Kathryn L. Cleonan

Steps in a Literature Block

By Kathryn L. Cloonan

1. **Setup / Background / Semantic Mapping**

2. **Share a piece of literature . . .**
   Story — oral as well as written
   Song
   Flip Chart
   String Story
   Big Book
   Flannel Board Story
   Student Made Book

3. **Personalize It**   **READ IT!**

4. **Put It Into Print**   **READ IT!**

5. **Model It**   **READ IT!**

6. **Expand It — Recreate It**
   Big Book or Class Book
   Mini Books
   Puppets
   Bulletin Board Stories
   Mobiles
   Wall Stories
   Overhead Transparency Stories
   Tutorette Stories
   Masks, Plays, Etc.
   Innovations

7. **Make the Writing Connection**
   Slot Stories
   Signs
   Posters
   Letters to a Character in the Story
   Letter to the Author
   "News" Article
   Adding Another Chapter
      Different Ending, etc.
   Writing Their Own Stories

Kathryn L. Cloonan

Concepts of Print

1. Displays book handling skills
2. Can tell letters from words
3. Has left to right directionality
4. Has some letter / sound connection
5. Knows where to start on a page
6. Can do one-to-one matching

Reading Strategies

1. **Semantic — meaning**
   Illustrations
   Prior knowledge
   Context of the sentence

2. **Syntactic — the structure of our language**

3. **Graphophonics — phonics**
   Letter / sound connections
   Rhyming words

Supportive Features of Text

Emergent Reading Materials

1. Consistent placement of text
2. Illustrations clearly match text
3. Simple vocabulary using children's natural language
4. Rhythm, rhyme, and repetition
5. Text parallels developmental stages of writing

Early Reading Materials

1. Longer sentence length
2. Book language
3. Variety of genres
4. Pictures enhance but do not consistently match text
5. Less repetition

Fluent Reading Materials

1. Short chapters
2. Increased variety of genres
3. Encourage integrating / utilizing many strategies
4. Encourage development of reading interests
5. Move the reader toward greater independence

Kathryn L. Cloonan

Steps to Guided Reading
for Emergent Readers

1. Select the text

    What are the needs of the children?

    Will the children have a high level of success?

    Does this book support their growth in skills and strategies?

2. Prepare ahead of time

    Look at illustrations.

    Plan the questioning.

3. Setting the scene

    Talk about the cover, author and illustrator.

4. Do a "Picture Walk"

    Read the title page.

    Talk through the illustrations.

5. Let the children read the text.

6. Return to the text.

    Discuss the story.

    Invite them to read their favorite page.

    Have children reread story in pairs.

7. Respond to the text.

    Discussion

    Reread

    Respond with writing, dramatization or arts and crafts.

Kathryn L. Cloonan

Steps to Guided Reading with Early Readers

1. Select the text

2. Prepare ahead of time
   Look at illustrations.
   Plan the questioning.

3. Set the scene
   Discuss cover, author and illustrator.
   Semantic / cognitive mapping.

4. Do a "Word Walk"
   Use 'focused questioning'.
   Students 'dip into the text'.
   Read text to find answers and confirm by reading section orally.

5. Review "How can you figure it out?"

6. Students read the story individually.

7. Return to the text.
   Discuss the story.
   Invite them to read their favorite page.
   Have children reread story in pairs.

Kathryn L. Cloonan

Guided Reading for Fluent Readers

Steps:

1. Story introduction
2. Silent reading / occasionally whisper reading
3. Discussion
4. Follow-up activity

Strategy Coaching:

Focus on self-correcting

Focus on cross-checking

Focus on self-monitoring

Kathryn L. Cloonan

Getting Ready for Literature Circles

1. Read the pages you agreed to AHEAD of time.

2. Bring your book folder with you to 'Circles'.

3. Keep track of unusual words on your chart.

4. Put 'flags' by at least two parts you would like your group to discuss such as:
   * part that you liked the best
   * part that surprised you
   * part that was most exciting
   * part that was confusing
   * * _____

5. Write two questions or comments to present to your group.

Kathryn L. Cloonan

Julie's Picture

M	Meaning (Semantics)
S	Structure (Syntax)
V	Visual (Graphophonic)

✓ ✓ ✓ ✓
Julie painted a picture.

✓ *paints* ✓ ✓
She painted a face.

✓ ✓ ✓
She painted eyes.

✓ ✓ ✓ ✓ *mouth*
She painted a big smile.

✓ ✓ *like* ✓
She painted long hair.

✓ ✓ ✓ ✓ ✓
Julie looked at her picture.

✓ ✓ ✓ *painting* ✓ ✓ ✓
It was a picture of her mom!

✓ ✓ ✓ ✓ ✓
Julie took the picture home
after school.

That ✓ ✓ ✓ ✓ ✓ ✓
"This is for you, Mom," said Julie.

✓ ✓ ✓ ✓ ✓ ✓ ✓
"It's me!" said Mom. "Thank you, Julie!"

Kathryn L. Cloonan

238

Running Record Analysis

Name _____ Date _____ Age _____

Text _____ Level _____ Seen / Unseen

Running Words: _____ Accuracy: $\dfrac{\text{Success}}{\text{Running}}$ x 100 = ⬚ _____ %

Self Corrections: _____ SC Rate: _____

Strategies Used:

Strategies to Coach:

Comprehension:

M.	Meaning	
S.	Syntax	
V.	Visual	

Continuous Running Record Summary

Name _____ Date _____

Date	Title	Level	Seen/ Unseen	Accuracy	S.C.	Comment

"Sing Me a Story, Read Me a Song"

Monday:
1. Teacher introduces a new song on a chart.
2. Sing together
3. Children each get a copy of the song to go in their own books called "Sing That Again".

Tuesday:
1. Teacher introduces the (same) song.
2. Sing together
3. Read together
4. Children illustrate their song.

Wednesday:
1. Sing together
2. Read together
3. Invite a "Leader Reader"
4. "Text Talk" — Discuss skills, pattern, or mechanics. Children can read their songs to a partner and play "Can you find".

Thursday:
1. Sing together
2. "Leader Readers"
3. "Text Talk"
4. Children highlight pattern or skill in their own book. Children take their "Sing That Again" books home to read.

Friday:
1. Sing together
2. "Leader Reader"
3. Plan together — Plan innovations, Big Books or mini-books

Kathryn L. Cloonan

SING ME A STORY — READ ME A SONG

INTEGRATING MUSIC INTO THE WHOLE LANGUAGE CLASSROOM
By Kathryn L. Cloonan

PURPOSE

1. Instill a love for reading and music.
2. Make use of simple, delightful materials that have rhythm, rhyme, repetition.
3. To give children early successes in reading.
4. Give children an opportunity to make the connection between print and what they say and sing.
5. Build sight vocabulary by frequently seeing words in meaningful, predictable context.
6. Enrich decoding/reading skills through meaningful print.

STEPS

SHARE IT — Sing Lots of Songs Often
PRINT IT — Print a Favorite on Chart Paper
ILLUSTRATE IT — Make a Big Book, Make Mini Books
READ IT — Let the Children Read It

RESOURCES

Record and Tapes

Sing Me a Story, Read Me A Song, Kathryn Cloonan
Whole Language Holidays — Stories, Chants and Songs, Kathryn Cloonan
Peter, Paul and Mommy, Peter, Paul and Mary
Elephant Show Record, Sharon, Lois and Bram
Special Delivery, Fred Penner
The Cat Came Back, Fred Penner
Learning Basic Skills Through Music, Hap Palmer
We All Live Together, Volumes 1, 2, 3 & 4, Greg Scelse and Steve Millang
Doing the Dinosaur Rock, Diane Butchelor
You'll Sing a Song and I'll Sing a Song, Ella Jenkins
Singable Songs for the Very Young, Raffi
More Singable Songs for the Very Young, Raffi

Resource Books

Sing Me a Story, Read Me a Song, Book I, Kathryn Cloonan. Rhythm & Reading Resources, 1991.
Sing Me a Story, Read Me a Song, Book II, Kathryn Cloonan, 1991.
Whole Language Holidays, Books I and II, Kathryn Cloonan. Rhythm & Reading Resources.

SONGS

WE HAVE A FRIEND

We have a friend and
her name is Amy
Amy is her name
Hello, Amy-Hello, Amy
Hello, Amy
We're so glad you're here.
Innovation:
    Change names of children

TWINKLE TWINKLE LITTLE STAR

Twinkle, twinkle little star
How I wonder what you are.
Up above the world so high.
Like a diamond in the sky.
Twinkle, twinkle little star
How I wonder what you are.

HICKORY, DICKORY DOCK

Hickory, Dickory Dock
The mouse ran up the clock
The clock struck one
The mouse ran down
Hickory, Dickory Dock
Innovations:
    The clock struck 2, 3, 4, etc.

BAA, BAA, BLACK SHEEP

Baa, Baa Black Sheep
Have you any wool?
Yes sir, yes sir three bags full.

One for my master
One for the dame
One for the little boy
that lives down the lane.

Baa, Baa, Black Sheep
Have you any wool?
Yes sir, yes sir three bags full.
Innovation:
    Color Words
    Baa, Baa, Purple sheep, etc.

BINGO

There was a farmer
Had a dog and Bingo was his name-o.
B I N G O
B I N G O
B I N G O
And Bingo was his name-o.

ON A SPIDER'S WEB

One elephant went out to play
On a spider's web one day.
He had such enormous fun
He asked another elephant to come.

Two elephants went out to play
On a spider's web one day.
They had such enormous fun
They asked another elephant to come.

Three elephants, four elephants,
Five elephants, six elephants,
Seven elephants, eight elephants,
Nine elephants................

Ten elephants went out to play
They had such enormous fun
They asked everyone to come.
Innovations: Change with theme or holidays — black cat, Christmas elf, leprechaun, dinosaur, Panda bear, etc.

FIVE SPECKLED FROGS

Five green and speckled frogs
Sat on a speckled log
Eating the most delicious bugs.
    YUM!   YUM!
One jumped into the pool
where it was nice and cool
Then there were four green speckled frogs.
Four...etc., Three...etc.,
Two...etc., One...etc.
Then there were NO green speckled frogs.

Kathryn L. Cloonan

THE WHEELS ON THE BUS

The Wheels on the bus go
    round and round
    round and round
    round and round
The wheels on the bus go
    round and round
All through the town.
Innovations:
1. doors . . . open and shut
2. children . . . up and down
3. wipers . . . swish, swish, swish
4. babies . . . wah, wah, wah
5. snakes . . . Sss, Sss, Sss
6. bears . . . growl, growl, growl, etc.

I KNOW AN OLD LADY

I know an old lady who swallowed a fly
I don't know why she swallowed a fly . . .
perhaps she'll die.

I know an old lady who swallowed a
    spider
(that wiggled and jiggled and tickled
    inside her)
She swallowed the spider to catch the fly
But I don't know why she swallowed
    the fly
perhaps she'll die.

I know an old lady who swallowed a bird
She swallowed the bird to catch the spider
(that wiggled and jiggled and tickled
    inside her)
She swallowed the spider to catch the fly
But I don't know why she swallowed
    a fly
perhaps she'll die.

I know an old lady who swallowed a cat
She swallowed the cat to catch the bird
She swallowed the bird to catch the spider
(that wiggled and jiggled and tickled
    inside her)
She swallowed the spider to catch the
    fly
But I don't know why she swallowed
    the fly
perhaps she'll die.

I know an old lady who swallowed a dog
She swallowed the dog to catch the cat
She swallowed the cat to catch the bird
She swallowed the bird to catch the spider
(that wiggled and jiggled and tickled
    inside her)
She swallowed the spider to catch the fly
But I don't know why she swallowed
    the fly
perhaps she'll die.

I know an old lady who swallowed a goat
She swallowed the goat to catch the dog
She swallowed the dog to catch the cat
She swallowed the cat to catch the bird
She swallowed the bird to catch the spider

(that wiggled and jiggled and tickled
    inside her)
She swallowed the spider to catch the fly
But I don't know why she swallowed the
    fly
perhaps she'll die.

I know an old lady who swallowed a horse
She's Full, of course!
Innovations: Change the animals she
    swallowed

TEN IN THE BED

There were ten in the bed
And the little one said,
"Roll over, Roll over"
So they all rolled over and one fell out
    And they gave a little scream
    And they gave a little shout

Please remember to tie a knot in your
    pajamas
Single beds were only made for
1, 2, 3, 4, 5, 6, 7, 8
Nine in the bed, etc.
Eight etc., Seven etc.
Six-five-four-three-two . . . etc.
One in the bed and the little one said,
"I've got the whole mattress to myself"
(repeat last line three more times)
    GOOD-NIGHT!

LITTLE COTTAGE IN THE WOODS

"Little cottage in the woods (Touch
fingertips of both hands together to
form a triangle shape for the house.)
"Little man by the window stood."
(Form "glasses" shapes with forefinger
and thumb of each hand making a
circle — put hands up to eyes in that
shape, against face.) "Saw a rabbit
hopping by" (Make rabbit "ears" by two
fingers held up on one hand and "hop"
them about.) "Frightened as could be."
(Arms held across chest "shake" in mock
fear.) "Help me, help me, help me, he
said." (Raise arms overhead and down
several times.) "Before the hunter shoots
me dead: (Form "guns" with forefingers
and "shoot.") "Come little rabbit, come
inside" (Beckon with hand.) "And happy
we will be." (Stroke the back of one hand
with the other as though tenderly petting
a rabbit.)

LITTLE SKUNK

Oh! I stuck my head in a little skunk's
hole — and the little skunk said, "God
bless your soul." Take it out! Take it out!
Remove it! But I didn't take it out and the
little skunk said, "If you don't take it out

Kathryn L. Cloonan

you'll wish you had." Take it out! Take it
out! Psssss — I removed it.

MICHAEL FINNAGIN

There once was a man named Michael
    Finnagin
He had whiskers on his chin-a-gain
The wind came along and blew them
    in-again
Poor old Michael Finnagin . . . begin-
    again.

There once was a man named Michael
    Finnagin
He went fishing with a pin-again
Caught a whale that pulled him in-again
Poor old Michael Finnagin . . . begin-
    again.

There once was a man named Michael
    Finnagin
He was fat and then grew thin-again
Ate so much he had to begin again
Poor old Michael Finnagin . . . begin-
    again

TINY TIM

I had a little turtle,
His name was Tiny Tim
I put him in the bathtub
To see if he could swim.
He drank up all the water.
He ate up all the soap.
And now he's home sick in bed
With a bubble in his throat.

THE ANTS GO MARCHING

The ants go marching one by one
Hurrah! Hurrah!
The ants go marching one by one
Hurrah! Hurrah!
The ants go marching one by one
the little one stops to suck his thumb
And they all go marching down —
into the ground — to get out — of the
rain —
BOOM, BOOM, BOOM, BOOM,
BOOM, BOOM, BOOM, BOOM,
two by two . . . tie his shoe
three by three . . . climb a tree
four by four . . . shut the door
five by five . . . jump and dive
six by six . . . pick up sticks
seven by seven . . . wave to heaven
eight by eight . . . climb the gate
nine by nine . . . look behind
ten by ten . . . pat a hen

GOOD-BYE

We have a friend and her name is Amy,
Amy is her name. Good-bye, Amy,
    good-bye Amy
Good-bye, Amy, we'll see you tomorrow.
Innovation: Change names of children.

243

HOLIDAY SONGS

TRICK OR TREAT

They'll be Trick or Treating here on
Halloween, **Trick or Treat!**
They'll be Trick or Treating here on
Halloween, **Trick or Treat!**
They'll be Trick or Treating here,
They'll be Trick or Treating here,
They'll be Trick or Treating here on
Halloween, **Trick or Treat!**

2. They'll be knocking at our doors on
Halloween, **Knock! Knock!**
3. Ghosts will all go "Boo!" on Halloween, **Booooooooo!**
4. Black cats all meow on Halloween,
Meeeeeeeeeeow!
5. We will all have fun on Halloween,
Hurray!

ONCE I HAD A PUMPKIN

Once I had a pumpkin, a pumpkin, a
pumpkin
Once I had a pumpkin with no face at all.
With no eyes and no nose and no mouth
and no teeth.
Once I had a pumpkin with no face at all.

Then I made a Jack-o-Lantern, Jack-o-
Lantern, Jack-o-Lantern.
Then I made a Jack-o-Lantern . . . with
a big funny face.
With big eyes and a big nose and a big
mouth and big teeth.
Then I made a Jack-o-Lantern . . . with
a big funny face.

DOG HAIR STEW

© 1991 Kathryn L. Cloonan

Ten black cats were left by themselves
on Halloween night with nothing to do.
So they decided to make their own
Dog Hair Stew.

First they got a very large pot
And filled it with water that was
extremely hot.
Their goal was to make a horrible brew
More horrible even, than last year's stew.

Cat #1 flicked his tail in a wave
And said, "Here's some slime from a
nearby cave."
"And here's some juice from a
skunkweed plant."
Said Cat #2 as he joined in the chant.

Cat #3 said, "Heh, Heh, wait till you see
what I brought.
The eyes of two dead fish I finally got!"
"Let me add some bat liver oil,"
meowed Cat #4,
A skinny cat named "Skin and Bones."

Cat #5 said, "Here's a couple of frogs
and a snake.
This is my very favorite stew to make."
One by one the cats came by
Adding secret ingredients with a meow
and a cry.

The oldest cat carefully stirred it round
and round
While the fire crackled with an ominous
sound.
The 10th cat hissed with eyes aglow,
"Here's the hair of a dog so stir it in
slow."

Now the cats they pranced and danced
around their Dog Hair Stew
Then drank every drop of their mysterious brew.
Then all at once the cats gave a very
loud wail
And their hair stood up straight from
their head to their tail.

"Happy spooky Halloween!", they said
with a wink,
"Dog Hair Stew is our favorite drink!"
And for the rest of the year
They had nothing to fear . . .

For each time a dog was seen,
Their hair stood up straight and they
looked so mean
Not a dog would dare
give them a scare.

And the cats would wink an eye and
say,
A little Dog Hair Stew on Halloween
day
Keeps even the meanest dogs away.

SCAT THE CAT

I'm Scat the Cat
I'm sassy and fat
And I can change my colors
Just like that! (Snap)

THIS IS THE CANDLE

This is the candle
This is the candle
That glowed in the jack-o-lantern.

This is the mouse
That lit the candle
That glowed in the jack-o-lantern.

This is the cat
That chased the mouse
That lit the candle
That glowed in the jack-o-lantern.

This is the ghost
That said "BOO!" to the cat
That chased the mouse
That lit the candle
That glowed in the jack-o-lantern.

This is the moon
That shown on the ghost
That said "BOO!" to the cat
That chased the mouse
That lit the candle
That glowed in the jack-o-lantern.
That shouted "Happy Halloween!"

ONE LITTLE SKELETON

One little skeleton, hopping up and
down
One little skeleton, hopping up and
down
One little skeleton, hopping up and
down
For this is Halloween!

2. Two little bats, flying through the air.
3. Three little pumpkins, walking in a
row.
4. Four little goblins, skipping down
the street.♪
5. Five little ghosties, popping in and out.

FIVE LITTLE PUMPKINS

Five little pumpkins sitting on a gate.
The first one said, "My, it's getting late!"
The second one said, "There are bats in
the air".
The third one said, "I don't care!"
The fourth one said, "Let's run, let's run."
The fifth one said, "Halloween is fun!"
OOOOOOOOOOOO went the wind.
Clap out went the lights.
And five little pumpkins rolled out of
sight.

BRAVE LITTLE PILGRIM

The brave little Pilgrim went looking for
a bear.
He looked in the woods and everywhere.
The brave little Pilgrim found a big bear.
He ran like a rabbit! Oh! what a scare!

FIVE FAT TURKEYS

Five fat turkeys are we.
We slept all night in a tree
When the cook came around
We couldn't be found

Let's fly to the tallest tree
There we'll be safe as safe can be.
From the cook and the oven you see
It surely pays on Thanksgiving days
To sleep in the tallest trees!!

244

Kathryn L. Cloonan

WE WISH YOU A MERRY CHRISTMAS

We wish you a Merry Christmas
We wish you a Merry Christmas
We wish you a Merry Christmas
and a Happy New Year!

Let's all do a little jumping
Let's all do a little jumping
Let's all do a little jumping
and spread Christmas cheer.

Let's all do a little twirling
Let's all do a little twirling
Let's all do a little twirling
and spread Christmas cheer.

We wish you a Merry Christmas
We wish you a Merry Christmas
We wish you a Merry Christmas
and a Happy New Year!

S.A.N.T.A.

There was a man who had a beard.
   and Santa was his name-o.
S.A.N.T.A.
S.A.N.T.A.
S.A.N.T.A.
And Santa was his name-o!

There was a man who had a beard.
   and Santa was his name-o.
S.A.N.T.Ho!
S.A.N.T.Ho!
S.A.N.T.Ho!
And Santa was his name-o!

(Leave off one more letter and replace it
with a "Ho" until the final verse is "Ho,
Ho, Ho, Ho, Ho.")

FIVE LITTLE REINDEER

Five little reindeer prancing up and down
Five little reindeer prancing up and down
Five little reindeer prancing up and down
For Christmas time is near.

2. Four little Santa elves trimming up a
tree . . .

3. Three little jingle bells ring, ring,
ringing . . .

4. Two little snowflakes twirling in the
night . . .

5. One little sleigh speeding through the
snow . . .

MY DREIDEL

I have a little dreidel.
I made it out of clay.
And when it's dry and ready
My "dreidel" I shall play.

chorus
Oh dreidel, dreidel, dreidel
Oh little top that spins
The children all are happy
When Hanukkah begins.

My dreidel's always playful
It loves to spin all day.
A happy game of dreidel
My friends and I shall play
(repeat chorus)

OH VALENTINE!
© 1991 Cloonan

Oh Valentine! Oh Valentine!
I hope that you'll be mine.
I took my time and wrote this rhyme
Especially for you.

Oh! Valentine! Oh! Valentine!
I hope that you'll be mine.
With crayons, paper, and some glue
I've made this card for you.
Oh Valentine! Oh Valentine!
I hope you'll be mine.
And on this very special day
There's just one thing to say . . .
"I love you!"
"Happy Valentine's Day!"

HERE'S A LETTER

Here's a letter, here's a letter.
One for you.
One for you.
Guess what's in the letter.
Guess what's in the letter.
I love you!
I love you!
(Verses two & three are done in a round)

ONE LEPRECHAUN WENT OUT TO PLAY

One leprechaun went out to play
On a bright St. Patrick's day.
He had such enormous fun
He asked another leprechaun to come.

Two leprechauns went out to play
On a bright St. Patrick's day.
They had such enormous fun
They asked another leprechaun to come.

Three, four, five, six, seven, eight, nine

Ten leprechauns went out to play
On a bright St. Patrick's day.
They had such enormous fun
They asked everyone to come!

LITTLE PETER RABBIT

Little Peter Rabbit
Had a fly upon his nose.
Little Peter Rabbit
Had a fly upon his nose.

Little Peter Rabbit
Had a fly upon his nose.

And he swished until it flew away.
(repeat)

Kathryn L. Cloonan

"Sing That Again"

HEY THERE NEIGHBOR!
Hey there, neighbor!
What do you say?
It's going to be a wonderful day!
Clap your hands and boogie on down.
Give 'em a bump and pass it around!
(or sit on down)

HI! MY NAME IS JOE!
Hi! My name is Joe and I work in the button
(doughnut) factory.
I have a wife, a dog, and a family!
One day my boss came to me and said,
"Hey Joe, are you busy?"
I said, "No."
He said, "Well, then work with your right hand."
• Repeat each time adding one more body part: left
hand, right foot, left foot, head
Last line, last time:
I said, "YES!!!"

TONY CHESTNUT
Toe knee chestnut
Nose eye love you.
Toe knee nose.
Toe knee nose.
Toe knee chestnut nose I love you . . .
That's what toe knee nose.

HI DE HAY! HI DEE HO!
Leader: *Hi dee hay! Hi dee ho!*
Group: **Hi dee hay! Hi dee ho!**
Leader: *Igglee wigglee wogglee wo!*
Group: **Igglee wigglee wogglee wo!**
Leader: *Raise your voices to the sky.*
Group: **Raise your voices to the sky.**
Leader: *Mrs. _____'s class is walking by*
Group: **Mrs. _____'s class is walking by.**
Leader: *Count off!*
Group: **1, 2, 3, 4, 5**
Leader: *Break it on down now!*
Group: **6, 7, 8, 9, 10 . . .**
Leader: *Let's do it all once again!*

RISE RUBY RISE!
Down in the valley two by two.
Down in the valley two by two.
Down in the valley two by two.
Rise Ruby Rise!

2nd verse:
We can do it your way two by two.
We can do it your way two by two.
We can do it your way two by two.
Rise Ruby Rise!

3rd verse:
We can do it my way two by two.
We can do it my way two by two.
We can do it my way two by two.
Rise Ruby Rise!

Mr. Rhythm and Rhyme
1. Mr. Jingle, Mr. Jangle, Mr. Rhythm and Rhyme
   I woke up this morning, I was feeling so fine.
   I went to my mother and my mother said,
   "You've got the rhythm in your head?"   tap tap
   I've got the rhythm in my head!   tap tap
   You've got the rhythm in your head!   tap tap
   We've all got the rhythm in our heads.   tap tap
2. hands   clap clap
3. hips   woo woo
4. feet   stamp stamp
5. Mr. Jingle, Mr. Jangle, Mr. Rhythm and Rhyme
   I woke up this morning, I was feeling so fine.
   I went to my mother and my mother said,
   "See if you can do it quiet instead."   shh! shh!
                                           stamp stamp
                                           woo woo
                                           clap clap
                                           tap tap
                                           shh! shh!
                                             shh! shh!

Sing That Again is available in both instrumental and vocals versions.

Kathryn L. Cloonan • 5125 N. Amarillo Drive • Beverly Hills, FL 34465

Kathryn L. Cloonan

"Sing That Again"

I THINK YOU'RE WONDERFUL
(R & K Grammer)

(Refrain)
I think you're wonderful.
When somebody says that to me,
I feel wonderful,
as wonderful as can be.
It makes me want to say
the same thing to somebody new.
And by the way I've been meaning to say
I think you're wonderful, too.

1. When we practice this phrase
   in the most honest way,
   Find something special
   in someone each day.
   We lift up the world
   one heart at a time.
   It all starts by saying
   this one simple line . . . Refrain

2. When each one of us
   feels important inside
   loving and giving and
   glad we're alive,
   Oh! what a difference
   we'll make in each day.
   All because someone
   decided to say . . . Refrain

* I'M BEING SWALLOWED BY A BOA CONSTRICTOR
(Silverstein)

I'm being swallowed by a boa constrictor
I'm being swallowed by a boa constrictor
I'm being swallowed by a boa constrictor
And I don't like it very much.

Oh, No! Oh, No! He's up to my toe
He's up to my toe, Oh Gee! Oh Gee!
He's up to my knee, he's up to my knee.
Oh fiddle! Oh fiddle! He's up to my middle!
He's up to my middle. Oh Heck! Oh Heck!
He's up to my neck, he's up to my neck!
Oh Dread! Oh Dread! He's up to my _____ slurp!

* A TEEPEE IS MY HOME
A teepee is my home.
Of deerskins it is made.
A place on top where smoke can go.
It stands in forest shade.
The river runs nearby.
And there is my canoe.
I paddle up and down the stream.
Beneath the sky of blue.

GOOD MORNING!!
Leader: *Good Morning!*
Group: **Good Morning!**
Leader: *How are you?*
Group: **How are you?**
Leader:
  It's so nice to see you again.
  With a one and a two and a How-do-you-do.
  DING-DONG
  It's so nice to see you again.
Leader: *Here's _____*
Group: **Hi _____**
Leader: *Here's _____*
Group: **Hi _____**
Leader: *Here's _____*
Group: **Hi _____**

All Together:
  It's so nice to see you again.
  With a one and a two and a How-do-you-do.
  DING-DONG
  It's so nice to see you again.

Leader: *Here's _____*
Group: **Hi _____**
Leader: *Here's _____*
Group: **Hi _____**
Leader: *Here's _____*
Group: **Hi _____**

All Together:
  It's so nice to see you again.
  With a one and a two and a How-do-you-do.
  It's so nice to see you again.
  It's so nice to see you again.

WADDALEE ACHEE

Waddalee Achee
Waddalee Achee

Doodle lee doo
Doodle lee doo (repeat)

It's the simplest song
There isn't much to it.
All you have to do is
Doodle lee doo it.

I know the rest
But the part I like best
Is the doodle lee
Doodle lee — doo!
Woo!

Sing That Again is available in both instrumental and vocal versions.
Kathryn L. Cloonan • 5125 N. Amarillo Drive • Beverly Hills, FL 34465

* Available on SING ME A STORY, READ ME A SONG
▲▲ Available on WHOLE LANGUAGE HOLIDAYS

Kathryn L. Cloonan

247

"Time to get up!"

said the _____

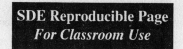
Kathryn L. Cloonan

248

Tattletale Application

Name _____   Boy ☐   Girl ☐

Address _____   _____

_____

_____   How old are you? _____ years

Grade _____   Teacher _____

School _____   Favorite Color _____

Four (4) nice things about _____

1. _____

2. _____

3. _____

4. _____

Writer's Lists

What are you an expert on?

1. _____

2. _____

3. _____

4. _____

What would you be willing to teach someone else?

1. _____

2. _____

3. _____

4. _____

What would you like to learn more about?

1. _____

2. _____

3. _____

4. _____

Kathryn L. Cloonan

Writer's Checklist

Yes, I can . . .

Dates checked

Draw a picture and tell about it.						
Draw a picture and write letters.						
Begin to leave spaces between words.						
Write the first letters in words.						
Write the first and last letters in words.						
Write some middle letters.						
Write some whole words.						

Write sentences.						
Put a period at the end of a sentence.						
Start a sentence with a capital letter.						
Use "super words"						
Give a story a title.						

Use a capital I for myself.						
Use . , ? or ! at the end of a sentence.						
Capitalize the first letter of a name.						
Spell some / most words correctly.						
Proof read my writing.						
Fix some mistakes.						
Find dictionary spelling for some words.						
Use spelling dictionary to correct words.						
Use quotation marks.						
Write paragraphs.						
"Rewrite" to make my best better.						
Write many different types of stories.						

Benefits	Process	Purpose

Writing

Encourages self-expression
Makes letter-sound connections
Builds fluency in ideas

Getting great ideas down on paper

Conference I

Makes the connection between their ideas and the printed word
Supports inventive spelling / corrective spelling

Communicating ideas
Learning new skills in
- phonics
- decoding skills
- grammar
- spelling
- punctuation
- sight words

Conference II

Builds self-confidence by acceptance
Enhances creativity
Increases communication skills through making choices and decisions

Creating, planning, and expressing ideas for a finished product

Publishing

Encourages further efforts
Builds self-respect and self-concept

Modeling correct spelling, punctuation, sentence formation, and publishing

Illustrating

Increasing comprehension

Builds the connection between print and ideas
Encourages sight vocabulary

Encouraging creativity

Reading

Building sight vocabulary

Builds sight vocabulary
Enhances decoding strategies
Builds reading fluency

Celebrating

Celebrating with an Authors' Tea

Encourages a love for reading and writing
Enhances acceptance of others
Increases awareness of "presenting" to others
Enriches sight vocabulary
Builds a collection of readable materials
Encourages learning more about a subject

Builds self-confidence
Enriches organizational and planning skills
Models respect and love for literature
Gives *all* children an arena for success
Offers a completed reading and writing cycle that is relevant to children

Kathryn L. Cloonan

Author's Story Planner

This is about _____

_____

I am pretending to be _____
so I can tell this story from his/her point of view.

It takes place _____

_____

The problem is _____

_____

However, _____

_____

Then _____

The problem is solved when _____

_____

The story ends _____

_____

How Well Do You Know Your Characters?

Character's name: _____

Boy or girl: _____ Age: _____

What does your character look like?
Draw a picture of your character.

Where does he or she live? _____

Who does he or she live with? _____

Character's Favorites

Pets	Foods	Friends

Kathryn L. Cloonan

Your Character's Feelings

What makes your character . . .

Happy	Sad

Mad	Scared

What are some things that are important to your character?
What are your character's biggest problems?

Kathryn L. Cloonan

255

AUTHOR'S PLANNING PAGE

Name: _____

Title: _____

Dedicated to: _____

Because: _____

About - Me - The Author: _____

_____

_____

I would like my book:

    Handwritten   _____

    or

    Typed   _____

I would like the words this size:

VERY LARGE   LARGE   SMALL

I would like the color of the cover to be: _____

1. I have chosen my paper: _____

2. I have talked with my Publisher: _____

3. I have a picture of me: _____

4. I have done my illustrations: _____

5. My book is all put together: _____

I DID IT!!!

About the Author

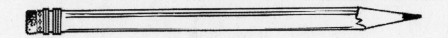

_____ _____ _____
      name

lives in _____

_____

_____ likes _____
      name

_____

_____ got the idea for _____
      name   his/her

book from _____

_____

Our Authors' Tea Plans

This is our _____ Authors' Tea.

It will be on _____. It will start at _____.

_____ and _____ will pass out programs.

_____ will do the welcome.

_____ will explain comments.

_____ will introduce _____.
Read   Comments   Applause!

_____ will introduce _____.
Read   Comments   Applause!

_____ will introduce _____.
Read   Comments   Applause!

_____ will introduce _____.
Read   Comments   Applause!

_____ will introduce _____.
Read   Comments   Applause!

Mrs. Cloonan will call all 5 authors up together and give each one a hug and a ribbon.

Applause for our authors!!

Authors will go to their special autograph signing desks.

Parents and teachers can ask for autographs. Boys and girls will start refreshments.

Then parents have refreshments and boys and girls go to authors and ask for autographs.

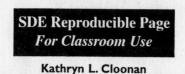

❧ Especially Honoring ❧

Author of

Autograph

❧ Especially Honoring ❧

Author of

Autograph

Reading Coaches

Purpose: Build fluency and confidence

Materials: Any book at reader's **<u>comfort</u>** reading level and checkers' card (optional)

Steps:

1. First reading coach reads aloud for 3-5 minutes.

2. Second reader reads aloud SAME text for 3-5 min.

3. One reader summarizes/sequences major events. Second reader adds interesting details.

Coaching: If reader makes a mistake:

1. Wait until reader has finished complete sentence. If reader does not self-correct say, **"Try that again, please."**

2. If they don't correct their mistake, point to the word and say, **"This is _____."**

3. Reader repeats the word.

4. Coach says, **"Good, now try the whole sentence again."***

*Extra points for positive comments.

Kathryn L. Cloonan

Reading & Writing Responses

Story Staircase

Title _____

This story begins when _____

The problem is _____

The next thing that happens is. _____

Then _____

After that, _____

The problem is solved when _____

Questions and Answers

Title _____

Our Questions	The Book's Answers

What and Why

Title _____

What Happens	Why

Warning!!!

Title _____

Watch Out for 'Foot in Mouth Disease'

What is it?

Who is likely to get it?

What are the symptoms?

What is the cure?

How can you make sure you don't get it?

Did You Know

Title _____

Did You Know That. . .

Topic	New Information About It

Opinion or Fact

Title _____

Opinions	Facts

Report Card

Title _____

Student _____

Subject	Grade	Comments

Kathryn L. Cloonan

Language Arts Block

Small Group Instruction	Morning Centers	Literature Extension

Writing Activities

1. Adding to idea notebook

2. Reading to get ideas or forms

3. Collecting information with partner

4. Illustrating for a new book

5. Reading "step-by-step" directions

6. Filling in a Character Chart

7. Writing a letter requesting information

8. Making a story board for a new book

9. Writing a practice copy

10. Giving suggestions to another author

11. Conferencing with a friend

12. Revising or checking (editing)

13. Writing a final copy

14. Writing comments to an author

15. Looking at the resource books

16. Filling in Author's planning page

17. Filling out invitations to an Author's Tea

18. Writing a thank-you note to someone for information or for coming to an Author's Tea

19. Practicing reading for an Author's Tea

20. Practicing signing your name!

Kathryn L. Cloonan

Voices

*Laughter is the
shortest distance
between two people.*

— *Victor Borge*

Smart Ways to Handle

KIDS WHO

PICK ON

Activities and strategies

to help bullies—and

the kids they target—

change their behavior.

by William J. Kreidler

Mark, a third grader in suburban Boston, doesn't want to go to school. His physical symptoms are real—headaches, dizziness, nausea—but his mother notices that these symptoms are most pronounced on Monday mornings. After her persistent questioning, Mark admits that every day at lunchtime he is being harassed by a bully in his grade. "But don't tell anyone," Mark pleads. "He says he'll beat me up if I tell."

Eileen, a fifth grader in rural Iowa, has organized a campaign to exclude Abby. Eileen has spread rumors about Abby, and the campaign has escalated to include tripping her and taking possessions from her desk and hiding them.

These incidents are part of what Ronald Stephens, executive director of the National School Safety Center, calls "one of the most underrated but enduring problems in schools today." And while teachers typically report that only 3 to 5 percent of students pick on other

kids during the year, student surveys indicate that 15 to 20 percent is closer to the truth. (And surprisingly, there is nearly twice as much of this behavior in grades 2 to 4 as there is in grades 6 to 8.) This does not mean that teachers aren't observant or that they don't care.

"So much of this behavior is hidden," says teacher Nancy Beardall, who has created a successful antibullying program. "I had an incident the other day that, had my head been turned two inches to the left, I would have missed completely."

To help you stop kids who pick on others from disrupting your classroom climate, this article provides:

WILLIAM J. KREIDLER, *Instructor's* Caring Classroom columnist, was a classroom teacher for 20 years. He now works for Educators for Social Responsibility in Cambridge, Massachusetts, developing materials and leading workshops in conflict resolution. His latest book is *Adventures in Peacemaking: A Guide for Afterschool Programs* (Educators for Social Responsibility, 1996).

OTHERS

Illustrations: Jimmy Holder

"We Don't Have Bullies at My School!" —and 4 Other Myths About Bullies

Now and then most children are intentionally mean to others, but they don't make a habit of this behavior. Bullies do. Dan Olweus, the Norwegian psychologist who pioneered the systematic study of bullying, points out that a bully intends to hurt another child, does so over and over again, and is more powerful than the target—either because he or she is physically bigger or has more status and power in the classroom. The bully may directly intimidate, threaten, or name-call. More discreetly—usually behind the other child's back—he or she may spread rumors, covertly damage the child's possessions, or exclude him or her from activities.

Whatever the tactic, it is often difficult to pick out bullies—and their targets—because we often misattribute characteristics of both. To help you spot each type of child, below we dispel five myths. See how many you ascribed to until now.

Myth #1:
"I don't have bullies in my classroom. Bullies are mostly a problem in large classes or large schools."
FACT: Bullying occurs at about

the same rate no matter how large or small a class or a school is. In addition, rural schools seem to have a higher rate of bullying than urban or suburban schools.

Myth #2:

Bullies have low self-esteem.
FACT: Bullies tend to score very high on self-esteem measures, and compared to other children, they suffer from less anxiety and insecurity. Because they exhibit little understanding of how their targets feel, bullies see themselves in a positive light. At the same time, they often see themselves as victims. A bully assumes another child didn't accidentally bump into him, the other child *meant* to. This thinking helps bullies justify their behavior: "I've got to get them before they get me."

Myth #3:

Bullies fail or are frustrated in school.
FACT: Some bullies do poorly in school, others do quite well.

Myth #4:

Targets of bullies are children who have a physical difference (i.e., they are overweight, have red hair or an accent, and so on).
FACT: External differences play a very small role. Instead, targets tend to have in common internal characteristics, such as lack of confidence and social skills, low self-esteem, and an aversion to confrontation and conflict.

Myth #5:

Most bullies are boys.
FACT: Girls are nearly as likely as boys to bully. The difference is in how girls bully. They are less likely to be physically aggressive, and instead bully through verbal harassment, exclusion from activities, name-calling, starting rumors, and so on. While much boy bullying is done one-on-one, girls are more likely to bully in a group.

Tips to Get Bullies to Kick the Habit

1 KEEP RECORDS.
Each time you verify a bullying incident, record the time, date, place, and names of children involved. Also keep a record of what intervention strategies you try.

2 TALK PRIVATELY.
Remind the child of your school and classroom rules and consequences regarding bullying. If it is a group of children who are bullying, talk with each child individually.

3 EMPHASIZE THE POSITIVE.
Because bullies generally have high self-esteem, esteem-raising activities are not very useful. Instead, focus on the social skills bullies lack. For example, bullies rarely feel empathy, so activities that enhance students' ability to see other points of view are helpful. Get bullies involved in cooperative activities, and supervise them so they don't create a new arena for bullying. Praise them when they demonstrate respectful behavior. Changing patterns is not easy, so look for small signs of success.

4 DEVELOP A BEHAVIOR CONTRACT.
Because many bullies repeat specific types of behavior, individual behavior contracts can help. For example, one contract might state: "I will not trip anyone, and if I do the consequence will be missing recess for two days." Have the child sign the contract.

5 CONTACT PARENTS.
Parents need to know if their child engages in bullying behavior. Dan Olweus has found that 50 percent of the time, the parents of a bully are alarmed to hear of this behavior and cooperate with the school in setting limits.

Activities to Break the Cycle of Bullying

B ullying is learned behavior," says bully expert Dan Olweus, "and that means it can be unlearned" if you send a consistent message—"We don't tolerate bullying here"—and balance that with more positive themes. These activities either address bullying directly or emphasize caring, respect, and safety in the school community.

HOLD CLASS MEETINGS ABOUT BULLYING
Primary/Intermediate:
Bully experts recommend a 20-minute class meeting at least once a

week about some aspect of the topic. At your first meeting, ask children what bullying means to them and have them brainstorm a list of related behaviors. Although children may want to name names, steer the discussion away from finger-pointing (invite anyone who is having trouble to speak to you privately). If you feel you need a definition of bullying, here's one that works well: "Bullying is when people who are stronger, older, or more popular treat another person disrespectfully over and over again." Emphasize the disrespect, power difference, and repetition.

R-E-S-P-E-C-T
Primary/Intermediate:
Discuss what respect is and isn't. Then, throughout the year, keep referring to these principles. For example, have children write and illustrate stories about respect, make a banner, and interview one another and adults about respect. Have kids share what they learn on a bulletin board, in a school newspaper, in a letter home, or over the PA.

Help for the Child Who Is Picked On

1 HAVE A PLAN FOR REPORTING BULLIES.
Bullying is vastly underreported because children are intimidated. Encourage all kids—targets and observers—to report incidents. Explain that this is not tattling, but information you need to make school safe for everyone. Reinforce that you are committed to keeping targets safe from reprisal.

2 TALK PRIVATELY.
Let the student know that it is not his or her fault. Listen to the child's feelings and explain that you will do all you can to help. Strategize with chronic bully targets by rehearsing responses. The first time you do this, have the child play the bully so you can model realistic ways to react. Also, help targets develop friendships by teaming them up with more socially skilled students for cooperative projects.

3 HELP KIDS RESIST BULLIES.
Targets typically reward bullies by giving them

an emotional payoff—the satisfaction of seeing how the behavior hurts—or material benefit—handing over lunch money, toys, or other possessions. While not responding the way the bully wants can be difficult, it's a powerful strategy. Remind kids that standing up for oneself doesn't mean countering aggression with aggression. Teach children to take slow breaths, keep a passive face, and to repeat to themselves, "I can handle this."

4 TEACH ASSERTIVE SKILLS.
Ignoring a bully is often not enough—he or she keeps at it. Teach all children to be assertive by standing straight, looking the bully in the eye, and saying "Stop bothering me" or "Don't do that. I don't like it" or "I'll report you if you don't stop." Then teach children to walk away.

Primary: Create a bulletin board titled THUMBS-UP BEHAVIOR AND THUMBS-DOWN BEHAVIOR. Explain that thumbs-up behavior leads to a caring, respectful classroom, while thumbs-down behavior is the opposite, and ask kids for examples of each. Then have children draw and label pictures that illustrate these behaviors, and post their work.

Intermediate:
Make a T-chart on the board and label it RESPECT LOOKS LIKE… and RESPECT SOUNDS LIKE…. Have the class identify behaviors for each side. Make a similar chart for disrespect.

FINE-TUNE YOUR RULES
Primary/Intermediate:
Work with your class to formulate rules against bullying based on the themes of respect and caring. Try the "therefore" approach: state a guiding principle of the class in positive terms, insert the word *therefore*, and then list three specific behaviors that are allowed or not. For example: "In this class we treat each other with caring and respect, *therefore* we don't bully other people, put them down, or tease them," and "In this class we call people what they want to be called, *therefore* we don't make fun of or laugh at people's names or call them mean names." Be sure to include a range of consequences, such as a warning, missing recess, going to the office, or a call home.

BULLIES IN BOOKS
Primary/Intermediate:
Talking about books that feature bullies is a safe way to open discussions about this topic. (For a list of titles, see page 76.) Children who may not feel comfortable discussing their own experiences will talk about someone in a story. Have children role-play the situation in the book to try out several different responses to bullies, or have them write or draw a new ending to the story. Also, try these discussion starters:
- What kinds of bullying behavior did you see in this book?
- What strategies did the target character use to confront the bully? What worked or didn't?
- What else could the target have done? What might've happened?

Continued on page 76

Schoolwide and Community Strategies

Action to thwart bullying must go beyond classroom activities or individual intervention. Here are some ideas to build awareness on the part of adults and create schoolwide policies.

- Make bullying the topic of a school staff meeting.
- Invite a bullying expert to your school.
- Share an article or other resource about bullying.
- So you can better tailor your approach to bullying, have students fill out a bullying questionnaire to help determine how much of this behavior is going on.

- Inform the community—parents, police, health-care workers, and community leaders —about bullying and its costs.
- Declare your school a Bully-Free Zone and create clear rules and consequences for it.
- Develop schoolwide themes of respect and caring.

- How do you think the characters felt during the bullying?
- Why do you think the bully acts as he or she does?
- Where does the bully get his or her power?
- What could the people who observed the bullying have done?

FEND FOR YOURSELF
Primary/Intermediate:
Give students make-believe bully situations as dry runs for handling the real thing.

Present to the children a hypothetical bully situation and have them brainstorm to solve it. Emphasize that everyone deserves to be treated with respect—even the bully—and all responses should be nonviolent. Make and post a chart of the class's "Dealing with Bullies" strategies. Then give the students another situation and have them role-play it in teams of three, with students taking the parts of the bully, the target, and the bystander.
Primary:
Have kids create comics that illustrate ways to respond to bullying.

Intermediate: Have kids create a onetime or ongoing newspaper about bullying such as "The Bully-Free Times" (or a more positive name), or write a bullying supplement to an existing school paper. Contents might include articles explaining what bullying is, criteria for a positive and safe school, editorials, and interviews.

Kids may even create antibullying superheros, but remind them that their assistance must be respectful and nonviolent.
Intermediate:
Ask students to develop skits on bullying and successful responses to present to younger children or at a PTA meeting. Some of the books about bullying below lend themselves well to dramatization. For example, when one elementary school dramatized *Oliver Button Is a Sissy,* they included a talent show because the book's plot revolves around a school show.

Editor's Note: Several of these activities were suggested by Carol Wintle, director of the Bullies and Scapegoats Project of Educators for Social Responsibility.

Resources

Choose children's books about bullies carefully. Avoid advocating fighting or revenge.

HELPFUL ORGANIZATIONS

National School Safety Center, 4165 Thousand Oaks Blvd., Westlake Village, CA 91362; *(805) 373-9977*

Bullies and Scapegoats Project, Educators for Social Responsibility, 23 Garden St., Cambridge, MA 02138; *(617) 492-1764*

Institute for Families in Society, University of South Carolina, Columbia, SC 29208; *(803) 777-5510*

PRIMARY BOOKS

Oliver Button Is a Sissy by Tomie de Paolo (Harcourt Brace, 1979); *grades 1–3*

Herbie's Troubles by Carol Chapman (Dutton, 1981); *grades K–3*

Chrysanthemum by Kevin Henkes (Greenwillow, 1991); *grades K–3*

King of the Playground by Phyllis Reynolds Naylor (Macmillan, 1994); *grades K–2*

Joshua T. Bates Takes Charge by Susan Shreve (Knopf, 1993); *grades 2–4*

INTERMEDIATE BOOKS

The Eighteenth Emergency by Betsy Byars (Viking, 1973); *grades 3–6*

The Hundred Dresses by Eleanor Estes (Harcourt Brace, 1974); *grades 2–5*

Wendy and the Bullies by Nancy Robinson (Scholastic, 1980); *grades 3–5*

The Bully of Barkham Street by Mary Stolz (HarperCollins, 1985); *grades 4–6*

Stick Boy by Joan T. Zeier (Macmillan, 1993); *grades 5–6*

Turning Around the "Down"

by Irv Richardson

Sooner or later it happens to everyone who teaches a classroom full of young people. You realize that things in the classroom aren't what you know they should be . . . kids are squabbling with each other, the assigned work isn't getting done, your energy isn't spent on teaching but instead on putting out the small brush fires combusting all over the classroom. The class has entered a negative cycle that needs an immediate "direction correction."

When I found my class headed into a negative spiral, quick action on my part was the first and most important step in turning the situation around. By following certain steps I was able to act like the cowboy who jumps on the back of the horses of the runaway stagecoach and slowly brings back order and direction back to the classroom. You can use the same steps:

STEP ONE: Realize that the class is comprised of individuals.

The way to turn the class around is to think about each individual member of the class. I found it effective to go through the class list and decide whether each individual student was making positive or negative contributions to the class. If I felt a student was making positive contributions, I would put a "+" next to the student's name. If I felt the student wasn't making positive contributions or being a productive member of the class, I would put a "−" next to that name.

After proceeding through the entire class list, I would go back and note the individuals I felt were not making positive contributions. Almost always, I found that there were many more "plusses" than "minuses." It wasn't the entire class that wasn't being productive; it was usually just a few individuals who were giving me my negative impression of the class.

STEP TWO: Realize that to change the behavior of the students, you must first change the behavior of the most important person in the class — you.

If the tone and the classroom climate are going to change, it is up to the teacher to initiate the change. Changing your behavior means that you have to pay greater attention to the things that are going well, and then decide upon specific steps you can take to help the students who aren't making good use of their time in class.

Go back to your class list. For each student whose name has a plus, write down one or two specific things the student is doing that you want to recognize as helping the class. It might be that he is getting his work done well or is helping keep the classroom neat or organized. Perhaps she is showing problem-solving or leadership skills.

For the students with a "−" after their names, think about the one behavior or action that you feel is most disruptive to the class. Perhaps someone is physically hurting classmates or not finishing classwork. List the specific behavior that you want to eliminate.

STEP THREE: Now that you've listed both positive and negative student behaviors, you need to develop specific plans to recognize positive behaviors and to work at changing the negative behaviors.

A good method is to divide your plan into two parts:

1. What you plan to do for each individual student; and
2. How you plan to share both your praise and concerns with the class.

Write a personal note to the children you feel are contributing to the class, expressing your appreciation and thanking them. (An alternative is to write the letter to the children's parents.) This will not only give the children recognition for their contributions, it will also reinforce your belief that there are indeed positive things happening in your classroom.

You can also make a list of the positive behaviors on a chart (without listing the names of specific individuals) and display that in the classroom.

For students whose behavior needs to change, develop specific steps to help each student change his or her behavior. For example, if you have a student who constantly interrupts you, you need to discuss his behavior with him privately, and explain that the behavior interferes with the other students' ability to learn. Let him know that you will be keeping track of the interruptions, and that you and he will work together to change his behavior.

Develop a plan that involves reasonable, related and respectful consequences for the student's disruptive behavior, and provide alternative ways for the student to act when confronted with situations that tend to initiate this type of behavior.

You can also list the unacceptable classroom behaviors on a chart and display it (without listing the culprits.) Discuss the list and the reasons that these behaviors are not good for the class.

Communicate with the students' parents, either in a note or by phone, explaining your concerns about their children's behavior, and explaining the steps you plan to take to help their children develop more positive behaviors.

STEP FOUR: Let your class know that your own behavior is going to change — and why.

The first time I used this process, I came into the classroom ready to change things and didn't inform the students that I was going to be using a different approach toward some classroom behaviors. This created a lot of tension when the students became aware that I was acting differently toward them.

It's better to explain to the class why you came to the decision to change things — there are some things happening in class that make it difficult for the class to run smoothly, etc. — and what you plan to do to alter the negative behaviors and reinforce positive behaviors. Discuss the lists you've made, get the students' input, and make them a part of the process.

STEP FIVE: Hold class meetings.

Class meetings are an excellent way to involve the students in the smooth functioning of the class. In my classroom we held class meetings on a regular basis, using the class meeting format suggested by Jane Nelsen in her book, *Positive Discipline*. As Dr. Nelson suggests in her book, we held our class meetings for four reasons:
   1. to give compliments
   2. to help each other
   3. to solve problems
   4. to plan events

I used one of these regularly scheduled class meetings to bring up my concerns about how things were going in our classroom. I shared the positive behaviors (without student names) that I thought were helping us as a class; then I shared the unhelpful behaviors (again, without the names of the responsible students), that I felt were not making positive contributions to our class. Often this list would bring snickers along with some furtive glances, as students identified those responsible for the behavior.

I used the meeting to let the class know I would be sending home notes to parents, and that these notes would share the positive things happening in the class, as well as ask for the parents' help in solving some of the problems individual students were having.

We also used the meeting to solicit student opinions about how they felt the class was going and what things they felt were, and were not, going well. As a class, we listed the things we could do to help make the class go more smoothly.

I also let the students know that I would be meeting soon with some individuals in the class to talk about specific plans that I had to help those individuals.

STEP SIX: Follow through.

Once you've analyzed the situation, developed plans, and discussed those plans with the class, you need to follow through. By following through with your plans on a consistent basis, you will emphasize the importance of your students' ability to work as a group, as well as your confidence in their ability to change. A byproduct of this is that you will discover, as I did, that your own confidence in your ability as "class manager," capable of positively affecting the classroom environment, will grow.

"Write 'Em Up!"

A classroom management tool you can use the next time students interrupt you with a complaint

BY CAROL ANN PERKS

> "A complaint file is not the only way to achieve peaceful classroom management, of course, but it does have a distinct advantage over other strategies."

"Ms. Perks, he keeps bothering me."

"Ms. Perks, she said I was stupid."

"Ms. Perks, she keeps copying me."

Chants! Heard throughout the day in classrooms nationwide, these spontaneous, well-learned mantras interrupt and distract teachers and students. Delaying answers to these chants, however, can create louder and larger choruses.

I sought enlightenment over the last six years and, through trial and error, I'm now at the point of nirvana. I've developed a system that answers the needs of students and rescues the teacher from these disturbing "chants" of no immediate consequence.

Necessary materials. You'll need a few materials to implement the system, but they're neither elaborate nor expensive. Once you have the following items, you're ready to roll:

- **File folders.** House them wherever you file student test papers.
- **A "teacher's mailbox."** You can make a simple mailbox by turning the front of a file folder one-quarter of the way down and then stapling the folder on two sides. On the front, write something like this: "Write Your Problems, Gripes, Complaints, Questions" and below it, "Teacher's Mailbox." Hang it in a convenient place,

A file folder and some staples are the only things you need to create a mailbox.

such as the entryway or next to the Rules and Behavior Chart (if you have one).

- **Notebook paper and pencils.** These can be supplied by the children.

How it works. The system ignites with the first chant. For example:

"Ms. Perks, Jon's bothering me, and I can't do my work." Krystal flips her book.

I look up from whatever it is I'm doing – monitoring a group of students at the computer station perhaps – and quickly evaluate the situation as "not life threatening" I say firmly, "Write him up!"

Jon insists, "It's not fair, she …"

Before he finishes, I say, "Write her up!"

"But Ms. Perks …"

"Be sure to date and time it." I end the discussion and continue conferencing.

Jon and Krystal begin writing feverishly, glaring at each other every once in a while as their pencils fly across the paper. Both are silently seething and thinking with confidence and satisfaction that forever more in the history of this third grade, their complaint will sit, ready and waiting, in their rival's file. They're sure that at some future date, an administrator or parent will inquire about the other student's "record" of behavior and then the student will "get what's coming!"

They strut to "Ms. Perk's Mailbox," and then return to their class work with the added comfort that at the end of the day, or at the first opportunity, a discussion will take place.

Yes, students are allowed to stop their work to write and file a complaint. That's part of the success of the system. It enables students to stop and redirect their negative energies and feeling into analyzing and writing about their problems.

Complete complaints. Written complaints can't be just a scrawled sentence or two. The complaint must follow formal letter writing guidelines and be written in legible cursive handwriting. Each complaint must also include:

- The time and date of the incident.
- The pattern of *who* is involved, *where* it happened and either *why* or *how* it happened.
- An opinion statement as to how this incident can be avoided in the future.
- Suggestions about how the teacher should handle similar incidents.

By the time the discussion takes place, everyone will have "chilled out," thought it out, and be able to speak with a more enlightened viewpoint. If not, you go over the students' Who, What, Why, Where, When, Opinion and Suggestions statements. You then *guide* them to a satisfactory outcome.

Filing complaints. The students' complaint letters are kept in a file. You need have only one file, from A to Z, for those students with one or two complaints. Three complaints against a child and he or she earns the "privilege" of having his or her own complaint folder.

The child with three complaints will probably need his or her own folder because the file will usually include a "written conference for the record" with the parent, and maybe a follow-up or a meeting with a counselor or both. The files are not color-coded, by the way.

A complaint file is not the only way to achieve peaceful classroom management, of course, but it does have a distinct advantage over other strategies.

When you have to communicate with a

Carol Ann Perks spent last year teaching third grade at Joe Hall Elementary School in Miami, FL.

child's parents, anecdotal records written by the student's peers carry far more significant weight than records written from the teacher's point of view. It's easy to see why. The parents will undoubtedly read statements that conflict with their child's version of an incident. When parents read from other students that their child's disruptive behavior is violating other children's right to learn, they're usually more inclined to listen to a workable plan.

"Paper trail." Complaint files are also valuable when a behavior problem comes to the attention of administrators. When a principal receives a call from an irate parent about something done to his or her child by a teacher or another student, it can be very helpful if the principal has access to a "paper trail" file. With peer anecdotal

*"**Ms. Perks'** Mailbox." is within easy reach of any child who wants to file a complaint.*

records, the principal is in a far better position to mediate the situation, taking everyone's point of view into account.

"Write 'Em Up," an effective and democratic classroom management tool, is a learning benefit for students' language arts, problem-solving and social skills, while it helps the teacher in her or his communication with students, parents and administrators.

It also eases a persistent problem in the classroom. Students learn to analyze a situation before they engage in "chanting" and hear the response, "Write 'Em Up!" ↓

***Carol Ann** discusses an incident with two children who have "chilled out" and are ready to find a solution.*

Susan Mandel Glazer on

Teaching Diverse Learners

Doing What We Shouldn't

We mean well, but sometimes we employ teaching strategies that are counterproductive.

We do lots of things that we shouldn't – especially with kids who find learning a problem. For example, we often confuse different, or lack of, experiences with lack of ability. Instead of enhancing curriculum so that these students can succeed, we lower expectations for them. We do this by slowing down the curriculum so they'll "get it."

> **"***Be a model for your students by creating high self-expectations.***"**

What do students get? In addition to a poor self-concept, they get last year's instructional materials again and go through the usual regimen of learning wherein teachers explain by definition rather than by modeling the desired behaviors. Then the students are assigned work and are expected to complete it within a prescribed time period.

When students finish the previous year's slower-paced, teacher-explained and assigned activity, they're administered adult-made tests where they're expected to demonstrate what they've learned.

Ability groups. "Learning" means getting the right answer, rather than understanding how that answer is achieved. When tests are scored, teachers often sort the children into ability groups (if not actually, at least in our minds) according to test scores.

Susan Mandel Glazer is Director of the Center for Reading and Writing at Rider University, Lawrenceville, NJ, and a Teaching Editor of *Teaching K-8*.

Recently, I was invited to Brunei to conduct workshops for teachers. I know little about Brunei's customs, but based on my experiences with thousands of teachers over the years, I made some assumptions.

I dressed informally for a workshop so that I could become actively involved with the participants. Since it was summer, I chose a short-sleeved suit and wore a sleeveless blouse under the jacket. For comfort, I wore matching walking shorts that looked like a skirt.

Dress code. My lack of experience in the culture led to an inappropriate judgment about the country's professional dress code. You see, Brunei, although located in the South China Sea, is a Muslim country with social and religious customs much like those found in the Mideast.

I realized this when I entered the lecture hall and saw the men seated on one side of the room and the women on the other side. The men wore ties and the women wore skirts long enough to cover their ankles, a matching loose shirt with long sleeves and a veil-style head covering.

My face must have showed my embarrassment. My bare arms and head seemed more visible than the wall-sized photograph of the country's sultan.

My host noticed my discomfort and remarked, "Don't be upset. Westerners usually come dressed as you are."

He was "lowering the expectations" and also "sorting me into an ability group" because I'd failed the cultural knowledge test. Although he intended to comfort me, his comment made me feel even worse.

I got through the morning session, trying not to show my discomfort. I never took the jacket off, even though the temperature was over 90 degrees; nor did I sit for fear of exposing more of my legs. I was invited to lunch, but I requested an expedition to the nearest women's store, where I clothed myself in traditional dress.

"Passing the test." No one needed to explain by definition why I'd failed the initial test. The firsthand experience did, however, cause me to act quickly in order to "pass the test with the right answer."

What could have been a sure failure turned out to be a great success, for the process helped me solve the problem. I also avoided being "ability grouped" with other consultants who had arrived in similar Western clothing.

I recall my friends explaining the dress code, but the explanation by definition had little impact on my behavior. The real situation, however, functioned to facilitate learning about the dress code and joining it. The situation also played havoc with my emotions, encouraging me to act immediately.

Kim's problem. What does this have to do with learners with problems? Eight-year-old Kim's short-term memory deficit resulted in an inability to spell or write by hand so that others could read her materials. As she said, "I need to see the letters all together or I forget what they look like." Although her tested intelligence and social skills proved

to be far above average for her age, her teachers insisted that she was capable of only C+ work.

Kim had been schooled in teacher-centered classrooms. Her teachers, who knew she had problems with spelling, gave her words of two, three and four letters to learn. The teachers selected the words from the "most frequently misspelled" word list.

Kim was expected to learn and remember content delivered orally by teachers. After explaining, the teachers frequently assigned worksheets to test students' recall. This approach didn't work for Kim. She needed functional, realistic and exciting activities in order for her to read and write successfully.

> **"** *Children perform as we expect them to. Expect big things and you'll usually get them. Be a model for your students by creating high expectations.* **"**

Exemplary program. Kim was placed in an exemplary program where children were able to select from a group of science and social studies projects. The focus was on learning strategies to help her collect information and then write about what she learned. Providing the child with a road map for accomplishing tasks were such strategies as KWL, Request Procedure and SQ4R. (Note: For more information on these strategies, ask your school's reading specialist or write to Susan Glazer, care of *Teaching K-8*, for examples.)

It was amazing to see Kim take off. She chose to study horses as they relate to farming, for they were her favorite topic. She learned strategies as quickly and efficiently as children who were considered gifted. Her spelling was still atrocious, but the amount of knowledge gained from books, conversations

and media was outstanding.

In addition to learning more about horses, Kim found out how to skim and scan in order to look for specific information. She learned to use appropriate referencing procedures (APA style) if her report required a bibliography.

Using illustrations. She found out that the text was more informative when illustrations were used. She collected photos, drew and photocopied pictures, matching them on pages with print of the same content. Kim learned about copyright law, how to develop a title page and how to construct a table of contents.

There were no isolated teacher explanations. When it was necessary to learn a skill in order to move forward on the project, the teacher or a classmate coached Kim in the task. A list of things to complete – sort of a contract between Kim and the teacher – aided the process. Kim was excited, creative, successful, independent, involved and, most of all, secure with the learning process.

Step-by-step strategies. Kim was put in charge of her own learning. She was provided with strategies that guided her step by step to succeed. The success and the option to make decisions built her self-esteem and therefore her desire to learn. The learning pace was accelerated by her own activity. The expectations were the same for Kim as for other students. The test of success was the product itself.

If you're doing some of the things noted at the beginning of this, *stop*! Children perform as we expect them to. Expect big things and you will usually get them. Be a model for your students by creating high self-expectations.

Strategies and environments for learning and testing growth that are realistic, functional and meaningful must be created for *all* students. ↯

Inclusion and the

Here's what research shows so far about inclusion's effect on *non*disabled students.

By Debbie Staub

Inclusion is receiving lots of attention, both in school districts across the country and in the popular media. Most of that attention is focused on how inclusion affects the students with disabilities. But what about the students who *don't* have disabilities?

As a project coordinator for the Inclusive Education Research Group at Emily Dickinson School in Redmond, Washington, I've been in contact with hundreds of teachers, parents, and students affected by inclusion, and I've done extensive research on the subject. Of course, each inclusion situation is unique: Some teachers receive more training than others, some schools provide classroom aides and others don't, some classrooms have one disabled student while others have several, and so forth. Regardless of the circumstances, though, I've found that teachers and parents usually want to know what the research says about these two main concerns:

1. Will the nondisabled students' learning suffer because of inclusion? Only a few studies have addressed this question. So far, these studies have shown no slowdown in nondisabled children's learning in inclusive classrooms. Surveys conducted with parents and teachers involved in inclusive settings generally show that they see no harm to the nondisabled children and that they have positive opinions about inclusion. In fact, one survey of more than 300 parents of elementary-age children shows that 89 percent would enroll their children in an inclusive classroom again.

2. Will nondisabled children receive less attention and time from their teacher? Only one study has directly investigated this issue. In that study, researchers randomly chose six nondisabled students in classrooms that had at least one student with severe disabilities (all of the classrooms had support from paraprofessionals). Then they chose a comparison group of nondisabled students in noninclusive classrooms. The researchers compared the amounts of instructional time and found that the presence of students with severe disabilities had no effect.

And time lost to interruptions wasn't significantly different, either.

The glass is half full

So in a nutshell, the research conducted thus far shows that being in an inclusive classroom doesn't *hurt* the nondisabled students. But does it *help* them? Teachers surveyed indicate that nondisabled students gain these important benefits from relationships with their disabled classmates:

Friendships. One of the most important functions of friendship is to make people feel loved, safe, and cared for. Researchers have documented cases in which meaningful, long-lasting friendships that benefit both students have emerged between disabled and nondisabled students. For example, one study chronicles the friendship that Stacy, a nondisabled 12-year-old, and Cary, a 13-year-old with Down's syndrome, have had for more than four years. A teaching assistant explains how she sees Stacy benefit from this relationship: "Stacy sees the growth Cary is making, and she is a big part of that success. She also benefits because Cary makes her feel good—always choosing to sit with her, always goofing around with her."

Social skills. Nondisabled children become more aware of the needs of others, and they become skilled at understanding and reacting to the behaviors of their friends with disabilities.

Self-esteem. One study documents the friendship between Aaron, a nondisabled sixth grader, and Cole, a classmate with severe disabilities. Aaron's ability to understand Cole's behavior has helped him take on a leadership role that he wasn't able to assume in the past, resulting in an increase in Aaron's self-esteem. "This has given Aaron a special place in the classroom, and he feels really good about himself," his teacher says.

Personal principles. Nondisabled students grow in their commitment to their own moral and ethical principles and become advocates for their disabled friends. For example, Cary's classmates became very vocal about making sure that she wasn't pulled out of the class unnecessarily. Developing these strong

Photos: ©1995 PhotoDisc, Inc. (page 76); Penny Gentieu/Tony Stone Images (page 77).

276

Other Kids

personal principles will benefit students throughout adulthood.

Comfort level with people who are different. On surveys and in interviews, nondisabled junior-high and high-school students say they're less fearful of people who look different or behave differently because they've interacted with individuals with disabilities. One seventh grader says. "Now I'm not like, 'Uh, she's weird.' She's normal! I've gotten to work with people with disabilities, so I know that." Parents notice the difference in their children, too. An interesting side effect is that these parents report that they feel more comfortable with people with disabilities because of their children's experiences.

Patience. Nondisabled students who've developed relationships with disabled classmates report that they have increased patience with "slower" learners.

Getting the payoff

So how do you realize these powerful benefits with your nondisabled students? What techniques and practices can you use? Surprisingly, many of the techniques you're already using contribute to these results.

Create a classroom that fosters kindness, consideration, empathy, concern, and care for others. Support this kind of atmosphere with these practices:

- Hold class meetings in which students can express themselves and their perceptions of how things are going.
- Use cooperative learning.
- Plan ahead to make sure all students are included in free-time activities.
- Teach social skills such as how to communicate clearly, resolve conflicts, and solve problems. Also, be sure that

> Nationwide, 50 percent of disabled students aged 6–11 are in regular classrooms. The same holds true for 30 percent of disabled students aged 12–17. Overall, inclusion is up 10 percent over the past five years.
>
> *Source: U.S. Department of Education, Office of Special Education Programs.*

your special-education teacher works with the disabled students on these skills, too.

Celebrate the experiences and differences that each child brings to the classroom. You can do this in a variety of ways:

- Model acceptance of diverse abilities, backgrounds. and behaviors.
- Be careful to include all students in class activities.
- Establish buddy and peer-tutoring programs.

One caution: Be aware of how often you ask or just expect nondisabled students to assume helping roles. True friendships are more likely to grow when children cooperate and interact often and of their own choosing.

Down the road

The research conducted so far points us in the right direction for improving the inclusion experience. Yet each question we answer leads to more to explore. These questions can be challenging to study because inclusion situations vary. We've just begun to discover the effects of inclusion on *all* students—disabled and nondisabled alike. ✳

Debbie Staub. Ph.D., is a project coordinator at the University of Washington's Consortium for Collaborative Research on Social Relationships. The group studies the impact of social relationships for children with and without severe disabilities. She's currently working on a book about friendships between elementary-school students with and without disabilities. You can contact her at EEU WJ-10, University of Washington, Seattle, WA 98195.

Staub's research is supported in part by Cooperative Agreement H086A20003. The content and opinions expressed do not necessarily reflect the position or policy of the U.S. Department of Education, and no official endorsement should be inferred.

Inclusion and Me: One Student's Perspective

By Allison Brand

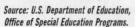

In second grade, I was in a class with 50 students. All of them were different in their own ways. But there was one girl named Megan who had Down's syndrome. We both helped each other in our own ways. I helped her with drawing, reading, and writing. She helped me understand that friends comes in all sizes, looks, personalities, and abilities.

In fourth grade, I was one of the first kids introduced to Erin, who has autism. I became her seat partner, and we became friends. This was Erin's first year at our school. It was her first year in an inclusive classroom. She was probably scared. She didn't talk, and she would kick and run away if you tried to talk to her. As the year went on, she learned that nobody else kicked. She learned that kicking just got her into trouble. She had been in special-education classrooms before, and maybe everybody else kicked, too. After being in a regular classroom, she learned that kicking was not okay.

In fifth grade, Erin and I were in the same class again. She would talk to a few of us. When she came out to recess, she would play on the bars with us. She didn't kick anymore. That was a big change from fourth grade, when she didn't want anything to do with us.

Now that we are sixth graders, Erin talks. She will say hi or bye and will answer my questions and talk to some people. I go to PE with Erin on Tuesdays. She will play basketball, do jumping jacks, or whatever is required. I also helped Erin in music for a while. She would be the loudest singer in the class. We also would pass out papers to the first graders. I really like working with Erin because it's fun and it makes me feel good knowing that I am helping her. I hope we will always be friends.

Allison Brand was a sixth grader at Emily Dickinson School in Redmond, Washington, when she wrote this essay.

Your experience counts. Tell us about your experience with inclusion. You can reach us at *Learning* Magazine, 1607 Battleground Ave., Greensboro, NC 27408; (910) 272-8020 (fax); or learning@vcom1.com. We may publish your letter in an upcoming column.

ERIC

Clearinghouse on Handicapped and Gifted Children
THE COUNCIL FOR EXCEPTIONAL CHILDREN
1920 Association Drive • Reston, VA 22091-1589
(703) 264-9474 • FAX (703) 264-9494

ERIC
Digest

OCTOBER 1992

EDO-EC-92-2

#E512

PROVIDING AN APPROPRIATE EDUCATION TO CHILDREN WITH ATTENTION DEFICIT DISORDER

Clarification of Terms

Throughout this digest, ADD will be used to refer to *attention deficit disorder*, or *attention deficit hyperactivity disorder* (ADHD). In the past, the term *minimal brain dysfunction* was also used.

Children with ADD

It is estimated that children with ADD constitute 3% to 5% of the current school-age population, which would represent 1.35 to 2.25 million children. Most experts agree that ADD is a neurobiological disorder that can have multiple causes. Research indicates that children with ADD are likely to have a biological relative with ADD. In addition, evidence also suggests that neurologic, neurochemical or, in some cases, toxic factors may be involved. Other factors such as medical conditions, medication side effects, familial functioning, or environmental conditions may exacerbate an existing disorder or contribute to the development of ADD-like problems in some children (Parker, 1992).

Diagnosis

As with all other disabling conditions, evaluation of children suspected of having ADD should be a multistep, multidisciplinary procedure. First the assessment should determine whether a child meets criteria for diagnosis of ADD; then, further assessment should determine the degree to which the child's educational performance is adversely affected. This information will help determine what types of educational services are necessary to assist the student.

The first step requires gathering information about the child from a number of sources and in a variety of ways. Medical information; parent or guardian descriptions of the child's physical, mental, social, and emotional development; school information; descriptions of social behavior and classroom adjustment; and assessment of the child's cognitive functioning are essential to making an accurate diagnosis. Because the behavior of children thought to have ADD can vary widely in different situations and environments, experts recommend obtaining information from many sources, and observing the child in different settings and at different times. Evaluations of children suspected of having ADD often include rating scales completed by parents and teachers.

School Responsibilities

Schools must provide appropriate educational services to students who have been identified as having ADD. In September 1991, the Department of Education issued a policy clarification on the topic of children with attention deficit disorder (Davila, Williams, & MacDonalt, 1991). The memorandum was intended to clarify state and local responsibility under federal law for meeting the needs of children with ADD in the educational system as a whole.

The responsibility for meeting the educational needs of children with ADD rests with the entire educational system, not just with particular sectors. Thus, if the needs of these children are to be fully met in the schools (whether through general or special education programs), increased coordination, collaboration, and consultation will have to occur among regular educators, special educators, administrators, and related services personnel. The report recognizes that:

> Regular classroom teachers are important in identifying appropriate educational adaptations and interventions for many children with ADD.

> State and local districts should take the necessary steps to promote coordination between special education and regular education programs.

> Regular education teachers and other personnel need training to develop a greater awareness of children with ADD and of adaptations that can be implemented in regular education programs to address the instructional needs of these children.

Children who are experiencing educational difficulties, whether from ADD or some other cause, often fail to receive any assistance until *after* difficulties, such as distractibility, disorganization, or inability to complete assignments on time, have caused them to fall significantly behind their classmates. By the time children have experienced such failure, they generally have already lost a great deal of academic ground. In addition, school failure may contribute to, or worsen, a student's feelings of low self-esteem, depression, or anxiety.

Federal Laws Affecting Children with ADD

Both the Individuals with Disabilities Education Act (IDEA) and Section 504 of the Rehabilitation Act of 1973 provide coverage for children with ADD. When the disability adversely affects educational performance, eligibility for special education should be approached through the processes of IDEA. When the disability does not affect educational performance but does substantially limit one or more major life activities, eligibility should be approached through Section 504. The following are highlights of each law as it affects the education of children with ADD.

1. Individuals with Disabilities Education Act, Part B:

- Requires that state and local districts make a free appropriate public education (FAPE) available to all eligible children with disabilities.

- Requires that the rights and protections of Part B of IDEA are extended to children with ADD and their parents.

- Requires that an evaluation be done, without undue delay, to determine if the child has one or more of 13 specified disabling conditions and requires special education and related services.

- Requires that children with ADD be classified as eligible for services under the "other health impaired" category in instances where ADD is a chronic or acute health problem that results in limited alertness that adversely affects a child's educational performance. Children with ADD can also be served under the categories of "learning disabilities" or "seriously emotionally disturbed," if the evaluation finds these conditions are also present.

- Does not allow local districts to refuse to evaluate the possible need for special education and related services of a child with a prior medical diagnosis of ADD solely by reason of that medical diagnosis. On the other hand, a medical diagnosis of ADD does not automatically make a child eligible for services under Part B (IDEA).

- Requires that a full and individual evaluation of the child's educational needs must be conducted in accordance with requirements in Part B (IDEA). These requirements include:

    A multidisciplinary team must perform the evaluation. At least one teacher or other specialist with knowledge in the area of ADD must be on the team.

- Requires that a due process hearing take place, at the request of the parents, if there is disagreement between the local district and the parent over the request for evaluation, the evaluation, or the determinations for services.

2. Section 504 of the Rehabilitation Act of 1973:

- Prohibits discrimination on the basis of disability by recipients of federal funds.

- Provides appropriate education for children who do not fall within the disability categories specified in Part B (IDEA). Examples of potential conditions not typically covered under Part B (IDEA) are:

    communicable diseases (HIV, tuberculosis)
    medical conditions (asthma, allergies, diabetes, heart disease)

temporary medical conditions due to illness or accident drug/alcohol addiction

- Requires that a free appropriate public education be provided to each qualified child who is disabled but does not require special education and related services under Part B (IDEA). A free appropriate education (FAPE) under Section 504 includes:

    Regular or special education and related aids and services that are designed to meet the individual student's needs and are based on adherence to the regulatory requirements on education setting, evaluation, placement, and procedural safeguards.

- Guarantees parents the right to contest the outcome of an evaluation if a local district determines that a child is not disabled under Section 504.

- Requires the local district to make an individualized determination of the child's educational needs for regular or special education or related aids and services if the child is found eligible under Section 504.

- Requires the implementation of an individualized education program (IEP). One means of meeting the free appropriate public education requirements of Section 504 is to follow the IEP guidelines as set forth in the regulations for Part B (IDEA).

- Requires that the child's education must be provided in the regular education classroom unless it is demonstrated that education in the regular environment with the use of supplementary aids and services cannot be achieved satisfactorily.

- Requires that necessary adjustments be made in the regular classroom for children who qualify under Section 504.

References

Davila, R. R., Williams, M. L., & MacDonalt, J. T. (September 16, 1991). Clarification of policy to address the needs of children with attention deficit disorders within general and/or special education. Washington, DC: U.S. Department of Education, Office of Special Education and Rehabilitation Services.

Parker, H. (1992). *The ADD hyperactivity handbook for schools.* Plantation, FL: Impact.

Note. This digest is adapted from two sources:

Children with ADD: A Shared Responsibility. Based on a Report of The Council for Exceptional Children's Task Force on Children with Attention Deficit Disorder (1992). Reston, VA: The Council for Exceptional Children, 1920 Association Drive, Reston, VA 22091. Order No. P385.

Irland, B. (1992, Winter). Making It Perfectly Clear; ADD/ADHD Students Can Qualify for Services. *The Scoop.* National Learning Differences Network, 82 S. Townline Road, Sandusky, MI 48471.

This publication was prepared with funding from the Office of Educational Research and Improvement, U.S. Department of Education, under contract no. RI88062007. The opinions expressed in this report do not necessarily reflect the positions or policies of OERI or the Department of Education.

ERIC

Clearinghouse on Disabilities and Gifted Education
THE COUNCIL FOR EXCEPTIONAL CHILDREN
1920 Association Drive • Reston, VA 22091-1589
(703) 264-9474 • FAX (703) 264-9494

ERIC Digest

July 1993

EDO-EC-93-5

#E522

ADHD and CHILDREN WHO ARE GIFTED

James T. Webb and Diane Latimer

Howard's teachers say he just isn't working up to his ability. He doesn't finish his assignments, or just puts down answers without showing his work; his handwriting and spelling are poor. He sits and fidgets in class, talks to others, and often disrupts class by interrupting others. He used to shout out the answers to the teachers' questions (they were usually right), but now he daydreams a lot and seems distracted. Does Howard have Attention Deficit Hyperactivity Disorder (ADHD), is he gifted, or both?

Frequently, bright children have been referred to psychologists or pediatricians because they exhibited certain behaviors (e.g., restlessness, inattention, impulsivity, high activity level, daydreaming) commonly associated with a diagnosis of ADHD. Formally, the Diagnostic and Statistical Manual of Mental Disorders (DSM-III-R) (American Psychiatric Association) lists 14 characteristics that may be found in children diagnosed as having ADHD. At least 8 of these characteristics must be present, the onset must be before age 7, and they must be present for at least six months.

DSM-III-R DIAGNOSTIC CRITERIA FOR ATTENTION-DEFICIT HYPERACTIVITY DISORDER*

1. Often fidgets with hands or feet or squirms in seat (in adolescents may be limited to subjective feelings of restlessness).
2. Has difficulty remaining seated when required to.
3. Is easily distracted by extraneous stimuli.
4. Has difficulty awaiting turns in games or group situations.
5. Often blurts out answers to questions before they have been completed.
6. Has difficulty following through on instructions from others (not due to oppositional behavior or failure of comprehension).
7. Has difficulty sustaining attention in tasks or play activities.
8. Often shifts from one uncompleted activity to another.
9. Has difficulty playing quietly.
10. Often talks excessively.
11. Often interrupts or intrudes on others, e.g., butts into other people's games.
12. Often does not seem to listen to what is being said to him or her.
13. Often loses things necessary for tasks or activities at school or at home (e.g., toys, pencils, books).
14. Often engages in physically dangerous activities without considering possible consequences (not for the purpose of thrill-seeking), e.g., runs into street without looking.

Almost all of these behaviors, however, might be found in bright, talented, creative, gifted children. Until now, little attention has been given to the similarities and differences between the two

groups, thus raising the potential for misidentification in both areas—giftedness and ADHD.

Sometimes, professionals have diagnosed ADHD by simply listening to parent or teacher descriptions of the child's behaviors along with a brief observation of the child. Other times, brief screening questionnaires are used, although these questionnaires only quantify the parents' or teachers' descriptions of the behaviors (Parker, 1992). Children who are fortunate enough to have a thorough physical evaluation (which includes screening for allergies and other metabolic disorders) and extensive psychological evaluations, which include assessment of intelligence, achievement, and emotional status, have a better chance of being accurately identified. A child may be gifted *and* have ADHD. Without a thorough professional evaluation, it is difficult to tell.

How Can Parents or Teachers Distinguish Between ADHD and Giftedness?

Seeing the difference between behaviors that are sometimes associated with giftedness but also characteristic of ADHD is not easy, as the following list shows.

Behaviors Associated with ADHD (Barkley, 1990)	Behaviors Associated with Giftedness (Webb, 1993)
• Poorly sustained attention in almost all situations	• Poor attention, boredom, daydreaming in specific situations
• Diminished persistence on tasks not having immediate consequences	• Low tolerance for persistence on tasks that seem irrelevant
• Impulsivity, poor delay of gratification	• Judgment lags behind development of intellect
• Impaired adherence to commands to regulate or inhibit behavior in social contexts	• Intensity may lead to power struggles with authorities
• More active, restless than normal children	• High activity level; may need less sleep
• Difficulty adhering to rules and regulations	• Questions rules, customs and traditions

Consider the Situation and Setting

It is important to examine the situations in which a child's behaviors are problematic. Gifted children typically do not exhibit problems in all situations. For example, they may be seen as

*Note. Reprinted with permission from the *Diagnostic and Statistical Manual of Mental Disorders, Third Edition, Revised,* Washington, DC, American Psychiatric Association, 1987.

ADHD-like by one classroom teacher, but not by another; or they may be seen as ADHD at school, but not by the scout leader or music teacher. Close examination of the troublesome situation generally reveals other factors which are prompting the problem behaviors. By contrast, children with ADHD typically exhibit the problem behaviors in virtually all settings—including at home and at school—though the extent of their problem behaviors may fluctuate significantly from setting to setting (Barkley, 1990), depending largely on the structure of that situation. That is, the behaviors exist in all settings, but are more of a problem in some settings than in others.

In the classroom, a gifted child's perceived inability to stay on task is likely to be related to boredom, curriculum, mismatched learning style, or other environmental factors. Gifted children may spend from one-fourth to one-half of their regular classroom time waiting for others to catch up—even more if they are in a heterogeneously grouped class. Their specific level of academic achievement is often two to four grade levels above their actual grade placement. Such children often respond to non-challenging or slow-moving classroom situations by "off-task" behavior, disruptions, or other attempts at self-amusement. This use of extra time is often the cause of the referral for an ADHD evaluation.

Hyperactive is a word often used to describe gifted children as well as children with ADHD. As with attention span, children with ADHD have a high activity level, but this activity level is often found across situations (Barkley, 1990). A large proportion of gifted children are highly active too. As many as one-fourth may require less sleep; however, their activity is generally focused and directed (Clark, 1992; Webb, Meckstroth, & Tolan, 1982), in contrast to the behavior of children with ADHD. The intensity of gifted children's concentration often permits them to spend long periods of time and much energy focusing on whatever truly interests them. Their specific interests may not coincide, however, with the desires and expectations of teachers or parents.

While the child who is hyperactive has a very brief attention span in virtually every situation (usually except for television or computer games), children who are gifted can concentrate comfortably for long periods on tasks that interest them, and do not require immediate completion of those tasks or immediate consequences. The activities of children with ADHD tend to be both continual and random; the gifted child's activity usually is episodic and directed to specific goals.

While difficulties and adherence to rules and regulations has only begun to be accepted as a sign of ADHD (Barkley, 1990), gifted children may actively question rules, customs and traditions, sometimes creating complex rules which they expect others to respect or obey. Some engage in power struggles. These behaviors can cause discomfort for parents, teachers, and peers.

One characteristic of ADHD that does not have a counterpart in children who are gifted is variability of task performance. In almost every setting, children with ADHD tend to be highly inconsistent in the quality of their performance (i.e., grades, chores) and the amount of time used to accomplish tasks (Barkley, 1990). Children who are gifted routinely maintain consistent efforts and high grades in classes when they like the teacher and are intellectually challenged, although they may resist some aspects of the work, particularly repetition of tasks perceived as dull. Some gifted children may become intensely focused and determined (an aspect of their intensity) to produce a product that meets their self-imposed standards.

What Teachers and Parents Can Do

Determining whether a child has ADHD can be particularly difficult when that child is also gifted. The use of many instruments, including intelligence tests administered by qualified professionals, achievement and personality tests, as well as parent and teacher rating scales, can help the professional determine the subtle differences between ADHD and giftedness. Individual evaluation allows the professional to establish maximum rapport with the child to get the best effort on the tests. Since the test situation is constant, it is possible to make better comparisons among children. Portions of the intellectual and achievement tests will reveal attention problems or learning disabilities, whereas personality tests are designed to show whether emotional problems (e.g., depression or anxiety) could be causing the problem behaviors. Evaluation should be followed by appropriate curricular and instructional modifications that account for advanced knowledge, diverse learning styles, and various types of intelligence.

Careful consideration and appropriate professional evaluation are necessary before concluding that bright, creative, intense youngsters like Howard have ADHD. Consider the characteristics of the gifted/talented child and the child's situation. Do not hesitate to raise the possibility of giftedness with any professional who is evaluating the child for ADHD; however, do not be surprised if the professional has had little training in recognizing the characteristics of gifted/talented children (Webb, 1993). It is important to make the correct diagnosis, and parents and teachers may need to provide information to others since giftedness is often neglected in professional development programs.

References

American Psychiatric Association (1987). *Diagnostic and statistical manual of mental disorders, Third edition, revised.* Washington, DC: Author.

Barkley, R. A. (1990). *Attention deficit hyperactivity disorder: A handbook for diagnosis and treatment.* Guilford Press: New York.

Clark, B. (1992). *Growing up gifted.* Macmillan: New York.

Parker, H. C. (1992). *The ADD hyperactivity handbook for schools.* Plantation, FL: Impact Publications.

Webb, J. T. (1993). Nurturing social-emotional development of gifted children. In K. A. Heller, F. J. Monks, and A. H. Passow (Eds.), *International Handbook for Research on Giftedness and Talent,* pp. 525-538. Oxford: Pergamon Press.

Webb, J. T., Meckstroth, E. A., and Tolan, S. S. (1982). *Guiding the gifted child: A practical source for parents and teachers.* Dayton: Ohio Psychology Press.

* * * * *

James T. Webb, Ph.D., is Professor and Associate Dean, School of Professional Psychology, Wright State University, Dayton, Ohio and senior author of *Guiding the Gifted Child.*
Diane Latimer, M.A. is at the School of Professional Psychology, Wright State University, Dayton, Ohio.

ERIC Digests are in the public domain and may be freely reproduced and disseminated.

This publication was prepared with funding from the Office of Educational Research and Improvement, U.S. Department of Education, under contract no. RR93002005. The opinions expressed in this report do not necessarily reflect the positions or policies of OERI or the Department of Education.

ERIC

Clearinghouse on Disabilities and Gifted Education

The Council for Exceptional Children
1920 Association Drive • Reston, VA 22091-1589
1-800-328-0272 • 703-264-9474 • FAX 703-264-9494 • Internet ericec@inet.ed.gov

ERIC Mini-Bib

September 1995

Readings And Resources On
Attention Deficit Disorders(ADD)/
Attention Deficit Hyperactivity Disorders (ADHD)

Crook, W. G. (1991). *Help for the hyperactive child.* Professional Books, PO Box 3246, Jackson, TN 38302. 245pp.

This guide for parents focuses on treating hyperactivity and attention deficit disorders, as well as related behavior and learning problems, through allergy detection, nutritional changes, and avoidance of environmental toxins, rather than drug treatment. Suggestions are given to parents, teachers and other professionals including; dietary changes, good nutritional supplements, food allergies, lifestyle changes, control of candida, psychological support and discipline and helping the child succeed in school.

DuPaul, G. J., & Stoner, G. (1994). *ADHD in the schools: Assessment and intervention strategies.* Guilford Publications Inc., 72 Spring Street, New York, NY 10012. 269pp.

This book addresses school-related problems associated with attention deficit hyperactivity disorder (ADHD), such as academic underachievement, noncompliance with classroom rules, and problematic peer relationships. Eleven appendices provide examples of ADHD identification criteria, a teacher handout on ADHD medications, an ADHD self-report rating scale, suggested readings, and samples for professional communications.

Fouse, B., & Brians, S. (1993). *A primer on attention deficit disorder.* (Fastback 354).Phi Delta Kappa, PO Box 789, Bloomington, IN 47402-0789. 45pp. (ED370319 microfiche only)

This pamphlet explains briefly what is known about attention deficit disorder (ADD) to help parents and educators have a more positive influence on the ADD child's life. It begins with definitions of terminology, characteristics of preschool, school-age, and adult individuals with ADD, and causes of ADD. It discusses special problems associated with ADD, including academic problems, behavior problems, interpersonal difficulties, and self-esteem difficulties. Strategies effective in managing ADD are outlined, including medical management, behavioral strategies, cognitive-behavioral therapy, modifications in assignments and tests, and instruction in learning strategies.

Friedman, R. J., & Doyal, G. T. (1992). *Management of children and adolescents with attention deficit-hyperactivity disorder.* (3rd ed.) Pro-ed, 8700 Shoal Creek Blvd., Austin, TX 78758-6897. 198pp.

This book combines medical and psychological research findings with clinical experience gained from work with children with attention deficit hyperactivity disorder (ADHD) and their families. The book begins with definitions and statistical information, and then goes on to review medical, psychological, and educational management programs.

Gordon, S. B., & Asher, M. J. (1994). *Meeting the ADD challenge: A practical guide for teachers.* Research Press, 2612 N. Mattis Ave., Champaign, IL 61821. 188pp.

This book is designed to help classroom teachers meet the challenge of serving students with attention deficit disorder (ADD) by presenting practical information about the needs and treatment of these children and adolescents. A five-stage model for behavioral assessment is described, involving problem identification, measurement and functional analysis, matching intervention to students, assessment of intervention strategies, and evaluation of the intervention plan. Specific assessment methods for use within this model are then discussed, and basic issues to be addressed prior to the design of an intervention strategy are analyzed.

Hartman, T. (1994). *Focus your energy: Hunting for success in business with attention deficit disorder.* Pocket Books, Simon & Schuster Consumer Group, 1230 Avenue of the Americas, New York, NY 10020. 138pp.

This book examines common characteristics of individuals with attention deficit disorder (ADD) who have succeeded in business, and draws on these findings to provide suggestions for adults with ADD. Guidelines for finding appropriate jobs in existing businesses are provided, as are tips on starting one's own business. Specific suggestions focus on how to harness and manage ADD in the workplace, including goal-setting, running meetings, and interpersonal relationships.

Johnson, D. D. (1992). *I can't sit still: Educating and affirming inattentive and hyperactive children. Suggestions for parents, teachers and other care providers of children to age 10.* ETR Associates, PO Box 1830, Santa Cruz, CA 95061-1830. 800-321-4407. 178pp.

Causes, symptoms and challenges related to attention deficit hyperactivity disorder are discussed, with a strong emphasis on cultivating students' self-esteem. Diagnosis of attention problems is described, as are treatments such as behavior management, drug therapy, and cognitive-behavioral therapy. Self-esteem is approached as a combination of feeling valued, feeling in control, feeling capable and avoiding embarrassment. Methods for parents, teachers and students to moderate and control their frustration and anger are described.

Johnston, R. B. (1991). *Attention deficits, learning disabilities, and Ritalin: A practical guide.* (2nd ed.) Singular Publishing Group, Inc., 4284 41st St., San Diego, CA 92105-1197; 800-521-8545. 178pp.

This book reviews practical aspects of identifying learning and attention disabilities; examines the problems and pitfalls in diagnosis and treatment; explores the expectations, limitations, and precautions necessary in using Ritalin® (brand name for methylphenidate); attempts to demystify what physicians do; addresses the dynamics of an effective team approach; and argues the need to demedicalize learning and attention disabilities.

Lerner, J. W. (1995). *Attention deficit disorders: Assessment and teaching.* Brooks/Cole Publishing Co., 511 Forest Lodge Rd., Pacific Grove, CA 93950. 259pp.

This book on attention deficit disorders (ADD) is designed to prepare current and prospective teachers and other school personnel to teach and work with students with ADD in the schools. The book reviews assessment methods, the diagnostic process and testing instruments; describes methods that regular teachers can use in the classroom; describes interventions used by special educators; and discusses the challenges faced by the parent of a child with ADD, methods of counseling, and home management for parents. Issues involved in using medications and the kinds of medications administered to children with ADD are reviewed.

Moss, R. A., & Dunlap, H. H. (1990). *Why Johnny can't concentrate*. Bantam Books, 666 Fifth Ave., New York, NY 10103. 225pp.
This book explains the components of attention deficit disorder (ADD) in children, acknowledges the diversity of children with these dysfunctions and the limitations of the labels used to categorize them, and offers suggestions regarding the practical management of these children. The book offers a general picture of the characteristics of ADD and the process of diagnosis, and provides chapters that look at ADD in four age groups: preschoolers, early elementary school, late elementary and junior high, and adulthood. The book also provides specific information to equip parents to help their children and to find qualified professionals when needed.

Nadeau, K. (Ed.) (1995). *A comprehensive guide to attention deficit disorder in adults: Research, diagnosis, and treatment.* Brunner/Mazel Publishers, 19 Union Square West, New York, NY 10003. 408pp.
This book is written for professionals who diagnose and treat adults with attention deficit disorder (ADD), it provides information from psychologists and physicians on the most current research and treatment issues regarding our understanding of ADD as a neurobiological disorder. Authors examine ADD with and without hyperactivity and describe a wide range of assessment tools that can be useful in developing a full diagnostic picture of different conditions that must be addressed in treating adults with the disorder.

Nadeau, K. G., & Dixon, E. B. (1991). *Learning to slow down and pay attention*. Chesapeake Psychological Services, P.C., 5041 A & B, Backlick Rd., Annandale, VA 22003. 52pp.
This booklet designed for children with problems of attention, impulsivity, and concentration, is to be read along with their parents. Sections include a check list for students to assess their problems at school, at home, and with friends; ways that other people can help the student, such as a talking with a counselor; and things the student can do to help himself or herself. Tips on doing homework, getting ready for school, paying attention in class, and solving problems are included. The book is written in easy-to-understand language and illustrated with cartoons.

Nadeau, K. G. (1994). *Survival guide for college students with ADD or LD*. Brunner/Mazel Publishers, 19 Union Square West, New York, NY 10003. 56pp.
This book is written for college students with attention deficit disorders, hyperactivity, or learning disabilities who are applying to or are already enrolled in college. Chapters include questions to consider in choosing a college, on-campus accommodations, coping strategies, specific tips for organizing important information and managing time, choosing a major, career guidance, tutoring, learning self-advocacy, and resources and services available elsewhere in the community.

Neuville, M. B. (1995). *Sometimes I get all scribbly*. (Rev.ed.) Pro-ed, 8700 Shoal Creek Blvd., Austin, TX 78757-6897. 159pp.
This first-person account of life with a child with attention deficit hyperactivity disorder (ADHD) addresses the author's struggles to help and understand her son. The story is a mother's testament to the day-to-day, moment-to-moment existence of life with a child who is hyperactive. It validates the struggles and triumphs of their lives.

Paltin, D. M. (1993). *The parents' hyperactivity handbook: Helping the fidgety child*. Plenum Publishing Corporation, 233 Spring St., New York, NY 10013. 800-221-9369. 291pp.
This book is written to provide information and suggestions on aspects of attention deficit hyperactivity disorder (ADHD) which parents of children with ADHD find most challenging. The first part of the book deals with behavior problems rooted in inattention, impulsivity, and hyperactivity. Aspects of childrens' affective development are discussed, including relationships among children and the interaction among self-concept, self-esteem, and self-mastery. The second part of the book then addresses specific issues such as medication, discussing ADHD with affected children, and working with schools and teachers.

Quinn, P. O. (Ed.). (1994). *ADD and the college student: A guide for high school and college students with attention deficit disorder*. Magination Press, Brunner/Mazel Publishers, 19 Union Square West, New York, NY 10003. 800-825-3089. 113pp.
This handbook was designed to help high school and college students who have attention deficit disorder (ADD) make a successful transition to college life. Chapters examine various aspects of ADD and its effects on college preparation and selection.

Quinn, P. O., & Stern, J. M. *Putting on the brakes: Young people's guide to understanding attention deficit disorder (ADHD)*. (1991). 64pp.; *The "Putting on the Brakes" activity book for young people with ADHD*. (1993). 88pps. Brunner/Mazel, Publishers, 19 Union Square West, New York, NY 10003.
This guide and accompanying activity book were designed to teach children between 8 and 13 the facts about attention deficit hyperactivity disorder (ADHD)and how to gain a sense of control. Tips are provided for organizing their lives through time management, improved study habits, and developing test taking skills. The activity book uses pictures, puzzles, and other techniques to assist in the learning of a wide range of skills.

Rief, S. F. (1993). *How to reach and teach ADD/ADHD children: practical techniques, strategies, and interventions for helping children with attention problems and hyperactivity*. Council for Exceptional Children, 1920 Association Drive, Reston, VA 22091-1589. 800-232-7323. 256pp.
This book provides information, techniques, and strategies to help students with attention deficit disorder (ADD) or attention deficit hyperactivity disorder (ADHD) succeed. This book is organized into 30 sections that provide practical guidance on such topics as: preventing behavioral problems in the classroom through effective management techniques; multisensory strategies for teaching academic skills; learning styles; cooperative learning techniques; protocol and steps for referring students and communicating effectively with parents, physicians, and agencies; and how administrators can help teachers and students to succeed.

Weaver, C. (Ed.)(1994). *Success at last!: Helping students with AD(H)D achieve their potential*. Heinemann, 361 Hanover St., Portsmouth, NH 03801-3912. 800-541-2086. 290pp.
This book presents a collection of papers on attention deficit hyperactivity disorder (ADHD) from parents, classroom teachers, teacher educators, researchers, curriculum specialists, administrators, and other stakeholders. Sections cover understanding and educating students with attention deficit (hyperactivity) disorders, student support services, different instructional paradigms, and seeing how ADHD students flourish when teachers change. Appendices include a U.S. Department of Education Memorandum on ADHD.

Weiss, L. (1992). *Attention deficit disorder in adults*. Taylor Publishing Company, 1550 W. Mockingbird Lane, Dallas, TX 75235. 217pp.
This book explores the manifestations of attention deficit disorder (ADD) in adults and what can be done to cope with its effects. Adults who live with ADD share their stories, as do their spouses and family members. Treatment options such as medication, group therapy, and creative visualization are described. Coping strategies for individuals hoping to control their temper, bolster self-esteem, and manage attention problems within an independent adult lifestyle are presented.

Wodrich, D. L. (1994). *Attention deficit hyperactivity disorder (ADHD)*. Paul H. Brookes Publishing Co., PO Box 10624, Baltimore, MD 22185-0624; 800-638-3775. 291pp.

This book aims to provide current information on attention deficit hyperactivity disorder (ADHD) in a clear, concise fashion to help parents deal with the various manifestations of this problem and the impact it has on their family life, as well as on the child's interpersonal life at home and at school. Information is presented on the various types of educational programs that might be useful for children with ADHD, and sources of financial help are discussed.

Materials From Federally Funded Research Projects:

In 1991 the U.S. Dept. of Education, Office of Special Education Programs (OSEP), funded four centers to synthesize the existing research on assessment and intervention practices to meet the needs of children with ADD. Titles are: *Assessment and Characteristics of Children with Attention Deficit Disorder* (ED363084), Arkansas Children's Hospital; *A Synthesis of the Research Literature on the Assessment and Identification of Attention Deficit Disorder* (ED363087), University of Miami; *Research Synthesis on Education Interventions for Students with Attention Deficit Disorder* (ED363085), Research Triangle Institute, NC; and *The Effects of Stimulant Medication on Children with Attention Deficit Disorder* (ED363086), University of California-Irvine. A fifth project was funded to investigate and report on promising classroom practices for children with attention deficits: *Promising Practices in Identifying and Educating Children with Attention Deficit Disorder* (ED363088) Federal Resource Center for Special Education, University of Kentucky.

A practitioner-oriented piece based on the above ADD research and other research on academic interventions for difficult-to-teach students was produced by Research Triangle Institute, NC: *Promising Classroom Interventions for Students with Attention Deficit Disorder* (ED363086).

The Chesapeake Institute, Washington DC published several documents based on the federally funded research syntheses: *Attention Deficit Disorder: Adding up the Facts* (ED370334), *Attention Deficit Disorder: Beyond the Myth* (ED370335), *Attention Deficit Disorder: What Teachers Should Know* (ED370336), *Attention Deficit Disorder: What Parents Should Know* (ED370337), *Where Do I Turn? A Resource Directory of Materials About Attention Deficit Disorder* (ED370333), *Teaching Strategies: Education of Children with Attention Deficit Disorder* (ED370332), *Executive Summaries of Research Syntheses and Promising Practices on the Education of Children with ADD* (ED363083).

The first in a series of policy briefs on ADHD has been produced by the Appalachia Educational Laboratory, Charleston, WV: *ADHD-New Legal Responsibilities for Schools* (ED378750).

Documents with an ED number can also be ordered for a fee through EDRS (ERIC Document Reproduction Service): 1-800-248-ERIC.

Videos:

A.D.D. Warehouse, 300 NW 70th Avenue, Suite 102 Plantation, FL 33317. 800-233-9273.
1-2-3 MAGIC: Training Your Preschooler & Preteen to Do What You Want Them to Do!
ADHD/ADD Video Resource for Schools with Attention without Tension
Educating Inattentive Children: A Guide for the Classroom;
How to Use Time-out Effectively
Understanding A.D.D.
Understanding Attention Disorders: Preschool through Adulthood
The Video SOS! Help for Parents
Why Won't My Child Pay Attention?

CACLD (Connecticut Association for Children with Learning Disabilities), 18 Marshall Street S., Norwalk, CT 06854. 203-838-5010.
Understanding Attention Deficit Disorder

CEC (Council for Exceptional Children), 1920 Association Drive, Reston, VA 22091-1589. 800-232-7323.
Facing the Challenges of ADD: A Kit for Parents & Teachers (2 videos)
A.D.D. from A to Z (4 videos)

Filmakers Library, 124 E. 40th Street, New York, NY 10016. 212-808-4980.
Out of Control

LDA (Learning Disabilities Association), 4156 Library Road, Pittsburgh, PA 15234. 412-341-1515.
Living with A.D.D.

Guilford Publications, 72 Spring St., New York, NY 10012. 800-365-7006.
ADHD What Can We Do?
ADHD What Do We Know?

JKL Communications, PO Box 40157, Washington, DC 20016. 202-223-5097.
The ABC's of ADD
Succeeding in the Workplace

National Professional Resources, Inc., Dept. B-2, 25 S. Regent Street, Port Chester, NY 10573. 914-937-8879.
It's Just Attention Disorder--A Video Guide for Kids
Inclusion of Children & Youth with Attention Deficit Disorder

StarBase One Limited, Box 1447, Nevada City, CA 95959.
Peer Support ADHD ADD Teens Speak Out!

University of Kentucky, Medical Television, 207 HSLC, 760 Rose St., Lexington, KY 40536-0232.
Attention Deficit Hyperactivity Disorder: Diagnosis and Management; A Training Program for Teachers

University of Minnesota, Dept. of Professional Development and Conference Services, 214 Nolte Center, 315 Pillsbury Drive, SE, Minneapolis, MN 55455-0139.
Creative Approaches to Attention Deficit Hyperactivity Disorder: Active Partnerships

Journals:

Attention, CHADD (Children with Attention Deficit Disorder), 499 Northwest 70th Ave., Suite 101, Plantation, FL 33317; 305-587-3700.
Journal of Learning Disabilities, Pro-ed, 5341 Industrial Oaks Blvd., Austin, TX 78735-8809; 512-451-3246.
Learning Disabilities Quarterly, Council for Learning Disabilities, PO Box 40303, Overland Park, KS 66204; 913-492-8755.

Journals (*Special Issues*):

Exceptional Children. Issues in the Education of Children with Attention Deficit Disorder, Vol.60 No.2, Oct/Nov 1993 Council for Exceptional Children, 1920 Association Dr., Reston, VA 22091-1589; 800-232-7323.
Intervention in School and Clinic. Attention-Deficit/Hyperactivity Disorder: Academic Strategies, Comprehensive Assessment, Students with ADHD in the Inclusive Classroom, Vol.30 No. 4, Mar 1995, Pro-ed, 5341 Industrial Oaks Blvd., Austin, TX 78735-8809; 512-451-3246.
Topics in Language Disorders. ADD and Its Relationship to Spoken and Written Language, Vol.14 No.4, Aug 1994, Aspen Publishers, Inc., 200 Orchard Ridge Dr., Gaithersburg, MD 20878; 800-638-8437.

Newsletters:

ADDendum (for and by ADD adults)
c/o CPS 5041A Backlick Road
Annandale, VA 22003
ADD-ONS, PO Box 675, Frankfort, IL 60423

ADDult News Newsletter of ADDult Support Network, 2620 Ivy Place, Toledo, OH 43613

Brakes, Magination Press, Brunner/Mazel Publishers, 19 Union Square West, New York, NY 10003; 800-825-3089.

CH.A.D.D.E.R, and *CH.A.D.D.E.R. Box* Newsletters of CHADD (Children with Attention Deficit Disorder), 499 NW 70th Ave., Suite 308, Plantation, FL 33317.

Challenge, newsletter of ADDA (Attention Deficit Disorder Association), PO Box 2001, West Newbury, MA 01985.

Resources:

Attention Deficit Disorder Association (ADDA)
PO Box 972
Mentor, OH 44061
800-487-2282

Attention Deficit Information Network (AD-IN)
475 Hillside Avenue
Needham, MA 02194
617-455-9895

Children with Attention Deficit Disorder (CHADD)
499 NW 70th Avenue, Suite 308
Plantation, FL 33317
305-587-3700
(call for number of your local CHADD group)

National Information Center for Children and Youth with Disabilities (NICHCY)
PO Box 1492
Washington, DC 20013
800-695-0285

Note. This bibliography was compiled by Janet Drill and Barbara Sorenson.

Internet Resources:

Gopher sites: gopher sjuvm.stjohns.edu
   St. John's University
   Electronic Rehabilitation Resource Center
   Norman Coombs, Jay Leavitt

   gopher hawking.u.washington.edu
   University of Washington
   Dean Martineau (demar@u.washington.edu)

FTP Sites: ftp://com13.netcom.com/pub/lds/add/add.faq
   ftp://mcs.com:/mcsnet.users/falcon/add
   ftp.netcom:/pub/lds/add

Worldwide Web: These homepages have disability-related information:
   http://www.seas.upenn.edu/~mengwong/add/20q.html
   http://www.seas.upenn.edu/~mengwong/add/gifts.html
   http://www.usfca.edu/usf/westford/westford.html
   http://www.eskimo.com/~jlubin
   http://www.eskimo.com/~dempt
   http://www.digimark.net/a+/ada.htlm (Americans w/Disabilities)
   http://disability.com (disability resources, products, and services)
      Site features disability tips of the month,
      One Step Ahead newsletter, Disability Mall.
      Site is sponsored by Evan Kemp Associates, a company managed by people with disabilities.
      For more info, contact: webmaster@eka.com

If you subscribe to America Online (AOL), there are several weekly ADD conferences in the Issues in Mental Health Forum (use the keyword IMH).

If you subscribe to CompuServe, there is an ADD Forum (GO ADD), a DISABILITIES FORUM (GO DISABILITIES), and an EDUCATION Forum (GO EDFORUM) that address special needs.

If you subscribe to Delphi, there are two forums: ADDvantage Mental Health and ADD Parents Playhouse.

==

INTERNET LISTSERVs:

To subscribe (be added) to a listserv:
   Send an e-mail message to the listserv address.
   Leave the Subject line blank.
   In the body of the message, type ONLY the following:

   SUBSCRIBE [list name] yourfirstname yourlastname
   Majordomo lists only: SUBSCRIBE (listname) your e-mail address

   For example: SUBSCRIBE ADA-LAW Mary Smith

List Name	Subscription Address	Post Messages To
ADD-PARENTS	majordomo@mv.mv.com	add-parents@mv.mv.com
ADDULT	listserv@sjuvm.stjohns.edu	addult@sjuvm.stjohns.edu
ADD-EMP-SUPPT-L	listserv@netcom.com	add-emp-suppt-l@netcom.com
LD-LIST	ld-list-request@east.pima.edu	ld-list@east.pima.edu
SO_ADD_SUPPORT-L	listserv@netcom.com	so_add_support-l@netcom.com

NEWSGROUPS:
alt.support.attn-deficit: This is a USENET news group. (Ask your system administrator how to gain access to newsgroups.)

Note. We do NOT verify the technical accuracy nor any claims made in the announcements nor do we necessarily agree with them. We do not warranty or guarantee any services that might be announced. Use at your own risk.

==

This publication was prepared with funding from the Office of Educational Research and Improvement, U.S. Department of Education, under contract no. RR93002005. The opinions expressed in this report do not necessarily reflect the positions or policies of OERI or the Department of Education.

What Happens Between Assessments?

by Jay McTighe

Not only assessment needs to change. Curriculums and instructional strategies, too, must reflect a *performance* orientation. Here are seven principles for performance-based instruction.

Growing concern over the inadequacy of conventional tests has spurred interest in performance assessments, such as performance tasks, projects and exhibitions. To many supporters, these performance assessments are better suited than traditional tests to measure what really counts: whether students can apply their knowledge, skills, and understanding in important, real-world contexts. More teachers are using performance assessments in their classrooms, and such assessments are beginning to influence district- and state-level testing programs as well.

Increasing the use of performance assessments — in and of itself — will not significantly improve student performance, however. To borrow the old farm adage: "You don't fatten the cattle by weighing them." If we expect students to improve their performance on these new, more authentic measures, we need to engage in "performance-based instruction" on a regular basis.

But what does it really mean to teach for performance? Working the past six years with hundreds of teachers using performance assessments, I have seen how the development of assessment tasks and evaluative criteria can influence instruction. Based on this experience, I offer seven principles of performance-based instruction,

illustrated by vignettes from classrooms in which these principles are being applied.

Establish Clear Performance Targets

As part of a unit on nutrition, a middle school health teacher presents her students with the following performance task.

> You are having six of your friends over for your birthday party. You are preparing the food for the party, but your mother has just read a book on nutrition and tells you that you can't serve anything containing artificial sweeteners or lots of salt, sugar, or saturated fats. Plan a menu that will make your friends happy and still meet your mother's expectations. Explain why your menu is both tasty and healthy. Use the USDA Food Pyramid guidelines and the Nutrition Facts on food labels to support your menu selection. [1]

To teach effectively, we need to be clear about what we expect students to know, understand, and be able to do as a result of our instruction. But performance-based instruction calls for more. We also need to determine *how* students will demonstrate the intended knowledge, understanding, and proficiency. When establishing performance targets, consider Gardner's (1991) contention that developing students' *understanding* is a primary goal of teaching. He defines understanding

as the ability to apply facts, concepts, and skills appropriately in new situations.

The principle of *establishing clear performance targets* and the goal of *teaching for understanding* fit together as a powerful means of linking curriculum, instruction, and assessment. A performance-based orientation requires that we think about curriculum not simply as content to be covered but in terms of desired *performances of understanding*. Thus, performance-oriented teachers consider assessment up front by conceptualizing their learning goals and objectives as performance applications calling for students to demonstrate their understanding. Performance assessments, then, become targets for teaching and learning, as well as serving as a source of evidence that students understand, and are able to apply, what we have taught.

Establishing clear performance targets is important for several reasons. Teachers who establish and communicate clear performance targets to their students reflect what we know about effective teaching, which supports the importance of instructional clarity. These teachers also recognize that students' attitudes and perceptions toward learning are influenced by the degree to which they understand what is expected of them and what the rationale is for various instructional activities. Finally, the process of establishing performance targets helps identify curriculum priorities, enabling us to focus on the essential and enduring knowledge in a crowded field.

Strive for Authenticity in Products and Performances

Fifth graders conduct a survey to gather data about community attitudes toward a proposal that public school students wear uniforms. The students organize the data and then choose an appropriate graphic display for communicating their findings. Finally, students write letters to the editor of the local paper to present their data and their personal views on the proposal. A direct link to the larger world is established when two student letters are published in the newspaper.

Leading reformers recommend that schools involve their students in authentic work. Performance tasks should call upon students to demonstrate their knowledge and skills in a manner that reflects the world outside the classroom. Although diagramming sentences may help students understand sentence structures and parts of speech, this is not really an authentic activity, because few people outside of school diagram sentences. When students engage in purposeful writing (for example, to persuade an identified audience), however, they are using their knowledge and skills in ways much more congruent with the demands of real life.

As in the larger world, authentic work in schools calls for students to apply their knowledge and skills, with the result typically being a tangible product (written, visual, or three-dimensional) or a performance. These products and performances have an explicit *purpose* (for example, to explain, to entertain, or to solve a problem) and are directed toward an identified *audience*. Because real-world issues and problems are rarely limited to a single content area, authentic work often provides opportunities for making interdisciplinary connections.

Emphasizing authentic work does not lessen the importance of helping students develop basic skills. On the contrary, basic knowledge and skills provide an essential foundation for meaningful application. The "basics" are not ends in themselves, however; they serve a larger goal: to enable students to thoughtfully apply knowledge and skills within a meaningful, authentic context.

Research and experience confirm that when learners perceive classroom activities as meaningful and relevant, they are more likely to have a positive attitude toward them (McCombs 1984, Schunk 1990). In addition, many teachers have observed that when given the opportunity to produce a tangible product or demonstrate something to a real audience (for example, peers, parents, younger or older students, community members), students often seem more willing to put forth the effort required to do quality work.

Remember that what we assess sends a strong signal to students about what is important for them to learn. When authentic performance tasks play a key role in teaching and assessing, students will know that we expect them to apply knowledge in ways valued in the world beyond the classroom.

Publicize Criteria and Performance Standards

Before beginning a laboratory experiment, a high school science teacher reviews the Science Department's performance list for a lab report with her students. The list, containing the criteria for a thorough report, clearly conveys the teacher's expectations while serving as a guide to the students as they prepare their reports. Before she collects the reports, the teacher allows students to exchange papers with their lab partners, give feedback to one another based on the performance list criteria, and make needed revisions.[2]

> When students have opportunities to examine their work in light of known criteria and performance standards, they begin to shift their orientation from "What did I get?" to "Now I know what I need to do to improve."

Like the problems and issues we confront in the real world, authentic classroom performance tasks rarely have a single, correct answer. Therefore, our evaluation of student products and performances must be based upon judgment and guided by criteria. The criteria are typically incorporated into one of several types of scoring tools: a rubric, a rating scale, or a performance list. With all of these tools, the criteria help to spell out the qualities that we consider to be most significant or important in student work.

Teachers at elementary schools in Anne Arundel County, Maryland, use a "Writing to Persuade" rubric to help students learn the qualities of effective persuasive writing. A large poster of the rubric, containing the criteria in the form of questions, is prominently displayed in the front of the classroom to provide an easy reference for teachers and students. For example: "Did I clearly identify my position?" "Did I fully support my position with facts or personal experiences?" "Did I effectively use persuasive language to convince my audience?"

Evaluative criteria clearly are essential for summative evaluations, but teachers also are recognizing their role in *improving* performance. By sharing the criteria with students, we begin to remove the mystery of how work will be evaluated, while highlighting the elements of quality and standards of performance toward which students should strive. Teachers also can help students internalize these elements of quality by having them use scoring tools themselves to evaluate their own work or that of their peers. When students have opportunities to examine their work in light of known criteria and performance standards, they begin to shift their orientation from "What did I get?" to "Now I know what I need to do to improve."

Provide Models of Excellence

A middle school art teacher displays five examples of well-constructed papier-maché sculptures of "figures in action." The examples illustrate the criteria by which the sculptures will be evaluated: composition (figure showing action), strength and stability of armature (underlying structure), surface construction (application of papier-maché), finishing techniques (texture, color, details), and overall effect. The teacher notes that the quality of her students' sculptures has markedly improved since she began sharing and discussing actual models of excellence.

Providing students with lists of criteria or scoring rubrics is a necessary piece of performance-based instruction — but it isn't always sufficient. Not every student will immediately understand the criteria or how to apply them to their own work ("What do you mean by well organized?"). Wiggins (1993) suggests that if we expect students to do excellent work, they need to know what excellent work looks like. Following his idea, performance-based instruction calls for providing students with models and demonstrations that illustrate excellence in products or performances.

This approach, of course, is not unknown in schools. Effective coaches and sponsors of extracurricular activities often involve their club or team members in analyzing award-winning school newspapers or yearbooks, or reviewing videotapes of excellent athletic or dramatic performances. But providing models of quality work is also an essential piece of performance-based instruction in classrooms.

Teachers can use examples of excellent work during instruction to help students understand the desired elements of quality. Some teachers also present students with examples of mediocre and excellent work, asking them to analyze the differences and identify the characteristics that distinguish the excellent examples from the rest. In this way, students learn the criteria of quality through tangible models and concrete examples. In some classrooms, students actually help to construct the scoring tools (rubric, rating scale, or performance list), based on their growing knowledge of the topic and the criteria they have identified in the examples. (The potential benefits of providing students with tangible examples underscore the value of saving examples of student work from performance tasks for use as models in future years!)

Some teachers are wary of providing models of quality, fearing that students may simply copy or imitate the examples. This is a real danger with activities for which there is a single correct answer (or one "best" way of accomplishing the task). With more open-ended performance tasks and projects, however, we can minimize this problem by presenting students with multiple models. In this way, students are shown several different ways to satisfy the desired criteria, thus discouraging a cookie-cutter approach.

By providing students with criteria *and* models of excellence, teachers are often rewarded with higher quality products and performances. In addition, they are helping students become more self-directed; students able to distinguish between poor- and high-quality performance are more likely to be able to evaluate and improve their own work, guided by a clear conception of excellence.

Teach Strategies Explicitly

An elementary teacher introduces his students to two strategies — summarizing and predicting — to enhance their comprehension of text materials. He describes each strategy and models its use by thinking aloud while applying it to a challenging text. During the lesson, the teacher refers to large posters spelling out a written procedure and visual symbol for each strategy. Following the lesson, he distributes bookmark versions of the posters. Over the next two weeks, each student works with a reading buddy to practice using the strategies with both fiction and nonfiction texts while the teacher monitors their progress and provides guidance.

In every field of endeavor, effective performers use specific techniques and strategies to boost their performance. Olympic athletes visualize flawless performances, writers seek feedback from "critical friends," law students form study groups, coaches share tips at coaching clinics, busy executives practice time management techniques.

Students also benefit from specific strategies that can improve their performance on academic tasks. For example, webbing and mapping techniques help students see connections, cognitive reading strategies boost comprehension (Palinscar and Brown 1984); Haller, Child, and Walberg 1988), brainstorming techniques enhance idea generation, and mnemonics assists retention and recall.

Few students spontaneously generate and use strategies on their own, however, so we need to explicitly teach these thinking and learning strategies. One straightforward approach is to use the direct instruction model, in which teachers

1. introduce and explain the purpose of the strategy;

2. demonstrate and model its use;

3. provide guided practice for students to apply the strategy with feedback;

4. allow students to apply the strategy independently and in teams; and

5. regularly reflect on the appropriate uses of the strategy and its effectiveness.

In addition to direct instruction, many teachers find it helpful to incorporate thinking and learning strategies into tangible products, such as posters, bookmarks, visual symbols, or cue cards (McTighe and Lyman 1988). For example, students in a middle school mathematics class I am familiar with have constructed desktop spinners depicting six problem-solving strategies they have been taught. When working on open-ended problems, the students use the spinners to indicate the strategy they are using. Their teacher circulates around the room, asking students to think aloud by explaining their reasoning and problem-solving strategies. Later, she leads a class discussion of solutions and the effectiveness of the strategies used. The spinners provide students with a tangible reminder of the value of using strategies during problem solving. These and other cognitive tools offer students practical and concrete support as they acquire and internalize performance-enhancing strategies.

Use Ongoing Assessments for Feedback and Adjustment

A middle school social studies teacher notes that the quality of her students' research reports has markedly improved since he began using the writing process approach of brainstorming, drafting, reviewing feedback, and revising. Through the use of teacher and peer reviews of draft reports, students are given specific feedback on strengths, as well as on aspects of their reports that may be unclear, inaccurate, or incomplete. They appreciate the opportunity to make necessary revisions before turning in their final copy.

The Japanese concept of *Kaizen* suggests that quality is achieved through constant, incremental improvement. According to J. Edwards Deming, guru of the Total Quality Management movement, quality in manufacturing is not achieved through end-of-line inspections; by then, it is too late. Rather, the quality is the result of regular inspections (assessments) *along the way*, followed by needed adjustments based on the information gleaned from the inspections.

How do these ideas apply in an academic setting? We know that students will rarely perform at high levels on challenging learning tasks on the first attempt. Deep understanding or high levels of proficiency are achieved only as a result of trial, practice, adjustments based on feedback, and more practice. Performance-based instruction underscores the importance of using assessments to provide information to guide improvement throughout the learning process, instead of waiting to give feedback at the end of instruction.

Once again, effective coaches and sponsors of clubs often use this principle as they involve their students in scrimmages, dress rehearsals, and reviews of bluelines. Such activities serve to identify problems and weaknesses, followed by more coaching and opportunities to practice or revise.

The ongoing interplay between assessment and instruction so common in the arts and athletics is also evident in classrooms using practices such as nongraded quizzes and practice tests, the writing process, formative performance tasks, review of drafts, and peer response groups. The teachers in such classrooms recognize that ongoing assessments provide the feedback that enhances their instruction and guides student revision. *Kaizen*, in the context of schools, means ensuring that assessment enhances performance, not simply measures it.

Document and Celebrate Progress

Early in the school year, a middle school physical education teacher has her students analyze their current fitness levels based on a series of measures of strength, endurance, and flexibility. The initial results are charted and used to establish personal fitness goals. The teacher then guides students in preparing individualized fitness plans to achieve their goals. Subsequent fitness tests at the middle and end of the year enable the teacher and her students to document their progress and, if necessary, establish new goals. The teacher believes that the focus on improvement based on a personal benchmark allows every student to achieve a measure of success while cultivating the habits necessary for lifelong fitness.

Perhaps one of the greatest challenges in this current era of school reform is the gap between our goal of higher standards of performance for all and the realization that some students are functioning well below these lofty standards. Many educators struggle daily with this tension: How do we preserve students' self-esteem without lowering our standards? How do we encourage their efforts without conveying a false sense of accomplishment? Perceptive teachers also recognize that students' own beliefs about their ability to be successful in new learning situations are a critical variable. Confronted with rigorous performance standards, some students may well believe that the target is beyond their grasp and may not, as a result, put forth needed effort.

There are no easy solutions to this dilemma. But reflect for a moment on the natural inclination displayed by parents and grandparents of toddlers and preschoolers. They regularly support new performance by encouraging small steps ("C'mon, you can do it!"), celebrating incremental achievements ("Listen, everyone! She said, 'dada'!"), and documenting growth (witness the refrigerator displays ranging from scribbles of color to identifiable pictures). These celebrations encourage children to keep trying and to strive for greater competence. They focus on what youngsters *can do* and how they have

Performance tasks should call upon students to demonstrate their knowledge and skills in a manner that reflects the world outside the classroom.

improved as a means of spurring continued growth.

Performance-based instruction demands a similar tack. Acknowledging the limitations of one-shot assessments, such as tests and quizzes, as the primary measures of important learning goals, some educators are moving toward creating collections of student work over time. One manifestation of this is the growing interest in and use of portfolios. Consider an analogy with photography. If a test or quiz represents a snapshot (a picture of learning at a specific moment) then a portfolio is more like a photo album — a collection of pictures showing growth and change over time.

Just as portfolios can be extremely useful as a means of documenting student progress, they also provide a tangible way to display and celebrate student work. Grade-level teams at North Frederick Elementary School in Frederick, Maryland, for example, sponsor a "portfolio party" each fall and spring. Parents, grandparents, school board members, central office staff, business partners, and others are invited to review student work collected in portfolios. Before the party, teachers guide students in selecting examples from their portfolios that illustrate progress in key learning areas. During the party, students present their portfolios to the guests, describe their work during the year, highlight the progress they have made, and identify related goals for future improvement.

Principal Carolyn Strum says the school's portfolio program has had at least four benefits: (1) the systematic collection of student work throughout the year helps document student progress and achievement; (2) student work serves as a lens through which the faculty can reflect on their successes and adjust their instructional strategies; (3) school-to-home communication is enhanced as students present and explain their work to their parents and other adults; and (4) students assume greater ownership of their learning and display obvious pride when involved in selecting and showing off their accomplishments and growth.

Developing content standards, creating more authentic performance assessments, and establishing rigorous student performance standards will not — in and of themselves — substantially boost student achievement. But the seven principles above reflect promising ways that teachers and schools are beginning to rethink their curriculum and instructional strategies to ensure that *performance* is more than something measured at the end of a unit. ∎

[1]This performance task was developed in 1994 by R. Marzano and D. Pickering, Mid-Continent Regional Educational Laboratory Institute, Aurora, Colorado.

[2]For a detailed discussion and examples of classroom performance lists, see M. Hibbard and colleagues, (1996), *Performance-Based Learning and Assessment*, (Alexandria, Va.: Association for Supervision and Curriculum Development).

References

Haller, E., D. Child, and H. Walberg. (1988). "Can Comprehension Be Taught: A Qualitative Synthesis." *Educational Researcher* 17, 9:5-8.

Gardner, H. (1991). *The Unschooled Mind.* New York: Basic Books.

McCombs, B. (1984). "Processes and Skills Underlying Intrinsic Motivation to Learn: Toward a Definition of Motivational Skills Training Intervention." *Educational Psychologist* 19: 197-218.

McTighe, J., and F. Lyman. (1988). "Cueing Thinking in the Classroom: The Promise of Theory-Embedded Tools." *Educational Leadership* 45, 7: 18-24.

Palinscar, A., and A. Brown. (1984). "Reciprocal Teaching of Comprehension Fostering and Comprehension Monitoring Activities." *Cognition and Instruction* 1: 117-176.

Schunk, D. (1990). "Goal Setting and Self-Efficacy During Self-Regulated Learning." *Educational Psychologist* 25, 1: 71-86.

Wiggins, G. (1993). *Assessing Student Performance: Exploring the Limits and Purposes of Testing.* San Francisco, Calif.: Jossey-Bass.

Jay McTighe is Director of the Maryland Assessment Consortium, c/o Urbana High School, 3471 Campus Dr., Ijarnsville, MD 21754 (e-mail: jmctighe@aol.com)

Voices

Childhood is the most basic human right of children.

— *David Elkind*

How Did You Know the Answer Was *Boxcar?*

by Sherry Walton and Kathe Taylor

Like it or not, we're stuck with standardized, multiple-choice tests for the foreseeable future. Why not help children learn to use this testing format to develop new problem-solving strategies and approaches to learning and to *showing* what they've learned?

Please check the statements that you think are correct:

1. Despite the movement toward authentic assessment, most states in this country still use multiple-choice, standardized tests for student placement and to judge the effectiveness of public schools.

2. Many children first encounter standardized tests in the 1st grade, and they continue taking them through early adulthood.

3. Most four-year colleges use SAT or ACT scores as part of their admission criteria and give little indication of changing in the foreseeable future.

4. Students from lower socioeconomic levels perform less well on standardized tests than do other students, threatening their access to higher education and many professions.

5. All of the above are true.

6. None of the above are true. Performance-based tests are fast replacing multiple-choice, standardized tests.

As these statements suggest, the use of standardized, multiple-choice tests is a complicated issue. One problem is that of equity: Some groups of students tend to perform better on these tests than do others. African-American, Native American, and Hispanic students; girls; children from lower socioeconomic levels; and children with particular learning styles generally perform less well than do middle-class, Euro-American boys, and Asian-American students.

This equity issue has broad implications for two reasons. First, public officials and school administrators often use these scores as a basis for important decisions about school funding and access. Second, nationally-normed, psychometrically sound instruments are used pervasively in the United States, in part because they are easy to administer and score and the cost per student is low. This is true even in states like Vermont, where portfolio assessment is gaining ground. Given political realities, standardized tests aren't going to go away any time soon.

> We believe that we must find ways to use standardized tests and the skills upon which they depend to engage students in authentic teaching and learning.

Some educators maintain that because these tests don't fit the educational philosophy underlying authentic student performance, we should simply ignore them. Taking this high road may be philosophically comfortable, but it could harm children who have little choice about participating in standardized tests. Further, for most children, taking these tests *is* an authentic experience — as in real, not imaginary. Students will face these tests over and over again in the course of their lives.

This brings us to our position. We believe that we must find ways to use standardized tests and the skills upon which they depend to engage students in authentic teaching and learning. Only by doing so can we mitigate the inequities of standardized testing. As one African-American graduate student put it:

> It doesn't matter whether the tests measure knowledge or not. When children of color can't do well on them, they can't get into good colleges. They can't get good jobs. We need to know how to help children do better on these tests so the tests won't act as barriers to educational and economic opportunity.

No Surprises?

One possible approach occurred to us two years ago after the annual publication of test scores in our local newspaper. Sure enough, there were few surprises. Nearly all the schools composed primarily of middle- and upper-middle class kids delighted in scores that were quite acceptable. The other schools — including a school that was home to most of the town's homeless children, a school with the highest English-as-a-second-language population, and an elementary school we'll call the "Jane Doe" school — did not do so well.

In some of these schools there was talk of changing the curriculum to more closely approximate the test format. Some teachers developed workshops to reteach the skills on which the children scored poorly. Others maintained that the tests were irrelevant and should be ignored. Meanwhile, administrators were fielding questions from concerned parents and central office officials. Principals felt pressured, teachers felt frustrated, children were upset, and many parents were simply confused.

What was surprising about the results at Jane Doe was that (1) students were predominantly white and middle class and (2) the school's test scores did not reflect the quality and quantity of the learning going on there. The teachers at Jane Doe had developed a coherent, educationally sound curriculum based on learning as a developmental process. The students, parents, and teachers were involved in well-planned, authentic learning experiences.

Significantly, no one asked whether these students understood tests as a particular kind of thinking, problem-solving, and literacy. The underlying assumption was that whatever the tests were measuring, kids in some schools just didn't have enough of it. But the question that we found most compelling was this: Did these children — and children at the other low-scoring schools — understand *how* to demonstrate what they knew under timed, multiple-choice conditions?

Putting Performance in Context

Following conversations with teachers at Jane Doe, we began to explore whether they could enrich their curriculums by using standardized test formats to get students to use new problem-solving strategies and approaches to learning. We also began to consider how teaching for authentic student performance might be related to equity issues and test-taking.

We ended up collaborating with teachers at the Jane Doe School. As we worked with them, we learned about the school's educational environment and the students' test-taking knowledge and problem-solving skills. We also came to understand the children's emotional needs and the teachers' needs, concerns, and insights.

Based on this information, we designed a series of workshops to help teachers and students explore what various types of test questions really ask of the test-taker. We also developed workshop materials for the students and extensive scripts for the teachers to use in coaching the students. Unlike other test preparation programs, ours required engaging students in improving their problem-solving skills by examining correct answers.

During one workshop, for example, a child had been attempting to answer the question, "the freight train carried apples and oranges in its _____." The answer was *boxcar*. The child asked plaintively, "How did you know the answer was boxcar?" A classmate then realized how he associated information from the *Boxcar* children's book with this question. That response helped other children explain that answering a question with information from outside the school is a legitimate strategy.

> When children chose correct answers for nonstandard reasons, teachers and students could explore other explanations. Such incidents moved the workshops beyond simple test preparation and helped teachers use assessment as a catalyst for learning.

Situations like this were repeated many times as students helped one another discover new problem-solving strategies. The problems students brought up helped to clarify why they chose certain answers — reasons that often were very different from what teachers assumed. For example, one question listed four months — November, September, April and December — and asked students to select the one month that didn't fit in

this group. One child chose December, the correct response. But when asked to explain her choice, she did not give the "right" reason — December alone has 31 days. Instead, she said that December is when Christmas comes.

When children chose correct answers for nonstandard reasons, teachers and students could explore other explanations. Such incidents moved the workshops beyond simple test preparation and helped teachers use assessment as a catalyst for learning.

Authentically Good Performance

The workshops were successful beyond anyone's expectations. When the school's test scores were published the following spring, Jane Doe was the only school in the district whose scores improved significantly. And the improvement was dramatic: many children's scores had risen by as much as 20 or 30 percentile points between 1994 and 1995. In reading, the median percentile rank rose from 56 to 75; in math, it went from 33 to 57; and in language, from 35 to 66.

The curriculums in these content areas had not changed from one year to the next. Neither had the school's developmental approach to learning. What did change was the children's knowledge of how to take a standardized test.

Even more important than the scores were the children's and teachers' reactions to the workshops and their test-taking experiences. Children who had reported having few test-taking strategies, as well as considerable anxiety and little confidence in their ability to perform, became confident mentors for younger children. They told their fellow students how to remain calm, how to avoid getting stuck, how to eliminate choices, and how to approach particular types of questions efficiently. They explained why they didn't need to worry about the way other kids were rustling the pages of their test booklets. And they reassured them that it was okay to not know everything.

In general, the children spoke of feeling happy about having performed a challenging task well. The teachers, many of whom took a dim view of standardized tests, reported that the workshops helped them to better understand their students as learners and problem solvers. By paying attention to the tests as one type of literacy and performance experience, they were better able to teach for authentic student performance and better able to help their students understand their ability to successfully negotiate the standardized test.

> ... what we offered was a process that combined practice in a number of things: attempting unfamiliar formats, receiving immediate feedback, exploring reactions and feelings, and generating and actively discussing different problem-solving approaches.

Assessment as a Learning Experience

At Jane Doe we collaborated further with the teachers and students as they prepared for a different test. We also went on to coach teachers at an elementary school with a number of homeless students, a rural elementary school, and an elementary school with very good test scores. The average scores for three schools improved substantially, and results are not yet in for the fourth.

What we taught the children to do through the workshops was simple but fundamentally different from many test preparation programs. We had no new test strategies to offer. Rather, what we offered was a process that combined practice in a number of things: attempting unfamiliar formats, receiving immediate feedback, exploring reactions and feelings, and generating and actively discussing different problem-solving approaches. Through this teacher-guided, but student-centered, process, children learned how to show what they knew. ■

Sherry Walton is a faculty member at Evergreen State College, Olympia, WA 98505 (e-mail: waltonsl@elwha.evergreen. com). **Kathe Taylor** is Assistant Director for Assessment and Academic Policy, Higher Education Coordinating Board, 917 Lakeridge Way, P.O. Box 43430, Olympia, WA 88504 (e-mail: kathet@hecb.wa.com).

Voices

The goal of observation is understanding, not some imagined objectivity. If a teacher is invested in and fascinated by a child — if the child is a "favorite" — that is not a problem, the teacher will always be working to understand and teach that child. The problem is when the child is unseen, invisible, or not cared for — and this is not a problem of objectivity but of commitment. Pushing oneself to see and observe this child — and every child — is an act of compassion and an important part of teaching.

— **William Ayers**

To Teach: The Journey of a Teacher, NY: Teachers College Press, 1993. Quoted in *Taking Note* (Stenhouse).

WHAT *to* Write

BY BRENDA MILLER POWER

Sometimes I learn the most when I am uncomfortable, unsure, and attempting new things. As you use new tools to observe and note events in your classroom, you may gain new learning and insights. But your first days and hours of taking notes may cause moments of discomfort and uncertainty. In fact, if your notes are to improve, chances are you have to seek out that discomfort by pushing yourself to reconsider what you write about.

This insight came to me the first time I took classroom notes that were completely random and unfocused. Previously, I had never tried to take notes without doing some mental sorting and censoring of myself. But on this day many years ago, I sat in a first-grade classroom, taking notes as a group of girls participated in writing workshop. In this class, students were allowed to talk about whatever they wanted to talk about during workshop time, to write about whatever they wanted to write about. Here are some of my notes:

> Tammy is starting to write. She says, "I need a pink crayon. Sarah's got all the pink crayons." Sarah replies, "I do not. I brought my own crayons from home, see?" She pulls out a set of markers, throws a pink crayon at Tammy.

For ten minutes, all I did was write as fast as I could, detailing this insipid little scene of kids arguing over the crayons and who had a right to possess them. Most previous mornings, I would have quickly moved to another table. But on this morning, I was determined to follow the advice of my graduate school professor. He had admonished me that week to stay put in one spot and write as much as I could about whatever I saw, not censuring my writing.

> You have to give yourself permission to write freely. Words, phrases, random and seemingly trivial details need to land on the page when you are learning to take notes.

When I looked over my notes that afternoon, I could actually feel my face getting red. "Tammy then grabbed a pink crayon from Lisa." These were the scribblings of a moron! There wasn't a shred of insight into the writing processes of these kids. Here I was, almost finished with a graduate degree in literacy, and this was the best I could muster in my notetaking?

But the more I looked at these notes, the more I realized the kids spent *a lot* of time arguing over material goods in the writer's workshop. This led me eventually to see some of the underlying tensions in the workshop between the egalitarian values of the teacher and the more materialistic values of the kids. Some of my most original research began the day I stopped censuring my notes and really concentrated on just writing down what I saw.

You have to give yourself permission to write freely. Words, phrases, random and seemingly trivial details need to land on the page when you are learning to take notes. These notes shouldn't have a polished feel to them. They will lack insight. I think teachers do a whole lot of editing of what they are seeing and writing when they take notes because they don't want to be in the position I was, seeing what I had written as simplistic, rough, uninsightful. But that is exactly what you're going to need if you want to get fresh perspectives on some of the intractable issues in your classroom.

Too often, we write our observations within a firmly established context of what we think our classroom *is*. We want to believe we've created a democratic place, where reading and writing are valued, where students treat each other fairly. This may be true much of the time. But the times when it is not true are the times when both teachers and students are ripe for learning. Raw notes — just writing what you see, as fast as you can, without editorial comment or deletions — can get you to that clear picture of what your classroom is.

These raw notes are the raw materials from which your research or assessments can grow. They will contain gems, nuggets of truth that will shape the rest of your notetaking agenda. But these nuggets will have to be mined in the future.

The notes you take quickly each day won't be the whole narrative, the complete story. And they shouldn't have the smooth feel of telling the whole story of any child or day in the classroom. But they will have the ingredients you need to tell the story of one student, one class, or one curricular idea.

Taking raw notes is the process of gathering raw ingredients. You will need time later to measure, weigh, mix, and cook what you've gathered into some kind of final product. But remember that this does come *later*. You're on a shopping expedition now, getting the freshest, most useful materials out of your classroom.

As you begin to take notes, keep the following principles in mind. They will help you continue your observations when you're feeling unconfident about your skills.

Write the Unwritable

Most teachers seem to follow that Midwestern principle of better living in their notetaking — if you can't say something nice, don't say anything at all. But the most interesting and useful information in your classroom may make you blush. Give yourself permission to write the most inconsequential garbage in the world. You're trying to see students in new ways, and that requires really being open to what you're seeing around you. If you get stuck, consider these questions: What surprises you? Bothers you? Worries you? Write down observations that would make you cringe if others read them — Melissa whacking John on the arm during the science experiment (is it anger or first love?); the whole class discussion of *Charlotte's Web* that shows only half the class read the assigned chapters; the planned lesson on quotation marks that blossoms into an unexpected and animated discussion of idioms. If you get stuck, give yourself some prompts to keep going. Write "I see," "I hear," or "I wonder" and fill in your own blanks.

Just Count

If words get in the way for you, begin your notetaking by keeping tally sheets. Many teachers have had terrible experiences as writers, and it's not surprising that they struggle to write anything when it's time to take notes. If you are one of these teachers, you may want to ease into notetaking by keeping tally sheets. To tally, you begin with a list of students you

Figure 5.1

Marilyn's Discussion Group Tally

Discussion Group

Discussion Group	Teacher	Karen	Susan	Beth	Joe	Tim	Totals
Elaboration	4	0	8	5	4	2	23
Feedback	15	0	4	1	1	0	21
Topic Change	0	0	0	0	0	0	0
Interruptions	0	0	1	0	0	0	1
Directions	2	0	0	0	0	0	2
Procedure	0	9	5	9	7	8	38
Questions	24	3	8	5	3	3	46
Reading	0	1	1	1	1	1	5

Discussion Group	Teacher	Karen	Susan	Beth	Joe	Tim	Totals
# of Turns	43	13	26	21	17	13	133
# of Words	464	94	198	360	242	132	1490
Average Words per Turn	10.8	7.2	7.6	17.1	14.2	10.2	11.2

Discussion Group	Teacher	Students	Girls	Boys
# of Turns	43	90	60	30
# of Words	464	1026	652	374
Average Words per Turn	10.8	11.4	10.9	12.5
% of Turns	32.3	67.7	45.1	22.6
% of Words	31.1	68.9	43.8	25.1
# of Words Read	0	303	176	127
% of Words Read	0	100	58.1	42

Discussion Group	Girls	Boys
# of Turns Each	20	15
# of Words Ea.	217	187
% of Turns Ea.	15	11.3
% of Words Ea.	14.6	12.6

Figure 5.2

Gail's Reading
Clues Checklist

Reading Clues Checklist

Teacher _Mrs. Bussiere_ Date _____

GROUP & BOOK	PHONETIC	SEMANTIC
#2 Geraldine's Big Snow (continuation)	IIII ④	HHT HHT II ⑫
#3 Let's Tell Time	⓪	HHT HHT I ⑪
#1 The Snow	IIII ④	HHT ⑤
#1 Ten Bears in My Bed	IIII ④	HHT HHT I ⑪
#2 Little Bear's Friend Chapter 2	II ②	HHT ⑤

Figure 5.3

Joni's Tally
of Gender
Differences
in Literature
Discussion
Groups

Students and Teacher Response

Student Names	Responses	*Lost on a Mountain in Maine*
Josh	45	
Ken	16	
Justin	32	
Edward	39	
Matt	46	
Total Student	178	
Teacher	40	
Total Number & T.	218	
Students Names	Responses	*Sarah, Plain and Tall*
Abby	23	
Betsy	42	
Sarah	7	
Total Student	72	
Teacher	58	
Total Number & T.	130	

are observing in their whole class or small group. You check off who talks and how often each student contributes to the group.

Marilyn Chesley wanted to look at the kinds of talk in her small fourth-grade literature groups and to know who talked the most. Her tally sheet began with a notation for who spoke how often and gradually changed to considering the kinds of responses in the literature group (see Figure 5.1).

Gail Bussiere was concerned that she might be treating students differently in her reading groups. So she tallied the number of semantic or phonetic cues she gave to different readers in groups, and then she compared totals in these different groups (see Figure 5.2).

Joni Cooke was looking at gender differences in her literature discussion groups. She looked at same-sex groups discussing different books and noted not only how much students talked, but also what the differences were in her

response pattern when she worked with all-boy and all-girl groups (see Figure 5.3).

Tina Meserve wanted to see how different instructional contexts affected the responses of her students. So she tallied the number of responses by students during three different periods: a student-directed problem-solving period; a music class led by another teacher; and a child-abuse presentation by an advocacy group (see Figure 5.4).

Heidi Stanhope was concerned about the participation of her special needs students in small group activities, so she sat in as an observer on two different groups that mixed her special needs students with other class members, and noted how many responses came from each student (see Figure 5.5).

Many teachers find that tallying oral responses is the best way into notetaking. One teacher wrote after completing a tally sheet, "This gives me just enough infor-

mation to know where to begin. I hardly knew what to look for when I started this project. Now I have some idea of what to look at and write about."

Work to Eliminate Prefab Judgments in Your Notes

By "prefab" judgments, I mean those insights in your notes that are based not upon what you're seeing but upon your preconceptions of what your classroom is like and how learning occurs in it.

Prefabricated homes come with all the design, materials, and construction predetermined. In many respects, they are as comfortable a home as those of an original design. But nothing about them is original — all the design and thinking has been done for the potential owner before the purchase.

Many times words and phrases show up in rough notes that demonstrate our own prefab thinking about students. We use words, phrases, and ideas we are comfortable with, but they can be a leap to a conclusion about our students and teaching that isn't warranted.

For example, you might write, "John seems to take risks and trusts his answers during the reading discussion." "Taking risks" and "trust" may reflect attributes that are valued in your classroom, but what exactly does this notation mean? It's better to write down what you saw and heard that day during the reading discussion — "John spoke out for the first time this year in reading group, saying, 'Carrie took my idea.' " Later, a pattern may emerge in your notes and observations that shows John fits *your* definition of a risk taker. But that jargon needs a clear definition, and you need to allow patterns to develop in your notes and observa-

Figure 5.4

Tina's Tally of Different Instructional Contexts (✔ indicates response by student; Ⓥ indicates response initiated by teacher [for music class only])

	Student Directed Problem-Solving Discussion	Music Class Teacher Directed Lesson	Child Abuse Presentation from Child Advocacy Group
Carrie	✔✔✔✔	ⓋⓋ	
Kate	✔✔✔✔✔✔		✔
Amy	✔✔✔✔	Ⓥ	✔
Philippa	✔✔✔✔		✔✔✔
Mandy	✔✔		
Jennifer	✔✔✔	✔	✔
Kimberly	✔✔		
Ashley	✔✔✔		✔✔
Carol	✔✔	ⓋⓋ	
Nicole		✔✔✔	✔✔
Bob	✔✔✔		✔
Richard	✔✔✔✔✔	✔✔	✔✔✔✔✔
Tommy	✔✔✔✔✔✔✔	✔✔✔✔✔	✔✔
Scott	✔✔✔✔✔✔✔✔	✔	✔✔✔✔
Mike	✔✔✔	✔✔	✔
Kyle	✔✔✔✔✔✔✔	✔✔✔✔✔✔✔✔	✔✔✔✔
Tim	✔✔✔✔✔	✔✔	
Teddy			

Figure 5.5

Heidi's Tally of the Participation of Her Special Needs Students

Reading Group

Reading Group	Teacher	Matt	Josh	Aaron	Kim	Nicole	Totals
Elaboration	6	1	1	0	1	0	9
Feedback	37	0	1	0	0	0	38
Topic Change	0	0	1	0	0	0	1
Interruptions	0	6	4	0	2	0	12
Directions	21	0	0	0	0	0	21
Procedure	0	2	3	0	1	0	6
Questions	15	0	0	1	0	1	17
Reading	0	9	10	6	5	6	36

Reading Group	Teacher	Matt	Josh	Aaron	Kim	Nicole	Totals
# of Turns	70	20	18	7	9	6	130
# of Words	412	95	78	43	52	39	719
Average Words per Turn	5.9	4.8	4.3	6.1	5.8	6.5	5.5

Reading Group	Teacher	Students	Girls	Boys
# of Turns	70	60	15	45
# of Words	412	307	91	216
Average Words per Turn	5.9	5.1	6.1	4.8
% of Turns	53.9	46.2	11.6	34.6
% of Words	57.3	42.7	12.7	30
Words Chorally Read		206		
Words Read Individually		206		

Reading Group	Girls	Boys
# of Turns Each	7.5	15
# of Words Ea.	45.5	72
% of Turns Ea.	5.8	11.5
% of Words Ea.	6.3	10

tions over time before that judgment can be made.

As you start to take notes, the following activities can help you figure out what to write.

1. Practice with videotape segments.

Bring a videotape of your students at work to a meeting with a colleague or group, and then practice taking notes together. Compare what different group members write. What are the differences in your notes? In your perceptions? These discussions can help you develop a focus for improving your notes. For example, your colleague might include lots of quotes in the actual dialect of the students. In contrast, your strength might be a rich description of the social environment. Your colleague might note that one student is especially disruptive. You might see the same interactions differently — as a positive step for a student who has been inhibited in groups before. Talk about the differences in your notes, the influences that create those differences, and specific strategies you might develop for improving your notes.

> You might write, "John seems to take risks and trusts his answers during the reading discussion." "Taking risks" and "trust" may reflect attributes that are valued in your classroom, but what exactly does this notation mean?

2. Spend a week just counting.

Zero in on one issue that is important to you as a teacher, and see if you can find a way to tally responses, rather than write descriptions of what's going on. All you need to get started is a class list and an issue of interest. Some things you can count include:

- the number of turns taken by children;
- the frequency of change in the topic of conversation;
- the number of different students who change the conversation topic;
- the number of boys' versus girls' utterances;
- the number of responses in science workshop versus responses in writer's workshop;
- the ratio of your talk to children's talk;
- the number of new drafts of writing each child starts in one week.

Once you have a week or two of tallies, think about what you've learned from the tallies and how you might revise your notetaking to reflect this new knowledge.

3. Revise your notetaking forms.

If you know what the focus of your research or assessment will be, it makes sense to revise your record keeping forms to include a place for notes on this issue. Look at the forms you use now and see if there is a way to revise them to include space to write about "reading strategies" or "gender issues" or "social interactions." This will help remind you what you need to write about each day and keep you focused on your research and assessment topics.

NOTES

NOTES

NOTES

NOTES

NOTES

Lots of Websites!

Some of these websites were contributed by Char Forsten, Irv Richardson, and Elizabeth Quinn. Others were pulled from the books listed on pages 317-318 of the bibliography section; still others were discovered by the editor.

Be aware that, while these sites were accurate and operational at the time of publication, they may have moved or disappeared in the meantime. Also, some of these sites are suitable for young students, while others are more appropriate for older students and teachers. While they may contain technical information that is over the heads of young children, some have photographs that the younger children will enjoy.

A few of the websites have been mentioned by presenters, but are included here with additional information.

General Directories and Resources for Teachers

U.S. Department of Education
http://www.ed.gov/pubs/pubdb.html

A database of U.S. Department of Education publications in ERIC (Education Resource Information Center).

Library of Congress
http://www.loc.gov

Great resource; many online exhibits.

Teacher's Edition Online
http://www.teachnet.com

Directory of links to various topics of interest to educators.

Yahoo Education Resources
http://www.yahoo.com/Education/

A wealth of information for K-12 educators regarding current topics, teaching methods, state standards, resources, and conferences. Also a search engine.

The Teacher Resource Page
http://grove.ufl.edu/~klesyk

Sites for children and teachers; schools on the net; online projects; places to publish student writing.

Global School Net Foundation
http://www.gsn.org/gsn/gsn/index.html

Links students and teachers to schools around the world.

Yahooligans!
http://www.yahooligans.com/

Great website and guide for kids! Around the World, Art Soup, and School Bell are just a few of the available selections. This also acts as a search engine for kids.

Websites By Topic

Across the Curriculum

The Exploratorium
http://www.exploratorium.edu/

A museum of science, art, and human perception with over 650 interactive exhibits. Great site for students and teachers.

Classroom Connect Classroom Web on the Net
http://ns.wentworth.com:80/classweb/

Visit classrooms around the world; create your own school page and post it on the Web.

ADD/ADHD

National Foundation of Gifted and Creative Children
http://www.nfgcc.oa.net/

This is a serious site created by people concerned about the overuse of the ADD/ADHD diagnosis. It talks about creative children and their characteristics, which can be mislabeled ADD/ADHD, and discusses the misuse of Ritalin. Anyone dealing with attention deficit disorder in the schools should check out this site.

The Arts

Crayola Home Page
http://www.crayola.com/art_education

Lots of valuable information, including instructional techniques on using Crayola materials.

The Dance Page
http://www.ens-lyon.fr/~esouche/danse/dance.html

Ballet and modern dance; major dance companies, dancers, directors and choreographers around the world. Lots of photos.

Corporation for Public Broadcasting
http://www.cpb.org/teachers/index.html

Includes information on the Annenberg/CPB Math & Science Project; projects for teachers and students.

PBS
http://www.pbs.org

Information relating to programs on PBS. The whole site is suitable for upper elementary students. Links include "Kid's TV" and "Learn With PBS."

Current Events

USA Today
http://www.usatoday.com

Bring the popular daily newspaper into your classroom. The publisher copies its easy-to-read, attractive format online. A great way for your students to keep up on current events and trends.

Welcome to the White House
http://www.whitehouse.gov

Learn about the President and Vice-President, take a tour of the White House, find out about issues, events, and White House communications. Links to websites for all branches of the Federal Government. A multilevel resource.

Geography/Social Studies/Multicultural Studies

Maps
http://pubweb.parc.xerox.com:80/map/

A map of the world; click on it, and you can zoom into a specific region in increments. Includes longitude and latitude information.

Native Americans

http://web.maxwell.syr.edu/nativeweb
and
http://hanksville.phast.umass.edu/misc/NAculture.html

Both sites have information on many of the Native American Nations. History, cultural information, issues, biographies. Expect discussions of serious topics of concern to Native Americans.

Discovery of Paleolithic Painted Cave at Vallon-Pont-d'Arc
http://www.culture.fr/culture/gvpda-en.htm

One of the editor's all-time favorite sites. The stone-age artwork in this cave rivals any art found in the museums of the world.

The African American Mosaic
http://www.loc.gov/exhibits/african/intro.html

Library of Congress resource, with links to many sites covering the history and culture of African Americans. Other great sites disappeared from the Internet, or were not operating, before publication. Try searching using the term "African Americans". Couldn't find a site specifically for kids, but there must be some!

Gifted Students

Center for Talent Development
http://www.yahoo.com/education/k_12/gifted_youth/

Stanford Education Program for Gifted Youth (EPGY)
http://kanpai.stanford.edu/epgy/pamph/pamph.html

This is a directory of programs on the Internet for gifted students.

See also ADD/ADHD

Language Arts

The Electronic Library
http://www.cs.cmu.edu/Web/books.html

An index of online books, including banned books ("Little Red Riding Hood"!)

The Internet Public Library Author's Page
http://ipl.sils.umich.edu:80/youth/AskAuthor/

Links to authors' pages.

Children's Literature Web Guide
http://www.ucalgary.ca/~dkbrown/index.html

This site has lots of information on children's literature, including "Authors on the Web." Authors featured include Eric Carle and Diane Duane.

Haiku

Two sites for haiku, each with links to other sites. The first site has audio clips; the second is from Japan, and is a little more in-depth.
http://www.lsi.usp.br/usp/rod/poet/haiku.html
and
http://mikan.cc.matsuyama-u.ac.jp/~shiki/intro.html

WebINK
http://ipl.sils.umich.edu:80/webink/

An Internet newsletter for children from the Internet Public Library. Children can subscribe for $19.95 a year and receive a downloaded copy and a print copy of the full newsletter. Plenty of good information is accessible for nonsubscribers.

Mathematics

Eisenhower National Clearinghouse for Mathematics and Science Education
http://www.enc.org/

Math and science resources and opportunities available to K-12 educators.

Abacus
http://www.ee.ryerson.ca:8080/~elf/abacus/

All about the abacus—Chinese, Japanese, and Aztec. History, how to use it.

Parents

The PTA
http://www.pta.org

Great site for parents and for teachers wanting methods of working with parents. Lots of information here on how parents can help their children learn.

Science

Animals

The Electronic Zoo
http://netvet.wustl.edu/e-zoo.htm

Both domestic and wild animals; lots of photos.

The Penguin Page
http://www.vni.net/~kwelch/penguins/

Lots of facts, artwork on all penguin species; video clips available for computers, along with a program you can download onto your computer which will play the videos. This site has a serious tone.

Children's Butterfly Site
http://www.mesc.nbs.gov/butterfly.htm

Great kids' site, lots of butterfly photos.

International Wolf Center
http://www.wolf.org

Photos and wolf sounds (scared the editor's cat!)

Live Keiko Cam
http://www.aquarium.org/keikohome.htm

This site includes a photo of Keiko the Orca who starred in "Free Willy"; the photo is taken in his tank, and is updated every 30 seconds. Very cool.

Astronomy, the Solar System and Space Flight

The Aurora Page
http://www.geo.mtu.edu/weather/aurora
Information on the aurora borealis suitable for grades 3-6; great photos.

The Starchild Project
especially for kids
http://starchild.gsfc.nasa.gov/
A wonderful site which deals with the solar system, the universe, and "space stuff"— essentially NASA's space program. The internet surfer can access Level I or Level II in each category, which includes information and activities. A great tool when developing adaptations for different levels of learners within the classroom. Some activities include audio.

QUEST—NASA's Space Missions.
http://quest.arc.nasa.gov/
Resources and interactive projects related to a number of NASA's space missions.

Mission to Mars
http://mars.sgi.com/default.html
Includes photos and current scientific information received from the probe.

NASA Space Shuttle Launches
http://www.ksc.nasa.gov/shuttle/missions/missions.html
A child who surfs into this website may never be seen again! Volumes of information on each shuttle launch, bios of the astronauts, missions, payloads, and on and on.

The Nine Planets
http://seds.lpl.arizona.edu/nineplanets/nineplanets/nineplanets.html
Volumes of information on the planets, their satellites, and other parts of the solar system; with beautiful accompanying photos.

Biology

Nano World
http://www.uq.oz.au/nanoworld/images_1.html
Great photos of very tiny organisms as seen through a microscope. Includes photos of human sperm and ovum.

Earth Sciences

Note: Many of the topics in this section about weather, oceanography, earthquakes, volcanoes, and so on are integrated within each site, and by links to other sites. Also check out the NASA sites in the astronomy section; much of the information about the earth has been obtained from this agency's projects. It's an interdisciplinary world we live in!

The Field Museum
http://www.bvis.uic.edu/museum
Dinosaurs and the geologic eras both before and during the reign of dinosaurs. Attractive illustrations, both audio and video clips.

Active Tectonics
http://www.muohio.edu/tectonics/activetectonics.html
Very advanced scientific information on earthquakes (too advanced for elementary students) but has photos of aftermath of Northride, California earthquake.

El Nino
http://www.pmel.noaa.gov/toga-tao/el-nino/home.html
Lots of facts, charts and graphs based on the scientific monitoring of El Nino, the "disturbance of the oceanic atmospheric system in the tropical Pacific." The shift in this current has created severe rain and flood conditions in the northern hemisphere, and drought (and resulting famine) in the southern hemisphere. Links to other oceanographic, geology, and space-related sites. Pretty technical, but a great way to demonstrate climate on a global scale.

NASA EOS ID Volcanology Team
http://www.geo.mtu.edu/eos
Includes data on a project which involves the launching of satellites in 1998 which will observe active volcanoes on Earth over a period of fifteen years. This site includes links to teacher workshops on volcanology.

Michigan Technological University Volcano page
http://www.geo.mtu.edu/volcanoes
Includes worldwide volcano reference map, active volcanoes around the world.

Volcano World
http://volcano.und.nodak.edu/
Suitable for elementary students; features "Rocky the Volcano"; lots of good, readable information.

Defense Meteorological Satellite Program
http://web.ngdc.noaa.dmsp/dmsp.html

A lot of very technical information here, received from a system of satellites which monitor meteorological, oceanographic, and solar physics. Is over the heads of most elementary students, but there are some great diagrams of the satellites, as well as great photos of the earth from space. (Includes photos of tropical storms.)

The Weather Underground
http://www.wunderground.com/

Students can type in their location and get the current weather and a three-day forecast for their area. Very cool!

The Weather Unit
http://faldo.atmos.uiuc.edu/WEATHER/weather.html

Ready to use, cross-curricular lesson plans on weather for grades 2 to 4.

U.S. Geologic Survey (USGS)
http://www.usgs.gov/

Excellent ecology site. Links to the following:

The Learning Web
http://www.usgs.gov/education

A great site with plenty of resources for K-12 teachers and students.

Physics

The Wonders of Physics
http://sprott.physics.wisc.edu/wop.htm

A great site. This is the web page of Professor Julian Clinton Sprott, who travels the country giving dramatically entertaining and educational physics demonstrations to students of all ages. Included here is information on how to get him to your school or area, how to get his videotapes, and the manuscript of an unpublished book with instructions for many physics activities.

See also Math

Especially For Girls

It's a fact that although both boys and girls are excited about computers in elementary school, by the fifth grade girls' enthusiasm seems to lag, as they perceive computers as a boy's interest. Very few young women are choosing computer science as a career. The following websites, some serious and some fun, are either of high interest to girls or are a good resource for teachers to use when planning instruction for girls.

Cynthia Lanius' Home Page
http://cml.rice.edu/~lanius/

Lessons and resources for teachers and students on math and computers includes the Girls Online Computer Club.

National Museum of Women in the Arts
http://www.nmwa.org

Bios, pictures of artwork of women in history.

WWWomen
http://www.wwwomen.com/

A searchable directory on topics of interest to women. Good resource for teachers, contains sensitive material that some segments of the parent population might object to if exposed to students. Not for younger students.

Encyclopedia of Women's History
http://www.teleport.com/~megaines/women.html

Written and submitted by K-12 students.

Women's National Basketball Association
http://www.wnba.com/

Kristi Yamaguchi

Here are three websites for the famous Olympic skater, all with great photos.

Kristi's Fan Page
http://www.skate.org/yamaguchi/

Kristi's Official Home Page
http://www.kristi.org/

The Kristi Yamaguchi Web Page
http://www.polaris.net/~shanhew/

Child Advocacy Organizations

Children's Defense Fund
25 E. St. NW
Washington, DC 20001

Learning Disabilities / Inclusion

A.D.D. Warehouse
300 Northwest 70th Ave. Suite 102
Plantation, FL 33317
1-800-233-9273
FAX: (954) 792-8545
Internet: www.addwarehouse.com
   Books, tapes, videos on ADD and hyperactivity

Paul H. Brookes Publishing Co. (catalog available)
P.O. Box 10624
Baltimore, MD 21285-0624
1-800-638-3775

Centre for Integrated Education and Community
24 Thome Crescent
Toronto, Ontario M6H 2S5

CH.A.D.D. (Children with Attention Deficit Disorder)
499 NW 70th Ave., Suite 308
Plantation, FL 33317
(305) 587-3700

The Council for Exceptional Children
1920 Association Drive
Reston, VA 22091-1589
(703) 620-3660
   (publishes *Exceptional Children, Teaching Exceptional Children* and *CEC Today*.)

Down Syndrome News
National Down Syndrome Congress
1605 Chantilly Dr., Suite 250
Atlanta, GA 30324
1-800-232-6372

Exceptional Children's Assistance Center
PO Box 16
Davidson, NC 28036
(704) 892-1321
1-800-962-6817 (NC only)
FAX: (704) 892-5028

The Exchange
The Learning Disabilities Network
72 Sharp St., Suite A-2
Hingham, MA 02043
(617) 340-5605

Impact
Publications Office
Institute on Community Integration
University of Minnesota
109 Pattee Hall, 150 Pillsbury Dr. S.E.
Minneapolis, MN 55455
(612) 624-4512

Inclusion Press International
24 Thome Crescent
Toronto, Ontario M6H 2S5
(416) 658-5363
FAX: (416) 658-5067
e-mail: Compuserve: 74640, 1124
Web Page: http: //inclusion.com

Learning Disabilities Association (LDA)
4156 Library Rd.
Pittsburgh, PA 15234
(412) 341-1515
FAX: (412) 344-0224

MPACT (Missouri Parents Act)
8631 Delmar, Suite 300
St. Louis, MO 63124
1-800-995-3160

Parents Active for Vision Education (P.A.V.E.)
National Headquarters
9620 Chesapeake Drive, Suite 105
San Diego, CA 92123
Phone: (619) 467-9620
1-800-PAVE-988
Fax: (619) 467-9624
   This organization believes that undetected vision disorders often contribute to learning problems in school.

PEAK (Parent Center, Inc.)
6055 Lehman Dr., Suite 101
Colorado Springs, CO 80918
(719) 531-9400
FAX: (719) 531-9452
   Inclusion resources, practical tools for educating ALL students in general education classrooms

Whole Language Hotline

In the fall of 1991, the Center for the Expansion of Language and Thinking (CELT) began sponsoring a crisis hotline to support teachers and administrators who come under attack for their child-centered practices.

For further information, contact: The Center for Establishing Dialogue in Teaching and Learning (CED)
325 E. Southern Ave., Suite 107-108
Tempe, AZ 85282
1-602-894-1333 • FAX 602-894-9547

Publications

Children's Literature

Book Links: Connecting Books, Libraries and Classrooms
American Library Association
50 Huron St.
Chicago, IL 60611

The Bulletin of the Center for Children's Books
University of Illinois Press
1325 S. Oak St.
Champaign, Il 61820

CBC Features
Children's Book Council
568 Broadway, Suite 404
New York, NY 10012

Children's Literature and Reading
(special interest group of the
International Reading Association)
Membership: Dr. Miriam A. Marecek
                        10 Marchant Rd.
                        Winchester, MA 01890

The Horn Book Magazine
11 Beacon St., Suite 1000
Boston, MA 02105

The Horn Book also publishes *The Horn Book Guide to Children's and Young Adult Books*, a semi-annual publication reviewing nearly 4000 hardcover trade books each year.

Journal of the Children's Literature Council of Pennsylvania
226 East Emaus St.
Middletown, PA 17057

Journal of Children's Literature
Children's Literature Assembly
Membership: Marjorie R. Hancock
                        2037 Plymouth Rd.
                        Manhattan, KS 66503

The Kobrin Letter (reviews nonfiction books)
732 Greer Rd.
Palo Alto, CA 94303

The New Advocate
Christopher-Gordon Publishers, Inc.
480 Washington St.
Norwood, MA 02062

Reading Is Fundamental (RIF)
600 Maryland Ave. S.W.
Suite 600
Washington, D.C. 20024-2569
(202) 287-3220
    *For information on starting a RIF program
    or for parent brochures.*

The WEB (Wonderfully Exciting Books)
The Ohio State University
Room 200 Ramseyer Hall
29 West Woodruff
Columbus, OH 43210

Early Childhood / Developmental Education

Childhood Education
Journal of the Association for Childhood
        Education International
Suite 315
11501 Georgia Ave.
Wheaton, MD 20902

Early Childhood News
Peter Li, Inc.
330 Progress Road
Dayton, OH 45449
(513) 847-5900

Early Childhood Today
Scholastic, Inc.
555 Broadway
New York, NY 10012

Young Children
National Association for the Education of Young Children
        (NAEYC)
1509 16th St. NW
Washington, DC 20036-1426
1-800-424-2460

General Education — Classroom Focus

Creative Classroom
Children's Television Workshop
P.O. Box 53148
Boulder, CO 80322-3148

Instructor Magazine
Scholastic, Inc.
555 Broadway
New York, NY 10012-3999

Learning
1607 Battleground Avenue
Greensboro, NC 27408

The Private Eye Newsletter
7710 31st Avenue NW
Seattle, WA 98117
e-mail: ruef@halcyon.com
Phone: (206) 784-8813
Fax: (206) 784-2172
website: http://www.the-private-eye.com/ruef/

Teaching K-8
40 Richards Ave.
Norwalk, CT 06854

General Education — Issues/Research Focus

*The American School Board Journal /
    Executive Educator*
National School Boards Association
1680 Duke St.
Alexandria, VA 22314

Democracy and Education
The Institute for Democracy and Education
College of Education
313 McCracken Hall, Ohio University
Athens, OH 45701-2979

Education Week
P.O. Box 2083
Marion, OH 43305
Editorial:
4301 Connecticut Ave. NW #250
Washington, DC 20008

Educational Leadership
Journal of the Association for Supervision and
    Curriculum Development (ASCD)
1250 N. Pitt St.
Alexandria, VA 22314-1403

FairTest
The National Center for Fair & Open Testing
342 Broadway
Cambridge, MA 02139
    FairTest has serious issues with standardized tests
    as they are administered and used in today's
    schools, and offers alternative options, including
    performance assessments methods.

Phi Delta Kappan
Eighth and Union
P.O. Box 789
Bloomington, IN 47402
Journal of Phi Delta Kappan International
The professional fraternity in education

Principal
National Association of Elementary School
    Principals (NAESP)
1615 Duke St.
Alexandria, VA 22314-3483

*The Responsive Classroom: A Newsletter for
    Teachers*
Northeast Foundation for Children
71 Montague City Rd.
Greenfield, MA 01301
1-800-360-6332

The School Administrator
American Association of School Administrators
1801 North Moore St.
Arlington, VA 22209

Teaching Voices
The Massachusetts Field Center for Teaching
    and Learning
University of Massachusetts
100 Morrissey Blvd.
Boston, MA 02125

TIP (Theory into Practice)
Subscription Dept.
The Ohio State University
174 Arps Hall
1945 N. High St.
Columbus, OH 43210-1172

Language *(See also Whole Language, this section)*

Language Arts
National Council of Teachers of English
1111 W. Kenyon Rd.
Urbana, IL 61801-1096

Literacy
The International Institute of Literacy Learning
Box 1414
Commerce, TX 75429

Primary Voices K-6
National Council of Teachers of English
1111 W. Kenyon Rd.
Urbana, IL 61801-1096

The Reading Teacher
International Reading Association
P.O. Box 8139
Newark, DE 19714-8139

(IRA also publishes *Journal of Adolescent and
Adult Literacy, Reading Today, Reading Research
Quarterly; Lectura y Vida* — a Spanish language
journal.)

Math and Science

Science and Children
National Science Teachers Association
1840 Wilson Blvd.
Arlington, VA 22201-3000

Teaching Children Mathematics
National Council of Teachers of Mathematics
1906 Association Dr.
Reston, VA 22091

Whole Language

The Whole Idea
The Wright Group
19201 120th Ave. NE
Bothell, WA 98011

Whole Language Network
Teaching K-8
40 Richards Ave.
Norwalk, CT 06854

*The Whole Language Teachers Association
    Newsletter*
P.O. Box 216
Southboro, MA 01772

WLSIG Newsletter
Whole Language Umbrella

President: Sharon Murphy
                Faculty of Education
                Ross Building, York University
                4700 Keele St.
                North York, ON M3J 1P3 Canada
                (416) 650-8059
                FAX (416) 650-8097

Send   Whole Language Umbrella - Membership
membership   Ross Building, York University
inquiries to: 4700 Keele St.
                North York, ON M3J 1P3 Canada
                (416) 650-8059
                FAX (416) 650-8097

Newsjournal: Jane and Jerry Bartow
                520 Kingsview Lane
                Plymouth, MN 55447

Publishers & Distributors of Math Books & Products

Creative Publications
5623 W. 115th Street
Worth, IL 60482-9931
(800) 624-0822

Crystal Springs Books
Ten Sharon Road, PO Box 500
Peterborough, NH 03458
(800) 321-0401

Cuisenaire
PO Box 5026
White Plains, NY 10602-5026
(800) 237-0338

Dale Seymour Publications
PO Box 10888
Palo Alto, CA 94303-0879
(800) 872-1100

Dandy Lion Publications
3563-L Sueldo
San Luis Obispo, CA 93401
(800) 776-8032

Delta Education
PO Box 3000
Nashua, NH 03061-9912
(800) 442-5444

Educational Electronics (Calculator Dist.)
70 Finnell Drive
Weymouth Landing, MA 02188
(617) 331-4190

Interact (Simulation Units)
1825 Gillespie Way, #101
El Cajon, CA 92020-1095
(800) 359-0961

The Math Shop
Quantexx
PO Box 694
Canfield, OH 44406
(800) 798-MATH

National Council of Teachers of Mathematics
PO Box 25405
Richmond, VA 23260-5405
(800) 235-7566

Scholastic, Inc.
2931 E. McCarty Street
Jefferson City, MO 65101
(800) 325-6149

Sources of Multiage Materials

Crown Publications
546 Yates Street
Victoria, British Columbia
Canada V8W 1K8
Phone: (604) 386-4636
FAX: (604) 386-0221
    Distributes books and videos for the Province
    of British Columbia Ministry of Education.

Crystal Springs Books
Ten Sharon Road
PO Box 500
Peterborough, NH 03458
Phone: 1-800-321-0401
FAX: 1-800-337-9929

Big Book Publishers

Creative Teaching Press, Inc.
P.O. Box 6017
Cypress, CA 90630-0017
1-800-444-4287

Richard C. Owen Publishers, Inc.
P.O. Box 585
Katonah, NY 10536
1-800-336-5588

Sundance Publishing
P.O. Box 1326
Littleton, MA 01460
1-800-343-8204

The Wright Group
19201 12th Ave. NE
Bothell, WA 98011
1-800-523-2371

Paperback Book Clubs

The Trumpet Club
P.O. Box 604
Holmes, PA 19043
1-800-826-0110

Troll Book Club
2 Lethbridge Plaza
Mahwah, NJ 07430
1-800-541-1097

Materials

Big Book Materials

Sticky pockets — Demco Library Supplies and Equipment, 1-800-356-1200

Velour paper — Dick Blick Art Supply, 1-800-345-3042

Grommets — Hardware stores

Alphabet & number stickers — Childcraft Education Corp., 1-800-631-5652

"Scribbles" Glitter Writers — Arts and crafts stores or Duncan Hobby, (209) 291-2515

Binding Machines and Spiral Binding

General Binding Corporation
One GBC Plaza
Northbrook, IL 60062
(847) 723-1500
Scholastic, Inc. — 1-800-724-6527

Book Racks/Easels

Fixturecraft Corp.
443 East Westfield Ave.
P.O. Box 292
Roselle Park, NJ 07204-0292
1-800-275-1145

Chart Paper/Sentence Strips

School Specialty – New England Division
P.O. Box 3004
Agawam, MA 01101-8004
1-800-628-8608

J.L.Hammett Company
P.O. Box 859057
Braintree, MA 02185-9057
1-800-333-4600

Computer Programs

Print Shop
Broderbund
500 Redwood Blvd.
P.O. Box 6121
Novato, CA 94948-6121
1-800-521-6263

SuperPrint
Scholastic
P.O. Box 7502
Jefferson City, MO 65102
1-800-724-6527

Educational Records Center

Catalog for Songs
3233 Burnt Mill Drive, Suite 100
Wilmington, NC 28403-2655
1-800-438-1637

Highlight Tape

Available through Crystal Springs Books
1-800-321-0401

Kinesiology

Brain Gym®
Developmental activities to help children learn more effectively
Educational Kinesiology Foundation
P.O. Box 3396
Ventura, CA 93006-3396
1-800-356-2109

Manatee Adoption

Save the Manatee Club
500 N. Maitland Ave., Suite 210
Maitland, FL 32751
(407) 539-0990
($10.00/year)

Metal Shower Curtain Rings

Department Stores

Plastic Rings/Bird Bands

Farm Feed Stores

Ribbons and Awards

Hodges Badge Company, Inc.
1-800-556-2440

Sea Monkey Eggs

Sea Monkeys
Transcience Corporation
P.O. Box 809
Bryans Road, MD 20616

Stencil Machines

The Ellison LetterMachine
Ellison Educational Equipment, Inc.
P.O. Box 8209
Newport Beach, CA 92658-8209
1-714-724-0555

Touch phonics Reading Systems

Manipulative Phonics System
4900 Birch Street
Newport Beach, CA 92660
(714) 975-1141
(800) 92-TOUCH (928-6824)
FAX (714) 975-1056

Whale Adoption

Whale Adoption Project
International Wildlife Coalition
634 N. Falmouth Highway
P.O. Box 388
N. Falmouth, MA 02556-0388
($15.00/year)

Wikki Stix

Available through Crystal Springs Books
1-800-321-0401

More Than Books

Expanding Children's Horizons Through Magazines

Publication Subscription Address	Interest Area/Age Group
Big Book Magazine Scholastic, Inc. P.O. Box 10805 Des Moines, IA 50380-0813 1-800-788-7017	General Interest 4-7
Boys' Life Boy Scouts of America 1325 Walnut Hill Lane P.O. Box 152079 Irving, TX 75015-2079	General Interest 7-18
The C.A.R.E. Package (Children's Authors Make Reading Exciting) Apple Peddler 25112 Woodfield School Rd. Gaithersburg, MD 20882-3715	Children's Authors 5-10
Classical Calliope 7 School St. Peterborough, NH 03458-1454	World History 9-16
Cobblestone 7 School St. Peterborough, NH 03458-1454	American History 8-14
* Creative Kids P.O. Box 8813 Waco, TX 76714-8813 1-800-998-2208 FAX: 1-800-240-0333 e-mail: Creative_kids@prufrock.com Submissions: Attn: Submissions Editor P.O. Box 6448 Mobile, AL 36660	Student Art/Writing 8-14
* Cricket P.O. Box 7433 Red Oak, IA 51591-4433 Submissions: 315 5th St., P.O. Box 300 Peru, IL 61354	Literature/Art 9-14
Faces 7 School St. Peterborough, NH 03458-1454	World Cultures 8-14
* Highlights for Children P.O. Box 269 Columbus, OH 43216-0269 Submissions: 803 Church St. Honesdale, PA 18431	General Interest 2-12
KIDS Discover P.O. Box 54209 Boulder, CO 80321-4209	Science/General Interest 5-12
Kids Life and Times Kids Life Submissions: Children's Television Workshop One Lincoln Plaza New York, NY 10023	Entertainment/Education 6-12

Publication Subscription Address	Interest Area/Age Group
Ladybug Red Oak, IA 51591	Literature 2-6
* Merlyn's Pen The National Magazines of Student Writing, Grades 6-12 P.O. Box 1058 East Greenwich, RI 02818	Student Writing 12-16
National Geographic World P.O. Box 2330 Washington, DC 20013-2330	Science/General Interest 8-14
* Odyssey 7 School St. Peterborough, NH 03458-1454	Space Exploration/ Astronomy 8-14
Plays 120 Boylston St. Boston, MA 02116-4615	Drama 6-18
Ranger Rick National Wildlife Federation 8925 Leesburg Pike Vienna, VA 22180-0001	Science/Wildlife Nature, Environment 6-12
* School Mates 186 Route 9W New Windsor, NY 12553	Chess for Beginners 7 and up
Scienceland 501 Fifth Ave. Suite 2108 New York, NY 10017-6107	Science 5-11
Sesame Street Magazine P.O. Box 52000 Boulder, CO 80321-2000	General Interest 2-6
Sports Illustrated for Kids P.O. Box 830609 Birmingham, AL 35283-0609	Sports 8-13
*Stone Soup The Magazine by Young Writers and Artists P.O. Box 83 Santa Cruz, CA 95063	Student Writing/Art 6-14
Storyworks Scholastic 555 Broadway New York, NY 10012-3999	Literature 8-11
3-2-1 Contact P.O. Box 51177 Boulder, CO 80321-1177	Science 8-14
Your Big Backyard National Wildlife Federation 8925 Leesburg Pike Vienna, VA 22184	Animals/Conservation 3-5

encourages children's submissions

Workshops and Conferences

The Society For Developmental Education
Ten Sharon Road, Box 577
Peterborough, NH 03458
1-800-924-9621
e-mail: sde.csb@worldnet.att.net
Check out our website at: http://www.socdeved.com

The Society For Developmental Education (SDE) presents workshops, conferences, and staff development inservices throughout the year and around the country for elementary educators on multiage, school readiness, inclusion education, multiple intelligences, character education, discipline, whole language, authentic assessment, math, science, and related topics.

SDE sponsors an International Multiage Conference each July. For information on dates and location, write or phone SDE at the address or number listed above.

Other Resources

ERIC

ERIC (Educational Resources Information Center) is a clearinghouse or central agency responsible for the collection, classification, and distribution of written information related to education. If you need help finding the best way to use ERIC, call ACCESS ERIC toll-free at 1-800-LET-ERIC. If you need specific information about multiage education, call Norma Howard at 1-800-822-9229.

A Value Search: Multiage or Nongraded Education is available for $7.50 and can be ordered from Publication Sales, ERIC Clearinghouse on Educational Management, 5207 University of Oregon, Eugene, OR 97403-5207. A handling charge of $3.00 is added to all billed orders.

National Association for Year-Round Education (NAYRE)
P.O. Box 711386
San Diego, CA 92171-1386
(619) 276-5296

The National Association for Year-Round Education (NAYRE) has its membership among schools who follow a year-round academic schedule; some members, for instance, have a nine-weeks-in-school, nine-week-vacation schedule, rather than giving students three months off during the summer. This type of year-round schedule provides academic continuity for teachers and students, plus frequent (and sometimes much needed) breaks.

NAYRE provides information on its programs and membership to interested parties.

International Registry of Nongraded Schools (IRONS)
Robert H. Anderson, Co-director (with Barbara N. Pavan)
PO Box 271669
Tampa, FL 33688-1699

IRONS is housed at the University of South Florida. It has been established to gather information about individual schools or school districts that are either in the early stages of developing a nongraded program or well along in their efforts. Its purpose is to facilitate intercommunication and research efforts. There is a phase one membership and a full membership.

Multiage Classroom Exchange
Teaching K-8
40 Richards Ave.
Norwalk, CT 06854

The Multiage Classroom Exchange puts teachers in contact with others who are interested in swapping ideas, activities, and experiences relating to the multiage, progressive classroom.

To join, send your name, address, age levels you teach, years of experience with multiage education, and a self-addressed, stamped envelope to the address listed. You'll receive a complete, up-to-date list of teachers who are interested in exchanging information.

Under Construction
Jane Meade-Roberts
202 Riker Terrace Way
Salinas, CA 93901
Phone (408) 455-1831 (to leave message)

Under Construction's goal is to assist teachers, parents and administrators in gaining an understanding of how children and adults construct knowledge, and to support experienced teachers who are working to understand constructivist theory and its implications for teaching. (Constructivism is a scientific theory of learning, based on Piaget's theory of cognitive development, that explains how people come to build their own knowledge and understand the things and people in their own world.)

The organization feels that multiage classrooms are wonderfully suited for helping adults learn more about how children develop and construct knowledge. Many of the teachers and parents in the group are currently involved in multiage classrooms or are interested in developing their understanding of constructivism so that they may begin a multiage learning environment for children in their own school.

Under Construction is an umbrella for several groups working toward this end. The Constructivist Network of Monterey County, which meets monthly, is largely composed of university personnel and some school teachers. The network provides a speaker series for the community. A focus group includes teachers involved in coaching and classroom visitations. The organization is collaborating with the local adult school to provide classes for parents of children in multiage classrooms, and has just begun to work with a new local university, with the object of working with people in the community. An advisory board oversees the organization.

The organization is funded by the Walter S. Johnson Foundation.

NEWSLETTER

MAGnet Newsletter
805 W. Pennsylvania
Urbana, IL 61801-4897

The MAGnet Newsletter provides information about schools that have implemented multiage practices.

Bibliography

(compiled by SDE Presenters)

Attention Deficit Disorder (ADD) / Attention Deficit Hyperactivity Disorder (ADHD)

Bain, Lisa J. *A Parent's Guide to Attention Deficit Disorders*. New York: Dell, 1991.

Barkley, Russell A. *ADHD in the Classroom (Video and Program Guide)*. New York: Guilford Publications, 1994.

Copeland, Edna D., and Love, Valerie L. *Attention Without Tension: A Teacher's Handbook on Attention Disorders (ADHD and ADD)*. Atlanta, GA: 3 C's of Childhood, 1990.

Hallowell, Edward M., and Ratey, John J. *Driven to Distraction*. New York: Touchstone, 1994.

Hartmann, Thom. *Attention Deficit Disorder: A Different Perception*. Penn Valley, CA, and Lancaster PA: Underwood-Miller, 1993.

Ingersoll, Barbara, Ph.D. *Your Hyperactive Child: A Parent's Guide to Coping With Attention Deficit Disorder*. New York: Doubleday, 1988.

Moss, Deborah. *Shelley, the Hyperactive Turtle*. Rockville, MD: Woodbine House, 1989.

Moss, Robert A., and Dunlap, Helen Huff. *Why Johnny Can't Concentrate: Coping with Attention Deficit Problems*. New York: Bantam Books, 1990.

Parker, Harvey. *The ADD Hyperactivity Handbook for Schools*. Plantation, FL: Impact Publications, 1992.

———.*The ADD Hyperactivity Workbook for Parents, Teachers, and Kids*. Plantation, FL: Impact Publications, 1988.

———.*The ADAPT Accommodation Planbook for Teachers*. Plantation, FL: Impact Publications, 1992.

———.*The ADAPT Student Planbook*. Plantation, FL: Impact Publications, 1992.

Quinn, Patricia O., M.D., and Stern, Judith M., M.A. *Putting on the Brakes: Young People's Guide to Understanding Attention Deficit Hyperactivity Disorder (ADHD)*. New York: Magination Press, 1991.

———. *The "Putting on the Brakes" Activity Book for Young People With ADHD*. New York: Magination Press, 1993.

Rief, Sandra. *How to Reach and Teach ADD/ADHD Children*. West Nyack, NY: The Center for Applied Research in Education, 1993.

Shapiro, Lawrence E. *Sometimes I Drive My Mom Crazy, But I Know She's Crazy About Me*. King of Prussia, PA: The Center for Applied Psychology, inc., 1993.

Taylor, John F. *Helping Your Hyperactive/Attention Deficit Child*. Rocklin, CA: Prima Publishing, 1994.

Anti-Hurrying

Elkind, David. *All Grown Up & No Place To Go*. Reading, MA: Addison-Wesley, 1984.

———. *The Hurried Child*. Reading, MA: Addison-Wesley, 1981.

———. *Miseducation: Preschoolers at Risk*. New York: Alfred A. Knopf, 1987.

Gilmore, June E.. *The Rape of Childhood: No Time to Be a Kid*. Middletown, OH: J & J Publishing, 1990.

National Education Commission on Time and Learning. *Prisoners of Time*. Washington, DC: U.S. Government Printing Office, Superintendent of Documents, 1994.

Packard, Vance. *Our Endangered Children*. Boston: Little, Brown & Co., 1983.

Postman, Neil. *The Disappearance of Childhood*. New York: Dell, 1982.

Uphoff, James K.. *Real Facts From Real Schools: What You're Not Supposed to Know About School Readiness and Transition Programs*. Rosemont, NJ: Modern Learning Press, 1990, 1995.

Uphoff, James K.; Gilmore, June; and Huber, Rosemarie. *Summer Children: Ready (or Not) for School*. Middletown, OH: The Oxford Press, 1986.

Winn, Marie. *Children Without Childhood*. New York: Penguin Books, 1984.

Assessment

Anthony, Robert. *Evaluating Literacy*. Portsmouth, NH: Heinemann, 1991.

Barrs, Myra et al. *The Primary Language Record: Handbook for Teachers*. Portsmouth, NH: Heinemann, 1988.

Baskwill, Jane, and Whitman, Paulette. *Evaluation: Whole Language, Whole Child*. New York: Scholastic, 1988.

Batzle, Janine. *Portfolio Assessment and Evaluation: Developing and Using Portfolios in the K-6 Classroom*. Cypress, CA: Creative Teaching Press, 1992.

Belanoff, Pat, and Dickson, Marcia, eds. *Portfolios: Process and Product*. Portsmouth, NH: Heinemann, 1991.

Clay, Marie. *An Observation Survey of Early Literacy Achievement*. Portsmouth, NH: Heinemann, 1993.

———. *Sand* and *Stones: "Concepts About Print" Tests*. Portsmouth, NH: Heinemann, 1980.

Clemmons, J.; Laase, L.; Cooper, D.; Areglado, N.; and Dill, M. *Portfolios in the Classroom: A Teacher's Sourcebook*. New York: Scholastic, Inc., 1993.

Cochrane, Orin, and Cochrane, Donna. *Whole Language Evaluation for Classrooms*. Bothell, WA: The Wright Group, 1992.

Daly, Elizabeth, ed. *Monitoring Children's Language Development*. Portsmouth, NH: Heinemann, 1992.

Goodman, Kenneth, ed. *The Whole Language Evaluation Book*. Portsmouth, NH: Heinemann, 1988.

Goodman, Yetta et al. *Reading Miscues Inventory: Alternative Procedures*. New York: Richard C. Owen Publishers, 1987.

Graves, Donald, and Sustein, Bonnie, eds. *Portfolio Portraits*. Portsmouth, NH: Heinemann, 1992.

Harp, Bill, ed. *Assessment and Evaluation in Whole Language Programs*. Norwood, MA: Christopher Gordon Publishers, 1993.

Johnston, Peter. *Constructive Evaluation of Literate Activity*. New York: Longman, 1992.

Kamii, C., ed. *Achievement Testing in the Early Grades: The Games Grownups Play*. Washington, DC: National Association for the Education of Young Children, 1990.

Keshner, Judy. *The Kindergarten Teacher's Very Own Student Assessment and Observation Guide*. Rosemont, NJ: Modern Learning Press, 1996.

Lazear, David. *Multiple Intelligence Approaches to Assessment: Solving the Assessment Conundrum*. IRI/Skylight Publishing, Inc., 1994.

Parsons, Les. *Response Journals*. Portsmouth, NH: Heinemann, 1989.

Picciotto, Linda. *Evaluation: A Team Effort*. Ont.: Scholastic, 1992.

Power, Brenda Miller. *Taking Note: Improving Your Observational Notetaking*. York, ME: Stenhouse, 1996.

Sharp, Quality Quinn. *Evaluation in the Literature-Based Classroom: Whole Language Checklists Grades K-6*. New York: Scholastic, 1989.

Tierney, Robert J.; Carter, Mark A.; and Desai, Laura E. *Portfolio Assessment in the Reading-Writing Classroom*. Norwood, MA: Christopher Gordon, 1991.

Traill, Leanna. *Highlight My Strengths*. Reed Publications, 1993.

Behavior / Discipline

Albert, Linda. *An Administrator's Guide to Cooperative Discipline*. Circle Pines, MN: American Guidance, 1989.

———. *Cooperative Discipline: How to Manage Your Classroom and Promote Self-Esteem*. Circle Pines, MN: American Guidance Service, 1996.

———. *Cooperative Discipline Elementary Kit*. (Three-video series, Implementation Guide, ten color posters, Cooperative Discipline book). Circle Pines, MN: American Guidance Service, 1996.

———. *Linda Albert's Advice for Coping With Kids*. Tampa, FL: Alkorn House, 1992.

———. *Responsible Kids in School and At Home: The Cooperative Discipline Way*. (Six-video series). Circle Pines, MN: American Guidance Service, 1994.

Bailey, Dr. Becky. *There's Gotta Be a Better Way: Discipline That Works!* Oviedo, FL: Loving Guidance, 1997.

Bluestein, Jane. *21st Century Discipline—Teaching Students Responsibility and Self-Control*. New York: Scholastic, 1988.

Braman, O. Randall. *The Oppositional Child*. Charlotte, NC: Kidsrights, 1997.

Burke, Kay. *What to Do with the Kid Who ... Developing Cooperation, Self-Discipline and Responsibility in the Classroom*. Palatine, IL: IRI/Skylight Publishing, 1992.

Canfield, Jack, and Siccone, Frank. *101 Ways to Develop Student Self-Esteem and Responsibility*. Needham Heights, MA: Allyn & Bacon, 1993.

Charles, C.M. *Building Classroom Discipline*. New York: Longman, 1992.

Coletta, Anthony. *What's Best for Kids: A Guide to Developmentally Appropriate Practices for Teachers & Parents of Children Ages 4-8*. Rosemont, NJ: Modern Learning Press, 1991.

Curwin, Richard L., and Mendler, Allen N. *Discipline with Dignity*. Alexandria, VA: Association for Supervision and Curriculum Development, 1993.

————.*Am I in Trouble? Using Discipline to Teach Young Children Responsibility*. Santa Cruz, CA: Network Publications, 1990.

Feldman, Jean. *Transition Time: Let's Do Something Different!* Beltsville, MD: Gryphon House, 1995.

Fox, Lynn. *Let's Get Together*. Rolling Hills, CA: Jalmar Press, 1993.

Glasser, William, M.D. *Control Theory in the Classroom*. New York: HarperPerennial, 1986.

————.*The Quality School: Managing Students Without Coercion*. New York: HarperPerennial, 1992.

————.*The Quality School Teacher: A Companion Volume to the Quality School*. New York: HarperPerennial, 1993.

Knight, Michael et al. *Teaching Children to Love Themselves*. Hillside, NJ: Vision Press, 1982.

Kohn, Alfie. *Punished by Rewards: The Trouble with Gold Stars, Incentive Plans, A's, Praise, and Other Bribes*. Boston: Houghton Mifflin, 1993.

Kreidler, William. *Creative Conflict Resolution: Strategies for Keeping Peace in the Classroom*. Glenview, IL: Scott, Foresman, & Co., 1984.

Kurchinka, Mary Sheedy. *Raising Your Spirited Child*. New York: Harper, 1991.

Kuykendall, Crystal. *From Rage to Hope: Strategies for Reclaiming Black & Hispanic Students*. Bloomington, IL: National Educational Service, 1992.

Mendler, Allen. *Smiling at Yourself: Educating Young Children About Stress and Self-Esteem*. Santa Cruz, CA: Network Publications, 1990.

————.*What Do I Do When? How to Achieve Discipline with Dignity in the Classroom*. Bloomington, IL: National Educational Service, 1992.

Nelson, Jane. *Positive Discipline*. New York: Ballantine Books, 1987.

Nelson, Jane; Lott, Lynn; and Glenn, Stephen. *Positive Discipline in the Classroom*. Rocklin, CA: Prima Publishing, 1993.

Redenbach, Sandi. *Self-Esteem: The Necessary Ingredient for Sucess*. Esteem Seminar Publications, 1991.

Reider, Barbara. *A Hooray Kind of Kid*. Folsom, CA: Sierra House Publishing, 1988.

Vail, Priscilla. *Emotion: The On-Off Switch for Learning*. Rosemont, NJ: Modern Learning Press, 1994.

Wright, Esther. *Good Morning, Class — I Love You!* Rolling Hills, CA: Jalmar Press, 1988.

————.*Loving Discipline A to Z*. San Francisco: Teaching From the Heart, 1994.

Cooperative Learning

Cohen, Dorothy. *Designing Groupwork: Strategies for the Heterogeneous Classroom*. New York: Teachers College Press, 1994.

Curran, Lorna. *Cooperative Learning Lessons for Little Ones: Literature-Based Language Arts and Social Skills*. San Juan Capistrano, CA: Resources for Teachers, Inc., 1992.

DeBolt, Virginia, with Dr. Spencer Kagan. *Write! Cooperative Learning and The Writing Process*. San Juan Capistrano, CA: Kagan Cooperative Learning, 1994.

Ellis, Susan S., and Whalen, Susan F. *Cooperative Learning: Getting Started*. New York: Scholastic, 1990.

Fisher, Bobbi. *Thinking and Learning Together: Curriculum and Community in a Primary Classroom*. Portsmouth, NH: Heinemann, 1995.

Forte, Imogene, and MacKenzie, Joy. *The Cooperative Learning Guide and Planning Pak for Primary Grades: Thematic Projects and Activities*. Nashville, TN: Incentive Publications, 1992.

Glover, Mary, and Sheppard, Linda. *Not On Your Own: The Power of Learning Together*. New York: Scholastic, 1990.

Johnson, David, and Johnson, Roger. *Cooperation and Competition: Theory and Research*. Edina, MN: Interaction Book Company, 1989.

————.*Learning Together and Alone*. Englewood Cliffs, NJ: Prentice Hall, Inc, 1991.

Kagan, Spencer. *Cooperative Learning*. San Juan Capistrano, CA: Resources for Teachers, Inc., 1994.

Reid, Jo Anne; Forrestal, P.; and Cook, J. *Small Group Learning in the Classroom*. Portsmouth, NH: Heinemann, 1989.

Shaw, Vanston, with Spencer Kagan, Ph.D. *Communitybuilding In the Classroom*. San Juan Capistrano, CA: Kagan Cooperative Learning, 1992.

Slavin, Robert. *Cooperative Learning*. Englewood Cliffs, NJ: Prentice-Hall, 1989.

————.*Cooperative Learning*. Boston: Allyn and Bacon, 1995.

Curriculum — Overview

Bredekamp, Sue, and Rosegrant, Teresa, eds. *Reaching Potentials: Appropriate Curriculum and Assessment for Young Children*, Vol. 1. Washington, DC: NAEYC, 1992.

Dodge, Diane Trister; Jablon, Judy R.; and Bickart, Toni S. *Constructing Curriculum for the Primary Grades*. Washington, DC: Teaching Strategies, Inc., 1994.

Fogarty, Robin. *The Mindful School: How to Integrate the Curricula*. Palatine, IL: IRI/Skylight Publishing, 1991.

Hall, G.E., and Loucks, S. F. "Program Definition and Adaptation: Implications for Inservice." Journal of Research and Development in Education (1981) 14, 2:46-58.

Hohmann, C. *Mathematics: High Scope K-3 Curriculum Guide* (illustrated field test edition). Ypsilanti, MI: High Scope Press, 1991.

Maehr, J. *Language and Literacy: High Scope K-3 Curriculum Guide* (illustrated field test edition). Ypsilanti, MI: High Scope Press, 1991.

National Association of Elementary School Principals. *Standards for Quality Elementary and Middle Schools: Kindergarten through Eighth Grade*. Alexandria, VA: NAESP, 1990.

Rowan, Thomas E., and Morrow, Lorna J. *Implementing the K-8 Curriculum and Evaluation Standards: Readings from the "Arithmetic Teacher."* Reston, VA: National Council of Teachers of Mathematics, 1993.

Short, Kathy, and Burke, Carolyn. *Creating Curriculum*. Portsmouth, NH: Heinemann, 1981.

Stevenson, S. Christopher and Carr, Judy F. *Integrated Studies in the Middle School: Dancing Through Walls*. New York: Teachers College Press, 1993.

Whitin, D.; Mills, H.; and O'Keefe, T. *Living and Learning Mathematics: Stories and Strategies for Supporting Mathematical Literacy*. Portsmouth, NH: Heinemann, 1990.

Curriculum — Integrated Activities (see pages 88-89 for math resources)

Bauer, Karen, and Drew, Rosa. *Alternatives to Worksheets*. Cypress, CA: Creative Teaching Press, 1992.

Beierle, Marlene, and Lynes, Teri. *Book Cooks: Literature-Based Classroom Cooking (4-6)*. Cypress, CA: Creative Teaching Press, 1992.

Brainard, Audrey, and Wrubel, Denise H. *Literature-Based Science Activities: An Integrated Approach*. New York: Scholastic, 1993.

Bruno, Janet. *Book Cooks: Literature-Based Classroom Cooking (K-3)*. Cypress, CA: Creative Teaching Press, 1991.

Cherkerzian, Diane. *The Complete Lesson Plan Book*. Peterborough, NH: Crystal Springs Books, 1993.

Cochrane, Orin, ed. *Reading Experiences in Science*. Winnipeg, Man.: Peguis, 1985.

Feldman, Jean R. *Wonderful Rooms Where Children Can Bloom!* Peterborough, NH: Crystal Springs Books, 1997.

Goin, Kenn; Ripp, Eleanor; and Solomon, Kathleen Nastasi. *Bugs to Bunnies: Hands-on Animal Science Activities for Young Children*. New York: Chatterbox Press, 1989.

Hiatt, Catherine; Wolven, Doug; Botka, Gwen; and Richmond, Jennifer. *More Alternatives to Worksheets*. Cypress, CA: Creative Teaching Press, 1994.

Huck, Charlotte, and Hickman, Janet, eds. *The Best of the Web*. Columbus, OH: Ohio State University, 1982.

Irvine, Joan. *How to Make Pop-ups*. New York: Beech Tree Books, 1987.

———.*How to Make Super Pop-ups*. New York: Beech Tree Books, 1992.

Jorgensen, Karen. *History Workshop*. Portsmouth, NH: Heinemann, 1993.

Kohl, MaryAnn, and Potter, Jean. *ScienceArts: Discovering Science Through Art Experiences*. Bellingham, WA: Bright Ring Publishing, 1993.

McCarthy, Tara. *Literature-Based Geography Activities: An Integrated Approach*. New York: Scholastic, 1992.

Ritter, Darlene. *Literature-Based Art Activities (K-3)*. Cypress, CA: Creative Teaching Press, 1992.

———.*Literature-Based Art Activities (4-6)*. Cypress, CA: Creative Teaching Press, 1992.

Rothstein, Gloria Lesser. *From Soup to Nuts: Multicultural Cooking Activities and Recipes*. New York: Scholastic, 1994.

Ruef, Kerry. *The Private Eye. Looking/Thinking by Analogy: A Guide to Developing the Interdisciplinary Mind*. Seattle: The Private Eye Project, 1992.

Short, Kathy G.; Schroeder, Jean; Laird, Julie; Kauffman, Gloria; Ferguson, Margaret J.; Crawford, Kathleen Marie. *Learning Together Through Inquiry: From Columbus to Integrated Curriculum*. York, ME: Stenhouse Publishers, 1996.

Spann, Mary Beth. *Literature-Based Multicultural Activities*. New York: Scholastic, 1992.

———.*Literature-Based Seasonal and Holiday Activities*. New York: Scholastic, 1991.

Steffey, Stephanie, and Hood, Wendy J., eds. *If This Is Social Studies, Why Isn't It Boring?* York, ME: Stenhouse Publishers, 1994.

Developmental Education / Readiness

Ames, Louise Bates. *What Do They Mean I'm Difficult?* Rosemont, NJ: Modern Learning Press, 1986.

Ames, Louise Bates; Baker, Sidney; and Ilg, Frances L. *Child Behavior (Specific Advice on Problems of Child Behavior)*. New York: Barnes & Noble Books, 1981.

Ames, Louise Bates, and Chase, Joan Ames. *Don't Push Your Pre-Schooler*. New York: Harper & Row, 1980.

Ames, Louise Bates, and Haber, Carol Chase. *He Hit Me First (When Brothers and Sisters Fight)*. New York: Dembner Books, 1982.

———.*Your Seven-Year-Old (Life in a Minor Key)*. New York: Dell, 1985.

———.*Your Eight-Year-Old (Lively and Outgoing)*. New York: Dell, 1989.

———.*Your Nine-Year-Old (Thoughtful and Mysterious)*. New York: Dell, 1990.

Ames, Louise Bates, and Ilg, Frances L. *Child Behavior*. New York: Barnes & Noble Books, 1955.

———.*The Child from Five to Ten*. New York: Harper & Row, 1946.

———.*Your Two-Year-Old (Terrible or Tender)*. New York: Dell, 1980.

———.*Your Three-Year-Old (Friend or Enemy)*. New York: Dell, 1980.

———.*Your Four-Year-Old (Wild and Wonderful)*. New York: Dell, 1980.

———.*Your Five-Year-Old, Sunny and Serene*. New York: Dell, 1979.

———.*Your Six-Year-Old, Loving and Defiant*. New York: Dell, 1979.

———.*Your Ten-to-Fourteen Year-Old*. New York: Dell, 1981.

Ames, Louise Bates; Ilg, Frances L.; and Haber, Frances L. *Your One-Year-Old (The Fun-Loving 12-to-24-month-old)*. New York: Delacorte, 1982.

Ames, Louise Bates, et al. *The Gesell Institute's Child from One to Six.* New York: Harper & Row, 1946.

Bluestein, Jane. *Being a Successful Teacher—A Practical Guide to Instruction and Management.* Belmont, CA: Fearon Teacher Aids, 1988.

Boyer, Ernest. *The Basic School: A Community for Learning.* Ewing, NJ: Carnegie Foundation for the Advancement of Learning, 1995.

———.*Ready to Learn: A Mandate for the Nation.* Princeton, NJ: The Foundation for the Advancement of Teaching, 1991.

Brazelton, T. Berry. *To Listen to a Child: Understanding the Normal Problems of Growing Up.* Reading, MA: Addison-Wesley, 1986.

———. *Touchpoints: The Essential Reference. Your Child's Emotional and Behavioral Development.* Reading, MA: Addison-Wesley, 1994.

———. *Working and Caring.* Reading, MA: Addison-Wesley, 1985.

Bredekamp, Sue, ed. *Developmentally Appropriate Practice in Early Childhood Programs Serving Children From Birth Through Age 8,* expanded edition. Washington, DC: National Association for the Education of Young Children, 1987.

Charney, Ruth Sidney. *Teaching Children to Care: Management in the Responsive Classroom.* Greenfield, MA: Northeast Foundation for Children, 1991.

Coletta, Anthony. *Kindergarten Readiness Checklist for Parents.* Rosemont, NJ: Modern Learning Press, 1991.

Elovson, Allanna. *The Kindergarten Survival Book.* Santa Monica, CA: Parent Ed Resources, 1991.

Grant, Jim. *Childhood Should Be a ~~Pressure~~ Precious Time.* (poem anthology) Rosemont, NJ: Modern Learning Press, 1989.

———. *Developmental Education in the 1990's.* Rosemont, NJ: Modern Learning Press, 1991.

———. *"I Hate School!" Some Common Sense Answers for Educators & Parents Who Want to Know Why and What to Do About It.* Rosemont, NJ: Programs for Education, 1994.

———. *Jim Grant's Book of Parent Pages.* Rosemont, NJ: Programs for Education, 1988.

———. *Worth Repeating: Giving Children a Second Chance at School Success.* Rosemont, NJ: Modern Learning Press, 1989.

Grant, Jim, and Azen, Margot. *Every Parent's Owner's Manuals. (Three-, Four-, Five-, Six-, Seven-Year- Old).* Rosemont, NJ. Programs for Education.

Hardin, Sonya, and Ridgley, Linda. *Ready, Set, Go! to Kindergarten.* Helping children transition from preschool to kindergarten. Video. Doulos Productions, P.O. Box 1351, Hickory, NC 28603-1351. 1-800-354-9982.

Hayes, Martha, and Faggella, Kathy. *Think It Through.* Bridgeport, CT: First Teacher Press, 1986.

Healy, Jane M. *Endangered Minds: Why Children Don't Think and What We Can Do About It.* New York: Simon and Schuster, 1990.

———. *Your Child's Growing Mind: A Guide to Learning and Brain Development From Birth to Adolescence.* New York: Doubleday, 1987.

Holt, John. *How Children Fail.* New York: Dell Publishing, 1964, 1982.

Horowitz, Janet, and Faggella, Kathy. *Partners for Learning.* Bridgeport, CT: First Teacher Press, 1986.

Karnofsky, Florence, and Weiss, Trudy. *How to Prepare Your Child for Kindergarten.* Carthage, IL: Fearon Teacher Aids, 1993.

Lamb, Beth, and Logsdon, Phyllis. *Positively Kindergarten: A Classroom-proven, Theme-based Developmental Guide for the Kinder-garten Teacher.* Rosemont, NJ: Modern Learning Press, 1991.

Mallory, Bruce, and New, Rebecca, eds. *Diversity and Developmentally Appropriate Practices: Challenges for Early Childhood Education.* New York: Teachers College Press, 1994.

Miller, Karen. *Ages and Stages: Developmental Descriptions and Activities Birth Through Eight Years.* Chelsea, MA: Telshare Publishing Co., 1985.

National Association of Elementary School Principals. *Early Childhood Education and the Elementary School Principal.* Alexandria, VA: NAESP, 1990.

National Association of State Boards of Education. *Right from the Start: The Report of the NASBE Task Force on Early Childhood Education.* Alexandria, VA: NASBE, 1988.

Northeast Foundation for Children. *A Notebook for Teachers: Making Changes in the Elementary Curriculum.* Greenfield, MA, 1991.

Reavis, George H. *The Animal School.* Rosemont, NJ: Modern Learning Press, 1988.

Singer, Dorothy, and Revenson, Tracy. *How a Child Thinks: A Piaget Primer.* Independence, MO: International University Press, 1978.

Wood, Chip. *Yardsticks: Children in the Classroom Ages 4-14.* Greenfield, MA: Northeast Foundation for Children, 1997.

Grade Replacement

Ames, Louise Bates. *What Am I Doing in This Grade?* Rosemont, NJ: Modern Learning Press, 1985.

———.*Is Your Child in the Wrong Grade?* Rosemont, NJ: Modern Learning Press, 1978.

Ames, Louise Bates; Gillespie, Clyde; and Streff, John W. *Stop School Failure.* Rosemont, NJ: Modern Learning Press, 1972.

Grant, Jim. *Worth Repeating.* Rosemont, NJ: Modern Learning Press, 1989.

Hobby, Janice Hale. *Staying Back.* Gainesville, FL: Triad, 1990.

Moore, Sheila, and Frost, Roon. *The Little Boy Book.* New York: Clarkson N. Potter, 1986.

Grade Replacement — Audio/Video

Ames, Louise Bates. *Part I: Ready Or Not: Here I Come!* and *Part II: An Evaluation of the Whole Child,* video. Modern Learning Press, 1983.

Gesell Institute of Human Development. *Ready or Not Here I Come!* Video/16 mm film. Modern Learning Press, 1984.

Grant, Jim. *Do You Know Where Your Child Is?* Video. Modern Learning Press, 1985.

———.*Grade Replacement.* Audiotape. Modern Learning Press, 1988.

———.*Jim Grant Live.* Audiotape. Modern Learning Press, 1985.

———.*Worth Repeating.* Video. Modern Learning Press, 1988.

Inclusion / Differently Abled / Learning Disabilities

Bailey, D.B, and Wolery, M. *Teaching Infants and Preschoolers with Handicaps.* Columbus, OH: Merrill, 1984.

Dudley-Marling, Curtis. *When School is a Struggle.* New York: Scholastic, 1990.

Dunn, Kathryn B., and Dunn, Allison B. *Trouble with School: A Family Story about Learning Disabilities.* Rockville, MD: Woodbine House, 1993.

Fagan, S.A.; Graves, D.L.; and Tressier-Switlick, D. *Promoting Successful Mainstreaming: Reasonable Classroom Accommodations for Learning Disabled Students.* Rockville, MD: Montgomery County Public Schools, 1984.

Friend, Marilyn, and Cook, Lynne. "The New Mainstreaming." *Instructor Magazine,* March 1992: 30-35.

Goodman, Gretchen. *I Can Learn! Strategies and Activities for Gray-Area Children.* Peterborough, NH: Crystal Springs Books, 1995.

———. *More I Can Learn!.* Peterborough, NH: Crystal Springs Books, 1997.

———. *Inclusive Classrooms from A to Z: A Handbook for Educators.* Columbus, OH: Teachers' Publishing Group, 1994.

Harwell, Joan. *Complete Learning Disabilities Handbook.* New York: Simon & Schuster, 1989.

Jenkins, J., and Jenkins, L. "Peer Tutoring in Elementary and Secondary Programs." In Effective Strategies for Exceptional Children, edited by Meyer, E.L.; Vergason, G.A.; and Whelan, R.J., 335-354, Denver, CO: Love Publishing Co., 1988.

Lang, Greg, and Berberich, Chris. *All Children are Special: Creating an Inclusive Classroom.* York, ME: Stenhouse Publishers, 1995.

McGregor, G., and Vogelsberg, R.T. *Transition Needs Assessment for Parents.* Philadelphia, PA: Temple University, 1989.

Perske, R. and Perske, M. *Circle of Friends.* Nashville, TN: Abingdon Press, 1988.

Phinney, Margaret. *Reading with the Troubled Reader.* Portsmouth, NH: Heinemann, 1989.

Rainforth, Beverly; York, Jennifer; and McDonald, Cathy. *Collaborative Teams for Students with Severe Disabilities.* Baltimore: Paul H. Brookes, 1992.

Rhodes, Lynn, and Dudley-Marling, Curtis. *Readers and Writers with a Difference: A Holistic Approach to Teaching Learning Disabled and Remedial Students.* Portsmouth: Heinemann, 1988.

Rosner, Jerome. *Helping Children Overcome Learning Difficulties.* New York: Walker and Co., 1979.

Society For Developmental Education. *Creating Inclusive Classrooms: Education for All Children.* Peterborough, NH: 1994.

Stainback, S., and Stainback, W. *Curriculum Considerations in Inclusive Classrooms: Facilitating Learning for All Students.* Baltimore: Paul H. Brookes, 1992.

———. *Support Networks for Inclusive Schooling.* Baltimore: Paul H. Brookes, 1990.

Stainback, S, Stainback, W., and Forest, M., eds. *Educating All Students in the Mainstream of Regular Education.* Baltimore: Paul H. Brookes, 1987.

Vail, Priscilla. *About Dyslexia.* Rosemont, NJ: Programs for Education, 1990.

———. *Smart Kids with School Problems.* New York: E.P. Dutton, 1987.

Vandercook, T., and York, J. "A Team Approach to Program Development and Support." In Support Networks for Inclusive Schooling: Interdependent Integrated Education, edited by Stainback, W. and Stainback, S., 95-122. Baltimore: Paul H. Brookes, 1990.

Villa, R., et al. *Restructuring for Caring and Effective Education: Administrative Strategies for Creating Heterogeneous Schools.* Baltimore: Paul H. Brookes, 1992.

The Internet

Editor's Note: All of these books contain website addresses, some of them suitable for teachers of K-12 classes, some for students of various ages, and some for both. The teacher needs to thoroughly explore each website to decide its appropriateness for a particular age group. Sometimes a listed site may not be appropriate for younger surfers, but will contain links to other sites that youngsters can enjoy. (There are meteorological sites, for instance, that have volumes of very technical scientific data, well beyond the understanding of elementary students, but which also contain really cool pictures of hurricanes.)

Websites come and go on the Internet; many of the websites in these books have already either disappeared or moved to another site. If you find that a particular site has vanished, a search of that topic will usually locate other usable sites.

Classroom Connect (Staff). *Educator's Internet Companion.* Lancaster, PA: Wentworth Worldwide Media, 1996.

Garfield, Gary, and McDonough, Suzanne. *Site Seeing the Internet Plain and Simple for Teachers, Parents & Kids.* Winnipeg: Peguis Publishers, 1996. The easiest and most fun book in this section.

McFedries, Paul. *The Complete Idiot's Guide to Creating an HTML Web Page.* Indianapolis: Que Corporation, 1996. Includes disk.

Place, Ron; Dimmler, Klaus; and Powell, Thomas. *Educator's Internet Yellow Pages: A Web Surfer Book.* Upper Saddle River, NJ: Prentice Hall PTR, 1996.

Virginia Space Grant Consortium. *The Educator's Guide to the Internet: A Handbook With Resources and Activities.* Menlo Park, CA: Addison-Wesley, 1997. Includes CD-Rom.

Williams, Bard. *The World Wide Web for Teachers*. Foster City, CA: IDG Books Worldwide (publisher of the "Dummies" series of books), 1996.

Issues in Education

Ledell, Marjorie, and Arnsparger, Arleen. *How to Deal with Community Criticism of School Change*. Alexandria, VA: Association for Supervision and Curriculum Development, 1993.

National Commission on Excellence in Education. *Nation at Risk: The Full Account*. USA Research Inc. Staff (ed.), 1984.

———. *Nation at Risk: The Full Account*. 2nd ed. USA Research Inc. Staff (ed.), 1992.

Rasell, Edith, and Rothstein, Richard, eds. *School Choice: Examining the Evidence*. Washington, DC: Economic Policy Institute, 1993.

Wortman, Bob, and Matlin, Myna. *Leadership in Whole Language: The Principal's Role*. York, ME: Stenhouse Publishers, 1995.

Wormtna, Robert. *Administrators Supporting School Change*. York, ME: Stenhouse Publishers, 1995, The Galef Institute.

Language Arts

Allen, JoBeth, and Mason, Jana, eds. *Risk Makers, Risk Breakers*. Portsmouth, NH: Heinemann, 1989.

Andrasick, Kathleen. *Opening Texts*. Portsmouth, NH: Heinemann, 1990.

Atwell, Nancie. *Coming to Know: Writing to Learn in the Middle Grades*. Portsmouth, NH: Heinemann, 1990.

———. *In the Middle: Writing, Reading, and Learning with Adolescents*. Portsmouth, NH: Heinemann, 1987.

———. *Side by Side: Essays on Teaching to Learn*. Portsmouth, NH: Heinemann, 1991.

———. *Workshop 1: Writing and Literature*. Portsmouth, NH: Heinemann, 1989.

———. *Workshop 2: Beyond the Basal*. Portsmouth, NH: Heinemann, 1989.

———. *Workshop 3: The Politics of Process*. Portsmouth, NH: Heinemann, 1991.

Barrett, F.L. *A Teacher's Guide to Shared Reading*. Toronto, Ont.: Scholastic TAB, 1982.

Barron, Marlene. *I Learn to Read and Write the Way I Learn to Talk*. Katonah, NY: Richard C. Owen Publishers, 1990.

Barton, Bob. *Tell Me Another*. Portsmouth, NH: Heinemann, 1986.

Baskwill, Jane. *Connections: A Child's Natural Learning Tool*. Toronto, Ont.: Scholastic TAB, 1982.

Baskwill, Jane, and Steven. *The Language Arts Sourcebook: Whole Language, Grades 5 and 6*. Toronto, Ont.: Scholastic TAB, 1991.

Baskwill, Jane, and Whitman, Paulette. *A Guide to Classroom Publishing*. Toronto: Scholastic TAB, 1988.

———.*Moving On: Whole Language Sourcebook for Grades 3 and 4*. Toronto, Ont.: Scholastic TAB, 1988.

———.*Whole Language Sourcebook: Grades K-2*. Toronto: Scholastic TAB, 1986.

Beeler, Terri. *I Can Read! I Can Write! Creating a Print-Rich Environment*. Cypress, CA: Creative Teaching Press, 1993.

Beierle, Marlene, and Lynes, Teri. *Teaching Basic Skills Through Literature: A Whole Language Approach for Teaching Reading Skills*. Cypress, CA: Creative Teaching Press, 1993.

Bird, Lois Bridge. *Becoming a Whole Language School: The Fair Oaks Story*. Katonah, NY: Richard C. Owens Publishers, 1989.

Bissex, Glenda. *GNYS AT WRK*. Cambridge, MA: Harvard University Press, 1980.

Bissex, Glenda, and Bullock, Richard, eds. *Seeing for Ourselves*. Portsmouth, NH: Heinemann, 1987.

Blake, Robert, ed. *Whole Language: Explorations and Applications*. New York: New York State English Council, 1990.

Borba, Michele, and Ungaro, Dan. *The Complete Letter Book: Multisensory Activities for Teaching Sounds and Letters*. Carthage, IL: Good Apple, 1980.

Bosma, Bette. *Fairy Tales, Fables, Legends, and Myths*. New York: Teacher's College Press, 1987.

Bromley, Karen. *Journaling: Engagements in Reading, Writing, and Thinking*. New York: Scholastic, 1993.

Brown, Hazel, and Mathie, Vonne. *Inside Whole Language: A Classroom View*. Portsmouth, NH: Heinemann, 1991.

Buchanan, Ethel. *For the Love of Reading*. Winnipeg, Man.: The C.E.L. Group, 1980.

Buncombe, Fran, and Peetoom, Adrian. *Literature-Based Learning: One School's Journey*. New York: Scholastic, 1988.

Buros, Jay. *Why Whole Language?* Rosemont, NJ: Programs for Education, 1991.

Butler, Andrea, and Turbill, Jan. *Towards a Reading-Writing Classroom*. Portsmouth, NH: Heinemann, 1984.

Butler, Dorothy. *Cushla and Her Books*. Boston: The Horn Book, 1980.

Calkins, Lucy M. *The Art of Teaching Writing*. Portsmouth, NH: Heinemann, 1986.

———.*Lessons from a Child: On the Teaching and Learning of Writing*. Portsmouth, NH: Heinemann, 1983.

———.*Living Between the Lines*. Portsmouth, NH: Heinemann, 1990.

Cambourne, Brian. *The Whole Story*. New York: Scholastic, 1988.

Cambourne, Brian, and Brown, Hazel. *Read and Retell*. Portsmouth, NH: Heinemann, 1990.

Cambourne, Brian, and Turbill, Jan. *Coping with Chaos*. Portsmouth, NH: Heinemann, 1988.

Clay, Marie. *Becoming Literate*. Portsmouth, NH: Heinemann, 1991.

———.*Observing Young Readers*. Portsmouth, NH: Heinemann, 1982.

———.*Reading Recovery: A Guidebook for Teachers in Training.* Portsmouth, NH: Heinemann, 1993.

———.*What Did I Write?* Portsmouth, NH: Heinemann, 1975.

Clifford, John. *The Experience of Reading: Louise Rosenblatt and Reader-Response Theory.* Portsmouth, NH: Heinemann, 1991.

Cloonan, Kathryn L. *Sing Me A Story, Read Me A Song* (Books I and II). Beverly Hills, FL: Rhythm & Reading Resources, 1991.

———.*Whole Language Holidays.* (Books I and II). Beverly Hills, FL: Rhythm & Reading Resources, 1992.

Collis, Mark, and Dalton, Joan. *Becoming Responsible Learners.* Portsmouth, NH: Heinemann, 1991.

Cochrane, Orin et al. *Reading, Writing, and Caring.* Katonah, NY: Richard C. Owen Publishers, 1985.

Crafton, Linda. *Whole Language: Getting Started, Moving Forward.* Katonah, NY: Richard C. Owen Publishers, 1991.

Cullinan, Bernice. *Children's Literature in the Reading Program.* Newark, DE: International Reading Association, 1987.

———. *Pen in Hand.* Newark, DE: International Reading Association, 1993.

Dakos, Kalli. *What's There to Write About?* New York: Scholastic, 1989.

Daniels, Harvey. *Literature Circles: Voice and Choice in the Student-Centered Classroom.* York, ME: Stenhouse Publishers, 1994.

Danielson, Kathy Everts, and Rogers, Sheri Everts. *Literature Connections Day-by-Day.* New York: Scholastic, 1994.

Davidson, Merrilyn et al. *Moving On With Big Books.* Auckland, New Zealand: Ashton Scholastic, 1989.

DeFord, Diane et al. *Bridges to Literacy.* Portsmouth, NH: Heinemann, 1991.

Department of Education, Wellington, New Zealand. *Reading in Junior Classes.* New York: Richard C. Owen Publishers, 1985.

Dewey, John. *The Child and the Curriculum* and *The School and Society.* Chicago: Phoenix Books, combined edition, 1956.

Drutman, Ava Deutsch, and Huston, Diane L. *150 Surefire Ways to Keep Them Reading All Year.* New York: Scholastic, 1992.

Dudley-Marling, Curtis, and Searle, Dennis. *When Students Have Time to Talk.* Portsmouth, NH: Heinemann, 1991.

Edelsky, Carole; Altwerger, Bess; and Flores, Barbara. *Whole Language: What's the Difference?* Portsmouth, NH: Heinemann, 1990.

Eisele, Beverly. *Managing the Whole Language Classroom: A Complete Teaching Resource Guide for K-6 Teachers.* Cypress, CA: Creative Teaching Press, 1991.

Fairfax, Barbara, and Garcia, Adela. *Read! Write! Publish!* Cypress, CA: Creative Teaching Press, 1992.

Ferreiro, Emilia, and Teberosky, Ana. *Literacy Before Schooling.* Portsmouth, NH: Heinemann, 1979.

Fisher, Bobbi. *Joyful Learning: A Whole Language Kindergarten.* Portsmouth, NH: Heinemann, 1991.

Five, Cora Lee. *Special Voices.* Portsmouth, NH: Heinemann, 1991.

Fletcher, Ralph. *What a Writer Needs.* Portsmouth, NH: Heinemann, 1992.

Fountas, Irene C., and Pinnell, Gay Su. *Guided Reading: Good First Teaching for All Children.* Portsmouth, NH: Heinemann, 1996.

Frank, Marjorie. *If You're Trying to Teach Kids How to Write, You've Gotta Have This Book.* Nashville, TN: Incentive Publications, 1979.

Freeman, Yvonne, and Freeman, David. *Whole Language for Second Language Learners.* Portsmouth, NH: Heinemann, 1992.

Froese, Victor, ed. *Whole Language: Theory and Practice.* Scarborough, Ont.: Prentice Hall, 1990.

Fulwiler, Toby, ed. *The Journal Book.* Portsmouth, NH: Heinemann, 1987.

———.*Programs That Work: Models and Methods for Writing Across the Curriculum.* Portsmouth, NH: Heinemann, 1990.

Furniss, Elaine, ed. *The Literacy Agenda.* Portsmouth, NH: Heinemann, 1991.

Garvey, Catherine. *Children's Talk.* Boston: Harvard Press, 1984. (Part of the Developing Child Series.)

Geller, Linda Gibson. *Word Play and Language Learning for Children.* Urbana, IL: National Council of Teachers of English, 1985.

Goodman, Kenneth. *What's Whole in Whole Language?* New York: Scholastic, 1986.

Goodman, Kenneth, et al. *Language and Thinking in School: A Whole-Language Curriculum.* Katonah, NY: Richard C. Owen Publishers, 1987.

———.*Report Card on Basals.* New York: Richard C. Owen Publishers, 1988.

Goodman, Yetta. *How Children Construct Literacy.* Newark, DE: International Reading Association, 1990.

Goodman, Yetta M.; Hood, Wendy J.; and Goodman, Kenneth S. *Organizing for Whole Language.* Portsmouth, NH: Heinemann, 1991.

Graves, Donald. *Build a Literate Classroom.* Portsmouth, NH: Heinemann, 1991.

———. *A Researcher Learns to Write.* Portsmouth, NH: Heinemann, 1984.

———. *Discover Your Own Literacy.* Portsmouth, NH: Heinemann, 1990.

———. *Experiment with Fiction.* Portsmouth, NH: Heinemann, 1990.

———. *Investigate Nonfiction.* Portsmouth, NH: Heinemann, 1989.

———. *Writing: Teachers and Children at Work.* Portsmouth, NH: Heinemann, 1983.

Graves, Donald, and Stuart, Virginia. *Write from the Start.* New York: New American Library, 1985.

Greenwood, Barbara. *The Other Side of the Story.* Toronto, Ont.: Scholastic TAB, 1990.

Gunderson, Lee. *A Whole Language Primer.* New York: Scholastic, 1989.

Haack, Pam, and Merrilees, Cynthia. *Ten Ways to Become a Better Reader.* Cleveland, OH: Modern Curriculum Press, 1991.

———.*Write on Target.* Peterborough, NH: The Society For Developmental Education, 1991.

Hall, Nigel, and Robertson, Anne. *Some Day You Will No All About Me: Young Children's Explorations in the World of Letters.* Portsmouth, NH: Heinemann, 1991.

Hancock, Joelie, and Hill, Susan, eds. *Literature-Based Reading Programs at Work.* Portsmouth, NH: Heinemann, 1988.

Hansen, Jane. *When Writers Read.* Portsmouth, NH: Heinemann, 1987.

Hansen, Jane; Newkirk, Thomas; and Graves, Donald, eds. *Breaking Ground: Teachers Relate Reading and Writing in the Elementary School.* Portsmouth, NH: Heinemann, 1985.

Harste, Jerome, and Short, Kathy. *Creating Classrooms for Authors: The Reading-Writing Connection.* Portsmouth, NH: Heinemann, 1988.

Harste, Jerome; Woodward, Virginia; and Burke, Carolyn. *Language Stories and Literacy Lessons.* Portsmouth, NH: Heinemann, 1984.

Hart-Hewins, Linda, and Wells, Jan. *Read It In the Classroom!* Portsmouth, NH: Heinemann, 1992.

Harwayne, Shelley. *Lasting Impressions: Weaving Literature into the Writing Workshop.* Portsmouth, NH: Heinemann, 1992.

Hayes, Martha. *Building on Books.* Bridgeport, CT: First Teacher Press, 1987.

Heald-Taylor, Gail. *The Administrator's Guide to Whole Language.* Katonah, NY: Richard C. Owen Publishers, 1989.

Heard, Georgia. *For the Good of the Earth and Sun: Teaching Poetry.* Portsmouth, NH: Heinemann, 1989.

Holdaway, Don. *The Foundations of Literacy.* New York: Scholastic, 1979.

———. *Stability and Change in Literacy Learning.* Portsmouth, NH: Heinemann, 1984.

Hopkins, Lee. *Pass the Poetry Please.* New York: Harper & Row, 1987.

Hornsby, David; Sukarna, Deborah; and Parry, Jo-Ann. *Read On: A Conference Approach to Reading.* Portsmouth, NH: Heinemann, 1986.

———. *Teach On.* Portsmouth, NH: Heinemann, 1984.

Hubbard, Ruth. *Authors of Pictures, Draughtsmen of Words.* Portsmouth, NH: Heinemann, 1989.

Hubbard, Ruth, and Power, Brenda. *The Art of Classroom Inquiry.* Portsmouth, NH: Heinemann, 1993.

Johnson, Paul. *A Book of One's Own.* Portsmouth, NH: Heinemann, 1992.

———. *Literacy Through the Book Arts.* Portsmouth, NH: Heinemann, 1993.

Johnson, Terry, and Louis, Daphne. *Literacy Through Litertaure.* Portsmouth, NH: Heinemann, 1987.

———. *Bringing It All Together.* Portsmouth, NH: Heinemann, 1993.

Karelitz, Ellen Blackburn. *The Author's Chair and Beyond.* Portsmouth, NH: Heinemann, 1993.

Kitagawa, Mary, and Kitagawa, Chisato. *Making Connections with Writing.* Portsmouth, NH: Heinemann, 1987.

Kovaks, Deborah, and Preller, James. *Meet the Authors and Illustrators: 60 Creators of Favorite Children's Books Talk about Their Work,* Vol. 1. New York: Scholastic, 1991.

———. *Meet the Authors and Illustrators: 60 Creators of Favorite Children's Books Talk about Their Work,* Vol. 2. New York: Scholastic, 1993.

Lamme, Linda. *Highlights for Children: Growing Up Reading.* Reston, VA: Acropolis Books, 1984.

———. *Growing Up Writing.* Reston, VA: Acropolis Books, 1984.

Lloyd, Pamela. *How Writers Write.* Portsmouth, NH: Heinemann, 1987.

Lynch, Priscilla. *Using Big Books and Predictable Books.* New York: Scholastic, 1987.

Madigan, Dan, and Koivu-Rybicki, Victoria T. *The Writing Lives of Children.* York, ME: Stenhouse, 1997.

Mann, Jean. *Literacy Labels* (six book set). Columbus, OH: Essential Learning Products, 1994.

McClure, Amy; Harrison, Peggy; and Reed, Sheryl. *Sunrises and Songs.* Portsmouth, NH: Heinemann, 1990.

McConaghy, June. *Children's Learning Through Literature.* Portsmouth, NH: Heinemann, 1990.

McCracken, Robert and Marlene. *Stories, Songs and Poetry to Teach Reading and Writing.* Chicago: American Library Association, 1986.

———. *Reading, Writing and Language: A Practical Guide for Primary Teachers.* Winnipeg, Man.: Peguis, 1995.

McKenzie, Moira. *Journeys Into Literacy.* Huddersfield: Schofield & Sims, 1986.

McTeague, Frank. *Shared Reading in the Middle and High School Years.* Portsmouth, NH: Heinemann, 1992.

McVitty, Walter. *Children and Learning.* PETA (Heinemann), 1985.

———. *Getting It Together: Organizing the Reading-Writing Classroom.* Portsmouth, NH: Heinemann, 1986.

Meek, Margaret, ed. *Opening Moves.* London: University of London Institute of Education, 1983.

Miller, Joan. *Sharing Ideas: An Oral Language Programme.* Melbourne: Nelson Publishing Co., 1988.

Mills, Heidi, and Clyde, Jean Anne. *Portraits of Whole Language Classrooms.* Portsmouth, NH: Heinemann, 1990.

Moffett, James, and Wagner, Betty Jane. *Student-Centered Language Arts, K-12, Fourth Edition.* Portsmouth, NH: Boynton/Cook, 1991.

Mooney, Margaret. *Developing Life-Long Readers.* Katonah, NY: Richard C. Owen Publishers, 1988.

Murray, Donald. *Learning by Teaching.* Portsmouth, NH: Boynton/Cook, 1982.

Myers, Miles. *The Teacher-Researcher: How to Study Writing in the Classroom.* Urbana, IL: National Council of Teachers of English, 1985.

NCTE and IRA. *Cases in Literacy.* International Reading Association and National Council of Teachers of English, 1985.

Newman, Judith, ed. *Whole Language: Theory In Use.* Portsmouth, NH: Heinemann, 1985.

———. *The Craft of Children's Writing.* Portsmouth, NH: Heinemann, 1985.

——— ed. *Finding Out Own Way.* Portsmouth, NH: Heinemann, 1990.

Newkirk, Thomas. *More Than Stories.* Portsmouth, NH: Heinemann, 1989.

———. *Nuts and Bolts.* Portsmouth, NH: Heinemann, 1993.

Nova Scotia Department of Education. *Language Arts in the Elementary School.* Curriculum Development Guide No. 86, 1986.

Olsen, Janet. *Envisioning Writing.* Portsmouth, NH: Heinemann, 1992.

Paley, Vivian. *Molly Is Three.* Chicago: University of Chicago, 1986.

———. *Wally's Stories.* Boston: Harvard Educational Press, 1981.

Parsons, Les. *Poetry, Themes, and Activities.* Portsmouth, NH: Heinemann, 1992.

———. *Writing in the Real Classroom.* Portsmouth, NH: Heinemann, 1991.

Pavelka, Patricia. *Making the Connection: Learning Skills Through Literature (K-2).* Peterborough, NH: Crystal Springs Books, 1995.

———. *Making the Connection: Learning Skills Through Literature (3-6).* Peterborough, NH: Crystal Springs Books, 1997.

Peetboom, Adrian. *Shared Reading: Safe Risks With Whole Books.* Toronto, Ont.: Scholastic TAB, 1986.

Peterson, Ralph, and Maryann, eds. *Grand Conversations: Literature Groups in Action.* New York: Scholastic, 1990.

———. *Life in a Crowded Place: Making a Learning Community.* Portsmouth, NH: Heinemann, 1992.

Picciotto, Linda Pierce. *Managing an Integrated Language Arts Classroom.* Ontario: Scholastic, 1995.

Pigdon, Keith, and Woolley, Marilyn. *The Big Picture: Integrating Children's Learning.* Portsmouth, NH: Heinemann, 1993.

Pinnell, Gay Su. *Teachers and Research: Language Learning in the Classroom.* Newark, DE: International Reading Association, 1989.

Raines, Shirley C., and Canady, Robert J. *Story Stretchers.* Mt. Ranier, MD: Gryphon House, 1989.

———. *More Story Stretchers.* Mt. Ranier, MD: Gryphon House, 1991.

———. *Story Stretchers for the Primary Grades.* Mt. Ranier, MD: Gryphon House, 1992.

———. *The Whole Language Kindergarten.* New York: Scholastic, 1993.

Rief, Linda. *Seeking Diversity: Language Arts With Adolescents.* Portsmouth, NH: Heinemann, 1992.

Romano, Tom. *Clearing the Way.* Portsmouth, NH: Heinemann, 1987.

Routman, Regie. *Transitions: From Literature to Literacy.* Portsmouth, NH: Heinemann, 1988.

———. *Invitations: Changing as Teachers and Learners K-12.* Portsmouth, NH: Heinemann, 1991.

———. *Literacy at the Crossroads: Crucial Talk About Reading, Writing, and Other Teaching Dilemmas.* Portsmouth, NH: Heinemann, 1996.

Sampson, Michael. *Pathways to Literacy.* New York: Holt, Rinehart & Winston, 1991.

Schell, Leo. *How to Create an Independent Reading Program.* New York: Scholastic, 1991.

Schickedanz, Judith. *Adam's Righting Revolutions.* Portsmouth, NH: Heinemann, 1990.

Schlosser, Kristin G., and Phillips, Vicki L. *Beginning in Whole Language: A Practical Guide.* New York: Scholastic, 1991.

———. *Building Literacy with Interactive Charts.* New York: Scholastic, 1991.

Schwartz, Susan. *Creating the Child-Centered Classroom.* Katonah, NY: Richard C. Owen Publishers, 1991.

Shannon, Patrick. *Becoming Political.* Portsmouth, NH: Heinemann, 1990.

———. *The Struggle to Continue.* Portsmouth, NH: Heinemann, 1990.

Shedlock, Marie. *The Art of the Storyteller.* New York: Dover Press, 1951.

Short, Kathy, and Pierce, Kathryn, eds. *Talking About Books.* Portsmouth, NH: Heinemann, 1990.

Silko, Leslie Marmon. *Storyteller.* New York: Seaver Books, 1981.

Smith, Frank. *Essays Into Literacy.* Portsmouth, NH: Heinemann, 1983.

———. *Insult to Intelligence.* Portsmouth, NH: Heinemann, 1986.

———. *Joining the Literacy Club.* Portsmouth, NH: Heinemann, 1988.

———. *Reading Without Nonsense.* New York: Teachers College Press, 1978.

———. *Understanding Reading.* Hillsdale, NJ: Lawrence Erlbaum Publishers, 1986.

Sobut, Mary, A., and Bogen, Bonnie Neuman. *Whole Language Literature Activities for Young Children.* West Nyack, NY: The Center for Applied Research in Education, 1993.

Somerfield, Muriel. *A Framework for Reading.* Portsmouth, NH: Heinemann, 1985.

Stephens, Diane. *What Matters? A Primer for Teaching Reading.* Portsmouth, NH: Heinemann, 1990.

Strickland, Dorothy. *Emerging Literacy: Young Children Learn to Read and Write.* Newark, DE: International Reading Association, 1989.

Sunflower, Cherilyn. *75 Creative Ways to Publish Students' Writing.* New York: Scholastic, 1993.

Taylor, Denny. *Family Literacy.* Portsmouth, NH: Heinemann, 1983.

———. *Learning Denied.* Portsmouth, NH: Heinemann, 1990.

Taylor, Denny, and Dorsey-Gaines, Catherine. *Growing Up Literate.* Portsmouth, NH: Heinemann, 1990.

———. *Learning Denied.* Portsmouth, NH: Heinemann, 1990.

Taylor, Denny, and Dorsey-Gaines, Catherine. *Growing Up Literate.* Portsmouth, NH: Heinemann, 1990.

Turbill, Jan, ed. *No Better Way to Teach Writing!* Portsmouth, NH: Heinemann, 1982.

Vail, Priscilla. *Common Ground: Whole Language and Phonics Working Together.* Rosemont, NJ: Programs for Education, 1991.

Van Manen, Max. *The Tone of Teaching.* Portsmouth, NH: Heinemann, 1986.

Ward, Geoff. *I've Got a Project.* Australia: PETA, 198. (Distributed in the United States by Heinemann, Portsmouth, NH)

Watson, Dorothy. *Whole Language: Inquiring Voices.* New York: Scholastic, 1989.

Weaver, Constance. *Reading Process and Practice.* Portsmouth, NH: Heinemann, 1988.

———. *Understanding Whole Language.* Portsmouth, NH: Heinemann, 1990.

Weaver, Constance, and Henke, Linda, eds. *Supporting Whole Language.* Portsmouth, NH: Heinemann, 1992.

Wells, Gordon. *The Meaning Makers.* Portsmouth, NH: Heinemann, 1986.

Wilde, Jack. *A Door Opens: Writing in Fifth Grade.* Portsmouth, NH: Heinemann, 1993.

Wollman-Bonilla, Julie. *Response Journals.* New York: Scholastic, 1991.

Language Arts — Bilingual

Whitmore, Kathryn F., and Crowell, Caryl G. *Inventing a Classroom: Life in a Bilingual, Whole Language Learning Community.* York, ME: Stenhouse Publishers, 1994.

Language Arts — Spelling and Phonics

Bean, Wendy, and Bouffler, Christine. *Spell by Writing.* Portsmouth, NH: Heinemann, 1988.

Bolton, Faye, and Snowball, Diane. *Ideas for Spelling.* Portsmouth, NH: Heinemann, 1993.

Booth, David. *Spelling Links.* Ontario: Pembroke Publishers, 1991.

Buchanan, Ethel. *Spelling for Whole Language Classrooms.* Winnipeg, Man.: The C.E.L. Group, 1989.

Cunningham, Patricia M. *Phonics They Use: Words For Reading and Writing. 2nd edition.* New York: HarperCollins College Publishers, 1995.

Cunningham, Patricia M., and Hall, Dorothy P. *Making Big Words: Multilevel, Hands-On Spelling and Phonics Activities. (Grades 3-6)* Torrance, CA: Good Apple, 1994.

———. *Making Words: Multilevel, Hands-On, Developmentally Appropriate Spelling and Phonics Activities. (Grades 1-3)* Torrance, CA: Good Apple, 1994.

Erickson, Rhonda. *The Amazing Alphabet Puppets.* Cypress, CA: Creative Teaching Press, 1995.

Fitzpatrick, Jo. *Phonemic Awareness: Playing With Sounds to Strengthen Beginning Reading Skills.* Cypress, CA: Creative Teaching Press, 1997.

Fry, Edward, Ph.D. *1000 Instant Words.* Laguna Beach, CA: Laguna Beach Educational Books, 1994.

———. *Phonics Patterns: Onset and Rhyme Word Lists.* Laguna Beach Educational Books, 1994.

Gentry, J. Richard. *My Kid Can't Spell.* Portsmouth, NH: Heinemann, 1996.

———. *Spel . . . Is a Four-Letter Word.* New York: Scholastic, 1987.

Gentry, J. Richard, and Gillet, Jean Wallace. *Teaching Kids to Spell.* Portsmouth, NH: Heinemann, 1993.

Lacey, Cheryl. *Moving on in Spelling: Strategies and Activities for the Whole Language Classroom.* New York: Scholastic, 1994.

Powell, Debbie, and Hornsby, David. *Learning Phonics and Spelling in a Whole Language Classroom.* New York: Scholastic, 1993.

Trisler, Alana, and Cardiel, Patrice. *My Word Book.* Rosemont, NJ: Modern Learning Press, 1994.

———. *Words I Use When I Write.* Rosemont, NJ: Modern Learning Press, 1989.

———. *More Words I Use When I Write.* Rosemont, NJ: Modern Learning Press, 1990.

Wagstaff, Janiel. *Phonics That Work! New Strategies for the Reading/Writing Classroom.* New York: Scholastic, 1995.

Wittels, Harriet, and Greisman, Joan. *How to Spell It.* New York: Putnam, 1982.

Learning Centers

Cook, Carole. *Math Learning Centers for the Primary Grades.* West Nynack, NY: The Center for Applied Research, 1992.

Ingraham, Phoebe Bell. *Creating and Managing Learning Centers: A Thematic Approach.* Peterborough, NH: Crystal Springs Books, fall 1996.

Isbell, Rebecca. *The Complete Learning Center Book.* Beltsville, MD: Gryphon House, 1995.

Marx, Pamela. *Classroom Museums: Touchable Tables for Kids!* New York: Scholastic, 1992.

Morrow, Lesley Mandel. *The Literacy Center: Contexts for Reading and Writing.* York, ME: Stenhouse, 1997.

Poppe, Carol A., and Van Matre, Nancy A. *Language Arts Learning Centers for the Primary Grades.* West Nynack, NY: The Center for Applied Research in Education, 1991.

———. *Science Learning Centers for the Primary Grades.* West Nyack, NY: The Center for Applied Research in Education, 1985.

Wait, Shirleen S. *Reading Learning Centers for the Primary Grades*. West Nynack, NY: The Center for Applied Research, 1992.

Waynant, Louise, and Wilson, Robert M. *Learning Centers, A Guide for Effective Use*. Paoli, PA: Instructo Corp., 1974.

Learning Strategies / Multiple Intelligences

Armstrong, Thomas. *In Their Own Way: Discovering and Encouraging Your Child's Personal Learning Style*. NY: Putnam, 1987.

———. *Learning Styles: Food for Thought and 130 Practical Tips for Teachers K-4*. Rosemont, NJ: Modern Learning Press, 1992.

———. *Multiple Intelligences in the Classroom*. Alexandria, VA: Association for Supervision and Curriculum Development, 1994.

———. *Seven Kinds of Smart: Identifying and Developing Your Many Intelligences*. New York: A Plume Book, 1993.

Banks, Janet Caudill. *Creative Projects for Independent Learners*. CATS Publications, 1995.

Bloom, Benjamin S. *All Our Children Learning: A Primer for Teachers and Other Educators*. New York: McGraw-Hill, 1981.

———,ed. *Developing Talent in Young People*. New York: Ballantine, 1985.

Cameron, Julia. *The Artist's Way: A Spiritual Path to Higher Creativity*. New York: Jeremy P. Tarcher/Putnam, 1992.

Campbell, Bruce. *The Multiple Intelligences Handbook: Lesson Plans and More . . . .* Stanwood, WA: Campbell & Associates, 1994.

Campbell, Linda; Campbell, Bruce; and Dickinson, Dee. *Teaching and Learning Through Multiple Intelligences*. Needham Heights, MA: Allyn & Bacon, 1996.

Carbo, Marie. *Reading Styles Inventory Manual*. Roslyn Heights, New York: National Reading Styles Institute, 1991.

Carbo, Marie; Dunn, Rita; and Dunn, Kenneth. *Teaching Students to Read Through Their Individual Learning Styles*. Needham Heights, MA: Allyn & Bacon, 1991.

Gardner, Howard. *Frames of Mind: The Theory of Multiple Intelligences*. New York: Basic Books, 1985.

———. *Multiple Intelligences: The Theory in Practice*. New York: Basic Books, 1990.

———. *The Unschooled Mind: How Children Think and How Schools Should Teach*. New York: Basic Books, 1990.

Gilbert, Labritta. *Do Touch: Instant, Easy Hands-on Learning Experiences for Young Children*. Mt. Ranier, MD: Gryphon House, 1989.

Grant, Janet Millar. *Shake, Rattle and Learn: Classroom-Tested Ideas That Use Movement for Active Learning*. York, ME: Stenhouse Publishers, 1995.

Lazear, David. *Multiple Intelligence Approaches to Assessment: Solving the Assessment Conundrum*. IRI/Skylight Publishing, Inc., 1994.

———. *Seven Pathways of Learning: Teaching Students and Parents About Multiple Intelligences*. Tucson, AZ: Zephyr Press, 1994.

———. *Seven Ways of Knowing: Teaching for Multiple Intelligences*. Palatine, IL: IRI/Skylight Publishing, Inc., 1991.

———. *Seven Ways of Teaching: The Artistry of Teaching With Multiple Intelligences*. Palatine, IL: IRI/Skylight Publishing, Inc. 1991.

New City School Faculty. *Celebrating Multiple Intelligences: Teaching for Success*. St. Louis, MO: The New City School, Inc., 1994.

Short, Kathy G.; Schroder, Jean; Laird, Julie; Kauffman, Gloria; Ferguson, Margaret J.; and Crawford, Kathleen Marie. *Learning Together Through Inquiry: From Columbus to Integrated Curriculum*. York, ME: Stenhouse, 1996.

Vail, Priscilla. *Gifted, Precocious, or Just Plain Smart*. Rosemont, NJ: Programs for Education, 1987.

———.*Learning Styles: Food for Thought and 130 Practical Tips for Teachers K-4*. Rosemont, NJ: Modern Learning Press, 1992.

Learning Theory

Bailey, D.B.; Burchinal, M.R.; and McWilliam, R.A. "Age of Peers and Early Childhood Development." Child Development 64: 848-62, 1993.

Hart, Leslie. *Human Brain, Human Learning*. New York: Longman Press, 1983.

Rogoff, Barbara. *Apprenticeship in Thinking: Cognitive Development in Social Context*. New York: Oxford University Press, 1990.

Vygotsky, Lev. S. *Mind in Society: The Development of Higher Psychological Processes*. Michael Cole et al, eds. Cambridge, MA: Harvard University Press, 1978.

———. *Thought and Language*. Alexey Kozulin, ed. Cambridge, MA: MIT Press, 1986. 256 pages.

Looping

Forsten, Char. *The Multiyear Lesson Plan Book*. Peterborough, NH: Crystal Springs Books, 1996.

Forsten, Char; Grant, Jim; Johnson, Bob; and Richardson, Irv. *Looping Q&A: 72 Practical Answers to Your Most Pressing Questions*. Peterborough, NH: Crystal Springs Books, 1997.

Grant, Jim. *The Looping Classroom*. Peterborough, NH: Crystal Springs Books, 1996. (Video) Two versions: one for teachers and administrators and one for parents.

Grant, Jim; Johnson, Bob; and Richardson, Irv. *The Looping Handbook: Teachers and Students Progressing Together*. Peterborough, NH: Crystal Springs Books, 1996.

Hanson, Barbara. "Getting to Know You: Multiyear Teaching," *Educational Leadership*, November 1995.

Jacoby, Deborah. "Twice the Learning and Twice the Love." *Teaching K-8*, March 1994.

Million, June. "To Loop or Not to Loop? This is a Question for Many Schools." *NAESP Communicator*. Vol. 18, Number 6, February 1996.

Multiage Education

American Association of School Administrators. *The Nongraded Primary: Making Schools Fit Children*, Arlington, VA, 1992.

Anderson, Robert H., and Pavan, Barbara Nelson. *Nongradedness: Helping It to Happen*. Lancaster, PA: Technomic Press, 1992.

Banks, Janet Caudill. *Creating the Multi-age Classroom*. Edmonds, WA: CATS Publications, 1995.

Bingham, Anne A.; Dorta, Peggy; McClasky, Molly; and O'Keefe, Justine. *Exploring the Multiage Classroom*. York, ME: Stenhouse Publishers, 1995.

Bridge, Connie A.; Reitsma, Beverly S.; and Winograd, Peter N. *Primary Thoughts: Implementing Kentucky's Primary Program*. Lexington, KY: Kentucky Department of Education, 1993.

Burruss, Bette, and Fairchild, Nawanna. *The Primary School: A Resource Guide for Parents*. Lexington, KY: The Prichard Committee for Academic Excellence and The Partnership for Kentucky School Reform, 1993. PO Box 1658, Lexington, KY 40592-1658, 800-928-2111.

Chase, Penelle, and Doan, Joan. *Full Circle: A New Look at Multiage Education*. Portsmouth, NH: Heinemann, 1994.

Davies, Anne; Politano, Colleen; and Gregory, Kathleen. *Together is Better*. Winnipeg, Canada: Peguis Publishers, 1993.

Fogarty, Robin, ed. *The Multiage Classroom: A Collection*. Palatine, IL: Skylight Publishing, 1993.

Gaustad, Joan. "Making the Transition From Graded to Nongraded Primary Education." *Oregon School Study Council Bulletin*, 35(8), 1992.

———."Nongraded Education: Mixed-Age, Integrated and Developmentally Appropriate Education for Primary Children." *Oregon School Study Council Bulletin*, 35(7), 1992.

———. "Nongraded Education: Overcoming Obstacles to Implementing the Multiage Classroom." 38(3,4) *Oregon School Study Council Bulletin*, 1994.

Gayfer, Margaret, ed. *The Multi-grade Classroom: Myth and Reality*. Toronto: Canadian Education Association, 1991.

Goodlad, John I., and Anderson, Robert H. *The Nongraded Elementary School*. New York: Teachers College Press, 1987.

Grant, Jim, and Johnson, Bob. *A Common Sense Guide to Multiage Practices*. Columbus, OH: Teachers' Publishing Group, 1995.

Grant, Jim; Johnson, Bob; and Richardson, Irv. *Multiage Q&A: 101 Practical Answers to Your Most Pressing Questions*. Peterborough, NH: Crystal Springs Books, 1995.

———. *Our Best Advice: The Multiage Problem Solving Handbook*. Peterborough, NH: Crystal Springs Books, 1996.

Grant, Jim and Richardson, Irv, compilers. *Multiage Handbook: A Comprehensive Resource for Multiage Practices*. Peterborough, NH: Crystal Springs Books, 1996.

Gutierrez, Roberto, and Slavin, Robert E. *Achievement Effects of the Nongraded Elementary School: A Retrospective Review*. Baltimore, MD: Center for Research on Effective Schooling for Disadvantaged Students, 1992.

Hunter, Madeline. *How to Change to a Nongraded School*. Alexandria, VA: Association for Supervision and Curriculum Development, 1992.

Kasten, Wendy, and Clarke, Barbara. *The Multi-age Classroom*. Katonah, NY: Richard Owen, 1993.

Katz, Lilian G.; Evangelou, Demetra; and Hartman, Jeanette Allison. *The Case for Mixed-Age Grouping in Early Education*. Washington, DC: National Association for the Education of Young Children, 1990.

Kentucky Department of Education. *Kentucky's Primary School: The Wonder Years*. Frankfort, KY.

———. *Multi-Age/Multi-Ability: A Guide to Implementation for Kentucky's Primary Program*. Frankfort, KY: Kentucky Department of Education, 1994.

Kentucky Education Association and Appalachia Educational Laboratory. *Ungraded Primary Programs: Steps Toward Developmentally Appropriate Instruction*. Frankfort, KY: KEA, 1990.

Maeda, Bev. *The Multi-Age Classroom*. Cypress, CA: Creative Teaching Press, 1994.

McAvinue, Maureen. *A Planbook for Meeting Individual Needs in Primary School*. Frankfort, KY: Kentucky Department of Education, 1994.

Miller, Bruce A. *Children at the Center: Implementing the Multiage Classroom*. Portland, OR: Northwest Regional Educational Laboratory; 1994.

———. *The Multigrade Classroom: A Resource Handbook for Small, Rural Schools*. Portland, OR: Northwest Regional Educational Laboratory, 1989.

———. *Training Guide for the Multigrade Classroom: A Resource for Small, Rural Schools*. Portland, OR: Northwest Regional Laboratory, 1990.

National Education Association. *Multiage Classrooms*. NEA Teacher to Teacher Books, 1995.

Nebraska Department of Education and Iowa Department of Education. *The Primary Program: Growing and Learning in the Heartland*. 2nd edition. Lincoln, NE, 1994.

Ostrow, Jill. *A Room With a Different View: First Through Third Graders Build Community and Create Curriculum*. York, ME: Stenhouse Publishers, 1995.

Politano, Colleen, and Davies, Anne. *Multi-Age and More*. Winnipeg, Canada: Peguis Publishers, 1994.

Province of British Columbia Ministry of Education. *Foundation*. Victoria, British Columbia, 1990.

———. *Primary Program Foundation Document*. Victoria, British Columbia, 1990. This and the accompanying Resource Document provide extensive resources that would be of great help in any multiage program.

———. *Primary Program Resource Document*. Victoria, British Columbia, 1990.

Rathbone, Charles; Bingham, Anne; Dorta, Peggy; McClaskey, Molly; and O'Keefe, Justine. *Multiage Portraits: Teaching and Learning in Mixed-age Classrooms*. Peterborough, NH: Crystal Springs Books, 1993.

Virginia Education Association and Appalachia Educational Laboratory. *Teaching Combined Grade Classes: Real Problems and Promising Practices*. Charleston, WV: Appalachian Educational Laboratory, 1990.

Multiage Education — Audio/Video

Anderson, Robert, and Pavan, Barbara. *The Nongraded School*. Bloomington, IN: Phi Delta Kappa. An interview with the authors of *Nongradedness: Helping It to Happen*. Video, 30 minutes.

Association of Supervision and Curriculum Development. *Tracking: Road to Success or Dead End?* Alexandria, VA: audiocassette.

Cohen, Dorothy. *Status Treatments for the Classroom.* New York: Teachers College Press, 1994. Video.

George, Yvetta, and Keiter, Joel. *Developing Multiage Classrooms in Primary Grades.* Ft. Lauderdale, FL: Positive Connections, 1993. Video, 22 minutes.

Goodman, Gretchen. *Classroom Strategies for "Gray-Area" Children.* Peterborough, NH: Crystal Springs Books, 1995. Video.

Grant, Jim. *Accommodating Developmentally Different Children in the Multiage Classroom,* 1993. Keynote address at the NAESP Annual Convention. Audiocassette available from Chesapeake Audio/Video Communications, Inc. (6330 Howard Lane, Elkridge, MD 21227, product #180).

———. *Avoid the Pitfalls of Implementing Multiage Classrooms.* Peterborough, NH: Crystal Springs Books, 1995. Video.

Katz, Lilian. *Multiage Groupings: A Key to Elementary Reform.* Alexandria, VA: Association for Supervision and Curriculum Development, 1993. Audiocassette.

Lolli, Elizabeth J. *Developing a Framework for Nongraded Multiage Education.* Peterborough, NH: Crystal Springs, 1995. Video.

Oakes, Jeannie, and Lipton, Martin. *On Tracking and Ability Grouping.* Bloomington, IN: Phi Delta Kappa.

Thompson, Ellen. *The Nuts and Bolts of Multiage Classrooms.* Peterborough NH: Crystal Springs Books, 1994. Video, 1 hour.

———. *How to Teach in a Multiage Classroom.* Peterborough, NH: Crystal Springs Books, 1994. Video, 25 minutes.

Ulrey, Dave, and Ulrey, Jan. *Teaching in a Multiage Classroom.* Peterborough, NH: Crystal Springs Books, 1994. Video.

Parent Involvement / Resources for Parents

Baskwill, Jane. *Parents and Teachers: Partners in Learning.* Toronto, Ont.: Scholastic, 1990.

Bettelheim, Bruno. *A Good Enough Parent.* New York: Alfred A. Knopf, 1987.

Bluestein, Jane, and Collins, Lynn. *Parents in a Pressure Cooker.* Rosemont, NJ: Modern Learning Press, 1990.

Butler, Dorothy, and Clay, Marie. *Reading Begins at Home.* Portsmouth, NH: Heinemann, 1982.

Clay, Marie. *Writing Begins at Home.* Portsmouth, NH: Heinemann, 1988.

Coletta, Anthony. *Kindergarten Readiness Checklist for Parents.* Rosemont, NJ: Modern Learning Press, 1991.

Dinkmeyer, Don; Dinkmeyer, James; and McKay, Gary D. *Parenting Young Children* (for parents of children under six), Circle Pines, MN: American Guidance Service, 1989.

Dinkmeyer, Don, and McKay, Gary D. *Systematic Training for Effective Parenting: The Parent's Handbook.* Circle Pines, MN: American Guidance Service, 1989.

Elovson, Allanna. *The Kindergarten Survival Book.* Santa Monica, CA: Parent Ed Resources, 1991.

Frede, Ellen. *Getting Involved: Workshops for Parents.* Ypsilanti, MI: High/Scope Press, 1984.

Grant, Jim. *Developmental Education in the 1990's.* Rosemont, NJ: Modern Learning Press, 1991.

———. *Jim Grant's Book of Parent Pages.* Rosemont, NJ: Programs for Education, 1988.

———. *Worth Repeating: Giving Children a Second Chance at School Success.* Rosemont, NJ: Modern Learning Press, 1989.

Grant, Jim, and Azen, Margot. *Every Parent's Owner's Manuals. (Three-, Four-, Five-, Six-, Seven-Year- Old).* Rosemont, NJ. Programs for Education. 16 pages each manual.

Henderson, Anne T.; Marburger, Carl L.; and Ooms, Theodora. *Beyond the Bake Sale: An Educator's Guide to Working with Parents.* Columbia, MD: National Committee for Citizens in Education, 1990.

Hill, Mary. *Home: Where Reading and Writing Begin.* Portsmouth, NH: 1995.

Karnofsky, Florence, and Weiss, Trudy. *How to Prepare Your Child for Kindergarten.* Carthage, IL: Fearon Teacher Aids, 1993.

Lansky, Vicki. *Divorce Book for Parents.* New York: New American Library, 1989.

Lazear, David. *Seven Pathways of Learning: Teaching Students and Parents About Multiple Intelligences.* Tucson, AZ: Zephyr Press, 1994.

LeShan, Eda. *When Your Child Drives You Crazy.* New York: St. Martin's Press, 1986.

Lyons, P.; Robbins, A.; and Smith, A. *Involving Parents: A Handbook for Participation in Schools.* Ypsilanti, MI: High/Scope Press, 1984.

Mooney, Margaret. *Reading to, With, and By Children.* Katonah, NY: Richard C. Owen Publishers, 1990.

Northeastern Local School District. *Every Child is a Promise: Early Childhood At-Home Learning Activities.* Springfield, OH, 1986.

———. *Every Child is a Promise: Positive Parenting.* Springfield, OH, 1986.

Rich, Dorothy. *Megaskills: In School and Life — The Best Gift You Can Give Your Child.* Boston: Houghton Mifflin, 1992.

Taylor, Denny, and Strickland, Dorothy. *Family Storybook Reading.* Portsmouth, NH: 1986.

Trelease, Jim. *Hey! Listen To This: Stories to Read Aloud.* New York: Penguin Books, 1992.

———. *The New Read-Aloud Handbook.* New York: Penguin Books, 1989.

Vopat, James. *The Parent Project: A Workshop Approach to Parent Involvement.* York, ME: Stenhouse Publishers, 1994.

Wlodkowski, Raymond, and Jaynes, Judith H. *Eager to Learn.* San Francisco: Jossey-Bass, 1990.

Teachers and Teaching

Erb, Thomas O., and Doda, Nancy M. *Team Organization: Promise — Practices and Possiblities.* Washington, D.C.: National Education Association of the United States, 1989.

Glatthorn, Allan A. *The Teacher's Portfolio: Fostering and Documenting Professional Development.* Rockport, MA: Pro>Active Publications, 1996.

Holly, Mary Louise. *Writing to Grow: Keeping a Personal-Professional Journal.* Portsmouth, NH: Heinemann, 1989.

Northern Nevada Writing Project Teacher-Researcher Group. *Team Teaching.* York, ME: Stenhouse, 1996.

Terry, Alice. *Every Teacher's Guide to Classroom Management.* Cypress, CA: Creative Teaching Press, 1997.

Thematic Learning and Teaching

Atwood, Ron, ed. *Elementary Science Themes: Change Over Time: Patterns, Systems and Interactions, Models and Scales.* Lexington, KY: Institute on Education Reform, University of Kentucky, 1993. Set of four pamphlets, 50 pages each.

Bromley, Karen; Irwin-De Vitis, Linda; and Modlo, Marcia. *Graphic Organizers: Visual Strategies for Active Learning.* New York: Scholastic, 1995.

Davies, Anne; Politano, Colleen; and Cameron, Caren. *Making Themes Work.* Winnipeg, Canada: Peguis Publishers, 1993.

Gamberg, Ruth; Kwak, W.; Hutchins, R.; and Altheim, J. *Learning and Loving It: Theme Studies in the Classroom.* Portsmouth, NH: Heinemann, 1988.

Haraway, Fran, and Geldersma, Barbara. *12 Totally Terrific Theme Units.* New York: Scholastic, 1993.

Herr, Judy, and Libby, Yvonne. *Creative Resources for the Early Childhood Classroom.* Albany, NY: Delmar, 1990.

Katz, Lilian G., and Chard, Sylvia C. *Engaging Children's Minds: The Project Approach.* Norwood, NJ: Ablex Press, 1989.

McCarthy, Tara. *150 Thematic Writing Activities.* New York: Scholastic, 1993.

McCracken, Marlene and Robert. *Themes* (9 book series). Winnipeg, Man.: Peguis, 1984-87.

SchifferDanoff, Valerie. *The Scholastic Integrated Language Arts Resource Book.* New York: Scholastic, 1995.

Schlosser, Kristin. *Thematic Units for Kindergarten.* New York: Scholastic, 1994.

Strube, Penny. *Theme Studies, A Practical Guide: How to Develop Theme Studies to Fit Your Curriculum.* NY: Scholastic, 1993.

Thompson, Gare. *Teaching Through Themes.* New York: Scholastic, 1991.

Tracking / Untracking

George, Paul. *How to Untrack Your School.* Alexandria, VA.: Association for Supervision and Curriculum Development, 1992.

Kohn, Alfie. *No Contest: The Case Against Competition.* Boston, MA: Houghton Mifflin, 1992.

Kozol, Jonathan. *Savage Inequalities: Children in America's Schools.* New York: Crown, 1991.

Oakes, Jeannie. *Keeping Track: How Schools Structure Equality.* New Haven: Yale University Press, 1985.

Tomlinson, Carol Ann. *How to Differentiate Instruction in Mixed-Ability Classrooms.* Alexandria, VA: Association for Supervision and Curriculum Development, 1995.

Wheelock, Anne. *Crossing the Tracks: How "Untracking" Can Save America's Schools.* New York: New Press, 1992.

NOTES

Index

NOTES